FATHERS AND SONS
IN ATHENS

Barry S. Strauss

*

FATHERS AND SONS IN ATHENS

Ideology and Society in the Era
of the Peloponnesian War

Princeton University Press
Princeton, New Jersey

Copyright © 1993 by Princeton University Press
Published by Princeton University Press,
41 William Street, Princeton, New Jersey 08540
In the United Kingdom: Princeton University Press,
Chichester, West Sussex

Library of Congress Cataloging-in-Publication Data

Strauss, Barry S.
Fathers and sons in Athens : ideology and society in the era
of the Peloponnesian War / Barry S. Strauss
p.
ISBN 0-691-03384-6
ISBN 0-691-01591-0 (pbk.)
1. Greek literature—History and criticism. 2. Greece—History—
Peloponnesian War. 431–404 B.C. 3. Fathers and sons—Greece—
Athens—History. 4. Literature and society—Greece—Athens.
5. Fathers and sons in literature. 6. Athens (Greece) in literature.
I. Title.
PA3074.S77   1994
880.9'355—dc20   92-13281

Second printing, and first paperback printing, 1997

Printed in the United States of America
by Princeton Academic Press

3 5 7 9 10 8 6 4 2

TO MARCIA

CONTENTS

PREFACE

Pity the Greeks: for two millennia and more, they have been the chief mirror in which the intellectuals of Europe and European-derived civilizations have chosen to see, not the Greeks as they were or might have been, but rather, themselves. Or envy the Greeks, for had they not made such a good mirror – had they not been so very susceptible to being used for the ends of others, had they not been so Protean, so plastic – they might not have lasted so long as the subject of the West's fascination. Just why the Greeks make such a good mirror may have as much to do with their own undying interest in self-fashioning as it does with the genius of their cultural artifacts. "Work unceasingly to fashion your own statue," says Plotinos in the third century AD. The statement would have a struck a resounding chord in classical Athens – in Alcibiades, for instance.

The Greeks have been variously represented: as aristocrats or democrats, as unravished brides of quietness or sexual misfits in need of a therapist's couch, as narcissists or altruists, as proto-racists or open-minded egalitarians. No historian, particularly not a historian of ideology, can underestimate the difficulty of getting past such preconceptions and trying to reconstruct the truth. The task is hard enough if one wants to study a debate in the Athenian assembly or a custom of the Athenian household. If, however, one aims to study both, that is, to combine social and political history, as this book does, then one must be prepared to wrestle not only with idealizations of the Greeks but with evidence that is often contradictory and intangible. Modesty is called for.

This is a book about fathers and sons, chiefly about fathers and sons in ancient Greece, specifically in Athens from about 450 BC to about 350 BC. Authors sometimes write with an ideal reader in mind. *Caveat lector* – let the reader beware, for I have kept several ideal readers in mind. Naturally I hope to engage other ancient historians and classicists in discourse and debate about the society, ideology and politics of late-fifth- and early-fourth-century Athens. I also hope to interest two other groups of scholars: anthropologists and historians – social, cultural, political – of other periods, both of whom have much to say about the underlying theoretical issues of this study. Although the use of anthropological methodologies and of comparisons to other eras of history may still be controversial among classicists, I trust that such practices have become common enough to make a long justification at the outset unnecessary. The reader can decide whether the references to anthropology and more recent history in the following pages are judicious or not.

In addition to addressing scholars, I would like to speak to a more general audience, to a reader, say, who has taken an undergraduate course in ancient Greece or in the history of the family but who lacks a specialized scholarly interest in the subject. In order to accommodate this reader, I have tried to avoid jargon, to explain all technical terms, and to translate all Greek. Unless otherwise stated, all translations are my own. I have also tried clearly to demarcate sections with mainly technical arguments, so the non-specialist reader can move on if he or she chooses.

There are many good reasons for scholars to reach out to non-specialists. I have been particularly motivated in this regard, however, by the prominence of the family in political ideology on both sides of the Atlantic in the 1980s and 1990s. By studying the family as ideology in classical Athens, we might be better equipped to debate the family as reality today. I offer this book as a modest contribution toward that end.

A generation ago, ancient historians usually used Latin spellings of Greek personal and place names rather than transliterations closer to the Greek originals: for example, Pericles not Perikles, Thucydides not Thoukydides, Corinth not Korinthos, Miletus not Miletos. Today, a variety of spelling systems are in use. Like other scholars, I have been consistently inconsistent: I have used Latin or Latin-derived spellings for famous names (Aristotle, Socrates, Athens, Mycenae) and Greek transliterations for less-known or little-known names (Kharmides, Andokides, Aigeus) and for Greek words (*kyrios, meirakion*).

A student of the history of fathers and sons cannot help but be aware of the debt owed to previous scholars. It is not merely a filial obligation but indeed a pleasure to acknowledge this debt. From studies in ancient history, to works on Athenian law, to interpretations of individual Greek dramas, to anthropological theory, to social-historical studies of the family, I have found a plethora of scholarly and stimulating material to read. The student of fathers and sons in classical Athens has indeed a rich inheritance.

I have also been very lucky in the support and encouragement my work has received. My research would not have been possible without fellowship grants from the National Endowment for the Humanities and without the willingness of the Department of History of Cornell University to allow me study leave. The Classics Department of the University of Toronto was a generous host during a visit in the spring 1990 semester. The office staff of Cornell's History Department as well as the reference and circulation departments of the John M. Olin Library at Cornell were helpful, as always. I presented earlier versions of some of my ideas in talks at Chicago, Oxford, Princeton, Santa Cruz, Stanford, and Toronto, where colleagues and friends shared their comments with me.

Princeton University Press sent the manuscript to two readers, whose extremely helpful comments I am pleased to acknowledge. All or parts of the manuscript were read as well by Isabel Hull, Philip Mitsis, Josiah Ober, and Hanna and Joseph Roisman, in whose debt I stand. The following individuals were generous in answering queries, offering advice, or discussing or supplying unpublished material: Fred Ahl, Kevin Clinton, Erich Gruen, Charles Hedrick, Donald Kagan, Nicole Loraux, Mary Beth Norton, Pietro Pucci, Jeffrey Rusten, Richard Saller, Alan Shapiro, Anne Steiner, and Michael Vickers. I would also like to thank Joanna Hitchcock, Miles Litvinoff, Lauren Osborne, Richard Stoneman, and Moira Taylor. I owe my father more than I can say. By far my greatest debt is to my wife, whose editorial assistance, encouragement, and patience were invaluable, and to whom this book is dedicated.

Ithaca, New York
August 1992

ABBREVIATIONS

ANCIENT AUTHORS AND TEXTS

Aesch.   Aeschylus
   Ag.   *Agamemnon*
   Cho.   *Choephoroi*
   Eum.   *Eumenides*
   Pers.   *Persians*
Aeschin.   Aeschines
Andok.   Andokides
Ant.   Antiphon
   Tetr.   *Tetralogy*
Apollod.   Apollodorus
   Epit.   *Epitome*
Ar.   Aristophanes
   Ach.   *Acharnians*
   Cl.   *Clouds*
   Eccl.   *Ecclesiazusae*
   Kn.   *Knights*
   Lys.   *Lysistrata*
   Thesm.   *Thesmophoriazusae*
Arist.   Aristotle
   Ath. Pol.   *Athênaiôn Politeia*
   Eth. Eud.   *Eudemian Ethics*
   Eth. Nic.   *Nicomachean Ethics*
   Poet.   *Poetics*
   Pol.   *Politics*
   Rh.   *Rhetoric*
Arr.   Arrian
   Anab.   *Anabasis*

Ath. Athenaeus
Dein. Deinarchus
Dem. Demosthenes
Diod. Diodorus Siculus
D.L. Diogenes Laertius
Dion. Hal. Dionysius of Halicarnassus
Eur. Euripides
  Hel. Helen
  Hipp. Hippolytos
  Med. Medea
  Supp. Suppliant Women
  Tro. Trojan Women
Hdt. Herodotus
Hes. Hesiod
  Op. Works and Days
  Th. Theogony
Hom. Homer
  Il. Iliad
  Od. Odyssey
Hyp. Hyperides
Isai. Isaios
Isoc. Isocrates
  Areop. Areopagitica
Lyk. Lykourgos
Lys. Lysias
  Agst. Theozot. Against Theozotides
Paus. Pausanias
Pl. Plato
  Alc. Alcibiades
  Ap. Apology
  Chrm. Charmides
  Cltphon. Cleitophon
  Euthphr. Euthyphro
  Grg. Gorgias
  Lach. Laches
  Lys. Lysis
  Menex. Menexenus
  Phdr. Phaedrus
  Prt. Protagoras
  Rep. Republic

Symp.   Symposium
Ti.   Timaeus
Plut.   Plutarch
  Alc.   Life of Alcibiades
  Comp. Thes. Rom.   Comparison of the Lives of
    Theseus and Romulus
  Kimon.   Life of Kimon
  Mor.   Moralia
  Nic.   Life of Nicias
  Per.   Life of Pericles
  Sol.   Life of Solon
  Them.   Life of Themistocles
  Thes.   Life of Theseus
Ps.-Dem.   Pseudo-Demosthenes
Ps.-Plut.   Pseudo-Plutarch
  Vita Andok.   Life of Andokides
Ps.-Xen.   Pseudo-Xenophon ("The Old Oligarch")
  Ath. Pol.   Athênaiôn Politeia
Soph.   Sophocles
  Ant.   Antigone
  El.   Electra
  OC   Oedipus at Kolonos
  OT   Oedipus Tyrannos
Theophr.   Theophrastus
  Char.   Characters
Thuc.   Thucydides
Xen.   Xenophon
  Ap.   Apology
  Cyr.   Cyropaedia
  Hell.   Hellenika
  Lac. Pol.   Lakedaimoniôn Politeia
  Mem.   Memorabilia
  Oec.   Oeconomicus
  Symp.   Symposium

COLLECTIONS AND REFERENCE BOOKS

ATL   B.D. Merritt, et al. The Athenian Tribute Lists. Vols. I–IV. Cambridge, Mass. and Princeton. 1939–53.

Diels and Kranz   H. Diels, Ed. Revised by W. Kranz. Die Fragmente der Vorsokratiker. 6th edn. Berlin, 1951.

FGrH   F. Jacoby. *Die Fragmente der griechischen Historiker.* 3
Teile in 14 vols. Berlin and Leiden. 1923–58.

IG   *Inscriptiones Graecae.* Berlin. 1873–.

Kassel and Austin   R. Kassel and C. Austin, Eds. *Poetae Comici
Graeci.* Berlin and New York. 1983–.

LSJ   Liddell and Scott. *A Greek–English Lexicon.* 9th edn. Rev.
H. Stuart Jones and R. McKenzie. Oxford. 1940.

RE   A. Pauly, G. Wissowa, and W. Kroll, Eds. *Real-Encyclopädie
der classischen Altertumswissenschaft.* Stuttgart. 1894–1978.

SEG   *Supplementum Epigraphicum Graecum.* Leiden. 1923–.

1

INTRODUCTION
Solidarity or conflict?

Yea, there thou makest me sad and makest me sin
In envy that my Lord Northumberland
Should be the father to so blest a son,
A son who is the theme of honor's tongue;
Amongst a grove, the very straightest plant;
Who is sweet Fortune's minion and her pride;
Whilst I, by looking on the praise of him,
See riot and dishonor stain the brow
Of my young Harry.

Shakespeare, *Henry IV, Part I*

CONTRADICTORY IMAGES

Scenes from a classical landscape: the place, the city of Athens and its territory, the approximately 1,000-square-mile region of Attica; the time, the era of the Peloponnesian War (431–404 BC, plus a decade or two on either side).[1] First, a vignette seen repeatedly in private houses all over Attica. About a week after the birth of a baby, the new father led the celebration of a ceremony called the *amphidromia*, literally the "walking or running around," in which he carried (possibly at a run and possibly naked) the newborn infant around the household hearth. A sacrifice probably followed and then a party, with food and wine and gifts from friends for the baby. Besides being a time of joy, the *amphidromia* ceremony had the serious purpose of introducing the newborn into the family through a ritual of initiation: for the Greeks, fire was an agent of purification, which was considered necessary after the bleeding that accompanies childbirth. Adding to the seriousness of the cer-emony was the knowledge of the alternative: that the father by

1

right could have rejected the infant as illegitimate, in which case he would have had it "exposed"; that is to say, abandoned somewhere, perhaps to die, perhaps to be adopted or enslaved. Having been accepted as legitimate, the child would be given a name, either at the *amphidromia* or at a second "tenth-day" *dekatê* celebration shortly afterward. So the first confrontation between an Athenian father and his child was one of stark inequality.[2]

For the second scene, imagine that same child and his or her father eighteen years later. The medical and demographic realities of Athens – a high infant mortality rate, a late age of marriage for men – render depressingly high the chances that one or both would now be dead. If they both did survive, though, and if the child was male, then in his eighteenth year, he and his father would be called before the local deme assembly in its annual registration of new citizens. The father would sponsor his son's candidacy and stand surety of the boy's qualifications: his attainment of the age of eighteen, his status as a free man, and his birth from two Athenian parents. The deme members would vote under solemn oath to approve or reject the candidate. Once approved by the deme and vetted by the council in Athens, the new citizen was legally free of his father's control and entitled to represent himself in court. Thanks to an act of paternal solidarity and support, the son was now a man.[3]

The next three scenes take us to death and beyond. Every year at the beginning of the Dionysia, the festival famous for the performance of tragedies and comedies, the state-supported "orphans" – in Athens anyone without a father might be considered an *orphanos*, even if he had a mother – were presented to the audience, to the citizens who had served *in loco parentis*, as it were (Thuc. 2.46.1; Lys. 2.75; Lys. *Agst. Theozot.* 2; Pl. *Menex.* 249c; Arist. *Pol.* 1268a9). Dressed in full suits of armor, the orphans had reached the age of eighteen and were about to cross the threshold into manhood, military service, and financial self-reliance (this last with the help of their patrimony, if any, of which they now obtained control). These orphans only included the sons of men who had fallen in Athens's battles ("because they were good men, their fathers died in war," as Aeschines puts it, 3.154) and not the sons of men who died of other causes. The special status of military orphans tells us something both about the high esteem for military prowess in Athens and about the emphasis put on the bond between father and son even after the father's death.[4]

A similar emphasis ought to have been apparent every time a father died, in a son's care to arrange a proper burial and to carry out all the necessary memorial ceremonies. Such punctiliousness may or may not have been the rule, but it was certainly a good card to play in court if one was after an inheritance and was claiming to have been adopted by the dear departed. On the subjects of death and solidarity, consider also the trial and execution in 390 BC of Nikophemos of the deme of Rhamnous and his son Aristophanes. Nikophemos had raised his son to follow in his footsteps in a career of public service. Together, the two men had organized a small fleet to help Athens's allies in Cyprus, and together, the two men had accepted an angry public's wrath when the fleet fell into Spartan hands. Father and son lived together, worked together, and died together.[5]

Thus, an introduction to Athenian father–son solidarity from cradle to grave, with many blanks left, which the following chapters will attempt to fill. These scenes create an impression of solidarity which must be balanced against an equally strong but opposite impression that the selection of other scenes could create. There is evidence of father–son solidarity in Athens, but there is also evidence of conflict.

Consider first the annual Oschophoria festival, whose main event was a procession from Athens to the sea at Phaleron, where a sacrifice was made. The paraders carried vine branches with the grapes still growing on them; called *oschoi*, these branches point to the agricultural origins of the Oschophoria. The ancients, however, also connected the festival with the myth of Athens's national hero, Theseus, and explained its colorful customs in light of the saga of his voyage to Crete, victory over the Minotaur, and return to Athens. Consider the explanations of (1) why the herald of the procession refused to wear the usual festive garland but put it around his staff instead, and (2) why the sacrifice was followed by cries of shock and confusion (*"Iou, iou"*) mixed with the usual hosannas (*"Eleleu"*). According to the legend, Theseus shipped off to Crete with a black sail of mourning hoisted; if he somehow managed to survive the ordeal of fighting the Minotaur and returned home safely, then he was supposed to change to a white sail, as a sign to his father, King Aigeus. Theseus did defeat the Minotaur, of course, but in the excitement of his return, he forgot to change his sail, and at the sight of the black sail, his father committed suicide by jumping from a cliff. The conquering hero

3

Theseus was now the new king of Athens, but he was also – not to put too fine a point on it – an indirect patricide. The news of Aigeus's death, according to the ancients, explains the mix of joy and sorrow in the Oschophoria procession. In the annual celebration of one of their many festivals, therefore, the Athenians re-enacted the curious drama of their national hero: an ambitious young man who accidentally provoked his father's death and immediately obtained his patrimony.[6]

Next, consider three scenes from Aristophanic comedies of the 420s and 410s. *Clouds* dramatizes the relationship between a father of about sixty and his son of nineteen or twenty. The spendthrift youth, who runs with a horsey set, and the old-fashioned frugal father do not understand each other. The mutual misunderstandings escalate when the father's plan to have the boy trained to outsmart creditors only ends up teaching him to talk back to his father; eventually the son beats the father on stage. Direct violence is avoided in *Wasps*, but here an old father, having turned over control of the household to his adult son, is held under virtual house arrest to keep him out of mischief in the courts. One of the many species that fetches up in *Birds'* Cloudcuckooland is the Father-Beater, who has to be talked out of his ardent desire to murder his father.[7]

Next, there is the case of the most notorious Athenian of his generation, Alcibiades (ca. 450–404), the very avatar of youth and of rebellion. Orphaned as a baby (it is somehow fitting that Alcibiades' father should have left the scene early on), Alcibiades was raised by the leading man of Athens, Pericles. The sources are full of anecdotes of Alcibiades talking back both to Pericles and in due course to virtually every older male in sight: his teachers, his father-in-law, and various older statesmen. Thucydides presents one of the most telling scenes of Alcibiades' career. In 415, as the leading champion of an expedition to conquer far-off Sicily, Alcibiades was accused of having enflamed the ambitions of the young men of Athens against the maturity and caution of the old – in other words, of having opened a generation gap.[8]

Read a few key ancient texts written in or about the Peloponnesian War era – Plato's dialogues, Sophocles' *Philoctetes*, many of Euripides' tragedies (especially *Alcestis*, *Hippolytos*, and *Orestes*), orations by Andokides, Isocrates, and Lysias in addition to Aristophanes and Thucydides – and it becomes easy to believe in the reality of this gap. To be young and rich and to come of age in

Athens in, say, the 420s, was to be part of a generation that had a taste for luxury, the money to pursue it, and the imperial swagger that came from that generation's leading position in the leading power of Greece. Yet their fathers too had been rich, luxury-loving, imperialist youths in their day (in spite of later protestations of purity). Two things made the generation of the 420s different from its predecessor: the training of the sophists and the brutality and upheavals of the Peloponnesian War, which freed the young to parade their power without inhibition or modesty.

People noticed. At first they may have been willing to wink at boys who were being boys. As the war dragged on, though, and as Athens began to lose the war, people lost their patience with the young and the arrogant. Consider a final case, that of Alcibiades' mentor, Socrates. Today perhaps the most revered of all ancient Athenians, in 399 Socrates was tried, convicted, and executed on charges of religious unorthodoxy and of corrupting the youth by his philosophizing. However damning these charges, there are good grounds for also placing the infamous trial in the context of political recrimination after Athens's defeat in the Peloponnesian War – a defeat in which Alcibiades and another protégé of Socrates, the notorious anti-democrat Kritias, had played dubious roles. Socrates was blamed for making these men into what they turned out to be. But the trial can also be seen, at least in part, as a reaction to the generation gap. Xenophon writes that Socrates' accusers, both the official and the unofficial ones, claimed that Socrates encouraged sons to have contempt for their fathers, and to obey him instead of them (Xen. *Ap.* 20, *Mem.* 1.2.49).[9]

We have, in sum, two contradictory sets of images of life in Athens in the age of the Peloponnesian War. On the one hand, there is paternal–filial solidarity, male bonding, Father & Son Co., and loyalty to the memory of the dear departed. On the other hand, there are sons preferring substitute fathers to the genuine article, there is a generation gap, violence between son and father, and even indirect patricide. Which set of images better depicts the reality of father–son relations in Peloponnesian-War-era Athens? Are they perhaps both correct, and was reality heterogeneous, depending on the individuals or the class in question? Or is neither accurate, but both are merely ideological obfuscations of sociological reality? Are complaints about father-and-son conflict and the generation gap in late-fifth-century Athens to be taken seriously or are they merely examples of a universal kind of grousing that can be found at any time in any society?

THEORETICAL INTERESTS

The attempt to sort out these questions was the genesis of this book. My primary purpose was, and is, to try to understand better the nature and meaning of father–son conflict in Athens of the Peloponnesian War era. This initial subject of inquiry, however, has led to a wider study of the symbolic and political meaning of fathers and sons in classical Athens. Thematically, the purview of this study has grown to include such subjects as ideology, political symbolism, social drama, and especially, the question of the boundary between public and private, between family and state in classical Athens.[10]

In terms of methodology, this study is eclectic. I have read in anthropology, literary criticism, psychology, comparative history, gender theory, and structuralist and post-structuralist theory, as well as in the ancient texts and traditional scholarly literature of classics and ancient history. I draw on ideas and insights from each of these disciplines, but I do not feel bound by any particular interpretive scheme. Such an approach may seem inconsistent to some, but I prefer to think of it as flexible, as one permitting light to be thrown on the subject from a variety of directions. In any case, the bulk of the work of this book has been the classicist's usual procedure of compiling, sifting, and analyzing ancient texts.

Fathers and sons: why not, as friends have asked, fathers and daughters, or mothers and sons or daughters, or parents and children? These are important questions. At a minimum, one wonders about the existence of comparative data on other parent–child dyadic relationships and the light such evidence might shed on the father–son bond. More importantly, a narrow focus on male–male relationships runs the risk of recapitulating Athenian ideology, which propagated the fiction of the invisibility of the female. Contrary to this ideology, not only were Athenian women visible, but they were an essential part of the ideology of that supposedly all-male phenomenon, Athenian democracy. According to the ancient conception, tyranny was characterized by loose morals and the ever-present threat that the tyrant might demand sexual favors from a subject's wife or daughter. In democracy, by contrast, the pride and freedom of the male citizen was symbolized by the subordination and seclusion, and hence the inviolability, of "his" women. (The ideology was powerful, even though in practice, few Athenian women were actually kept in seclusion.) Thus ancient democracy, like ancient republicanism more generally, was gendered, that is, it used the symbols and language of gender to express notions of political authority. In ideology as in reality, women were essential.[11]

Nor will it do to say that the father–son relationship provides a particular insight into Athenian patriarchy. So it does, but the patriarchal rule of fathers over sons, however important, necessarily presupposes the patriarchal rule of husbands over wives, who after all bear the sons in the first place. One cannot do justice to Athenian patriarchy, therefore, without studying male–female as well as male–male relationships.[12]

For several reasons, nevertheless, this study has been restricted primarily to the father–son relationship. First of all, as a monograph, its focus necessarily had to be restricted. Of course, that focus might have emerged as a series of comparative case-studies, for example, one father–son relationship, one mother–daughter relationship, and so on. A second consideration intervened, however: the privileged status of the father–son relationship in Athenian ideology, precisely because inter-male relationships were so charged with symbolic meaning in Athenian and Greek culture. The right relationship of father and son was as important a topic for Athenian patriarchy as the right relationship of male and female – but this can be no surprise to students of a society as androcentric as Athens; a society in which inter-male competition and status anxiety as well as male homoeroticism were all ordinary parts of public life. In private life, patrilineal succession – the transmission of property from father to son – was highly prized. In practice, it is true, the Athenian kinship system was bilateral rather than patrilateral; the absence of a son often led to the adoption of a daughter's son or collateral kinsman as heir. The ideological importance of patrilineal succession was nonetheless great. Fourth-century Athenian funerary inscriptions, for example, commemorate father and son far more often than father and daughter or mother and son or daughter: eloquent testimony of the relative ideological and economic differences between the sexes in Athens. In public life, only males could be actors on the stage of the polis. Furthermore, although the male game of political competition was not entirely bereft of cooperation, it often turned out to be a zero-sum game: one man's victory required another man's defeat. Yet this ethos ran counter to the nurture–obedience dynamic of the father–son relationship. Indeed, the father–son bond was a nexus of contradictions in the ideology of Athenian relationships.[13]

Because Athenian democracy not merely tolerated but demanded the subordination of women, there was little conflict between the democratic ethos of equality and a male citizen's power over his wife and daughters; the same of course was true of power over slaves. For the same reason that every man in the assembly felt that no other man was his *kyrios* (lord, master, someone holding power or authority), that same man prided himself on being the *kyrios* of other human beings in his own household: that is, the *kyrios* of his slaves, wife, daughters, and sons under the age of eighteen. For the Athenians, there was no contradiction between a political regime in which the common people were lord and master (a *politeia* in which the demos was *kyrios*) and a household in which a man was lord and master (*kyrios*) of the women. On the contrary: a man's mastery of his household was considered both to attest to and to mirror the mastery required of an Athenian citizen. A man who could not rule his wife could hardly rule Athens or the Athenian empire.[14]

On the other hand, since all male citizens were political equals, a father's power as *kyrios* of his sons until they turned eighteen was potentially problematic. There was plenty of room for tension between, for example, a seventeen-year-old ready to come into his own, and the father who was still his *kyrios*. The position of a twenty-year-old who was his own *kyrios* but who still depended on his father financially, as was frequently the case, might even have been more difficult. Hence, the peculiar symbolic character of the father–son relationship, which was located at the intersection of contradictory axes of democratic ideology: equality and hierarchy, cooperation and conflict. To sum up, this study focuses on Athenian father–son relationships to the exclusion of other relationships within the household because of the particular insight into the tensions within democratic ideology offered by the father–son nexus.

This study of fathers and sons has been conceived as a modest contribution to a much wider scholarly literature: one that in recent years has ranged over such related subjects as the Athenian notion of "the political," women in Athens, male–female and male–

male relationships, homoeroticism, and the family – in short, all aspects of that fundamental question, the interrelationship of public and private, both in Athens and in our own society. One such subject, Athenian patriarchy in the literal sense of "father rule," has received less attention than other topics; it is hoped that this study can direct greater attention to it.

Let us turn now briefly to this larger question of public and private. We usually think of Athenians as citizens, as *politai*, and for good reason: no one could deny the extraordinary contribution of the Athenians to the theory and practice of *ta politika* – politics – in later civilizations, including our own. It has been argued that Athens invented the notion of a separate, autonomous political realm; if the argument has sometimes been pushed to the point of extravagance, there is no doubt that Athens did endow politics with a significant degree of independence and rationality. Even in Athens, however, politics was not completely separate from its social and familial context. For example, politically enfranchised citizens of Athens (though citizens, women were excluded from politics) were all also sons and most of them fathers, either by blood or by adoption. Yet if we do think of Athenians as fathers or sons, we tend to do so in a spirit of strict separation of public and private and family and state: one was a father or son at home, not on the speaker's platform.[15]

Yet this strict separation is problematic. We need to be suspicious of the notion of *homo politicus* and of the supposed dichotomy between *homo politicus* and *homo economicus*, which is overly schematic and compartmentalized. In Athens, for example, the theoretical distinction (a) between the citizen community and everyone else and (b) between politics and everything else was not only vitiated by practice – for example by the constant mixing of citizens and non-citizens in daily life – but was expressed by recourse to the very categories that were supposed to be excluded. What, for example, defines an Athenian citizen? Age, parentage, and (for practical purposes) gender – all ostensibly "strictly nonpolitical" terms.[16]

Recent feminist theory has gone far in demonstrating the fallibility and ideological bias of a strict public–private distinction. If, as proponents of the theory argue, politics is "gendered," I would argue that politics is also – for want of a better term – "familialized." For example, if Athenian citizenship was a male preserve, it was also one that assured each citizen of the sanctity of his household. Politics uses the symbols and languages of the family to express notions of political authority. Athenian citizens, for example, had public names, modeled after patronyms; they were enrolled in groups that mixed the idiom of politics and kinship; and while they prized equality, they equated the supreme power of the Athenian people in the constitution with the power of an Athenian father in his household.[17]

My interest in this book is less in the family than in – that *faute de mieux* again – familialism, which Barrett and McIntosh define as a term referring to "ideologies modelled on what are thought to be family values and the rendering of other social phenomena like families."[18] This is a study less of the family as practice than of the family as ideology and as metaphor, and of the influence of relationships within the domestic domain on concepts and constructs in the politico-jural domain.[19]

We ancient historians have perhaps had a tendency to underestimate the importance of symbol, mythology, and ritual in Athenian politics. Important correctives have been offered in recent years, for example in the work of J.-P. Vernant and his followers in and out of France, and in the writings of such historians as W.R. Connor, S.C. Humphreys, and N. Loraux, among others. It has become clear that the references in the sources to father–son conflict need to be placed in a context that spans the gap between myth and politics; they need to be understood as part of a discourse about politics via mythic symbols.[20]

For the Athenians (as for us) paternal authority was intimately connected with political authority. Athenian parentage was a matter not only of familial but of political significance, both on the practical level of citizenship and on the symbolic level of national myth: the Athenians were the "children of the earth," the "children of Athena," the "children of Erechtheus," the "children of Theseus." Zeus, the chief god of Greece, the "father of gods and men" as the poets frequently call him, rebelled against his father Kronos, who had earlier attempted to kill him, and who was himself a patricide. Theseus, the national hero of Athens, was himself a bastard who was abandoned by his father and who, although later accepted by that father, eventually proved to be indirectly responsible for the father's death; years later Theseus also turned out to be responsible indirectly for the death of his own bastard son, Hippolytos.[21]

The discourse about father–son conflict in Peloponnesian-War-era Athens, therefore, was, among other things, a way of explaining or explaining away or protesting the political and social upheavals of the day, and in a language that gained its power from its connection both to everyday life (what could be more mundane and familiar than the family?) and to myth and ritual (what could be more sacred?). It was a discourse of private life that bestowed or questioned the legitimacy of events in Athens's public life.

I have tried to stay clear of any notion of the primitivism of kinship or the family, in spite of the pervasiveness of this idea in the works of such seminal nineteenth-century scholars as Fustel, Maine, and Morgan, among others. Recent writings have challenged their primitivist notions considerably. Much less am I arguing that Athenian politics was "really all about" kinship or quasi-kinship, or that kinship was its fundamental idiom.[22]

To be sure, Athenian democracy never divorced itself from the notion of kinship as much as the modern, Lockeian liberal state has. The polis frequently appropriated the language of kinship as a legitimizing tool: for example, in the notion of Athenian autochthony or descent from a mythical national hero or of the bonds between members of one of democratic Athens's ten tribes. For all the symbolic significance of such quasi-kinship ties, however, kinship ties beyond the household had little influence on the everyday give-and-take of the polis. As Lawrence Stone comments about the modern state, at the very moment that the emerging state undermined the kinship power network of the medieval aristocracy, it encouraged patriarchy within the household as a model of the new, royal patriarchy. Later, under the influence of Locke, the ideology of the modern state distanced itself further (though not entirely) from familial models.[23]

The household was a fundamental constituent of the ideology of the Athenian state. Polis and oikos were less antithetical institutions than mutual and interdependent ones. The two emerged together in the early Archaic era, when prosperity created a class of small farmers, the heads of households (oikoi) who became both the soldiers and citizens of a new political community: the polis. Marilyn Arthur aptly describes the classical oikos as "a small holding corporation composed of its male head, his wife, their children, and the slaves who served it and worked the land that was its economic base."[24] As Arthur argues, the polis was defined as the sum of its individual households or oikoi. Citizenship depended on legitimate birth in an oikos, but not on membership

11

in a larger kinship group. True, potential citizens were initiated into hereditary quasi-kinship groups called phratries, but even these groups were products and subdivisions of the democratic state.[25] Rather than thinking in terms of either/or – either the family or politics – or in terms of domination/subordination or top/bottom, it is better to think of interaction between two distinct and interdependent institutions and complexes of symbols; to think of a constant flow in both directions of comparisons and analogies – from family to politics and from politics to family.

The last half-dozen paragraphs have gone far afield from the question of father–son conflict in Peloponnesian-War-era Athens. The reader might well ask if a straightforward social history might not be more to the point. The short answer is no. A social history of the Athenian family in the later fifth century BC is greatly to be desired but, given the quality of the surviving ancient evidence, pulling off such a study would be no mean feat. Such a study would, moreover, have to be very broadly conceived, both to do justice to the intimate connection of the familial and the political in Athens and to explain why the conflict in question was largely an ideological one.

The long answer . . . the long answer requires a theoretical excursus to justify the claims that the Athenian family was politicized and that Athenian politics was familialized. Chapter 2 offers such an excursus. After presenting a basic thesis there about the ideological nature of familialism in Athens, I proceed to a discussion of the terminology of fathers and sons, and then to an explanation of what I mean by ideology, and to discussions of the interconnection of oikos and polis, and of what I call, following the anthropologist Victor Turner, the social drama.

A winding road through theory, the will o' the wisp of ideology, a shortage of hard evidence, and a conflict in what evidence there is: enough to make the most loyal reader of history wonder whether he or she really wants to stay the course! It may seem like a difficult journey, and perhaps the best way to ease it is to give some indication now of where it is going to lead. To do so, I propose to devote the remainder of this chapter to brief statements of my overall thesis, methodology, and choice of texts.

THE ARGUMENT

Father–son tension can be found throughout the entire period of ancient Greek culture, from the myth of Zeus and Kronos on. Indeed, two strains of argument about fathers and sons appear in the Greek tradition. Greek tradition is firm about the importance of filial piety, praising it in such figures as Telemakhos or Hektor, but the tradition is not as firm about filial piety as, say, the Old Testament. On the one hand, normative discourse constantly reiterates the need for sons to obey and respect their fathers and to care for them in their old age. We might call this the "major key" of Greek father–son discourse. On the other hand, the "minor key" of this discourse not only recognizes the likelihood of conflict and tension between fathers and sons, but has a certain admiration for it. The tradition makes clear, for example, that Zeus was not wrong to rebel against the tyranny of his father Kronos; Prometheus was heroic to rebel against the tyranny of the patriarch Zeus; Achilles was heroic to prefer death and immortal glory on the battlefield at Troy rather than to return to Phthia and take care of his aging father Peleus.

The major-key argument needs little explanation, for society (at least male society) has as much at stake in the security of paternal authority as the individual father does. If a father is not secure in his power in the family, how is a governor to be secure in his power in the polity? For precisely this reason, the minor-key argument does need explanation; why encourage a destabilizing tendency? One might employ a "safety-valve" explanation: better to acknowledge an inevitable problem than to try to repress it and risk an eventual explosion. Some father–son conflict indeed seems inevitable, given the universal struggle in all societies over the intergenerational transmission of power and property, and the universal alternation of dependence and independence.

The subject of father–son conflict appears, moreover, to raise questions of profound symbolic significance. A varied group of intellectuals – Freud and his followers, anthropologists, ethnologists, and historians of religion – have argued that patricide or the patricidal urge is at the root of civilization. Neither generational change, nor the acquisition of wealth, nor hunting would be possible without confronting the issues symbolized by patricide, they variously argue. From this perspective, too, one might argue that the strain of admiration for rebellious sons (symbolic if not actual patricides) in the Greek tradition is a healthy form of releasing tension.[26]

Beyond the safety-valve explanation, however, it is important to note, in a Foucauldian vein, how Greek social relations, which tended to be conceived of in zero-sum terms – that is, the desire to dominate rather than be dominated – left their mark on familial relations as well. A son who was too obedient to his father ran the risk of seeming too subordinate to another man. The specific emphasis of Athenian democracy on individual autonomy further intensified the problem. Both the Greek cultural tradition of the heroic youth and the Athenian democratic innovation of the autonomous citizen contributed to the admiration for filial rebellion which is present in our sources.[27]

Father–son tension was not unique to Peloponnesian-War-era Athens. Borrowing from Freud and Norman O. Brown, one could say that a major motif of ancient Greek civilization was the tension between patriarchy and fraternity, or the rule of elders versus the assertiveness and rebellion of youth banded together as brothers. Such a dynamic can be discerned in the Homeric quarrel between Achilles and Agamemnon or the revolt of Kypselos against the Bakkhiadai in the seventh century BC or the rebellion of Julian the Apostate against Constantius in the fourth century AD. Athens in the period of the Peloponnesian War is a particularly dramatic case, but by no means a unique or isolated one. On the other hand, the Athenians of that period did discuss father–son conflict more openly and vehemently than do people of most eras. Compare the *Iliad*, which hints at father–son tension discreetly, in, for example, Achilles' distance from Peleus or his attachment to his tutor Phoinix, a would-be patricide (of all things) – compare that with fifth-century tragedy and comedy, which puts father–son conflict on center stage in front of the whole polis. By so emphasizing this conflict, Peloponnesian-War-era literature turns it into a central ideological metaphor, one with considerable political as well as sociological relevance.[28]

Father–son conflict was well suited to be a central ideological symbol of the Athenian polis. Political discourse was already imbued with familial language, such as the notions of *kyrios* and of the "fatherland" (*patris*). When, in the decade of the 420s, the multiple shocks of war, a major epidemic, the sophistic revolution, and the death of Pericles – who had dominated politics for a generation – gave new energy to the anti-democratic movement and new prominence to young men in their twenties, father–son conflict was ready to come into its own. It was a theme perfectly suited to symbolize conflicts between generations, between tradition and novelty, between the differing conceptions of authority among oligarchs and democrats, and between go-slow "mature" war policies and "youthful" gung-ho adventurism.

A conflict in ideology, however, is not the same as a conflict in practice. While there was something of a generation gap in the Peloponnesian War, especially in the 420s, references to father–son conflict in contemporary texts may reveal more about Athenian perceptions than about Athenian deeds. Most surviving texts have little to say about anyone outside of a narrow, relatively wealthy, urbanized, and mainly citizen elite, and they only permit impressionistic statements about that limited group. Furthermore, the sources tend to concentrate on spectacular rather than on representative cases of rebellion – particularly on the case of Alcibiades. A final argument against the reality in practice of father–son conflict concerns rhetoric. From the rhetorical point of view, complaints about disobedient sons are much more effective in a period when the old pattern of general obedience is still largely intact, and when conflict therefore seems aberrant, than in a period of general filial rebellion. Unless the authority of the Athenian father was still basically intact, unless the oikos was still basically strong, then the rhetoric of conservatism and preservation would have little emotional power. Perversely, the prominence of father–son conflict as ideological symbol, therefore, points to its relative insignificance as reality in practice.

I attempt to substantiate these points in the following three chapters. After a discussion of methodology (Chapter 2), I offer a synchronic analysis of the classical Athenian discourses of father–son solidarity (Chapter 3) and father–son conflict (Chapter 4). Then I turn to a diachronic study of the ideology of father–son relations in Athens during the Peloponnesian War era (Chapters 5 and 6). In particular I examine the role of paternal–filial ideology in the Athenians' conception of their experience in the time of the Peloponnesian War, borrowing from the anthropologist Victor Turner's notion of social drama. Turner argues that political conflicts, like dramas, pass through ritualized stages implicit in the minds of political actors. Especially in times of crisis, such actors tend to act and speak according to their education in a culture's central myths. In a democracy like Athens, the political actors included the entire citizen body, or at least the demos in assembly and in the courts, and not just the leading orators and generals. Furthermore, the physical, rhetorical, and thematic (issues of war and peace, and so on) similarities between the theater and the assembly encouraged Athenians to apply a metaphor of drama to politics. Athenians, therefore, had reason to conceive of their historical experience as drama.[29]

Furthermore, Athenians had a tendency to conceive of their experience in the Peloponnesian War era as a drama of father–son conflict. At the outbreak of the war, Athens was governed by the strong hand of Pericles, a man in his sixties who was often compared to Zeus, the patriarch of the Olympian pantheon. When Pericles died in the third year of the war, Athenian politics was opened to new forces. One of them was the unusual prominence of young men (young by Athenian standards). Of these orators and politicians in their twenties and early thirties, none was more prominent than Pericles' former ward Alcibiades. Comic and tragic playwrights described Alcibiades-like characters in their plays in order to caricature a paradox: their countrymen's simultaneous pride in a season of youth and fear of youth rampant. Young men delivered speeches in the assembly and conducted prosecutions in the courts, but nothing bespeaks their influence more than the Sicilian Expedition of 415, which the politician Nicias described as a young man's adventure in which the older generation was intimidated into acquiescence (Thuc. 6.13.1–2). Nothing, that is, except the affair of the Herms on the eve of the expedition's departure, in which the mutilation of statues all over Athens one night was taken as both the sign of a political conspiracy and a symbol of the dangers of youthful excess.

The fallout from this affair and the failure of the Sicilian Expedition marked a turning point. Not only was Alcibiades forced into exile, but the season of youth had faded in the public mind. The most appealing symbol in Athenian politics over the next decade was not a young hero but rather the so-called *patrios politeia*, the ancestral, traditional, or paternal constitution. As a means of restoring order on the ideological plane (and perhaps thereby more generally), Athenians returned from the rule of the son to the rule of the father. At the beginning of the postwar era, the imputation of disloyalty to one's father was not to be taken lightly on the part of the accused, but rather needed to be parried and disproved, as evidenced by the trial of Andokides in 400. The accusation of having interfered in a father's control over his son was even more dangerous; without a convincing response, it could be fatal. As the trial, conviction, and execution of Socrates in 399 show, Athenians had restored the ideology of paternal rule – with a vengeance.

Taken as a whole, therefore, the texts of the Peloponnesian War era show not only a thorough mingling on the ideological plane of oikos and polis and of public and private, but a tendency to construct Athens's political and military experience in familial terms, specifically in terms of the paternal–filial metaphor. Over the course of the war Athenian ideology changed and changed again until it came full circle: from father to son to father again.

Having sketched out the main theses of this book, let me turn to a discussion of the texts on which the following pages focus.

TEXTS

Students of the classics have sometimes attempted to produce scholarly works "more lasting than bronze." This book has a more modest aim. It is meant to be a stimulating essay on the family as ideology in ancient Athens, but not the definitive statement on the subject. While I will advance new interpretations of specific points, I also hope to provoke debate on a theoretical question: the shape and scope of the boundary between public and private. A conceptual metaphor often shapes the broad outlines of an author's work; for example, a book can be said to have been "crafted" or its style may be called "polished" or "lapidary." This book has been shaped by a cinematic metaphor. Film is less permanent or definitive than sculpture, but it offers a great variety of perspectives. Like a cameraman, I have tried to "pan" over the spectrum of the subject of fathers and sons in Athens in the Peloponnesian War era, sometimes "zooming" in for detail, other times pulling back for depth.

It was clear from the outset of my work that it would take several large volumes to do justice to the full range of relevant ancient evidence. For example, virtually all of extant Attic tragedy and comedy is germane, as is much in oratory, philosophy, and the classical historians, as well as in the numerous post-classical anecdotal accounts (Plutarch, Athenaios, Aulus Gellius), commentaries, and scholia that are well known to classicists. Vase painting and sculpture have much to say about the famous families of myth;

inscriptions offer valuable evidence about the transmission of names and professions, mainly in the elite but with some reference to ordinary people as well. The more archaeologists learn about civic and domestic architecture in classical Athens, the more we may be able to say about the physical shape of the arena of familial relations within the household and about the analogues and differences between public and private space.

Yet this book is not several large volumes, but only a single monograph. Although I have attempted to read as widely as possible in the ancient evidence, I have had to sift and choose what I discuss here, focusing on a relatively few texts and omitting many others. Some of the principles of selection which I followed are easily stated, others more complex. The limits of space, of my own training, and of my interests as a historian dictated a focus on literary sources; relatively little will be said about archaeology, architecture, inscriptions, sculpture, and vase painting. No ancient historian can be entirely happy about such a decision, but every study must recognize some limits.

In chronological terms, the focus is on the years ca. 450–380 BC. To study that era's inherited cultural tradition, it has of course been necessary to refer to earlier texts. The limited number and variety of surviving texts of the Peloponnesian War period, moreover, has made it necessary from time to time to refer to later material, particularly to fourth-century oratory. Every effort has been made to avoid anachronism, for example, not to cite a speech of the 320s as evidence for a supposedly unique characteristic of the 420s; wherever possible I have tried to connect the later material to relevant Peloponnesian-War-era texts.

In short, this study has both diachronic and synchronic dimensions. Uniting these two approaches is not without its difficulties; the reader can judge whether the marriage has turned out to be harmonious.[30]

In terms of genre, this book focuses primarily on oratory, tragedy, and comedy, with somewhat less attention given to history and philosophy. The classical historians were relatively uninterested in social history and, while philosophy has a great deal to say about fathers and sons, one must be cautious about using it as a guide to popular mores or ideology. Dover makes a valuable distinction between works composed for public delivery, that is, oratory, drama, and inscriptions, and works composed for a small audience, such as philosophy or history; as he notes, the first set of texts are a much better guide to popular culture than the second. As Ober notes in a similar vein, texts written by the elite for a mass audience (for example, oratory) must be treated differently from texts written by the elite for an elite audience (for example, philosophy).[31] While the material on fathers and sons in Plato, Xenophon, and Aristotle – whom Winkler rightly calls an "eccentric coterie" – is too plentiful and rich to ignore, the following pages devote relatively more attention to oratory and drama.[32]

The principles of chronology and my intended audience helped to narrow down the texts to be studied here, but this still left far too much for a single volume. In the end, I was forced to make choices not only on thematic but also on personal grounds. I chose texts that were particularly relevant to my central themes: the alternation between solidarity and conflict in Greek normative discourse on fathers and sons, the centrality of father–son conflict as an ideological symbol of the Peloponnesian War era, the gap between ideology and societal reality, and the Athenian tendency to conceive of the war as a social drama of fathers and sons. But, however vague, sentimental, or unscientific a criterion, I also chose texts on architectonic and aesthetic grounds; that is, because they seemed to cap or support particular points of my argument particularly well.

For example, in my judgment, Euripides' *Hippolytos* is a text in which all the major themes of this book converge as in few others, and so it receives a long discussion. On the other hand, Euripides' *Alcestis* and *Orestes* or Sophocles' Oedipus plays receive relatively little attention: not because they lack relevance (far from it) but rather because they do not illustrate the argument as well as *Hippolytos* does. Similarly, some readers may question why so much attention is devoted to Andokides' speech "On the Mysteries," hardly a literary classic. The answer is that Andokides' text throws into stark relief the pivotal role of father–son conflict as both familial and political ideology.

The texts on which the following pages focus, therefore, have been chosen on a variety of grounds. The main texts studied include, among orators, Andokides, Lysias, and, to a lesser extent, Aeschines and the Demosthenic corpus. Four comedies of Aristophanes are discussed in some detail (*Birds*, *Clouds*, *Knights*, *Wasps*) as are the fragments of Eupolis's *Demes*. Among tragedies, Euripides' *Hippolytos* receives the longest discussion, followed by his *Suppliants* and *Herakleidai* and Sophocles' *Antigone*. Several passages in Thucydides, mainly relating to the debate on and departure of the Sicilian expedition, receive a close analysis. Plato's *Laches* and Xenophon's *Symposium*, both texts with a dramatic date during the Peloponnesian War but written later, receive considerable attention, as do Plato's and Xenophon's respective *Apology of Socrates* and the parts of Xenophon's *Memorabilia* of relevance to Socrates' trial. Numerous other texts from the fifth and fourth centuries BC, as well as the works of much earlier (such as Homer) and much later (for example, Plutarch) writers are also referred to from time to time.

2

INTELLECTUAL PATERNITY

Patiently, patiently, ever the father, you answer their questions.

> Carolyn Kizer, "Amusing Our Daughters."

Let us begin with a thesis statement about the Athenian family, particularly the father–son relationship, and about the interconnection of the familial and the political in classical Athens.

For Athenians, the father–son relationship served as a powerful, multivalent symbol of authority. It is but one example among many in classical Athens of the pervasive analogy between oikos and polis, and it was an important component in Athenian ideology. Because of the symbolic power of the family or household in classical Athenian culture, when Athenians tried to make sense of their history, one of the models they drew on was the familial model, and the father–son relationship in particular. To the Athenians themselves, the story of Athens was a story not just of citizens and constitutions but of fathers and sons.

The rest of this chapter is devoted to exploring the meaning of this statement.

SEMANTICS

To study the father–son relationship is to step on rich symbolic soil. The father–son nexus raises basic questions about creation and procreation, about transmission and transgression. It is a fundamental theme of the myths by which our society lives, from old myths, like Judaism or Christianity, to new ones, like psychoanalysis. For Freud, the father plays a crucial role in the institution of civilization, be it through ontogeny or phylogeny. Under the

21

first rubric comes what Freud describes as the resolution of the Oedipus Complex, in which a boy learns to obtain the maternal object of his desire by submitting to his father's power and resolving to become like him; under the second rubric comes Freud's anthropological myth of the totem, in which a tyrannical, primal father is murdered by his sons, only to have them in turn identify themselves with him and his strength. In either case, for Freud, patriarchy is a requisite of civilization. Lacan dispenses with Freud's anthropology, but he too emphasizes the role of the father as the instrument that teaches the infant about the laws and taboos of society – but Lacan means the symbolic rather than the real father. In the "Name of the Father," as Lacan puts it, drawing from both Freud and the Gospels, we signify difference (the separation of the infant from the mother), language, law, and the social order itself.[1]

To study parents and children is to study more than biology. While motherhood is visible, fatherhood is not, except in a hit-or-miss similarity of features between a child and its purported genitor. Paternity is hard to prove. According to Hesiod, only men of justice are rewarded with wives who are fertile and bear sons who resemble their fathers (Hes. *Op.* 235). The fragility of paternity is described clearly in the *Odyssey*, when Athena (in the guise of the mortal Mentes) remarks on the physical similarity between Telemakhos and his father Odysseus. Telemakhos, who has not seen Odysseus since infancy, is not so sure of his paternity, and replies:

> Friend, let me put it in the plainest way.
> My mother says I am his son; I know not
> surely. Who has known his own engendering?
>
> (Hom. *Od.* 1.214–16, tr. Fitzgerald)

The diffident Telemakhos refers to Odysseus as "he by whom they say I was begotten" (*Od.* 1.220).[2]

The uncertainty (before the modern technology of verification) of paternity makes it necessary for a culture and the individuals within it to construct, discursively, the ties that bind father and son.[3] While these are usually ostensible blood ties, they need not be; adoption is an obvious exception. Upon further reflection, the father–son relationship is defined by (and defines in turn) a complex web of interrelated concepts of, *inter alia*: authorship ("the wish is father to the thought"), authority ("the founding fathers"), creation ("to father a child"), generations ("fathers and sons"), obedience ("filial piety"), affection ("fatherly"), mentorship ("father-figure"), apprenticeship and education (*"Doktorvater"*), and servitude (as in the example of calling a porter a "boy" or a waiter's assistant a "busboy," even if they are both adults).

In his provocative critique of the study of kinship among anthropologists, Schneider highlights the synthetic nature of the father–son relationship. He points out the plasticity of the terms in Yapese (a Micronesian language) which were originally translated into English as "father" (*citamangen*) and "son" (*fak*). A reassessment shows that these terms denote neither consanguinity nor absolute states of *being*, but refer rather to codes of conduct and variable ways of *doing*. According to the traditional Yapese outlook, coitus had nothing to do with conception, and hence there was no consanguineous relationship between "father" and "son." What ties a *citamangen* and *fak* for the Yapese is not blood, but the authority and independence of the *citamangen* and the respectful obedience and dependence of the *fak*. The *citamangen* controls land and land-based resources (status and rank); the *fak* works the land for the *citamangen* and may expect to obtain control of it one day. In the usual course of things (and note that it is possible for the relationship to be terminated) the *citamangen* eventually grows elderly and becomes dependent on the *fak*, at which point the terminology is reversed: the older man becomes the *fak*, the younger man the *citamangen*. In short, among the Yapese, kinship is neither absolute, nor privileged, nor a universal idiom in terms of which all other relationships may be expressed. Kinship is not merely intertwined with but subordinate to what we might call political and economic factors.[4]

In Athens the notion of consanguinity was usually present (except in cases of adoption) in the father–son relationship (for example, Aesch. *Eum.* 657–666). The Yapese case is instructive, nevertheless, because it suggests the importance of authority, obedience and the control of resources in the way a particular culture construes that relationship. Schneider's emphasis on the integrity and specificity of native formulations is also instructive: we should not assume that the Athenians defined the father–son relationship the way the Yapese did, nor, for that matter, the way a particular modern culture does today. Yet the Yapese case does offer clues for resituating the Athenian father–son relationship in the wider context of Athenian society and culture. It also suggests an answer for the question of why fatherhood and sonship should have a political significance: because they can hardly be constructed without one.

A brief examination of the relevant classical Attic terminology demonstrates that in Athenian culture, consanguinity was not the only, although it was the primary, attribute of the father–son relationship: notions of authority and obedience were an integral part of the complex of meaning in which the relationship existed. Let us examine consecutively the terms for father and son.

Father

The ordinary word for father in Attic Greek is *patêr* (plural, *pateres*). There are also less specific terms that can denote "father," among other things, for example: *genetês*, "genitor" (from *gignomai*, "to become" or "to be born"); *goneus*, "father," "ancestor," or, in the plural *goneis*, "parents" (also from *gignomai*); and *tokeus*, "begetter" (from *tiktô*, "to bear") are less common.[5] *Patêr* and its numerous derivatives, frequently found in prose and poetry, are highly connotative in meaning. In Homer, for example, *patêr* can be a term of respectful salutation for any older man (LSJ s.v.). *Patêr* and the adjectival form *patrôios* are frequent epithets of Zeus from Homer to the classical period (LSJ s.vv.). The plural, *pateres*, is commonly used to mean "forefathers" or "ancestors," often in an appeal to the authority of the past (LSJ s.v.; e.g. Thuc. 2.36.2).[6]

Poets and philosophers use *patêr* metaphorically to mean "author" or "source," for example, Herakleitos's famous dictum: "War is the father of all (*Polemos pantôn men patêr esti*) and king of all, and shows some as gods, others as men; and makes some slaves and some free" (Frg. 53 Diels and Kranz, Hippolytos, *Refutatio Omnium Haeresium* 9.9.4). Plato plays with the notion of *tou logou patêr*, "the father of the discourse," which in context refers to the initiator of the discourse (*Symp.* 177d; cf. *Phdr.* 257b).[7]

Patêr-derivatives played an important role in Athenian politics, society, and economics. To consider only the most relevant examples, one's country was one's fatherland, *patris* (e.g. Lys. 2.6.7; Thuc. 7.69).[8] *Patrios, patrikos,* and *patrôios* are all adjectives derived from *patêr*, all meaning "of the father," with *patrios* and *patrôios* often meaning "hereditary." In Attic prose, *patrôios* is generally used for property and patrimony, while *patrios* usually refers to customs, laws, and traditions; *patrikos* often refers to friendship. So the customary or ancestral law of the land was literally "the paternal law," *patrios nomos*, or simply "the paternal things," *ta patria*. Traditional offices in the Athenian government such as the archon basileus or polemarch could be described as "ancestral" (*tôn patriôn*, as opposed to later "additions," *ta epitheta*, Arist. *Ath. Pol.* 3.2, 3.3). The local and time-honored religious shrines of fifth-century Attica were also "ancestral" (*patria*, Thuc. 2.2.16). Both sides in the late-fifth-century debate on the Athenian constitution, oligarchs and democrats alike, claimed to be proponents of the "ancestral" – literally the "paternal" – constitution, the *patrios politeia*, an agreeably emotion-laden and vague term. To do something according to the customs of one's fathers, particularly to carry out a religious rite, was called *patriazein* ("to take after one's father," Pollux 3.10).[9]

An inherited friendship was a "paternal friendship," *patrikê philia* (e.g. Isoc. 19.10). One's patrimony, the paternal estate, was literally "the paternal things," *ta patrôia* (LSJ s.v. *patrôios*; cf. Suda s.v. *patrôion*) or "paternal substance" (*patrôia ousia*, Isai. frg. 1 [D.H. *On Isaios* 8]; *patrikê ousia*, LSJ s.v. *patrikos*) or "paternal household" (*patrôios oikos*, Isai. 7.25) or "paternal allotment" (*patrôios klêros*, Isai. 3.30). The inherited gods of the Athenians were paternal gods, *patrôioi theoi*, and patriotic oratory witnessed frequent appeals to their authority (Thuc. 7.69; Xen. *Hell.* 2.4.21). Poetry from Homer on frequently refers to the "patrimonial hearth" (*hestia patrôia*, e.g. Hom. *Od.* 17.80; Soph. *El.* 881; Eur. *Med.* 681).[10]

One of the most interesting and politically complex of the *patêr*-derivatives is the notion of bearing one's father's name, a patronymic, for example, Pericles, son of Xanthippos, a custom usually referred to in Attic as being called *patrothen*, "from or after a father" (LSJ s.v.). A traditional appellation, the patronymic contains a wide range of connotative meaning. To refer to someone simply by his father's name might indicate formality or irony or the subject's youth or obscurity or his father's fame, as for example in the case of Lysis, a rich young teenager whom Socrates calls "son of Demokrates," after his prominent father (Pl. *Lys.* 204e; cf. Dem. 21.60). More often, however, the patronymic connoted seriousness, manliness, and that combination of formality and intimacy that demarcates a moment whose symbolic is greater than its literal significance. For example, after the battle of Lade in 494 (a disastrous loss for the Greeks) the Samians granted the relatively few men who had fought bravely for Samos the privilege of "having their names inscribed on a stele with the patronymic indicated (*patrothen*) because they were men of courage (*andrasi agathoisi genomenoisi*)" (Hdt. 6.14; cf. Pl. *Laws* 753b). In Homer, of course, it is common to address a warrior by his patronym: "Peleus's son Achilles," "son of Atreus," "Neleus's son Nestor," and so on.[11]

The patronymic conferred identity. It was, first of all, a recognition of legitimate birth, which was not taken for granted, as indicated by the cycle of paternity-affirming rituals an Athenian boy went through. Second, it was a declaration of social status. To be the son of Odysseus was to share in honor and glory; to be the son of Thersites was another matter. The difference is what makes the patronymic problematic for an egalitarian society, which is probably why Kleisthenes in the late sixth century promoted the use of the demotic name (based on residence) instead. Kleisthenes' reform of nomenclature was only partly successful. In the fifth century, some Athenians enthusiastically accepted the demotic, while others adhered to the patronymic; the choice can sometimes be correlated with democratic or oligarchic political sentiments. By the fourth century, a compromise had been worked out, by which it was common (either in speech or in writing) for an Athenian to use both the patronymic and the demotic, for example: Aristoteles, son of Euphiletos of Akharnai (*IG* II² 44).[12]

A third point is that the patronymic declared possession. The son's name would appear in the nominative case, the father's name in the genitive: for example, Pericles son of Xanthippos would be Periklês Xanthippou, literally "Pericles of Xanthippos" or "Xanthippos's Pericles." In a sense, therefore, the son was "of" the father, of his body and his oikos, and in the father's possession. In epic, the patronymic is usually indicated by the -*idês* or -*iadês* adjectival ending: for example, *Pêliadês Akhilleus*, "Peliad Achilles," that is, Achilles the son of Peleus, or Atreidês Agamemnon, "Atreid Agamemnon," that is, Agamemnon the son of Atreus. The adjectival form perhaps lays less emphasis on possession than does the genitive, though it too does qualify and limit a son's individuality.[13]

The persistence of the patronymic is primarily a datum of social and political history, pointing both to a certain conservatism and to the paradox of inherited inequality in a democratic society. It is an important psychological datum too, however, for the patronymic suggests a strong connection between one's father, one's name, and one's identity, especially one's public identity. Psychoanalytic theory suggests that the infant's admission to society and its laws comes through the symbol of the father. For the infant, the father may represent the authority that separates him from his mother's breast and creates the rules of civilization. More concretely, we each inherit from our father a status and a stance toward society. The father – the symbolic father, the family name, and the real, flesh-and-blood father – mediates between the individual and society.[14]

Demosthenes, for example, offers a fine insight into Athenian categories when he says that the opposite of having a renowned father or grandfather – which would spur a man to an active public life – is having ancestors whose deeds were paltry and without name: literally anonymous, *anônyma* (Dem. 10.73). To have a father who, for all practical purposes, lacked a name was to be, for the purpose of public life, nameless. A man who was not *patrônymos* was *anônymos*. On the other hand, a glorious patronym – a "great-named father" (*megalônumon . . . pater*, Ar. *Cl.* 569–70) – signified the promise of great deeds ahead.[15]

The *patêr*, therefore, was an important source of meaning and identity in Athenian culture. A detail in Aeschylus's *Oresteia* is revealing. Not least of the functions that Agamemnon fulfilled as father was that of exegete. In a prayer to Zeus (often referred to as "Zeus Patêr" in the *Oresteia*) asking him to raise his fallen house (*domos*) back up to greatness, Orestes cites his father Agamemnon's services to the god (Aesch. *Cho.* 246–263). Among them, Agamemnon transmitted the god's signs (*sêmata*) to mortals. Unless Zeus comes to the salvation of Orestes and Electra, the "father-bereft offspring" (*patrostêrês gonos*, 253), he will have no way to send his signs. For Orestes, it is only the father who gives the house its meaning in the divine order.

The name of our father, the friends of our father, the laws of our fathers, the gods of our fathers, the fatherland: these were commonplaces of Athenian culture, all pointing to an underlying assumption of the father's authority and the consequent value of an association with it. The whole complex of meaning is epitomized in a passage in Thucydides. In a state of high nervousness in 413 on the eve of the climactic battle between Athens and its enemies in the Great Harbor of Syracuse, the Athenian general Nicias

27

approaches his trierarchs individually and addresses them each *patrothen* (Thuc. 7.69), having already addressed the troops at large (7.62–64). He had little to say on the *patêr* theme in the first speech (*patris*, 7.61.1, is the only example), which makes its prominence in the second one all the more striking and melodramatic. His originality exhausted, Nicias falls back on commonplaces. Here is Thucydides' sardonic report of Nicias's remarks:

> Nicias, appalled by the position of affairs, realizing the greatness and the nearness of the danger now that they were on the point of putting out from shore, and thinking, as men are apt to think in great crises, that when all has been done they have still something left to do, and when all has been said they have not yet said enough, again called on the captains one by one, addressing each by his father's name (*patrothen*) and by his own, and by that of his tribe, and adjured them not to belie their own personal renown, or to obscure the hereditary virtues (*patrikai aretai*) for which their ancestors (*progonoi*) were illustrious; he reminded them of their country (*patris*), the freest of the free, and of the unfettered discretion allowed in it to live as they pleased; and added other arguments such as men would use at such a crisis, and which, with little alteration, are made to serve on all occasions alike – appeals to wives, children, and national gods (*theous patrôious*), – without caring whether they are thought commonplace, but loudly invoking them in the belief that they will be of use in the consternation of the moment. Having thus admonished them, not, he felt, as he would, but as he could, Nicias withdrew and led the troops to the sea.

> (Thuc. 7.69.1–3, tr. Crawley)

Here then is an impromptu Fourth-of-July oration, with the *patêr* theme taking the place of motherhood and apple pie (or, to use the current American idiom, of "family values").[16]

Son

In Attic prose, the clearest word for son is *huios*, possibly derived from a root meaning "to procreate" (LSJ s.v.). Son is often expressed as well by the vaguer word *pais*, "child" (possibly derived from a family of terms meaning "small"), which has such common connotations as "young person," "boy" or "girl," or "son" or "daughter."[17] The distinction between *huios* and *pais* is not always crystal clear, but it is sometimes marked, as in a speech of Isaios: "He [sc. our father] had four children (*paides*): we were two sons (*hueis*) and two daughters (*thugateres*)" (Isai. 2.3). *Pais* has perhaps more of a technical and legal sense than *huios*, as *pais* is also the term for any male citizen who had not yet come of age (Arist. *Ath. Pol.* 42.1). In Attic tragedy *huios* is rare, and *pais* is common as "child," "son," or "daughter" (LSJ s.v.). In Herodotus's Ionic prose, *pais* replaces *huios* as "son," generally excluding the notion of "daughter" (LSJ s.v.). For example, King Kleomenes of Sparta "died without a *pais* (*apais*), leaving only a daughter (*thugatêr*), whose name was Gorgo" (Hdt. 5.48). Like *pais*, *teknon* (from *tiktô*, "to give birth"; cf. *tokos*, "son," or "offspring") can mean "child," "son", or "daughter." "Son of" could also be denoted in Attic Greek, as noted above, by the genitive patronymic (for example, Plato Aristonos, "Plato son of Ariston") or, in epic, the *-idês*, *-iadês* adjectival endings. Various derivatives of *gignomai*, "to be born," can also mean "son," "child," or "offspring": *gonos* or *ekgonos*, the latter also meaning "grandson" or "descendant" (cf. *eggonos*).[18]

In epic and occasionally in high-faluting classical rhetoric, *huios* or *pais* is used to foster a sense of community: so Homer refers to the Achaeans as the "sons of the Achaeans" (*huies Achaiôn*, for example, *Il.* 1.162); in the account of Salamis in Aeschylus's *Persians*, a general battle cry calls the "sons of the Hellenes" (*paides Hellênôn*, 402) out to fight; in Sophocles' *Oedipus Tyrannos*, Oedipus refers to the people of Thebes as his children (*tekna*, e.g. 1, or *paides*, e.g. 58); orators in Herodotus speak of the Lydians as the "sons of the Lydians" (*hoi Lydôn paides*, 1.27) and the Ionians as the "sons of the Ionians" (*Iônôn paidas*, 5.49). Here, kinship, in the form of common descent, is the idiom of unity. A similar notion can be found in the practice of the doctors of Cos calling themselves *Asklêpiadai*, "sons of Asclepius," and in their organization as a guild, with each new student taking filial responsibility toward his masters. Similarly, consider Aristotle's remark on the village (*kômê*), which he considers, unlike the polis, to be primarily an extension of the household (*apoikia oikias*, *Pol.* 1252b17). Aristotle notes that some villagers call each other "milk-peers" (*homogalaktas*, *Pol.* 1252b18).[19]

Of the various terms for "son," *pais* has by far the greatest variety of connotative meanings. Attic Greek has numerous *pais*-derivatives for "childish things," among them: *paidzô*, "to play"; *paidia*, "a game"; *paideuô*, "to rear" or "to educate"; *paideia*, "upbringing," "education," or "childhood"; *paidagôgos*, "slave attendant for boys" or "teacher." More interesting are the extensions of *pais* in Athenian usage to denote status or hierarchy. First, *pais* can mean "slave," even if the slave is an adult; compare the demeaning use in the United States of "boy" for an adult African-American during the Jim Crow era. Second, *pais* or *paidika* can be used for the *eromenos*, that is, the "subordinate" (or "passive" or "receptive") partner in a pederastic relationship. According to conventional morality, a *pais/eromenos* was not supposed to be over the age of twenty or so, but there are examples nevertheless; and even conventional morality considers the *pais/eromenos* to be at his most attractive during late adolescence. Hence, once again, the *pais* was not necessarily a boy.[20]

One could say a great deal about each of these uses of *pais*. What is most interesting from the point of view of fathers and sons, however, is the readiness with which Athenian culture constructed analogous hierarchies.[21] Just as *pais* refers to a subordinate social relationship in the nuclear family, so it does in the wider circle of "oikos-management" (*oikonomia*), that is, the management of slaves, and in the wider circle still of extra-oikos erotic relationships.

IDEOLOGY AND EVERYDAY LIFE

The scholarly literature on the meaning of ideology is quite large. I have been influenced mainly by those theories that see ideology, and culture more broadly, as a system of meanings and symbols.[22] Ideology is defined herein as a system of meanings and symbols which attempts to create a collective consciousness and to maintain power. Ideologies are globalizing and competitive. They are also quite often subtle and embedded in the experience of ordinary life, particularly in words that suggest analogies between everyday life and politics – in, for example, the activities, status, and significance of a father, which evokes such notions as "fatherland," "founding fathers," "paternalism," and "patriarchy." Two other questions about ideology – the relative importance of explicit and inexplicit ideology, and the pursuit of stability – require brief further comment.

Let us take the relationship of explicit and inexplicit ideology first. One of the most important contributions of recent students of ideology has been to emphasize its presence in every stratum of society. The historian seeks examples of ideology not just in treatises or party platforms but in institutions and symbols of non-overtly political significance and finally in the language, actions, and habits of everyday life. This may be a matter of necessity for the always document-poor ancient historian, but it is, much more profoundly, an indication of the nature of society. First of all, as political anthropologists have argued, the less overtly political a symbol is, the more politically efficacious it may be. Second, the practice-oriented anthropology of Pierre Bourdieu and the sociology of Anthony Giddens have argued that the "constitution of society," as Giddens puts it, is more tangibly created in individual practices than in any formal written document. Bourdieu describes how, in a pre-capitalist society with precious few formal institutions, a system of dispositions – of language, of bodily deportment, of gift exchange, and so on – makes vivid and reproduces the dominant ideology. To take another example, in his study of a Cretan village, Michael Herzfeld demonstrates how, through language and through ritualized contests of sheep-stealing, shepherds create an indigenous "poetics of manhood." Recently historians of ancient Greece have begun to investigate the political and ideological significance of ordinary practices.[23]

Perhaps the ideological efficacy of an elite is to be measured less in the ability of the governors to express their power in official discourse than in their ability to have the governed express it all-but-spontaneously in the unofficial discourse of everyday life. Pericles says as much of Athens in his Funeral Oration: unlike Spartans, who require an education consisting of laborious exercises and strict isolation from foreigners for the inculcation of the rules of adulthood, Athenians become good soldiers and citizens freely and individually (Thuc. 2.38–39). Pericles' ideals are repeated in thousands of ways by thousands of Athenians in everyday life.

As many feminist scholars have argued, gender is one of the most basic of ideological symbols. Research about such diverse places as seventeenth-century Britain and its North American colonies and third-millennium BC Mesopotamia has shown that politics, no less than private life, is gendered – that is, it uses gender as an important category. Arguing in a similar vein, other feminist scholars have shown that politics is also "familialized," that it uses the family too as a category. I shall proceed from this important insight.[24]

Athenian sources frequently evince analogies between oikos and polis: from debates in the philosophers to speeches in tragedy and oratory to small but telling details of legal and political terminology. One of the things that made the father–son relationship an important and efficacious Athenian ideological symbol was its presence in a variety of settings and intensities, from the humble to the exalted, from the commonplace to the sacred. A part of everyday life within the domestic unit, fathers and sons played a significant role in Athenian communal and religious rituals too, and they were frequently the subject of Attic tragedy and comedy. Furthermore, as noted above, patêr and pais and their derivatives were words with strong political connotations. Hence, the pervasiveness of the father–son relationship contributed to its power as an ideological symbol.[25]

Of necessity, discussions of ideology get into questions of obtaining, maintaining, and reproducing power, which leads to our second question, stability. As Thompson points out, it is important to avoid a simple functionalist model, by which ideology would directly preserve the stability and equilibrium of the social order. The critics of functionalism have long since demonstrated its tendency to overestimate social stability and its failure to do justice to the phenomenon of change. In a similar vein, Thompson criticizes the familiar notion that ideology produces stability by generating consensus; as he notes, the stability of a complex society may owe more to the divisions among potential opposition groups than to any overall societal consensus. In other words, ideologies can produce stability through tension and fragmentation as well as through consensus.[26]

Athenian history and culture, moreover, similarly argue against a model of equilibrium or consensus. With its fundamental principles of freedom (eleutheria), equality (isonomia, isêgoria), and the alternation of ruling/being ruled (archein/archesthai) Athenian democracy suggests rather a model of strife and change, of flux and debate. So does the role of father and son in Athenian culture. To be sure, a society can use the father as a buttressing symbol of strict authority and tradition and use the son as a paradigm of obedience: consider, for example, Roman patriarchal ideology. The Athenian model of father–son relations, though, is more flexible and less certain – perhaps the very qualities that make it so interesting. Although Athenian (and Greek) normative discourse usually emphasizes the authority of the father, the obedience of the son, and their mutual affection, nevertheless a powerful minor key runs through ancient Greek history of, on the one hand, admiration for the independence and vigor of the son (from Achilles to Alcibiades to Alexander) and, on the other hand, recognition and fear of the hostility of the father (from Kronos to Laios to Philip of Macedon). In democratic Athens, father–son ideology balanced an emphasis on tradition (for example, democracy as *patrios politeia*, that is, the traditional – literally, paternal – regime) with admiration for the vigor of youth.[27]

To sum up, to speak of Athenian ideology is to speak of the system of symbols and meanings which attempted to create a collective consciousness and to maintain the power of democracy as a system of government and a way of life. A globalizing ideology, it provoked competitive counter-ideologies (most notably oligarchy, but also monarchy and a variety of philosophical utopias). It was present in the practices of everyday life as much as or more so than in official, elite discourse. If ideology succeeded in achieving social stability, it did so through tension and balance rather than through consensus. In some ways it masked unpleasant realities, in other ways it bestowed power on groups and individuals who may have lacked power otherwise.[28]

THE OIKOS

One of the most important sources of symbolic political power in Athens was the family. The closest Attic Greek equivalent to our word "family" is oikos, a much-discussed term among classicists. Like today's "family," oikos refers to the nuclear unit, sometimes with the addition of an aged parent; kin of the bilateral extended family were referred to as *anchisteia*, *suggeneia*, or *prosēkontes*; other terms, such as *oikeioi*, *philoi*, *anankaioi*, *epitēdeioi*, could refer to either family or friends. Our main sources for the term "oikos" are forensic speeches and philosophy, which are useful but problematic evidence. The Attic terminology of family and kinship is notably plastic; for example, as part of their rhetorical strategy, the orators do not hesitate to play with a term's meaning even in the same speech. Oikos can mean "house" (Ant. 2d.8) or "property" (Lys. 19.47) or "lineage" (from father to son) (Dem.

43.48) or "nuclear family" (Dem. 43.19) or "progeny" (43.12) or "persons within a household," including slaves (Arist. *Pol.* 1253b4–7); the related *oikia* can mean "property" (Isai. 6.18) or "persons" (Isoc. 19.7) but is more likely to be used as "house" (Xen. *Oec.* 1.5). Oikos and *oikia* can also mean "meeting house" (*IG* II² 1672, line 24) or "clubhouse" (*IG* II² 1241, lines 18, 32, 41; 2622, line 2) and, by extension, the people who meet there; the "oikos of the Dekeleians" (*IG* II² 1237, line 33) thus, according to an ingenious suggestion, may mean "the deme assembly of the Dekeleians," in reference to the building where that assembly met. Some texts emphasize the religious aspect of the oikos (for example, Homeric Hymn to Aphrodite 29–30; Lys. 1.27; Isai. 7.30). Oikos thus has a range of meanings: familial, territorial, architectural, economic, religious, and, less commonly, political. There is a greater emphasis on property and cult than in our "family." Much is made in Attic oratory of the importance of continuing the oikos from generation to generation and not letting it die out (for example, Isai. 7.30; Dem. 43.75, 83–84).[29]

This last argument is invariably self-interested, a way of strengthening a claim to an inheritance, but there is other evidence that Athenians saw the oikos as an institution that passed property and good character from father to son. The old Fustelian view of the oikos as an institution of ancestor worship or one looking toward a limitless future is no longer tenable; the Athenians generally seem to have had little interest in ancestors beyond the great-grandfather. Indeed, the oikos did not even possess any family surname to continue, although first names were passed on. On the other hand, the interest in transmitting education and property and thereby re-creating the oikos from generation to generation was immensely important. To be sure, the modern family, too, is a unit of child-rearing and property inheritance, but given the Athenian father's responsibility to his legitimate sons to teach them a trade, to initiate them into citizenship, and to pass his property on to them and no one else (except for what he gave his daughters as a dowry), the emphasis on intergenerational transmission was much greater in the oikos than it is in today's family. In short, the oikos was conceived of as much more of a diachronic unit than is today's family.[30]

Even when a text places its emphasis on the oikos as a group of persons, it rarely gives "oikos" the connotations of emotion and intimacy which our "family" has. Again, caution is required, given the male and property-oriented biases of our sources; no audience at a tragedy could doubt the importance of emotions in the oikos. On the other hand, even tragedy puts an emphasis on the importance for a young male of succeeding to his patrimony, an emphasis that – to our taste – seems highly incongruous. On the whole, therefore, it is probably more in keeping with Athenian categories to think of oikos as "household" in the primary instance and "family" only secondarily.[31]

The independent nuclear household seems to have dominated the architecture and economy of classical Athens. Small houses of five to seven rooms grouped around a court and separated from the world outside were the norm. Each household had its own, if generally simple and unpretentious, religious cult. The hearth, more likely a portable brazier than the fixed structure of idealizing literary sources, played a central role in the oikos's cult: communal meals, ceremonies of initiation and intergenerational continuity (for example, marriage or the *amphidromia*), and daily prayers and offerings. Funerals and memorial observances honored the dead and comforted the living, and fostered a sense of familial cohesion. As for membership in an extended family, that counted a great deal in inheritance claims and, at least theoretically, in the obligation to avenge homicide. Cousins moreover might become close friends or political allies. On the whole, however, the extended family played a relatively small role in Athenian life; the oikos predominated. It is not surprising that the oikos figures much more prominently in classical Athenian ideology than the extended family, nor that so many of the crises of tragedy and comedy take place in the household nucleus.[32]

As has often been pointed out, the architecture of the oikos was in general quite different from that of public buildings; in Athens, public and private space were broadly differentiated. Athenian ideology moreover tended to designate the oikos as "female" and meeting-places and buildings of the polis as "male." Independent oikoi, separate public and private architecture, gendered distinctions between household and political space: given such data, it is fair enough to wonder about the relevance to public life of the private relations of Athenian fathers and sons. What significance did the affairs behind the walls of the oikos have for the polis?[33]

A great deal: as frequently happens in the history of ideology, Athenian ideology was inconsistent on the subject of oikos and polis. An Athenian would see many symbolic markers of the independence of the oikos, but he would also see many indications that the oikos was a fundamental symbolic building block of the polis. At the same time as the independence and uniqueness of the polis were proclaimed, it was hedged around with the reassuring symbols of the oikos. The portable brazier found in Athenian private houses, for instance, was echoed in the public hearth in the town hall of the community, probably a successor to the royal hearth of the Mycenaean palace. The *andrôn* ("men's room") found in many private houses, used for dining and drinking parties, was echoed in civic buildings and temples. In short, the distinction between public and private, between oikos and polis, was only partial and incomplete.[34]

Let us look at the question of public and private in classical Athens in two stages: by first examining several recent theoretical perspectives, and then turning to the ancient evidence for the interrelationship of oikos and polis.

THE THEORY OF OIKOS AND POLIS: A MIDDLE WAY

There has been considerable divergence of opinion among scholars recently about the nature of the public–private distinction in Athens. Broadly speaking, some scholars emphasize the polis and public life, arguing that Athenian democracy, beginning with Cleisthenes, created its own political values; the private values of the oikos either were rendered separate and irrelevant or were utterly subsumed and transformed by the public values of the polis. For example, arguing (in the tradition of Hannah Arendt) for a pure political sphere, Meier sees in Athens the presence of "a clear dividing line between work and politics, between the house and the *polis*."[35] Hansen and Musti each emphasize the strong sense in classical Athens of a separation between public and private; Hansen emphasizes the self-segregation of the male citizens (from metics, slaves, foreigners, women, and children) in all things political.[36] Lanza and Vegetti argue for the all-pervasive ideological infuence of the polis, "the model of theoretical organization, the *analogia universalis* of every process of structuring of the religious, physical and psychological order."[37]

The other end of the spectrum is held by scholars who, from a variety of perspectives, emphasize the triumph of the private. Humphreys and Carter turn Meier on his head, as it were, by arguing for the growing appeal of private life for disillusioned members of the Athenian elite beginning in the late fifth century. Humphreys argues that because of a combination of factors in the fifth and fourth centuries – urbanization, increased social and residential mobility, and, above all, the elaboration of a new set of norms for behavior in public – "Athenians [became] newly conscious of polis and oikos as being separate and different."[38] A different case for the primacy of the private emerges in the work of Foucault and the classicists such as Winkler and Halperin whom he influenced. On the Foucauldian model, the state is subordinate to other power networks, the most important of which, in the case of classical Greece, are managing a household and governing oneself; in the latter category Foucault includes what is today called sexuality. Foucault describes Greek sexual practices as primarily hierarchical and polarized. He emphasizes what he calls the homology or isomorphism between sexuality and a polarized model of social relations often discernible in Greek culture, a model whose hallmarks were honor, competition, aggression, domination, the refusal to submit to others, and a contempt of compromise.[39] While Foucault's arguments depend heavily on the philosophers, rarely representative of ordinary Athenian life, Winkler and Halperin apply them to texts, such as oratory, which are of more direct value as historical evidence. Winkler is also much influenced by reading in the social and cultural anthropology of traditional Mediterranean societies, where an emphasis on the honor and shame of the household looms large. Focusing on the regulation by the polis of the body and particularly of male sexual misbehavior, Winkler and Halperin argue for the presence in public life of the hierarchical values of the bedroom; that is, for the predominance of the oikos.[40] We have come full circle.

In scholarship, unlike politics, compromise is not necessarily the best route, and yet it is important to recognize that there are substantial elements of truth in each of the above theses. The polis did have a remarkable hold on Athenian culture in all its forms, and at the same time some notion of public and private did emerge. Furthermore, the traditionally hierarchic values of Greek society were balanced by the emergence under democracy of a strong ethos of equality. Nevertheless, one must do justice to the importance of the oikos – or the father–son nexus within it – as a model and idiom in classical Athenian society. Rather than posit either the dominance of the polis or the strict separation of oikos or polis, we ought rather to recognize a complementary and homologous relationship between the two: notions of public and private constantly interacted, each shaping and changing the other.[41]

Whatever Foucault's strengths and weaknesses as a social thinker, certainly the straightforward application to Athens of the Mediterranean model is as problematic as it is provocative. Anthropologists themselves are by no means in agreement about the validity of Mediterranean society as a notion – Herzfeld, for instance, detects a certain First World *nostalgie de la boue*, and questions whether such often-evoked notions as "Mediterranean shame and honor" are not merely artificial constructs belonging to a discourse about northern and not southern society.[42]

Athenian democracy created new values in the minds of its participants. On the other hand, we go too far if we think that in creating new values Athenian democracy jettisoned all old values. For all its emphasis on equality within the citizen group, the Athenian polity was nonetheless divided into dominant (adult male citizen) and subordinate groups (women, resident aliens, foreigners, slaves, children). Even within the circle of citizenship, there was an emphasis on the alternation of governing and being governed, ruling and being ruled. It is noteworthy in this context that the same Attic Greek verb (in the active or passive voice) – *archein/archesthai* – means not only "to rule" or "to be ruled" but "to govern" or "to be governed" and "to hold public office" or "to be governed by a public official." This formula can be read as one that emphasizes sharing and orderly alternation. In the era of the Peloponnesian War, however, when the lines of power in the Athenian empire were particularly stark, the emphasis is perhaps more likely to have been on power disparities. Indeed, as many have noted, late-fifth-century Greek culture in general demonstrates a marked tendency toward hierarchy. For example, for the restive cities in the Athenian empire, the opposite to complete autonomy was not partial autonomy or power-sharing, but "slavery" (e.g. Thuc. 3.10.3).[43]

Equality received a novel emphasis in fifth- and fourth-century Athens but it did not entirely displace the desire "to be the best," that is to say, the search for personal honor. The career of virtually any politician of democratic Athens bears this out. Nor need we assume that because he developed new loyalties to associations outside the oikos the citizen shed his loyalty to the oikos every time he stepped out the front gate or entered the agora.

Consider the case of Polystratos of the deme of Deirades, a wealthy landowner among whose numerous public offices were those of *katalogeus* and *bouleutês* under the Four Hundred (see Lys. 20). After the restoration of democracy Polystratos was tried, convicted, and sentenced to a heavy fine; there followed (winter 410/409) a second trial and the threat of a fine which this time Polystratos could not afford to pay, having allegedly lost much of his wealth in the Decelean War. The result would have been loss of citizen rights (*atimia*) for himself and his grown sons, all of whom had served Athens in the Peloponnesian War (Lys. 20.35). In this second trial one of Polystratos's three sons defended his father on a charge of overthrowing democracy during the oligarchy of 411 (Lys. 20.11–13, 19, 27, 30, 33–36; Harpokration s.v. *Polystratos*). The son is moved not merely by filial piety but also by self-interest.[44] The details of Polystratos's case are extraordinary, but the requirement of family solidarity in the face of a public threat is not. Lysias 20 is a defense speech delivered by one of the sons. The speaker says, in conclusion:

> we find, gentlemen, that when someone puts forward his children with sobs and lamentations you take pity on the children for the disenfranchisement (*atimia*) that they will owe to him; and you overlook the fathers' transgressions on account of the children, of whom you cannot yet tell whether they will grow up to be good citizens or bad. But of us you can tell that we have zealously worked in your service, and that our father is clear of any transgression.... And our position is the contrary of that of other people: for others seek your indulgence by producing their children; but we seek it by producing our father here and ourselves, begging you not to render us disenfranchised (*atimoi*) instead of enfranchised (*epitimoi*), men without a polis (*apolidas*) instead of citizens (*politai*). Nay, pity both our father, an old man, and us. If you ruin us unjustly, what pleasure will there be for him in our society, or for us in company with each other, when we are unworthy both of you and of the polis?
>
> (Lys. 20.34–35, Loeb trans. modified)

Few texts do a better job of weaving together oikos and polis, and of suggesting that the two were inseparable. No doubt the sentiments expressed were in part for show, but only in part.

Abstractions are of great value in revealing underlying principles but in the ordinary course of events the ordinary *politês* is likelier to have made cross-references between categories rather than to have kept them separate. Rather than saying "this is oikos, this polis, and never the twain shall meet," he is likely, before making a decision, to have weighed a variety of factors from each sphere – and not merely to have weighed them, but to have compared, conflated, and even confused them. Athenian political oratory, for example, frequently strays from the issues at hand to venture into such matters as whether a public speaker is a good father or whether his father was a good man or whether his mother had to work to make a living or whether his private life is disposed in an orderly manner or not. In short, if Athens is not to be reduced to a so-called Mediterranean society whose public culture was dominated by considerations of honor and shame, neither are those considerations to be excised from our assessment of Athens. To the degree that Athenians constructed a dialogue between oikos and polis, their conception of society was more organic than disjointed. Athenian culture, in short, was complex.[45]

There is a parallel between our conception of an organic relationship between oikos and polis and certain of Aristotle's arguments in the *Politics*. Aristotle stakes out a middle ground on the subject of the relationship of oikos (or *oikia*) and polis. On the one hand, he opposes the enterprise of Plato's *Republic* to unify oikos and polis (*Pol.* 1260b27–1264b25). He also objects to a prevalent contemporary argument asserting an analogy between slave management and statesmanship: the first an activity within the household, the second an activity in the polis (*Pol.* 1252a8–18, 1255b15–20). Aristotle asserts a fundamental, qualitative distinction between polis and oikos, even if a small polis and large oikos each should contain about the same number of people (*Pol.* 1252a8–13). On the other hand, Aristotle considers oikos and polis to be intimately connected; indeed, he denies the possibility of creating an excellent polis if one leaves the oikos unregulated, in the private sphere as it were.[46]

To create an excellent polis, according to Aristotle, one must regulate the education of women and children, since women comprise half the free population, and children are the future "partners of the regime" (*Pol.* 1260b19–20). Aristotle argues that the oikos is not merely a unit of reproduction, but an institution which is the source of political order, friendship, and justice (*Eth. Eud.* 1242a40–b1; cf. 1242a22–27). Not only, therefore, is every polis

composed of oikoi, but the polis cannot be good unless its oikoi
are also good (*Pol.* 1253b2–3, 1260b8–20).[47]

Another important point is Aristotle's distinction between slave
management and other oikos activities. Aristotle maintains that
there are fundamental differences among what he considers to be
the primary relationships in the household (*Pol.* 1253b5–8): the
relationship of master and slave (*despotês* and *doulos*), husband
and wife (*posis* and *alochos*), and father and children (*patêr* and
tekna). Yet Aristotle considers the three relationships, however
great the differences among them, to be all part of the general
problem of ruling and being ruled. Moreover, while he draws a
sharp distinction between being a slavemaster and being a statesman (1253b18–21) Aristotle pursues the analogy between the art
of ruling and the paternal or matrimonial art: a husband rules his
wife like a statesman (*politikôs*), a father rules his children like a
king (*basilikôs*) (1259a37–b17).[48]

Aristotle, therefore, does not believe in a complete analogy
between oikos and polis, and still less in the desirability of unifying
the two. He nevertheless does not embrace a modern, liberal separation of public and private, arguing rather (a) that the rule of a
father over a wife is analogous to the rule of a magistrate over
free men, while the rule of a father over children is analogous to
that of a king over his subjects, and (b) that the political art should
include the regulation of the oikos.

OIKOS AND POLIS IN PRACTICE

Let us examine various indices of the interrelationship of oikos
and polis in classical Athens, with an emphasis on three points in
particular: (1) the legal requirements for citizenship and for holding
the office of archon, (2) the political myth of common descent,
and (3) the widely shared ideology that one could not be a good
citizen without being a good man in the oikos, or the reverse, that
misbehavior in the oikos was a sure sign of misbehavior in the
polis.

Citizenship first. Athenians had a varied terminology for citizenship. In addition to the usual *politês* (derived from polis) or *astos*
(derived from *astu*, "city") or "Athenian" (*Athênaios*), they spoke
of someone as "having a share in the city" (*metechô tês poleôs* or
metesti moi tês poleôs, Soph. *OT* 630; cf. Ar. *Lys.* 63; and numerous
fourth-century sources, e.g. Dem. 39.31, 57.1–2; Ps.-Dem. 59.111;

Arist. *Ath. Pol.* 26.4) or of having a share in its courts (Pl. *Laws* 768b) or sacred and public business (Dem. 39.35). What is interesting for our purposes is that Athenians spoke analogously of "having a share in one's paternal estate" (*tôn patrôiôn echeis to meros*, Dem. 39.35) or "a share in paternal shrines and tombs" (*hierôn kai taphôn patrôiôn metousiai*, Aeschin. 2.152). Polis and oikos were analogously shared institutions, and in both cases membership was exclusive and challengeable.[49]

Except for the rare cases of "adoption" into citizenship – note the similarity of terminology (*poiêsis*) between familial adoption and civic enfranchisement – the Athenian citizen-to-be had to prove his legitimate birth into an Athenian oikos. A candidate for Athenian citizenship had to prove that he was freeborn, eighteen years old, son of a citizen father and mother who were themselves children of Athenian fathers and who had been properly married; his qualifications had to be accepted by his deme and, in most cases, his phratry (Arist. *Ath. Pol.* 42.1). Nor could the candidate make his case without the active support of his family; there was no question of relying on documents from a state archive. Rather, the candidate needed to present as a witness his father or, should the father be deceased or abroad, his guardian. The representative of the oikos, the father or guardian, thus played a central role in the integration of the individual into the political community.[50]

The phratry (*phratria*) is in itself a good example of the interrelationship of oikos and polis. It was once thought that the Attic phratries were primitive survivals, kinship groups that predated the polis. The revisionist and widely accepted view nowadays is that phratries were never kinship groups; rather, phratries developed out of local associations, perhaps in the Dark Ages; in the classical era, they had a political as well as a social function, since phratry membership was one of the common proofs of citizenship if challenged. The phratry was one of many groups (for example, *genê, phylai, trittyes*, demes) that mediated between the polis and the individual – or, to be precise, between the polis and the oikos, since one was initiated into one's father's phratry, with the help of one's father or guardian, just as at the deme scrutiny. Although membership was hereditary, the phratry ideology of brotherhood and common fatherhood was mythical (note the annual phratry festival of the Apatouria, a term perhaps equivalent to *homopateres* or "same father"). The ideology contributed to Athenian male solidarity, while the scrutiny of the phratry initiation was another link in the chain connecting citizenship with membership in an oikos.[51]

Was the citizenry of Athens legally a collection of oikoi; was "the polis ... an aggregation of oikoi," as Wolff argues? An exaggeration, if it means that the polis was composed of a finite set of oikoi, each continued by one heir. The Athenians rather seem to have thought of each generation as reconstituting a new oikos, and in any case a father might have several heirs, each forming a separate oikos. On the other hand, there was, with but few exceptions, no possibility of citizenship without legitimate birth under lawful wedlock into an Athenian oikos, as verified by initiation into phratry and deme. According to the spirit of the law, therefore, the Athenian polis was indeed "an aggregation of oikoi"; this statement holds even truer when applied to the ideology of Athenian descent (below). The relationship between the individual and the polis was mediated by a series of segmentary institutions – oikos, phratry, and deme – that each relied on kinship as a membership criterion. Strictly speaking, this kinship was bilateral, but there was a strong patrilineal bias.[52]

To turn to the archonship, Aristotle's account (*Ath. Pol.* 55.2–3) of a candidate's scrutiny before the council is worth quoting:

> They ask, when they subject [a candidate] to the scrutiny (*dokimasia*), first "Who is your father and what is your deme? Who was your father's father, and who was your mother, and your mother's father and his deme?" Then they ask whether he has an Apollo Patrôios and Zeus Herkeios, and where the shrines are, then whether he has family tombs and where they are, then if he treats his parents (*goneas*) well, and whether he pays taxes, and if he has served on military campaigns.

As in the case of citizenship, there is much emphasis here on the candidate's parents, first as signs of citizen birth and second as evidence of acceptable moral behavior: a candidate must treat his living parents well and respect deceased parents' tombs. Perhaps it was the archon's eventual entry into the Areopagos council, that most traditional of institutions, that made filial duty (that most traditional of responsibilities) seem like an appropriate issue to explore. That question, however, was not the end of linking the archonship to the oikos. The reference to Apollo Patrôios is probably a question as to whether the candidate belongs to a phratry, with which the god was associated; again, the root issue is legitimate descent. Zeus Herkeios was a god of the oikos; the issue here is perhaps whether the candidate has a household with roots in Attica, as indicated by the household shrines. After so much attention to family, the questions about taxes and military service are almost jarring.[53]

The questions asked of would-be archons are a reminder that the maltreatment of one's parents by any Athenian, including the failure to provide for their food and shelter or to bury their corpses, was punishable by law (*nomos goneôn kakôseôs*). It is just one of many examples showing that in Athens, the personal, or at least the familial, was political. Indicative is the oath of the Athenian juror, in which one called down, as punishment for swearing falsely, destruction not only of oneself but also of one's family.[54]

Let us turn now to the civic myths of common descent, a second indication of the interrelationship of oikos and polis in Athens. The familial metaphor underlay the Athenian myths of national origins. Fifth-century drama frequently describes Athenians as descendants of the various mythical kings of Attica: most commonly as Erechtheidai (for example, Eur. *Supp.* 702; *Ion* 1050; Ar. *Kn.* 1015, 1030), but also as Kekropidai (Ar. *Kn.* 1055), Aigeidai (Ar. *Kn.* 1067), and Theseidai (Soph. *OC* 1066). As Loraux has demonstrated, the notion of common paternal descent from the first Athenian, Erichthonios (and through Erichthonios, descent from Athena and her father Zeus), was at the center of the metaphor. Fifth-century vase painting and drama and fourth-century funeral orations interpret autochthony, the Athenian claim to be born "of the earth itself" and thereby to be native to Attica, as a myth that gave all Athenian citizens a common and divine ancestry. Moreover, even though Erichthonios was born of Ge, or Mother Earth, and even though Athena, the eponymous deity of Athens, was female, the myth of autochthony places great emphasis on Athenian paternity.[55]

Paternity is stressed, first (and paradoxically), in the person of Athena, who along with Hephaistos, the myth says, fertilized Ge: Erichthonios and thus all Athenians traced their descent to Athena's father, Zeus. The sources often stress both Zeus's special closeness to his daughter (for example, Eur. *Tro.* 48) and Athena's status as a masculinized goddess who served as a patroness of males (e.g. Aesch. *Eum.* 736–738). Second, funeral oratory often points out that since Athenians were autochthonous, the earth was their fatherland as well as their mother (Lys. 2.17; Isoc. 4.25; Dem. 60.4; cf. Pl. *Menex.* 249a4–5, 249b7–c1). Athenian ideology often plays down the maternal role in the familial metaphor of autochthony. For example, in Euripides *Herakles* (ca. 416) Amphitryon compliments Theseus by remarking that "The fatherland (*patris*) that bore him (*tekousa tonde*) is blessed with children (*euteknos*)" (1405). Third, in another version of the autochthony myth, Athenians traced their descent through Ion (eponymous hero of the Ionians) to Apollo Patrôios, "the patrimonial Apollo." This myth was dramatized by Euripides in *Ion*, perhaps performed sometime late in the penultimate decade of the fifth century. Apollo Patrôios was patron deity of the phratry festival, the Apatouria; his cult appears to have grown in importance at the end of the fifth century and throughout the fourth.[56]

Since Athens was a fatherland (*patris*), it was possible to describe it, as one would a private patrimony, as something that had to be conserved and passed on to future generations, not something that one dared squander. In his Funeral Oration of 431/430, for example, Pericles praises both remote ancestors and his father's generation for acquiring an empire and for passing it down to contemporaries (Thuc. 2.36.1–2). The year before, King Arkhidamos of Sparta had advised his countrymen not to give up the discipline which their fathers had passed down to them (Thuc. 1.85.1). In the same debate, the Corinthians had warned the Spartan assembly not to let their hegemony of the Peloponnese grow less than what their fathers had left them (1.71.7). All three speakers use the verb *paradidômi* to describe their fathers' transmission of goods, the standard terminology for private inheritance (LSJ s.v.), which suggests the polis–oikos analogy.

The ideology connecting behavior in the oikos with behavior in the polis – a third index of the interrelationship of oikos and polis in Athens – is present in drama and abounds in the orators. Information about one's own private behavior, or that of members of one's oikos, greatly influenced a person's public reputation. Perhaps the *locus classicus* is Aeschines' formulation in his well-known prosecution of Timarkhos in 346 for having spoken in the assembly after a previous career of prostitution; Aeschines' conception of the interrelationship of public and private is a clarification of similar sentiments (though not concerning prostitution) in a fifth-century text, as will become clear presently.[57] In any case, in the era of the Peloponnesian War too, a citizen similarly lost his rights by speaking in the assembly after committing an act of prostitution: so Kleon brags in Aristophanes' *Knights* (877–880) of 424 BC.[58] Aeschines cites several classes of evil-doers prohibited by law from addressing the assembly; besides current or former prostitutes and cowards or deserters, they are: (1) anyone who beats his father or mother or fails to provide them with food or shelter, and (2) anyone who has squandered his patrimony (*patrôia*) or other inheritance (Aeschin. 1.28–30). Aeschines asks why Solon, the ostensible author of the law, should forbid a man who mistreats his parents from speaking. He answers: "Because if anyone is stingy in his behavior toward those whom he ought to honor on a par with the gods, why ever, [Solon says], would strangers (*allotrioi*) and the whole polis listen to him?" (Aeschin. 1.28; cf. Lys. 30.23). And why does Solon prohibit those who squander inheritances?

> Because he thought that the man who manages his own private household badly (*ton gar tên idian oikian kakôs oikêsanta*) would dispose of the common affairs of the city (*ta koina tês poleôs*) in a similar fashion; and the lawmaker [Solon] did not think it possible for the same man to be bad (*ponêros*) in private affairs (*idiai*) and good (*chrêstos*) in public affairs (*dêmosiai*); nor did he think the orator ought to come to the speaker's platform well versed in speeches but not in life.
>
> (Aeschin. 1.30)

Aeschines thus states the equation clearly: a man who does not manage his *oikia* well cannot manage the polis well; a man who mistreats his parents, his nearest and dearest, would do who-knew-what to his fellow citizens. In short, if you're bad in private, you'll be bad in public (cf. Aeschin. 3.77–78).

About a century earlier, Sophocles gave similar sentiments to the character of King Kreon in *Antigone*. In a long speech addressed to his son Haimon, Kreon connects the absolute loyalty which he says a son owes his father with the absolute obedience which he says a good man owes his ruler. He expects Haimon to understand why Kreon cannot tolerate the disobedience of his niece and ward Antigone, Haimon's fiancée:

> For if I nurse (*trephô*) unruliness in those who are kin by birth (*eggenê phusei*),

Then I shall indeed do so outside of the family (*exô genous*).
Whoever is a firm man (*chrêstos*) among the members of his
    oikos
Will be found to uphold justice in the polis too.
. . .
There is no greater evil than anarchy.
This destroys poleis, this leaves oikoi
Ravaged.

(Soph. *Ant.* 661–662, 672–674)

Once again, behavior in the oikos is analogous to behavior in the
polis.

Aeschines and Kreon have something else in common too, the
assumption of a private realm limited by public imperatives. As
king, Kreon claims the right to regulate burial when the corpse
was a traitor in life; as orator, Aeschines claims the right to regulate
vice when a vicious man speaks in the assembly. Kreon's claim
was controversial and vitiated by his arrogance and impiety, but
not Aeschines' claim: he won the case and Timarkhos was convicted (Dem. 19.284). Aeschines feels no need to apologize for
intruding into Timarkhos's affairs or to reassure the audience that
its privacy was safe. On the contrary, he says that by prosecuting
Timarkhos he was defending all Athenian fathers, sons and boys
– in other words regulating sexual behavior in general (2.180). And
not just sexual behavior, because he considers a conviction to
benefit all fathers by discouraging sons from squandering their
patrimonies (1.195).[59]

Similar themes – the analogy of oikos and polis, the blurring of
public and private – appear in Demosthenes, though with a slight
shift of emphasis to the applicability to public life of the model
of family harmony (25.89: *homonoia*):

For you, men of Athens, as I have said, observe a natural
benevolence (*philanthrôpia*) toward each other, and just as
families inhabit private households so you inhabit the polis
in public (*hôsper hai suggeneiai tas idias oikousin oikias,
houtô tên polin oikeite dêmosiai*).

(Dem. 25.88)

The suggestion, in other words, is that the polis should be one
big family. Interestingly, Demosthenes goes on to refer not to
brotherhood, as an orator might today, but to the relations between

47

young and old, specifically fathers and sons. Nor does he paint a rosy picture; rather he assumes conflict is inevitable. What the family offers as a model is not a utopia without conflict but a pragmatic mode of mediating conflict. "Wherever there is a father and grown-up sons, and perhaps their sons too, there are necessarily many desires and by no means similar ones; for youth has neither the same words nor the same deeds as old age" (Dem. 25.88).[60] How then is peace preserved? The orator explains: by mutual winks and nods and a moderation that neither needs to flaunt indiscretion nor insist on punishment. The polis too promotes harmony by a prudent retreat from confrontation (Dem. 25.89). Demosthenes' model is interesting in many ways, not least because it highlights the father–son relationship as the core of the oikos–polis analogy.[61]

The analogy between the role of the father as *kyrios* in the oikos and in the polis plays a subtle and revealing role in Lysias 1, "On the Murder of Eratosthenes." The speaker, one Euphiletos, stands accused of the premeditated murder of his wife's lover Eratosthenes; Euphiletos's defense is that he caught Eratosthenes *in flagrante*, and thus had the right by Athenian law to kill him. As an accused murderer, Euphiletos needs to demonstrate his law-abidingness to the court, but as a wronged husband, he needs to reassert his male authority before the men of Athens – to show that he can keep his house free of criminals and keep guard over his own wife (Lys. 1.36, 48). Throughout the speech, therefore, Euphiletos assimilates the restoration of his authority, as *kyrios* of his oikos, over those who have cuckolded him, to the theme of the restoration of the laws of the polis over an adulterer. For example, he claims to have declared to Eratosthenes when he caught him,

Not I but the law of the polis is going to kill you, which you transgressed and deemed less important than pleasure, and chose to commit so great a crime against my wife and my children rather than to obey the laws and be a person of orderly behavior.

(Lys. 1.26)

Euphiletos chooses his words carefully when describing his decision to kill Eratosthenes rather than to accept Eratosthenes' proposal of monetary compensation instead. "I would not yield to his proposed sum," Euphiletos says, "but I held that the law of the polis had greater authority [literally, "was more *kyrios*," *kyriôteron*], and I obtained satisfaction" (Lys. 1.29). The admirable Euphiletos has the good character to pass up money in obedience to his *kyrios*, the law, and so presumably he can master other temptations and assert his own status as *kyrios* in the oikos. He insists on an intimate connection between public and private, and asserts that he executed Eratosthenes less out of private motives than for the good of the whole polis (Lys. 1.47).[62]

To read the orators in search of analogies between paternal and political authority is to go from elegant, sophistic constructions to melodrama to puns and wordplay. There is melodrama aplenty, for example, in the often-repeated charge in the Demosthenic corpus that so-and-so, the alleged public miscreant, treated his own father swinishly. Androtion accuses Diodorus of killing his own father (Dem. 21.2, 24.7), Diodorus accuses Timokrates of failing to support his elderly father and of selling his son into prostitution (Dem. 24.200–203), Demosthenes asserts that Aristogeiton abandoned his father in prison and refused to bury him when he died (Dem. 25.54–55). One begins to suspect that the audience enjoyed the very predictability of such charges.

As for wordplay, a speaker in Lysias (21.24), for instance, says he would gladly deprive his children of their father (*patêr*) in order to die for the sake of the fatherland (*patris*). This little jingle sheds much light on the intimate connection between public and private in Athenian culture. Unlike the American revolutionary Nathan Hale, whose only regret was that he "had but one life to give for ... [his] country," the speaker appears to regret that he had but one fatherhood to give! Demosthenes (18.205–206) makes a similar pun: in the good old days of the ancestors (*progonoi*), he says, every Athenian considered himself to have been born not only to a mother or father (*patêr*, *mêtêr*, *goneis*) but to the fatherland (*patris*). The import is that every citizen is a son of the fatherland, and that he owes his country filial loyalty and obedience. In both Lysias and Demosthenes, quasi-filiation becomes the idiom of politics: wordplay, but serious and useful play. Andokides (1.106) wraps himself in the flag, as it were, by mentioning in the same breath Athenians' forefathers (*pateres*), his ancestors (*progonoi*), and the fatherland (*patris*). Later in the same speech he seeks the jury's sympathy by first reminding them of his lack of family (father dead, no brothers or children) and then exhorting them to behave toward him like a surrogate father, brothers, or children (Andok 1.148–149). Andokides won the case.[63]

49

Andokides' ploy calls to mind the well-known Athenian habit of bringing one's family to court to elicit the jurors' sympathy. The main idea was showing off the innocents who would suffer should anything untoward happen to their sole support, the defendant. The intended result, as Demosthenes puts it with stern disapproval, was to make pity prevail over the laws (Dem. 21.99, 195, cf. 224–225). Another important point was to make the best of the family's background in order to claim a record of distinguished public service. Nor should we forget plain old bathos: in antiquity, as today, there was nothing more efficacious than a mother's tears on her son's behalf. A final point should also be kept in mind: the implicit argument that a good family man must also be a good citizen, and therefore deserves acquittal.[64] For example, in his defense on a charge of treason, Aeschines does a good job of enumerating his family's supposed sacrifices for Athens and he certainly gets his relatives to the courtroom, including his mother and ninety-four-year-old father (Aeschin. 2.147–152; cf. Dem. 19.310). What he really handles nicely, however, is the oikos–polis analogy. Pointing out to the jurors his three children, Aeschines says that he has only brought them to court as "evidence" (*tekmêrion*) in response to one question:

> I ask, men of Athens, whether you think that, in addition to the fatherland (*patris*) and the company of my friends and my share in the shrines and tombs of my fathers (*hierôn kai taphôn patrôiôn metousiai*), I would have betrayed *them* to Philip – them, the dearest of all mankind to me. [Do you think] I would have preferred his friendship to their safety?
> (Aesch. 2.152; cf. Ps.-Dem. 7.17)

Clearly, a father like Aeschines could never have betrayed the fatherland!

Lysias's prosecution of Agoratos is similarly melodramatic and even more sophisticated, since it offers a metaphor within a metaphor. The analogy between honoring one's parents and fearing the gods, or between respecting one's friends and obeying the laws, was utterly conventional, to judge from its appearance on Isocrates' list of instructions to the young, a list of Polonius-like banality (Isoc. 1.16; cf. Pl. *Meno* 91a). Lysias exploits this conventionality nicely. The orator claims that Agoratos calls the Athenian people "father," and then he finds a way to turn the trope against Agoratos, arguing that Agoratos must be treated like a son who has violated his legal duty to provide for his father:

> In every way [Agoratos] deserves to die many times over; for the same man who says that he <was adopted> by the demos, the demos, whom he himself calls his father (*patêr hautou*), [this man] is found to have injured the demos. . . . Now whoever struck his birth father (*gonôi patêr*) and failed to furnish the necessities of life, and robbed his adoptive father (*poiêtos patêr*) of all his goods, how could he not thereby deserve the death penalty according to the law against maltreatment (*nomos kakôseôs*)?
>
> (Lys. 13.91)

Lysias serves warning here that two can play at the game of familial symbolism. Before appealing to the demos as its son, one had better be sure that he can prove himself to be a good son.

Like Lysias, Demosthenes (10.40–41) invokes the law against maltreatment of parents. For him the analogy is not explicitly one of father and son, but the related model of children (*tekna*) and parents (*goneis*) or a young man (*ho en hêlikia*) and his elders (*hoi presbuteroi*). The issue is the reluctance of the rich to pay liturgies, on the grounds that the poor get off scot free. Demosthenes compares this to an argument that children need not support their (aged) parents because their parents no longer support them – which would result in a violation of the law against maltreatment. He says: "So just as each one of us has a parent (*goneus*), so we must consider the citizens taken as a whole to be the common parents (*koinoi goneis*) of the whole polis" (Dem. 10.41).

Let us take stock of the evidence: both modern theories and the testimony of the ancients, primarily of the orators. Schneider has demonstrated the need to be wary of the notion of kinship as the underlying idiom of a culture. I am certainly not arguing that either the oikos or kinship or quasi-kinship more generally was the central underlying metaphor of Athenian political ideology (let alone the dominating fact of political practice). In fact, one could make a case for precisely the opposite thesis, and argue that the pervasiveness of democratic and public-spirited ideology in classical Athens had a tendency to make politics the idiom of familial ideology! Indeed, in the *Republic* Plato gives Socrates an argument in this vein. Expounding on the theme of democracy, Socrates comments:

In this kind of a polis [sc. a democracy] then doesn't liberty get into everything? ... It makes its way into private houses (*idiai oikiai*) and ends up breeding anarchy even among the animals. ... For example, ... a father (*patêr*) will accustom himself to behave like a child (*pais*), to fear his sons (*hueis*), while the son behaves like a father, and feels neither shame nor fear before his parents (*goneis*), in order to be free. A metic puts himself on a par with a citizen (*astos*) as does a foreigner (*xenos*). ... Altogether the young (*neoi*) are thought to be the equals of the old (*presbuteroi*) and compete with them in word and deed, while the elderly (*hoi gerontes*) accommodate themselves to the young, and are full of playfulness and pleasantries, thus aping the young for fear of appearing disagreeable and authoritarian (*despotikoi*).

(562e–563b tr. Grube modified; cf. *Laws* 701b).

Socrates' point is well taken, and it or its variants seem to have been well known in Athens. Aristophanes makes a similar point in *Clouds* and the thesis is probably implicit in the anti-democratic grousings of the "Old Oligarch," who comments on the ill effects of democracy on slaves and metics (Ps.-Xen. *Ath. Pol.* 1.10–12).

Rather than thinking in either–or terms, it is best to think of household and politics as interacting continuously, each shaping and changing the other. The analogy between oikos and polis was mutual; the relationship between oikos and polis, by and large, complementary rather than antithetical. The result is neither a neat nor an uncomplicated picture, but perhaps it is not far removed from reality.

Foucault argues that mastery or domination was what might be called the "root paradigm" of the concept of power in Athenian culture. As we have seen, this is an exaggeration: to do justice to such values of democracy as equality and concord, one can hardly make mastery the sole value of the Athenian polis – but it was an important value nonetheless. Recent work in anthropology and sociology emphasizes the significance both of everyday interactions and of non-overtly political behavior in creating the symbols of political power. If these approaches are valid, it follows that both the oikos and particularly the relationship within it that is most invested with questions of authority and power – the father–son relationship – were important symbols of political power in classical Athens.[65]

In Athens, the familial metaphor influenced political ideology in a number of different ways, three of which have been emphasized here: (1) the public interest in the private, familial background of citizens and archons, (2) the civic myth of common descent from a first father or from the Attic soil personified as a mother and a fatherland, and (3) the frequent argument that behavior in the oikos is an index of behavior in the polis.

A related point is the plasticity of the boundary between public and private in Athens. Athenian citizens (*politai*) were not merely cogs in a constitutional machine. They were sons both of an oikos (in which the father was himself an Athenian citizen and the mother was the daughter of an Athenian citizen father) and of the fatherland (*patris*). In many matters that we consider part of the private sphere, father was ready to enforce the conviction that he knew best.

THE SOCIAL DRAMA

"Have I played my role well in the comedy of life?" Augustus is supposed to have asked his friends as he neared death (Suetonius *Life of Augustus* 99.1). The notion that public figures in a society conceive of their activity in theatrical terms is one that the anthropologist Victor Turner pursued in many of his works. Like Geertz, Ortner, and other symbolic anthropologists, Turner conceives of culture as a system of meanings and symbols. Geertz, for instance, in a celebrated article, considers the meaning of the Balinese cockfight, which he sees as a "paradigmatic human event" that spells out both the ethos of the observer's culture and his own private sensibility.[66] Turner's work is marked by the notion of "social drama," the idea that political conflicts, like dramas, pass through ritualized phases which are implicit (consciously or unconsciously) in the minds of the actors. Turner's ideas and those of his followers may help us to understand the evolution of Athenian paternal ideology during the period of the Peloponnesian War. Likewise the Athenian case illuminates Turner's paradigm.[67]

Turner first studied politics as drama by analyzing the conflicts between individuals within the small kinship groups of the African Ndembu. He sees each of these conflicts as a "social drama," a public episode that passes through ritualized stages of breach, crisis, redress, and reintegration or lasting schism. Social dramas require individuals to choose between personal preferences and social obligations. Turner writes: "The situation in a Ndembu village closely parallels that found in Greek drama where one witnesses the helplessness of the human individual before the Fates; but in this case the fates are the necessities of the social process."[68] Hence, the cross-fertilization of drama and politics is inherent.

At various stages of his work, Turner alternately stressed the symbolic and functional aspects of social dramas, arguing that they might either reveal underlying structures or allow self-reflection, that they might provide a remedy for a societal crisis or serve as a liminal moment of societal transformation.[69] Social dramas might fulfill all these roles at once by providing a framework for action. Turner notes that the actions taken by various politicians often seem to be part of a self-contained drama whose script is not chosen by accident. He writes:

> What seems to happen is that when a major public dramatic process gets under way, people, whether consciously, preconsciously, or unconsciously, take on roles which carry with them, if not precisely recorded scripts, deeply engraved tendencies to act and speak in suprapersonal or "representative" ways appropriate to the role taken, and to prepare the way for a certain climax that approximates to the nature of the climax given in a certain central myth of the death or victory of a hero or heroes in which they have been indoctrinated or "socialized" or "enculturated."[70]

As an example, Turner notes the significance of the Christ myth in Mexican politics. He argues that in such disparate events as Hidalgo's insurrection of 1811 and the emperor Maximilian's choice in 1867 to eschew flight from Mexico, Mexican political actors chose martyrdom to " 'fulfill the prophecy', or fulfill the model presented by so many symbols of the Mexican cultural scene – symbols in which the processual myth that ends in the *via crucis* is represented."[71]

Turner's four phases (breach, crisis, redress, reintegration or schism) need hardly to be taken as canonical, but they provide a useful framework for analyzing the Peloponnesian War. The alternation of war and peace, of stability and revolution, of death and healing, would have made it easy for an Athenian who had lived through the war to conceive of his experience as one that went from breach to crisis to redress to reintegration or schism. For example, one might have conceived of the failure of Spartan–

Athenian diplomacy in 432 as the breach, the actual fighting from 431 to 405 as the crisis, the Spartan victory of 404 as the redress, and the victory of the democrats over the oligarchy of the Thirty in 403 as the reintegration. One could point to many other turning points: the death of Pericles, the plague, the Sicilian Expedition, the intervention of Persia, and so on. What is important is that Athens did pass through crisis and conflict, and that the civil war and final restoration of democracy in 404–403 served as a kind of reintegration.

By imposing such a framework on the ancient evidence, one runs of course the risk of anachronism. Foreign perspectives can provide fresh insights, however; moreover, the Athenians themselves quite consciously applied the metaphor of drama to their experience, public and private. The theater was a fundamental metaphor of classical Athenian culture. The Peloponnesian War contains most of the elements which Aristotle deems necessary for tragedy: it was (or could easily be conceived as) a complete whole with beginning, middle, and end; it offered action, beautiful speeches, reversal of fortune from good to bad; it excited pity and fear leading to a *katharsis* of the emotions. An Athenian theatergoer of the late fifth century need not have been disappointed by the dramatic public events of his own lifetime. The orators quoted from tragedy, compared their opponents to villains of the stage, imitated such staples of dramatic narrative structure as recognition scenes and reversals, and alternately adopted or mocked tragic diction and meter (e.g. Andok. 1.49–51, 129; Dem. 19.241–250; Lyk. 1.101–102). Kleon, if Thucydides is to be trusted, castigated the members of the Athenian assembly for behaving like "spectators (*theatai*) of speeches" rather than with deliberative sobriety (Thuc. 2.38.4). Hence, Athenians were conscious of the applicability of the theatrical metaphor to their public life.[72]

Myth was the bread and butter of Attic drama, especially tragedy. An Athenian who, like Turner's Mexicans, wanted to "fulfill the prophecies," who sought narrative paradigms by which to make sense of his own experience, would find plenty of material on stage. Attic drama, moreover, was a genre that offered links between public and private, and between oikos and polis. The stories of tragedy are usually set in mythical and royal oikoi, where affairs of state intersect with private, familial matters. Indeed, tragedy owes much of its emotional power to the manner in which it dissolves boundaries and blends genres. Hence, there was plenty of precedent in tragedy for an Athenian to describe politics in terms of the oikos or the oikos in terms of the polis.[73]

In his study of male Cretan peasants, Herzfeld combines Turner's theory of social drama with Goffman's work on self-presentation in everyday life. Herzfeld's peasants seek a reputation for being good men; they attempt to achieve this through "performances," dramatic actions that cannot fail but to leave others impressed. Successful performers draw their scenarios from larger categories of identification, such as ideological propositions and historical antecedents. Applying Herzfeld's stimulating model, we may consider the most important mythic scenarios which fifth-century Athenians drew from the theater and applied to their private or public "performances."[74]

Fifth-century tragedy offers any number of paradigms which an Athenian of the era of the Peloponnesian War might have applied to his personal drama or to the drama of Athens. The paradigm on which this book shall focus is one of father–son conflict, a theme evoked in numerous ways in Athenian life of the late fifth century, public and private; ways that, at least in ideology if not in practice, went well beyond the perennial tension between the generations to be expected in any society. In ways both consciously and unconsciously, the Athenians conceived of the social drama of the Peloponnesian War as a drama of fathers and sons. Before tracing the vicissitudes of paternal–filial ideology during the war, however, let us examine in Chapters 3–4 the inherited expectations and tension points in the Athenian ideology of fathers and sons.

APPENDIX TO CHAPTER 2
Patrios and *Patêr*

A skeptic might ask if the literal connection between *patrios* and *patêr* really meant much to Athenians, and to ordinary people as well as to the intelligentsia. A fair question, but several examples in the orators of wordplay and of jingly repetition suggest that the connection *did* mean something. While it seems to have been more common to connect *patêr* with such derivatives as *patrikos* or *patrôios*, the connection between *patêr* and *patrios* was sometimes made too. Let us take the more common cases first. Isaios (3.30–32), for example, tells the story of the claimant to her father's estate who is supposed to have been given an old family name by her father. The woman's husband, however, has no knowledge of any such name – and isn't it ironic, the orator asks, that someone claiming a patrimony (*ho klêros ho patrôios*) has no knowledge of his wife's paternal nomenclature (*touth' hupo tou patros keimenon tautêi*)? There is a similar juxtaposition of *patrôios* and *patêr* in Demosthenes' "Against Meidias," where the orator notes how large a patrimony Meidias has inherited from his father (21.157). In Isaios's "On the Estate of Nikostratos," where the identity of Nikostratos's father is in dispute, the orator uses in the same sentence the words "patronymic" (*to onoma patrothen*) and "fathers" (*pateres*) as virtual synonyms (Isai. 4.4). In "Against Aristokrates," Demosthenes (23.111) plays on the words *patêr* and *patrikos* ("hereditary"), noting that it was preferable for Philip of Macedon to have the Athenians rather than the Thessalians as allies, since the Athenians were his hereditary friends (*patrikoi philoi*) while the Thessalians had once expelled his father (*patêr*).

Sometimes *patrios* and *patêr* are connected closely, as in Euripides' *Ion*, performed perhaps in the penultimate decade of the fifth century BC. The chorus of that play describes the blessing of having children "in the ancestral chambers" (*en thalamois/patrioisi*, 476–477). Children inherit wealth from their fathers (*ek paterôn*, 479) and pass it on in turn to their own children. Children "bear defense and safety for their ancestral land (*gai patriai*) with a spear" (483). The juxtaposition here of *patêr* and *patrios* provides a strong sense of their semantic proximity. In the *Hippolytos* of 428 BC, the chorus juxtaposes *patêr*, *patrôios*, and *patrios*. Lamenting Hippolytos's unjust exile, they mention "a father's anger" (*patros orgas*, 1124), the "paternal household" (*patrôion ... domon*, 1136), and exile from the "ancestral land" (*patrias gas*, 1148).

Another revealing text is the pseudo-Demosthenic "Answer to Philip's Letter." A fourth-century BC political pamphlet rather than a genuine oration, and perhaps the work of Demosthenes' contemporary, the historian Anaximenes of Lampsakos, it is nonetheless revealing of the language which the educated thought might impress ordinary people.[1] The author uses several *patêr*-root words to rouse the Athenians to battle:

> Consider how shameful it would be if your fathers (*pateras*) faced many hardships and great risks in fighting the Lacedae-monians, but you were unwilling to defend vigorously the inheritance which they justly acquired for you; if a man from Macedonia was so bold that for the sake of extending his empire his whole body was wounded fighting in wars, but the Athenians, to whom it was ancestral practice (*patrion*) not to yield to anyone but to conquer all in wars, if they should forsake through laziness and weakness the deeds of their forebears (*progonôn*) and the interests of their fatherland (*patridos*).
>
> (Ps.-Dem. 11.21–22)

The author thus connects *patrios* to *patêr* through a series of puns. He argues that war with Macedon is both in the best interests of the fatherland (*patris*) and demanded by Athens's traditional (*patrion*) military prowess and by the deeds of the ancestors (*pateres*, *progonoi*).

Similar wordplay can be found in Isocrates' *Panegyrikos* (4.24–25). Isocrates discusses the Athenian claim to autochthony. He argues that the genuineness of this claim justifies the Athenian practice of referring to the polis by the same words that they apply to their nearest kin (*oikeiotatoi*): nurse (*trophos*), fatherland (*patris*), and mother (*mêtêr*). Note that the author treats *patris* (fatherland) as a virtual synonym for *patêr* (father). Lysias (2.17) speaks in a similar vein in his funeral oration: "being autochthonous, they [our ancestors] possessed the same mother (*mêtera*) and fatherland (*patrida*)." In his funeral oration, Demosthenes (60.4) notes that each Athenian can trace his existence back not only to his father (*patera*) and more distant ancestors (*tôn anô progonôn*) but also to their common fatherland (*patrida*).[2] To return to the *Panegyrikos*, Isocrates immediately goes on to say that only a "familial" origin (*archê tou genous*) as great as Athens's – only autochthony – could give the citizens of a country grounds for thinking highly of themselves, for justly laying claim to hegemony, and for frequently recalling their ancestral glories (*tôn patriôn pollakis memnêmenous*). The word for "ancestral" is *patrios*, and here the connection between *patrios* and parentage is extremely close.

Shortly afterward in the same tract (4.54–63) Isocrates advances a complicated argument to justify Athenian hegemony over Sparta. This argument offers an elegant illustration of the political implications of the father–son relationship, and it may also demonstrate, through oblique wordplay, the connection of *patrios* and *patêr*. Isocrates identifies Sparta with the Herakleidai (sons of Heracles), in mythology suppliants who obtained Athenian help and reclaimed their patrimony – the Peloponnesus. Isocrates equates the Spartans with the Herakleidai and hence with refugees, supplication, the receipt of favors, and obligation owed. On the other hand, he equates the Athenians with autochthony, asylum, the bestowing of favors, and a debt to call in. Moreover, he explicitly compares (4.56) the power of Athens to the greatness of Heracles himself – "their [the Herakleidai's] father" (*patêr*). By implication Athens is *in loco parentis* and Sparta is *in loco filii*. Perhaps the most interesting part of the argument is Isocrates' summation: in addition to the gratitude and fairness which might dictate Spartan submission to Athenian hegemony,

> it is certainly not ancestral custom (*patrion*) for immigrants to rule over the autochthonous, nor for those who receive benefits to rule over their benefactors, nor for those who had become suppliants to rule over those who give them asylum.
>
> (Isoc. 4.63)

There may be an element of wordplay in Isocrates' argument. It is not "ancestral" for the passive to rule the active, and it is not "paternal" for sons to rule those *in loco parentis*.

Did ordinary Athenians make as elegant puns of *patrios* and *patêr* as Euripides, Isocrates, and the author of pseudo-Demosthenes 11? Perhaps not, although there are examples of sophisticated wordplay among peoples far less urbanized and literate than fifth-century Athenians. By 413, in any case, after years of witnessing powerful images of filial disrespect and inter-generational conflict on the public stage, any connotation of "father" in a term of political discourse is likely to have been strong and evocative.

3

SOLIDARITY
Proud fathers, obedient sons

"I ought to tell you, I ... idolize my son. ...

"...And I don't only idolize him, Arkady Nikolaich, I am proud of him, and the height of my ambition is that some day there will be the following lines in his biography: 'The son of a simple army-doctor, who was, however, capable of divining his greatness betimes, and spared nothing for his education ...'" The old man's voice broke.

Turgenev, *Fathers and Sons*

When they arrived in the land of Goshen, Joseph had his chariot made ready and went up to meet his father Israel in Goshen. As soon as he appeared he threw his arms around his neck and for a long time wept on his shoulder.

Genesis 46:29

The subject of this chapter is the rules of behavior in Athenian father–son relations, what one might call the ideal pattern or the normative discourse of practice. Given the limitations of the sources, the study of practice here must mean largely the study of a number of statements – in law, oratory, drama, philosophy, art – as to how fathers and sons are supposed to behave toward each other. Ascertaining how they really *did* behave and, trickier still, how they really felt, is much more difficult.

The evidence in the following discussion is drawn from the era of the Peloponnesian War whenever possible, but the richer fourth-century documentation (especially oratory) is sometimes cited too, as well as other relevant material as early as Homer and as late as Plutarch. Although based on wide reading, the following discussion is offered less as an exhaustive commentary on the evidence than as a series of snapshots meant to illustrate several major

61

themes. After discussing the behavioral prescriptions in the law, we shall turn to the transmission of property, to sentiment, to education, and then to an overview of intergenerational relations across the life cycle. Since the subject is normative behavior, the emphasis in this chapter is on harmony and good relations between father and son. Since the subject, however, is Athens, that is, a society that paid more than its share of attention to filial rebellion, it is also necessary to give father–son conflict its due; we shall turn to that subject in Chapter 4.

LEGAL NICETIES

As has often been pointed out, the law is an imperfect and at times misleading guide to reality. By the same token, law remains an immensely valuable window into a culture: it provides one of the most authoritative models of what a society idealizes and also of what a society fears (indicated by its legal prohibitions). Moreover, as ancient historians are only too well aware, the law is sometimes all we have got to go on; we have to extrapolate or at least speculate about practice from the legalities. With these caveats in mind, we can turn to the father–son relationship as defined by surviving Athenian law.

First of all, the law established the father's authority over his sons and daughters. Until a son turned eighteen or a daughter married, the father was his or her *kyrios*: a figure of authority but no despot. Aristotle declares that the father governs his children like a king his subjects; it is a hierarchical relationship, but nonetheless one between free people (*Pol.* 1259a37–41, 1259b10–17). Athenian law and practice confirm philosophical theory. Affection, pride, and self-interest (the father hoped one day to depend on his children, when he was aged and they were grown), as well as a son's claim on his patrimony, all prevented the father from treating a child like a chattel.[1]

The powers of the Athenian father must not be examined through the prism of the better-known Roman *patria potestas* (paternal power). The ancient sources emphasize the differences between the two. Gaius, for example, says that "there are scarcely any other men who have as much power over their sons as we [Romans] do" (1.55). Dionysios of Halikarnassos writes:

The constitutions established by the Greeks have ordained

an altogether short time for sons to be ruled by fathers: some until they complete the second year from puberty [i.e. around age eighteen],[2] some as long as they remain bachelors, and some until their registration at the public offices, as I learned from the legislation of Solon and Pittakos and Kharondas, in which much wisdom is evidenced. They have ordained punishments if they disobey the fathers, but not heavy ones: they permit them [sc. fathers] to drive them [sc. sons] from the house (*oikia*) and not to leave them wealth (*khrêmata*), but nothing beyond. Accordingly, among the Greeks there is a great deal of unseemly behavior by children toward their fathers.

(Dion. Hal. 2.26)

Allowances must be made, of course, for the rhetorical bias of these sources who want to emphasize Roman uniqueness. Even on a superficial reading, however, the legal differences between Greek and Roman father–son relationships are striking. In practice, as recent research argues convincingly, the powers of the Roman *paterfamilias* (head of household) were considerably attenuated by affection within the family and by convention, which ruled out harsh punishments and prescribed a measure of financial independence for young men. The law gave the *paterfamilias* enormous powers, however, which were part of official ideology; they compare strikingly with the ideology of the Athenian father. The legal powers of the *paterfamilias* include the right to execute a misbehaving son and the complete control of the family property until death. The son, no matter how old, was not legally independent while his father was alive, nor could he become a *paterfamilias* himself until his father died, except by the undesirable means of being disinherited (*emancipatio*).[3]

By contrast, the Athenian father, once he had accepted an infant child as his own (see below), had no legal right to execute him or her. He was now expected to teach the growing boy a trade and, after the boy reached puberty, to initiate him into the patrilineal phratry and deme – that is, to have him recognized as an Athenian citizen. Unlike a young Roman, an Athenian became legally independent and free of his father's authority at age eighteen (Dem. 18.259, cf. 19.230), although, as we shall see, he often continued to be tied to his father by financial and emotional bonds. Moreover, the Athenian father had less leeway than the Roman about the

63

disposition of his property, being legally required to leave it to his son(s). If a father were found squandering the property that should be left for his heirs, he could be sued for idleness or mental incapacity. Even if the heir was still a minor, anyone could sue the father (at least for idleness; mental incapacity might have required a suit by the son himself after age eighteen) on his behalf (Hdt. 2.177; Ar. *Cl.* 844–846; Xen. *Mem.* 1.2.49; Aeschin. 1.30; Dem. 57.32; Plut. *Sol.* 22; Pollux 8.42; D.L. 1.55).[4]

So much for the differences. There were also similarities; if less than in Rome, the legal authority of the Athenian father over his children was nonetheless considerable. Until his majority, no child was able to enter into any contract (Isai. 10.10). He would be represented in any legal transaction by his father (for example, Ant. 3.2). The father also had the right to mandate that his son while a minor be adopted into another family; he could also appoint a guardian-to-be in case he should die while his son was still a minor. Before Solon had ended the practice, the father had moreover the right to sell his children and presumably, *a fortiori*, to pledge them as surety for a debt (Plut. *Sol.* 13.23). Around 400 BC, the enslavement of children for debt still appeared to be a danger outside of Athens (Lys. 12.98; Isoc. 14.48). Certain other powers of the father over the child hardly needed stating in legislation: the power to require a child's labor on the family farm or business, and the power to discipline a child, if necessary by beating.[5]

Procedures at the beginning and end of the child's developmental cycle bracket the father's legal authority. First, the Athenian father had the right to reject a newborn child. The father celebrated the birth of a child and made clear his acceptance of it as his own and as a member of the oikos at the ceremony of the *amphidromia*, which took place about a week after the child's birth. Formal naming would take place either at this ceremony or at a second one ten days after the child's birth (the *dekatê*). Before the *amphidromia* the father had the right to leave the child out for exposure, where it might die, be found and sold as a slave, or be adopted by a childless couple. There is little hard evidence and much controversy about the extent of exposure in classical Athens, but it is clear that some infants were indeed exposed, perhaps primarily sickly or deformed ones; as for healthy infants, girls were probably more likely to be victims than boys.[6]

Even after a son turned eighteen, the father continued to retain the right to discipline extraordinary misbehavior by "proclaiming a separation" (*apokêryxis*). By this action the son was removed from the household, left vulnerable to attacks on his citizenship, perhaps deprived of his name, and finally, cut off from his share in the patrimony. In practice, however, *apokêryxis* was probably resorted to only very rarely.[7]

The law mandated another tie between a father and his independent adult son, traditionally established by Solon (Plut. *Sol.* 22.1, 4). In old age, both parents had the right to be fed, housed, and cared for by their son: the right to *therapeia* (care, tending, service). In his Funeral Oration, Gorgias praises Athenians for the piety of their *therapeia* toward their parents (Diels and Kranz B6, 236 ll.13–14). It was also the son's responsibility to arrange for parental funeral and memorial rites (Isai. 2.18, 36–37; Dem. 57.70; Dein. 2.17–18; Xen. *Mem.* 2.213). Anyone, and not merely a wronged father, could file a special lawsuit against a son for alleged mistreatment of parents (*graphê goneôn kakôseôs*), including neglect or physical violence. It was considered outrageous for a son to beat his father or mother. Anyone who did so was forbidden to address the assembly, on penalty of *atimia* (Aeschin. 1.28), that is, exclusion from political and religious life. To add teeth to the enforcement procedures, the prosecutor in a suit for mistreating parents was freed of the usual penalties for withdrawing his case or for not gaining at least 20 per cent of the jurors' votes; the prosecutor was also permitted to address the jury without being bound by the usual time limit. The filial duty of caring for parents was reiterated in the public context of the annual scrutiny of the archons-to-be: men aged at least thirty, they were asked if they treated their parents well if alive or, if deceased, if they tended their graves (Arist. *Ath. Pol.* 55.3). Similarly, among the grounds on which an orator could be impeached and, if convicted, prohibited from addressing the Athenian people were beating one's parents or failure to provide food and housing for them (Aeschin. 1.28).[8]

To sum up, the Athenian father was his son's legal master until the boy turned eighteen. He was his guardian and representative in any judicial transaction. He had legal control of the ancestral estate and his wife's dowry even after his son's majority, but he was required to bequeath this estate to his son(s) and could be sued for squandering it. He had the power to reject an infant, but only in the first week or so of its life. He also had the power to sever a son's ties with the oikos and hence to disinherit him, but this may have been more theoretical possibility than practical reality. There was a considerable difference between the Athenian and the Roman father, both legally and ideologically; the practical difference may not have been so great, however. In any case, the Athenian father had formidable legal authority over his son.

THE ROOT OF ALL EVIL

The Athenian father–son relationship is not to be reduced to property, but neither is the economic dimension to be ignored. Athenian boys grew up knowing that one day they would inherit their share of their father's property. That knowledge, as Plutarch groused in a reference to fifth-century Athens, did not make "sons feel any gratitude nor be solicitous (*oude... therapeuousin*) nor show respect, because they wait for their inheritance as if it were a debt owed to them" (Plut. *Mor.* 497b).[9] By law, no Athenian father with a living son could write a will; that is, upon the father's death the property devolved automatically to the son. If there was more than one son, they would share the property equally, either in common or separately, after dividing it; there was no primogeniture. Daughters received their share of the estate in the form of a dowry upon marriage.[10]

By the year 410 BC (Lys. 32.6, our earliest surviving evidence) and during the fourth century, exceptions were apparently permissible. There are a half dozen cases of fathers who, despite having a living son, leave a will providing a portion of their estate for their wife or their daughter's dowry or making unequal distinctions between sons. In one case, the famous general Konon (died ca. 392) is said to have left only about 17 talents of his approximately 40-talent estate to his son Timotheos; the rest went to his brother, his nephew, and dedications at Delphi (Lys. 19.39–40). The evidence is slippery, however, for the estate was located not in Athens but in Cyprus, and the portions of brother and nephew might represent a guardianship of Konon's son. Above all, the self-interested speaker wants to demonstrate that the sons of wealthy fathers are not always as rich as one would expect. The evidence of Konon's case does not amount to much, therefore. All in all, the likeliest conclusion is that, while an Athenian father with living sons might leave some money to care for his wife and daughter, nevertheless, after 410 BC as before, he would leave the great bulk of his estate to his sons.[11]

When a boy reached adolescence, he might begin to anticipate his eventual coming into his patrimony: a delightful thought if "the old man" was "loaded," a burden to shoulder or escape if he was poor. Indeed, the following discussion about succession to the patrimony concerns a matter of interest primarily to those of great or middling wealth. But precisely how long would a young man of "great expectations" have to wait for his inheritance? "Until his father died" is the answer one might give, but the Athenian situation was not so simple and the demographics of death and generational spacing require further comment.

The age of majority at Athens, the age at which a young man was registered with his father's deme as an Athenian citizen, could represent himself in contracts, and was formally free of his father as *kyrios*, was eighteen. Having previously been registered in his father's phratry at age sixteen, the eighteen-year-old now finally had his name listed on the *lêxiarchikon grammateion*, the deme's list of citizens; as Demosthenes puts it, he was "enscribed among the men" (Dem. 19.230). Manhood did not automatically mean inheritance, however. An eighteen-year-old only came into his patrimony if his father had already died or if his mother was an *epiklêros*. Yet the demographic realities ensured that quite a few Athenians were included in these categories.[12]

The little evidence we have suggests that Athenians followed what historians of European demography call the Mediterranean type of marriage: women tended to marry for the first time in their late teens or early twenties, and men in their late twenties or thirties. The evidence also suggests that Athenian life expectancy was low (approximately 25 years at birth compared to approximately 70 years at birth in the middle-class West today) and that mortality rose sharply for men over fifty. These data have two important consequences here. First, there usually was a considerable age gap between father and son. If, for example, a man married at around the age of thirty, then when his son reached the age of majority, the father would be nearly fifty – and perhaps considerably older, in the (not unlikely) event that his wife did not give birth immediately to a son or in the (not unlikely) event that his first male child or children did not survive to adolescence. The second consequence, based on computer-generated models, is that only about half of the males who reached the age of eighteen would have a living father. Hence, about half of the population of Athenian young men took control of their patrimony at the age of eighteen.[13]

The other half, however, did not. Some would have to wait for their father to die. Again, given the demographic realities, this event might come sooner rather than later. Computer simulations suggest that in a pre-industrial population with Mediterranean-type marriage, only about a third of 25-year-olds would have a living father, and only about a fifth of 30-year-olds. Take, as a highly anecdotal example, the speaker of Isaios 2: *On the Estate of Menekles*, who was probably in his twenties when his father died. He took charge (with his brother) of dowering his sisters (Isai. 2.3–5), which shows that he was over eighteen, but he was unmarried (Isai. 2.18) and of the age to go on military campaigns (*en hêlikiai epi to strateuesthai*, Isai. 2.6), which suggests that he was not yet thirty. Still, there are enough references to old age in ancient Greek literature (e.g. Pl. *Laws* 929d–e) to ensure that some sons would have a long wait indeed. In *Wasps* (1351–1354), for example, Aristophanes parodies the impatience of young Athenians through the device of role reversal: old Philokleon promises a flute-girl that he will buy her freedom and make her his concubine "when his son dies" and he gets control of his property.[14]

It was not always necessary to wait for the old man to die, however. We have several examples of (a) fathers who shared their property with their sons and (b) fathers who retired from management of the oikos and turned it over to their son. Although these practices were not without problems, there were nonetheless many sound reasons for early sharing or transfer of the oikos. First of all, quarrels between brothers over the division of an estate after a father's death were a notorious source of trouble. Every Athenian knew the mythical case of Eteokles and Polyneikes, and there was no shortage of real-life examples. By settling matters and dividing an oikos before his death, a father lessened the risk of future troubles.[15] Second, daughters received their share of the family property upon marriage, and there was some logic to endowing sons then as well. Demosthenes, for example, refers to this case from the early fifth century:[16]

> Bouselos, men of the jury, was a member of the deme Oion, and to him were born five sons, Hagnias and Euboulides and Stratios and Habron and Kleokritos. And all these sons of

Bouselos grew to be men, and their father Bouselos divided
his property among them all fairly and justly, as was fitting.
And when they had divided the property among themselves,
each of them married a wife according to your laws, and
sons and sons of sons were born to them all, and there were
born five oikoi from the single oikos of Bouselos, and each
of them lived separately having his own oikos and producing
his own offspring.

(Dem. 43.19)

There is a third point: assuming a son married around the age
of thirty, a father would then be sixty or older and hence might
be ready to retire, which added an incentive for him to turn over
the oikos. It was customary in Athens for old men to retire
(Aeschin. 3.251) and be looked after by their children. Very rich
young Lysis, for example, could confidently expect that when he
was old enough – when he was *prudent* enough, that is, as Socrates
tried to correct him – his father would turn over to him both the
management of the household and his father's own person (Pl.
Lys. 209c).[17]

Comparative evidence from modern Greece is suggestive. In
several communities studied by anthropologists, the norm is for
the father to retire and turn over control of the household to the
son upon marriage. The most clear-cut case is that of the Sarakatsani,
the migratory shepherd community of Epiros studied by
Campbell. Among the Sarakatsani it is customary for the son to
marry around the age of thirty and for the father to retire shortly
thereafter, as soon as the son's first child is born. The community
considers it important that a male who is married and a parent
should be "master" (*noikokyros*, cf. the ancient *kyrios*) in his own
household.[18]

In the Piraeus families of Asia Minor refugees and their descendants
studied by Hirschon in the early 1970s, marriage similarly is
considered to mark the formation of a new household. "When
you give your child in marriage," people say, "he/she becomes
'master'/'mistress' (*noikokyros/noikokyra*)."[19] Once the children
are married a father relinquishes all authority over them. Transfer
of property at marriage is common in modern Greece, though not
the invariable rule.[20] What can be gained from the modern evidence
nonetheless is the fleshing-out of a paradigm in which the marriage
of the son(s) is the key moment at which the father retires and

transfers effective and perhaps also legal control of the family property. It is tempting to apply this model to classical Athens, and to suggest that, if a son had not already come into control of his patrimony through his father's death, he had a good chance of gaining that control at the time of his marriage, around the age of thirty.[21]

An Athenian son's duty to his elderly parents was buttressed by various public and legal sanctions. Parents nevertheless ran the risk of slights large and small, real and imagined.[22] For example, Aristophanes' Philokleon, prevented by his son from going to the law courts, is put under virtual house arrest in his own home – perhaps a comic exaggeration of real-life scenes. Plutarch pities the lot of elderly parents who are hurt by the sight of a son mistreating an honored slave or neglecting the family farm, plants, or animals (*Mor.* 480a). The speaker of Lysias 19 says (with a knowing smile, no doubt) that a father who distributes his estate among his sons (even just the ancestral estate, not to mention what he acquired on his own) keeps "no small amount" (*ouk elachista*) for himself; "for," he says, "all men want to be cared for (*therapeuesthai*) by their sons because they have property rather than to be in need of their sons because they are poor" (Lys. 19.37). In general only wealthy fathers had the requisite surplus property to make such an arrangement, however.[23]

Examples of fathers who gave some property to a son while retaining some for themselves are the comrades-in-arms Konon and Nikophemos, two of the wealthiest Athenians of their day (the 390s), who each left his son with "a competence" (*hikana*) while keeping the rest for themselves (Lys. 19.36). Another case is Euktemon, who had such a great estate that he and his son Philoktemon could both carry out liturgies while Euktemon (died ca. 364) was still alive (Isai. 6.14, 38).[24]

Some fathers retired or planned to retire in their son's favor. The speaker of Isaios 2, for one, served as gymnasiarch out of his adoptive father Menekles' property while the man was still alive (Isai. 2.43). The speaker's emphasis on how he took care of (*etherapeuon*, 2.18, 36) his adoptive father, though self-serving, perhaps suggests that the man had retired. The two brothers Euergos and Theophemos divided their estate by 356 BC while their father was still alive: Euergos, who was married, lived with the father, while the bachelor Theophemos lived alone (Dem. 47.34–35). Presumably, the father had retired and was cared for by

Euergos. Bouselos, discussed above, may be another example of a father who handed over the estate to his sons and then retired, though a man of his evident wealth may have been in a position to keep "no small amount" for himself.[25]

The position of the Athenian son vis-à-vis his patrimony is likely to have displayed considerable variation, therefore. Perhaps as many as half of the young men of Athens, their father dead, will have taken control of their patrimony in their eighteenth year. The other half will have had to wait longer. The majority will probably have been in control of their patrimony, or their share of it, after allowing for brothers' and sisters' shares, by the time of their marriage around age thirty. Others will have had to wait longer, but few will have had to wait much longer: computer modeling suggests that only about 12 percent of Athenian men would have had a living father by the time they reached age thirty-five.[26]

A son was likely to be well versed in his father's finances since one day they would be his. In a wealthy oikos, for example, a son might find himself involved in a lawsuit concerning money owed by or to his deceased or retired father, in which case a close working relationship with his father would be essential. For instance, Apollodoros, son of the late banker Pasion, strengthens his claim to money allegedly owed Pasion's estate by referring to Pasion's discussion of his finances with his two sons during his final illness (Ps.-Dem. 49.42–43). Pasion was twenty-four at the time of his father's death in 370/369 (Dem. 36.22). To take another case, in 411 BC at around the age of seventy, Polystratos sent a letter to his son in Sicily, where the son was serving as a privateer, detailing the affairs of the oikos (Lys. 20.27).[27]

From the point of view of affective relations between father and son, the years between eighteen and thirty were probably crucial. The son was now legally independent, his own *kyrios*, but the father was still in charge of the household's property. The older the son, the more eager he would be to come into his share. If the father trusted the son to manage the property well and to take care of his aging parents, then he would probably have been inclined to turn over control of the oikos. If not, the result might have been an impasse.

One can imagine a spectrum, from rivalry to delicate negotiations to mutual respect and affection, at every point on the economic scale. In less wealthy families, fathers and sons might share work on a farm or in a shop, or the sons might leave to find their fortune: as, for example, a mercenary, a cleruch, a laborer on the Periclean building projects, or a dockworker in Piraeus. The wealthiest fathers might find themselves stuck with a Pheidippides who, at about age nineteen, was squandering the estate of his poor father Strepsiades as if he already had title to it. On the other hand, they might be blessed with an Autolykos, the champion athlete who was the pride and joy of his father Lykon – not least because Autolykos was well mannered enough to declare that his father Lykon was, similarly, *his* pride and joy (Xen. *Symp.* 3.12–13).[28]

SENTIMENT: "THAT'S MY BOY!"

At the upper end of the social scale, an Athenian was expected to take pride in his father and his ancestry. Homer provides numerous models for this outlook, as does Pindar, and there are many examples of it thriving in Peloponnesian-War-era Athens. Andokides, for example, is proud not only of the usual generalships and public offices in his family but also of its antiquity. "The most ancient house of all," he calls it (Andok. 1.147), and other sources show that he traced his ancestry back through Odysseus and Telemakhos to the god Hermes. The young men of Plato's dialogues are often flattered with references to the greatness and fame of their families. Hippothales, for example, lover of Lysis, wrote verses about Lysis's father, grandfather, and ancestors, playing up their horses, wealth, victories at the Panhellenic games, and kinship with Herakles himself (Pl. *Lys.* 205c).[29]

It is unlikely that ordinary people were similarly captivated by their genealogies, but no matter how poor their oikos the norm was probably for them too to display pride in and hope for their sons. It was an Athenian commonplace that a father's children (daughters and sons) were to him "the dearest of the dear" (Ar. *Ach.* 326–329) or "the dearest of people" (Aeschin. 2.152). The rich made sacrifices at the birth of a child (Plut. *Mor.* 497a), but one did not have to be rich to rejoice (*getheô*) at the news that one's wife was going into labor, and then to hear the midwife say "it's a boy! a real lion of a boy and the image of his dad!" (Ar. *Thesm.* 507–516).[30]

People have children for various reasons: some material, some emotive, some reasons stated and some not. A life of marriage and parenthood was a given for almost everyone in the Athenian citizen class, and hence hardly needed to be explained. When Athenians did nevertheless discuss the motivations for having children, they tended to emphasize material factors (particularly support from children in old age and the assurance of a proper funeral) and the symbolic significance of children as a sign of the good life. In a kind of reproductive Calvinism, Athenian public opinion held that good sons demonstrated good parents. The emblematic case is Tellos of Athens, whom Solon cites as enviably happy because (among other things) he had noble sons and lived to see his grandchildren survive infancy (Hdt. 1.30; Plut. *Sol.* 27.6).[31]

Why people have children and why they say they have children are not always the same thing, however. The sources attest an important emotive dimension to Athenian parenthood beyond the desire for support, burial, and the satisfaction of prosperity.[32] Orators, playwrights, and philosophers all uphold the ideal that parents should feel friendship and loving affection (*philia* and *storgê*) for their children. Aristophanes thought it credible to show a father wanting to gratify his young son by buying him dice, or in having old Strepsiades reminisce about the days when he fed and "diapered" his infant son or, when the child had become a toddler, bought him a toy cart (Ar. *Wasps* 291–316, *Cl.* 863–864, 1380–1385).[33]

Perhaps more common than these genre scenes are depictions of masculine pride in one's son. The granddaddy of such scenes is in the *Odyssey* (11.467–540), when Odysseus meets the very unhappy shade of Achilles in Hades. After bitterly regretting his own untimely death, Achilles inquires first about his son Neoptolemos, and then and at greater length about his father Peleus. Achilles bemoans his inability to protect Peleus in old age as a son should. Odysseus knows nothing about Peleus, but he tells "the whole truth" (507) – whatever Odysseus, of all people, might mean by that – about Neoptolemos, zeroing in on Achilles' specific question about his feats of war. Odysseus describes Neoptolemos as the complete hero: unflinching, brave, a killer, victorious, unwounded, wealthy with plunder, well respected, and a good speaker. At the news, Achilles is transported, as Odysseus recounts later:

> So I spoke, but the shade of swift-footed Aiakides
> [sc. Achilles]

73

Went off taking long strides in the field of asphodel,
Glorying (*gethosunê*) that I had said his son was famous.

(Hom. *Od.* 11.538–540)

It is a striking scene, in two ways in particular. First, the news of
Neoptolemos's heroic deeds seems to erase Achilles' bad mood
completely, as if Neoptolemos had restored his life and virtually
erased the deficit created by Achilles' inability to champion *his*
father Peleus. Second, Odysseus's news creates a moment of
powerful emotion. Achilles feels the need to distance himself
abruptly – and not very politely – from Odysseus. It is as if
Achilles was compelled to create a private moment alone with the
idealized image of his son, that is, with the vicarious continuation
of his own arrested adulthood.

Pride in one's son is found, if less dramatically, in Odysseus's
family too. In the last scene of the *Odyssey*, for example, Odysseus,
his son Telemakhos and his aged father Laertes all prepare for
battle against the friends and families of the suitors. Odysseus
admonishes his son not to shame their forefathers (*paterôn genos*),
and Telemakhos replies manfully. It is Laertes, however, who gets
the most pleasure out of the interchange. He remarks:

What day is this now for me, dear gods? I truly rejoice!
My son and my grandson are holding a contest in courage
(*aretê*).

(Hom. *Od.* 24.514–515)[34]

Paternal pride in a son was a commonplace in later Greece,
enough so for Plutarch to remark that it was ponderous to praise
one's own son (he recommends instead the less egotistical practice
of praising a nephew [*Mor.* 492c]). The father's pride and egotism
(*philauton*, Plut. *Mor.* 492c) perhaps lay in the knowledge that he
had produced something good, or that he had reproduced himself,
or that he had assured the continuity of his own. Peisistratos, for
example, is supposed to have remarked upon his second marriage,
that the now-grown (*enêlikoi*) sons of his first marriage were such
gentlemen (*kaloikagathoi*) that he wanted to have more sons just
like them (Plut. *Mor.* 480d, cf. 189d).[35]

A father might take pride in seeing his son follow in his footsteps. In the fifth century, there is the example of the wealthy
general and tragic poet Karkinos son of Xenotimos of Thorikos
(born before 480), whose three sons (Xenotimos, Xenokles, and a

third whose name is not known) appeared as dancers in his plays. Xenokles (adult by 422) followed his father's example by writing tragedies, as did his son, also named Karkinos (born before 405). In *Wasps*, the elder Karkinos is called "blessed in his good children" (*makarie tês eupaidias*, 1512) and, because of their dancing skills, "delighted with his children" (1532).[36]

Wasps also names another father, one Automenes, as "blessed" (*makarios*, 1275) in his three sons: Ariphrades, Arignotos, and a third whose name is not known. The boys are called "extremely skilled craftsmen" (*hoti kheirotekhnikôtatous*, 1276): Arignotos as a lyre-player, the unnamed son as an actor, and Ariphrades as a practitioner of ... cunnilingus (1278–1279, 1283). Aristophanes takes the low road by emphasizing Automenes' role in begetting these sons with their peculiar talents (*paidas ephuteusas*, 1276) and by having him swear that Ariphrades acquired his talent "without any teaching from anyone" (1281) – in other words, like son, like father. Comic exaggeration, but it probably paints a realistic picture of Athenian fathers calling their sons "chips off the old block." Ariphrades may have been a comic poet, and perhaps Automenes (of whom nothing is known) really did brag about his natural *poetic* skill.[37]

We find another example of paternal pride in Xenophon's *Symposium*, a Socratic dialogue with the dramatic date of 421. The guests of honor at the drinking party in the home of Kallias in Piraeus are Lykon and his teenage son Autolykos. Father and son recline next to each other on a couch at the symposium. Famous for his good looks, Autolykos had just won the prize in the pankration (a combination of boxing and wrestling) at the Panathenaic games, and Kallias wanted to become his lover. The conversation at the symposium turned to the question of what possession or accomplishment each guest most prided himself in having. When it was Lykon's turn to answer, he responded, "Don't you all know that it is my son?" (Xen. *Symp.* 3.12). One of the guests suggests snidely that what Autolykos is proud of, on the other hand, is his prize. But Autolykos pipes up with the reply that no, indeed, what he is proud of is his father! Up to this point Autolykos had been sitting demurely beside his father, while the other guests reclined; it was customary for adult males alone to recline at an Athenian party. Now, Autolykos underlines his respect by reclining beside his father on the dining couch, a gesture perhaps even of affection and ease, perhaps even a manly gesture: children were not expected to speak at a symposium, but Autolykos's remark had delighted the audience (3.12–13). As syrupy as the scene is, as "goody-two-shoes" as Autolykos is, the smitten Kallias is overcome, and blurts out that Lykon is the richest man in the world; Lykon agrees, naturally (Xen. *Symp.* 3.13).

The conversation is of course stylized to suit the homoerotic and at times mock-serious themes of Xenophon's dialogue, but nonetheless it fits the Athenian pattern of paternal pride, as the end of the dialogue shows graphically. We approach this end after a Socratic discussion of education, politics, and love, much of which is aimed at lighting sparks between Kallias and Autolykos – who indeed do exchange rapt glances (8.42). Lykon, however, has the final word, or rather gesture. He and Autolykos leave the symposium, and Lykon accompanies his son, ever the athlete-in-training, on his customary walk. After their departure, an entertainment is provided by a small troupe: a "soft porn" mime of Dionysos and Ariadne kissing and petting, that leaves the audience so vehemently excited that the married men hurry off to their wives (9.2–7). Then comes the final scene of Xenophon's dialogue: "Socrates and those of the others who had stayed behind went out with Kallias toward Lykon and his son who were taking a walk" (9.7). The image of Socrates, Kallias, and the others observing the stroll of Lykon and his son may call to mind the image of Odysseus observing Achilles' stroll in the asphodel with thoughts of his heroic son. Each in his own way, Lykon and Achilles are pursuing an image of the ideal son who makes his father proud.

SENTIMENT: "DEAR OLD DAD"

In his interesting discussion of parents and children, Aristotle notes that the love between them was a mutual but nonetheless hierarchical emotion: children love (*philein*) their parents too, but not as much as their parents love them, because "the bond that ties the begetter to the begotten is closer than that which ties the generated to its author" (*Eth. Nic.* 1161b, tr. Ostwald). As Aristotle notes, the child loves his parent as his superior and benefactor, just as a mortal loves a god (*Eth. Nic.* 1162a; cf. *Pol.* 1259b11–12). Perhaps he might have added that a child's love for his or her parents is tempered by the knowledge of what those parents expect of him or her. As an analogue to a father's pride in his son, the son might feel pride in his father and paternal ancestry, as we have already seen. The son, however, was not granted the luxury of a stroll through the asphodel in rapt contemplation of his paternity. Rather, he was expected to work hard in order to prove himself worthy of his father. Autolykos, for instance, was considered admirable because he had put in a great deal of effort in order to win the prize in the pankration. In the long run, the prize would help him win attention and glory by improving his ultimate chances of helping his friends and his fatherland; more obviously and in the short run, it would bring honor (*kosmeô*) to himself and his father (Xen. *Symp.* 8.38).

A son inherited many things from his father, among them: his property, his debts, his reputation, and his friendships and enmities. While a father lived, his son (if he was old enough) was expected to help him fight his battles, whether military or legal. As Kreon says in *Antigone*, "men pray to have obedient sons at home who fight the enemy back in kind and honor the friend as much as their father does" (641–644). It only stands to reason, then, that a good son should continue these battles after the father's death. Perhaps the most famous case in ancient Greek culture of the avenging son is Orestes, who did not shrink from killing his own mother Klytaimnestra, as well as her lover Aigisthos, in order to avenge his father Agamemnon. The theme of son (and daughter) avenging the father pervades Aeschylus's *Oresteia*, a dramatic trilogy of 456. A black-figure kalyx *kratêr* of slightly earlier date illustrates the theme graphically. One side of the vase depicts the father Agamemnon being murdered in the vulnerability of his undergarments; the other shows the young heroic son, Orestes, slaying Agamemnon's murderer Aigisthos. An axe-wielding Klytaimnestra is present in both scenes. Incidentally, Orestes' dilemma is recapitulated in a speech of Antiphon (died 411), in which the speaker avenges his late father by prosecuting his stepmother for allegedly poisoning him (Ant. 2.1–2, 5, 17, 23–24).[38]

Orestes' quest for vengeance is not entirely altruistic; as he frequently states, one of his primary aims is to regain his patrimony (e.g. Aesch. *Cho.* 300–301, *Eum.* 754–760). The sources often demonstrate the belief on the part of a father or son that, sentiment aside, the generations have no practical choice but to maintain solidarity (e.g. Lys. 20.35). Euxitheos of Mytilene, defending himself in Athens on a charge of murdering Herodes, takes pains to defend his father against the accusation of having once joined the Mytilenian revolt against Athens in 427. Euxitheos portrays himself as a loyal son; he also deflects the prejudice that would accrue to him as the son of a rebel (Ant. 5.74–79).

The orators are full of examples of sons who kept up a friendship begun by their fathers, for example, a speaker in Isaios who announces that a certain two brothers are his friends as was their father before them (Isai. 4.1). Isaios's audience took it for granted that enmity could also be passed from father to son (Isai. 1.11). Perhaps one of the most important things a son inherited from his father was the older man's reputation. A man of achievement, Pindar notes, bequeaths his offspring "the grace of a good name as the best of possessions" (*Pythian Odes* 11.57–58). A father's good name could be immensely useful: in the courtroom, for example, it was common to recall one's father's liturgies (e.g. Isai. 4.27, 7.38), generalships (e.g. Lys. 10.27), or other services (e.g. helping Athens to import grain, Isoc. 17.57) as an argument in one's favor. It is not surprising that normative discourse urged fathers to garner a good reputation. Isocrates, for example, argues that happiness does not consist of money, but of winning the highest repute for oneself and as a legacy for one's children (Isoc. 4.76). A bad paternal reputation could be extremely problematic for a son, given the traditional belief, by no means extinct, that it was fair and just to visit the sins of the father on the children.[39]

The sources afford glimpses of the predicament of a son with a disreputable father – and hence *not* someone whose name a son would want to live up to. For example, Andokides attacks the orator Hyperbolos (assassinated in 411) as the son of a slave, and comedy falsely makes Hyperbolos's father a non-Greek, named Chremes, according to hostile historiography – his real, very Athenian name was Antiphanes.[40] In his defense before an Athenian jury on a charge of treason in 411, Antiphon counters the accusation that he was a revolutionary as his grandfather had been before him (Ant. frg. B.1.1). Theomnestos was accused around 384 (Lys. 10.4) not only of being a coward in battle but of being the son of a coward (Lys. 10.28, 11.10). Around 395 a prosecutor of Alcibiades, son of the notorious Alcibiades, argues that the son should have been a model citizen, in order "to make his own life an apologia for the crimes of his father" (Lys. 14.29); instead he was an alleged miscreant. The son made few concessions to his father's enemies, but instead, to use the prosecutor's tendentious language, "prides himself (*philotimeitai*) on his father's villainy" (Lys. 14.35). The son had put it more favorably in a defense speech made in regard to a different charge (it *was* difficult to be Alcibiades' son!) around the same time: "Because of the great number of individual points that might be raised on my father's behalf I am at a loss as to which of them to mention at present and which it is necessary to leave out" (Isoc. 16.39).[41]

Later in the fourth century it was standard procedure for political rivals to trade charges about each other's father. Aeschines (Aeschin. 2.93) calls Demosthenes' father a knife-maker (in reality he owned, among other things, a factory of slaves who made knives). Demosthenes smears Aeschines' father as a slave and schoolteacher (Dem. 18.129–131, 19.248–249). Demosthenes claims that Androtion has inherited his father Andron's *atimia* for public debt, while Androtion himself apparently accused someone of being the son of a male prostitute (Dem. 22.33–34, 61, 68, 24.168). Taking advantage of the usual economic connotation of *patrôios* (the standard word for "patrimony") the orator quips that "imprisonment runs in Androtion's family," literally, "being imprisoned is his patrimony" (*patrôion to dedesthai*, Dem. 24.125). He also makes hay of the fate of Aristogeiton's father, who died in debt to the state (Dem. 25.30, 77–78, 99).[42]

The sons of famous fathers were expected to follow in their footsteps, and the sons of disreputable fathers were expected to save what they could of their fathers' reputation. The sons of obscure fathers might redeem the reputation of their oikos by achieving greatness themselves. Whatever his background, therefore, a son was expected to achieve things in life that would exalt (*orthoô*, literally "set straight') the name of his father and his fatherland, for example, by fighting well as a hoplite (Pl. *Lach.* 181a–b). Sons of the upper classes were expected to lift up (*epairô*) their paternal oikos and exalt (*auxeô*) the fatherland (Xen. *Mem.* 3.6.2), but as the hoplite example shows, even men of less grand ancestry were expected to include, among their motives, the desire to do their fathers proud. A second-century BC gravestone inscription from Naxos expresses a sentiment that would have been at home in classical Athens: it attributes the ambitions of the deceased Kleophon, a young man in his twenties, to the desire to gratify his father Anaxippos. To return to fourth-century BC evidence, in a cliché-ridden speech (and hence a good guide to normative discourse) Isocrates urges young Demonikos, son of the recently diseased Hipponikos, to compete with the achievements of his father (Isoc. 1.12). Friendly, clean-cut competition of course –

Isocrates compares it to the way an athlete trains against his competitors (*ibid.*) – but even the friendliest of contests can incite jealousy. There was plenty of potential for tension in father–son competition.[43]

It is noteworthy that Demonikos is urged to compete not with a living father but with the memory of a dead one. Given the demographic realities, many Athenian teenagers would have been without a living father. A teenager might suffer from the absence of his father, as Telemakhos does for a long time (Hom. *Od.* 1.217–220, 16.188–189) or, guided by older mentors, he might have found the image of the absent father an inspiring role model (as Telemakhos does at last with the help of Athena). Alternatively, a son might still feel himself in competition with his father's image even when the father himself is dead, or he might find that image surviving as a powerful internal censor.[44]

If winning one's father's approval was a positive spur to a son's ambition, fear of his father's disapproval was a negative check on a son's failure. As usual, Homer provides the received opinion, in the celebrated speech of Glaukos before Troy:

> Hippolokhos begot me, and I claim that he is my father;
> He sent me to Troy, and urged upon me repeated injunctions,
> to be always among the bravest, and hold my head above others,
> not shaming the generation of my fathers, who were
> the greatest men in Ephyre and again in wide Lykia.
> Such is my generation and the blood I claim to be born from.
>
> (*Il.* 6.206–211, tr. Lattimore)

"Not shaming his father" was considered an important element in a man's motivation, important enough that it could, admittedly, become an obsession: consider the case of Ajax in Sophocles' tragedy of 442 or 441. *Ajax* indicates what a fifth-century Athenian imagined as the excesses to which the old-fashioned heroic mentality might be given: an overemphasis on revenge, an oversensitivity to shame, and an excessive fear of the father. Neither Ajax nor his half-brother Teukros can keep on an even keel when it comes to their father Telamon. Ajax alternates between images of a reverend and pious Telamon, a great warrior Telamon, and an unforgiving Telamon who would have contempt for his son's failure to

win the highest glory at Troy. For example, one of the reasons
Ajax gives for deciding on suicide is the thought of coming home
to his father empty-handed of honor. He says:

> What countenance can I show my father Telamon?
> How will he ever stand the sight of me
> If I come before him naked, armed with no glory,
> When he himself won chaplets of men's praise?
>
> (Soph. *Ajax* 462–465, tr. Moore)

Suicide seems the only way left of proving himself:

> An enterprise which will prove to my old father
> That the son of his loins is not by breed a weakling.
>
> (Soph. *Ajax* 470–472, tr. Moore)

Later in the play, after having failed to talk Ajax out of committing
suicide, Teukros thinks fearfully of his father, whom he imagines
as old and grouchy and likely to blame the whole thing on him:

> He's not much given to smiling, even when things go well.
> What will he not say? What reproach will he spare me?
> . . .
> Age makes him morose and stirs him up
> To causeless anger.
>
> (Soph. *Ajax* 1010–1012, 1017–1018, tr. Moore)

Sophocles describes here how the image of the father could be an
excessive censor in the psyche of the son.[45]

To sum up, then, on one level, a son's affective relationship to
his father was a matter of winning the father's approval and of
avoiding his censure by achieving great things in life. Needless to
say, there was a substantial element of competition in this interchange. On a second level, a son's affective relationship to his
father (and his mother) was one of support, help, and defense.
This protective and sustentative dimension increased as each of the
parties grew older. Athenian law was a watchdog in various ways
on sons who did not show the requisite care for their aging parents,
and public opinion also helped to enforce the rules. A good son
was also expected to help his father fight his battles while alive
and to continue his friendships and enmities after the father's
death. To grow into a good man, however, a boy had to be
properly educated, and in this a father's role was considerable.

BRINGING UP BABY

In addition to giving his children food and shelter, to passing on his property to his sons, and to dowering his daughters, an Athenian father was supposed to provide for his sons' education. No doubt much of this process took place on an elevated cultural level, but the sobering fact is that the father's role in a son's education sometimes came down to giving the boy a beating. Athenian sons were expected to obey and to respect their fathers – to honor and fear them and to show shame in their presence, as Demosthenes puts it somewhat strictly in a criminal case (Dem. 54.23; cf. Isai. 2.18, 36; Pl. *Rep.* 562e) – and fathers did not need to be shy about enforcing these qualities. Protagoras, both an advocate of higher education and an admirer of the humble way in which ordinary people raised their children, has this down-to-earth comment about the injunctions of a parent, nurse, or slave attendant to a son: "If he is willing, he obeys, but if not, they straighten (*euthunousin*) him, just like a bent and twisted piece of wood, with threats and blows" (Pl. *Prt.* 25d). Both a male child and a slave (of any age) could be called "boy" (*pais*) in Athens; Aristophanes clarifies the sense of the pun:

> *Chorus-leader*: What is it, boy? For it is fair to call anyone "boy" who gets a beating, even if he's an old man.
> (Ar. *Wasps* 1296–1297)

It might have been unusual to beat a nineteen- or twenty-year-old, as Strepsiades tries to do to his son Pheidippides in *Clouds*, but there was nothing unusual about a father beating or ordering a slave to beat a younger son. Lysis, for instance, who is perhaps in his early teens, considers beatings to be an ordinary part of life (Pl. *Lys.* 208d–209a). An element of physical coercion, therefore, was present in the cherished concept of *paideia*.[46]

But only an element. By all accounts, the father's role in a son's education was gentle as well as stern, advisorial as well as prescriptive. As Xenophon's Socrates says, on the subject of the many blessings that children owe their parents:

> Nor are parents contented only to provide food for their children, but as soon as they consider them capable of learning, they teach them whatever good things for living themselves know; and if there is something that they think that someone else is more competent to teach, they send [their

son] to him at their own expense and try to do everything they can so their children turn out to be as good as possible.

(Xen. *Mem.* 2.2.6)

Socrates' rival, the sophist Protagoras, likewise argues that

[Parents,] beginning with the smallest children and continuing as long as they live, both teach and admonish [their children]. As soon as [a child] understands what is said to him, the nurse, the mother, the *paidagôgos* and the father himself struggle that the child may be as good as possible.

(Pl. *Prt.* 325c)

Protagoras and Socrates too (despite his denials) took a professional interest in education and thus may put more of an emphasis on the importance of a father finding a good teacher for his son (who *could* they each have had in mind?) than normative discourse does otherwise. Indeed, before going any further, it is important to recognize the degree to which Athenian culture implicitly took a boy's education *out* of the hands of his father or the father's appointed teacher. By its emphasis on communal rites of passage, on same-age groups, and on the educational value of the theater and the assembly, Athens ensured even without state schools that the institutions of the polis had considerable influence on the education of its future citizens. Plato, a critic of Athens, complains in the *Laws* that in a truly good city a son would not belong to his genitor at all, but only to the polis (Pl. *Laws* 804d). Yet, even in Athens, custom ensured that a father have his son participate in communal educational experiences. The defendant in Antiphon's *Second Tetralogy* expresses Athenian ideology well when he says that he educated his son in the things that would most benefit the community (*to koinon*), expecting that both he and the boy would benefit (Ant. 2.2.b.3). Truant officers were unnecessary in a society where communal ideology was so often reinforced, and where a son could sue his father for not introducing him to the father's phratry or deme. The polis had many reasons for emphasizing communal education, primarily of course the wish to see itself safely reproduced, but not least among its reasons was the need to respond to the demographic realities: with so many boys likely to lose their father during their childhood, it was imperative to make some provision for their upbringing

83

beyond trusting to the sense of responsibility of a guardian or a mother's second husband.[47]

So the father was not expected to be the sole educator of his son. Still, a wide variety of evidence demonstrates that he was expected to play a central and supervisory role. There is, for instance, the sixth-century BC poet Theognis, who says to the young Kyrnos, "I shall give you good advice like a father to his son" (Theognis 1.1049).[48] Another case, from the late fourth century, is Theophrastos's greedy man. He keeps his sons home from school during the holiday-filled winter month of Anthesterion in order to save on tuition, but apparently he feels too responsible for their education to pull them from school altogether (*Char.* 22.6, cf. 30.14). Even a stupid man knows to teach his sons sports; what makes him stupid, in Theophrastos's mind, is his insistence on training the boys past the point of exhaustion (*Char.* 14.10). The wealthy Crito thinks there is something unmanly about Socrates' willingness to die in 399 when, by escaping, he could live and shoulder his proper responsibility for raising and educating his sons (Pl. *Ap.* 45d). In the late fifth century the wealthy Lysimachos, proud of his interest in his teenage son's education (unlike his own father, whom he blames for having failed to supervise his education), accuses the ordinary father of losing all interest in a son's upbringing when he becomes a *meirakion*, but he assumes that ordinary fathers do at least pay attention to a younger boy's education (Pl. *Lach.* 179a, e).[49]

Athenian culture's emphasis on familial reputation would also encourage a father to do what he could to educate his sons. To quote Socrates again, on the subject of the importance of educating sons: "The management of the father's entire estate (oikos) will depend on how the sons turn out, on whether they are upright or the opposite" (Pl. *Lach.* 185a). As the reference to "the father's entire estate" indicates, Socrates is addressing rich men here, and his tone is rather self-important. Nevertheless, his message would have resonated for the ordinary Athenian father as well: if you care at all about the future of your oikos and about its good name, then pay attention to the education of your sons.[50]

Unlike the wealthy speakers in Plato's *Laches*, a dialogue about education, the ordinary Athenian father would not have been in any position to buy his son special lessons in, for example, fighting in armor (Pl. *Lach.* 179d). Only a minority of sons would have the leisure time which is presupposed by Nikeratos's command from his father Nicias to memorize all of Homer (Xen. *Symp.* 3.5). The ordinary citizen could not provide his son with the battery of nurses, teachers, trainers, and slave attendants that the wealthy could order up, but even the poorest fathers had their educational responsibilities. It was customary for a father to teach his son his *technê* – agricultural skill or a craft or trade; indeed, it was a legal requirement, if Plutarch (*Sol.* 22.1) is to be trusted; according to Plutarch sons who had not been so educated were freed of the responsibility for providing for their fathers' old age. Plato notes the essential role usually played by the father in teaching his son "the paternal *technê*" (*Laws* 694c–695b). Only a small, destitute minority of Athenians would know no *technê*, but even they might have participated from time to time in the informal aspect of paternal education: for example, eating with their sons and telling them family stories (e.g. Pl. *Lach.* 179b-c) or taking them to temples or public buildings or local or national festivals.[51] A description in Plato, with a dramatic date of 420, paints a vivid picture:

> *Nicias*: Lysimachos, it seems to me that you really only know Socrates through his father, and that you haven't met him since he was a child, when perhaps, if he was accompanying his father among his demesmen, he may have drawn near you either in a temple or in some other gathering of the demesmen. Since he has grown up you have clearly not happened upon the man.
>
> (Pl. *Lach.* 187e)

Socrates grew up to be a hoplite, but future knights or rowers might also have been taken as children by their fathers to deme events.[52]

Formal education had to be paid for, and the access of poor boys to it was limited, but one should not assume that they were cut off from formal education entirely. Many poor boys (though we do not know how many) as well as probably most of the sons of the wealthy and the so-called hoplite class received a primary education from about the age of six to about the age of thirteen or fourteen (roughly at the time when a *pais* became a *meirakion*).[53] In any case, whatever primary education Athenian boys did receive included only reading, writing, music, and athletics. Only a tiny minority of Athenians went on to what might be considered higher education.[54]

Indeed, informal education was of immense importance for most Athenian boys. A father or an older male friend or relative could teach a boy to work the family farm or to follow the family craft or trade, instruct him in the rudiments of soldiery or rowing, and whatever inherited wisdom, know-how, and gossip was in the air. We do not know the details, but clearly some Athenian boys went through something like an apprenticeship with a master craftsman who was not their father; the sources mention builders, potters, and doctors. There were other informal sources of education for a boy, of course: what he learned on his mother's knee; childhood games and the physical training learned in the gymnasia, so useful for future military service; religious teaching, whether explicit or implicit in ritual and ceremony; the knowledge of neighbors, slaves, friends, and lovers; and the political knowledge he began to pick up upon attending the assembly from about the age of twenty.[55]

WERE THE RICH LIKE OTHER PEOPLE?

Let us look more closely at the question of how the great figures of Athenian public life provided for the education of their sons. It is a commonplace of the Platonic corpus that the great generals and political leaders of Athens were unable to pass on their talents to their sons, who never achieved greatness themselves. Socrates heightens the paradox by noting that these leaders spared no expense in their sons' education; what they failed to do, however, was to teach their sons their own particular skill (*technê*) or excellence (*aretê*). The great founder of the Athenian empire, Themistocles, for instance, had his son Kleophantos trained in horsemanship and every other skill that was being taught at the time. And yet, as Socrates asks, "Have you ever heard anyone, young or old, say that Kleophantos son of Themistocles was a good and wise man in the way his father was?"(Pl. *Meno* 93e). A rhetorical question, of course.[56]

The sons in question seem to have had a different perspective on the matter. In *Laches*, for instance, Lysimachos son of Aristides and Melesias son of Thoukydides each blames his own lack of success in public life on neglect by his famous father.[57] Laches takes up the point eagerly: "we blame our fathers because they allowed us to indulge ourselves when we became *meirakia* and meanwhile they worked on the affairs of others" (Pl. *Lach.* 179c). He continues:

> What Lysimachos said just now about his father [Aristides] and about Melesias's father [Thoukydides] seems to me to be very true, for them and us and everyone in public affairs: it is nearly always the case, as he says, that they pay little attention to their private affairs, whether concerning their children or anything else, and they arrange them carelessly.
>
> (Pl. *Lach.* 180b)

That two grown men, with teenage sons of their own, could still hold up their long-passed adolescence as the key to the rest of their lives speaks volumes about Plato's psychological acumen – and about his mastery of the deadpan. It also demonstrates how seriously Athenian sons took their fathers' responsibility to teach them their *technai*.

Some scholars have taken the Platonic criticism one step further, arguing that Athenian fathers generally, and not just the famous politicians and generals, were far too occupied with public affairs to pay proper attention to the upbringing of their children. The argument betrays a degree of idealizing the Athenian male as *homo politicus* and, in any case, it does not bear scrutiny. Back in the fifth century BC, Protagoras responded to Socrates' criticism by insisting that Athenian fathers did indeed teach their *technai* to their sons; when the sons of good men turned out poorly it had much more to do with the sons' lack of natural aptitude than with parental neglect (Pl. *Prt.* 327c). Nowadays we might turn Plato's argument around and point out the rarity of greatness, the complexity of the manifold factors that shape a growing child, and the psychological burden upon a son of a father's greatness, who sometimes responds by seeking a life of obscurity; it would be difficult to find any society, let alone Athens, where great men usually have great sons.[58]

The main counter to Plato, however, is this: rather than invariably turn out to be nonentities, the sons of famous Athenians often became respected practitioners of the same profession as their fathers; on occasion, they even achieved greatness. Undoubtedly, careerist fathers in Athens could have spent more time than they did in the personal supervision of their sons' upbringing, but they were perfectly capable of hiring appropriate teachers and masters for their sons. Moreover, an advanced education was neither the prerequisite nor the guarantee of political or military greatness.

An interesting fifth-century example is that of the general Miltiades, hero of Marathon, whose son Kimon also became a general, the hero of several battles and one of Athens's greatest politicians. Miltiades died in 489 when Kimon was a *meirakion*, and Kimon did not receive an advanced education, although Miltiades had presumably arranged a traditional Athenian primary education for the boy. Still, after his father's death, Kimon did go through a wild and disorderly phase, even inspiring rumors of incest with his sister Elpinike. Yet Kimon matured into a brilliant and disciplined general by his early thirties (Plut. *Kimon* 4–6). Kimon's sons were not nearly as distinguished, but neither were they no-accounts: Lakedaimonios was a hipparch and general, and his brother Thettalos was a leader of the political assault on Alcibiades in 415.[59]

Konon, general in the Peloponnesian War and Corinthian War, was the father of Timotheos, also to be a general in his day. Konon lived to see his son reach his twenties, and the collaboration between the two became a symbol of father–son solidarity. As a young man, probably in his early twenties, Timotheos seems to have accompanied Konon during his travels through the cities of Ionia in 394 BC after Konon's smashing victory over Sparta at Knidos. At any rate, Samos and Ephesos honored both father and son with statues at the time (Paus. 6.3.16).[60]

Pericles produced no son as great as himself, but neither did Napoleon, Bismarck, Lincoln, or Gandhi. But Pericles' only son to live past the age of about thirty, also named Pericles, did become a general, and Pericles also raised a ward who grew to achieve greatness – Alcibiades. (Another Periclean ward, Alcibiades' brother Kleinias, was, however, a conspicuous failure.) Alcibiades' father, also named Kleinias, who died in Alcibiades' early childhood, was himself a prominent politician. Kleinias had taken special pains over his sons' upbringing by appointing Athens's greatest politician as their guardian rather than making the usual choice of a close relative for the post.[61]

There are many other examples of fathers active in public life who produced sons who were active too. Andron, for one, a member of the oligarchy of the Four Hundred in 411, thought enough of his son Androtion's education to send him to study with Isocrates; the boy became a prominent orator and historian in the fourth century. Hagnon, a general and prominent official in the Peloponnesian War era, was the father of Theramenes, the well-known democratic politician turned oligarch in 411 and 404. One of the ten experienced *probouloi* (commissioners) appointed to guide the state in the crisis of 413, Hagnon played a small role in establishing the oligarchy of the Four Hundred, in which his son was an active participant. The extremely wealthy Hipponikos, general in the 420s, was father of Kallias, general in Corinth in 390 and ambassador to Sparta in 371. Diotimos of Euonymon, general in the 430s, was father of Strombichides, general in the late Peloponnesian War and eventually executed under the Thirty for his fervent support for democracy. Strombichides' son Autokles was in turn an Athenian general and ambassador in the first half of the fourth century. Finally, Nikophemos of Rhamnous, a close colleague of Konon in the 390s who played a prominent role in his fleet, was the father of Aristophanes, ambassador to Syracuse in 393 and, with Nikophemos, co-commander of a small Athenian expedition to Cyprus in 390. The Spartan capture of this expedition led eventually to the two men's execution back in Athens, but perhaps father and son felt some small satisfaction in having fought together, like Odysseus and Telemakhos.[62]

What these examples demonstrate is that men of prominence in Athenian public life did not necessarily produce sons who grew up to be failures. We catch only glimpses of a father's specific actions to further his son's education: Themistocles' emphasis on riding lessons for his son or Thoukydides' emphasis on wrestling for his sons; Kleinias's choice of Pericles as the guardian of his sons, or Andron's permission for his son Androtion to study with Isocrates. The overall picture is nevertheless clear. Fathers who could afford to arranged for their sons' education and, like their poorer co-citizens, attempted to teach them their own *technai*. At times they even succeeded.

ACROSS THE YEARS

Let us take a brief look at the cycle of a father's educational responsibilities to his son as the child grew from infancy to manhood. The Athenians had a keen awareness of the stages of a child's growth, and custom marked a number of transition points (some precise, others flexible) along the way. In terms of the father–son relationship, the stages of a boy's growth exhibited a certain tension between solidarity with the father and separation from him. The growing boy learned to be like his father and prepared to head his own oikos one day, but he also forged ties outside the oikos with his peers, with his kin, demesmen, and the members of quasi-kinship groups (the *genos* and the phratry) and his age-mates (*hêlikes*). Finally, he became a member of the citizen group of the polis – the official induction came in his eighteenth year, although there had been considerable previous preparation through ritual and informal education. As already noted, it was part of the father's educational responsibility to make sure that his son participated in such rituals. In his supervision of his son's education, therefore, the Athenian father was in the doubly ironic position of not only preparing someone to supplant him in the household, but also of moving someone away from and outside of his own paternal domain altogether. The *kyrios* helped to make a new *kyrios* who would one day share in the status of the Athenian demos as *kyrios* of the polis.[63]

It is usually argued that during his first few years, the young Athenian child was put under the care of his mother, other female relatives, and, if the family could afford one, a nurse. This is safe to believe, as long as one avoids the idealist-cum-misogynist argument (or, in a variation, the psychological exposé) that as *homo politicus*, the Athenian father avoided the home, especially drooling infants in the "women's quarters." No doubt the young child was primarily a woman's responsibility, but there is plenty of evidence of Athenian fathers enjoying the company of their infants and toddlers. Homer, Aristophanes, and Theophrastos all describe fathers playing with their young sons. Herodotus expects his audience to be shocked by the Persian custom whereby fathers avoided their sons for the first five years of a child's life, so as to avoid disappointment if the child died; by contrast, Athenian fathers clearly did see their young sons. As for the "women's quarters," recent research casts doubt on whether any but the very wealthiest families could afford such an extravagance. The literary evidence and the archaeological remains both indicate that most Athenian houses were small and cramped, so, like it or not, fathers would have had to get used to the presence of the young and messy. The father, therefore, was not the primary figure in the young child's life, but he was expected to be a presence nonetheless.[64]

Shortly after the birth of a son, the father would have to arrange formal ceremonies to acknowledge the child's paternity and to name him. At the next celebration of the Apatouria (an annual public festival in the autumn), on the day of the Koureotis, he would register the infant in his phratry, which required: the provision of a sacrificial victim, the payment of a fee to a priest, possibly the provision of food for a party afterward, and of course the attestation of his son's paternity. It is possible that this costly ceremony was optional, and that poorer men only registered their sons with the phratry once, when a boy turned sixteen; wealthier Athenians would have registered their sons twice.[65]

When a boy turned three, the father would arrange for him to participate in the Choes ("Pitchers"), the second day of the annual three-day Anthesteria festival in early spring. The Anthesteria was sacred to Dionysos, god of wine, and Choes marked the drinking of the new wine pressed the previous fall. The child participants in the festivities each received his own juglet and took his first taste of wine. The symbolic significance stems from Dionysos's powers as god of growth; the participation of children seems to have marked a stage in their development, perhaps a transition from infancy to childhood. These were also the first, tentative steps of transition from the household to the civic world, since Dionysos was a civic deity, and since children were formally introduced for the first time to their age-mates (*hêlikes*).[66]

Boys participated prominently in other Athenian festivals and celebrations as well: as members of choruses that sung poetry, sometimes competitively; as bearers of ritual boughs from house to house; as an intermediary (the "hearth child") between initiates and divinity at Eleusis; and in athletic contests. Eager fathers might play a role in getting their sons involved in a prominent and public ceremony, particularly when there was a prize to be won.[67] The singing choir-boys were a picture of innocence; the contrast between the participants and onlookers was a graphic evocation of the pathos of time, and of the transition between generations. Plato, for example, describes a grown-up Kritias recalling his own participation, at about the age of ten, in one of the boys' choruses competing in the recitation of poetry at the Koureotis (Pl. *Ti.* 21b). The scene is full of symbols of the father–son relationship: the day itself, in which sons are initiated into their fathers' phratry; the point, not missed by Kritias, that the contest had been established by "our fathers," that is, the ancestors; finally, the presence among the onlookers of young Kritias's ninety-year-old grandfather Kritias, after whom he had been named. The scene was a melodrama in miniature, a vignette of generational transition, heightened no doubt by Plato's artistry but able to be perceived by any father at the annual festival.[68]

The growing child would hear stories, myths, and nursery rhymes; in the *Republic*, Plato proposes state censorship of these tales because of their influence on an impressionable youngster, and he assumes that they are mainly told by mothers and nurses (376e–378e). But fathers sometimes told stories to their young children, too. Theophrastos's chatterbox, for example, allows his children to keep him up at night and to force him to tell them a story before they sleep (*Char.* 7.9). At about the age of six, the children of wealthier families would be put in the charge of a slave known as a *paidagôgos*, literally "child-leader," effectively "a mixture of nurse, footman, chaperon and tutor," as one scholar puts it in an idiom that calls to mind its Edwardian upper-class milieu, in turn nicely reminiscent of the degree to which the Athenian *paidagôgos* was a class luxury. Schooling, that is primary education, began at around the age of seven. Primary schooling was neither universal nor compulsory, but it was accessible to considerably more Athenian boys than was the care of a *paidagôgos*.[69]

The father whose sons were under the care of *paidagôgos* and teachers was relatively free of child-rearing responsibility, at least until primary education ended at around the age of fourteen; a minority of wealthy boys would continue under the care of teachers and trainers. In poorer families, fathers would have greater direct responsibilities and might begin teaching their sons the family trade or put them to work on the family farm at an early age. Regardless of social class, fathers would continue to spend time with their sons in the informal educational activities mentioned above. The fewer the formal educational opportunities open to the son, the larger the father's role as mentor may have loomed. Consider, for instance, Lysistrata's defense of herself as a person of culture in spite of being a woman (and therefore not able to attend school) because she had heard "many speeches from [her] father and older men" (Ar. *Lys.* 1124–1127). Likewise, a poor boy might think of his father and his father's friends and kinsmen as the keys to his education.

But only up to a point. For one thing, boys have friends, and friends sometimes seem a lot better informed about the world than one's father does, especially (at least nowadays) when a boy becomes a teenager. For another, many teenage boys had no father. This latter datum is surely not unrelated to the facts of life for some Athenian teenage boys, that is, pederasty. From the ages of about thirteen or fourteen to about twenty-one (the *meirakion* stage), a boy in the elite might be involved in love affairs with *neoi*, or young men in their twenties. This was a common pattern, but of course Athenian adolescents may have alternatively had sexual relations with other partners such as slaves, friends of the same age, friends of one's father, and – if a boy became a prostitute himself – paying clients. Boys may even have had sexual relations with girls![70]

As Dover argues in a sensitive and witty discussion, the father of a *meirakion* is likely to have given him mixed messages about love affairs with *neoi*: on the one hand, they were to be avoided, on the other hand, they were not so bad after all if the *neos* was decent, upright, famous, well connected, and rich – in other words, a role model for the son and a good contact for the father. Such a mixed message was perhaps inevitable, given the convention that the younger partner (the *eromenos*) be available to the older one (the *erastês*) but never let himself seem available. In Xenophon's *Symposium*, for example, Lykon serves as chaperon to his son Autolykos, and is not about to let the boy's would-be lover Kallias lay a hand on him, but he is perfectly content to let the two make eyes at each other in his presence. A *meirakion* who no longer had a living father was perhaps especially likely to have an *erastês*, since he would provide the boy with the missing older male role model.[71]

Aristophanes offers a characteristically wicked and intricate joke on the subject of fathers protecting their sons from a lover's predations. In *Birds*, the elderly Euelpides imagines that his fantasy city would be the kind of place

> Where the father of a good-looking boy will meet me and go on at me as if I'd done him a wrong: "That was a nice way to treat my son, Stilbonides ['Bright Eyes']! You met him when he'd had a bath, leaving the gymnasium, and you didn't kiss him, you didn't say a word to him, you didn't pull him close to you, you didn't tickle his balls – and you an old friend of the family [*patrikos philos*, i.e. inherited or paternal friend]!"
>
> (Ar. *Birds* 137–142, tr. Dover [1978] 137)

93

The humor here is a typical Aristophanic reversal. In real life, a father would no doubt treat an old man who was ogling his freshly bathed son as a wretched old pervert, and hardly as a desirable *erastês*. As a *patrikos philos* the old man was doubly misbehaving, for surely he could reserve his lechery for strangers.

There is more to the joke, though, for as a *patrikos philos*, Euelpides should have treated the boy in a fatherly manner – with affection, not lust. In the fantasy, though, the boy's father invites his paternal friend Euelpides to help himself to his son's body. Does this suggest a wish that "in a fatherly manner" might mean "with lust"? And since, as the well-known Greek proverb has it, "friends have all things in common" (e.g. Pl. *Phdr.* 279), is the father exposing his own incest fantasy by inviting his paternal friend to enjoy his son? In short, Aristophanes may be indulging in a perverse joke here that points nonetheless to what might have been genuine problems.[72]

The "teenage years" (roughly, the *meirakion* stage, from about thirteen or fourteen to about twenty-one) offered their own challenges, especially after eighteen, when the boy became *kyrios*. As he became a *neos*, a son might itch for control of his patrimony, and in the resulting father–son confrontation, sparks could fly, especially if the father was uneasy about turning property and authority over to his son. Perhaps the tensions were greatest among the wealthy, who had property worth fighting over. In *Clouds*, for example, Aristophanes explores a wealthy family's experience of cultural as well as financial conflict between a father of around sixty and his approximately twenty-year-old son.[73]

In this context, it is worth reconsidering what has been a common theme from Plato on, the notion of Athenian pederasty as a kind of substitute paternity, especially a substitute for the father's educational role. In the *Symposium*, for instance, Phaidros argues that an *erastês* is a much better check on a young man's shameful or cowardly behavior than any friend or even a father could be (178d). Scholars have sometimes criticized Athenian fathers for sloughing off their responsibility to their son onto his lover. This critique suffers from the same lack of evidence and idealizing bias as the previously cited argument that Athenian fathers systematically neglected their sons' professional education. Moreover, as Slater points out, pederasty had the salutary effect of counteracting father–son competition. Whether it had its origins in initiation rites or not, Athenian pederasty did bring the *mei-*

rakion into the orbit of a wider adult male world than his father's.[74]

If the *meirakion* perhaps distanced himself somewhat from his father, ties need not have been severed. The father had two important formal responsibilities to the teenage son, and informal contacts no doubt remained. The first formal responsibility was to register the boy in his father's phratry on the day of Koureotis at the Apatouria festival. The evidence is murky, but it appears that the ceremony took place when the boy was about sixteen, and that a ritual cutting of his hair was a marker of his coming manhood. For many, if not most fathers, this was a second registration, the boy having previously been registered as an infant. Once again, a father had to sponsor his son as well as to provide a sacrifice for the ritual, a fee for the priest, and perhaps food for a party afterward.[75]

The second formal responsibility was the registration of the son in the father's deme upon the boy's eighteenth birthday. An important ceremony of great legal and psychological significance, deme registration was a milestone of the boy's continuing integration into the community of citizens. Upon registration the boy became his own *kyrios*, which meant he could make contracts, and represent himself in court; he was now also eligible for military service.[76]

The procedure is fairly clear, at least for the late fourth century. The father or legal guardian would sponsor the son's candidacy at the deme assembly. There the deme members would vote under oath on the boy's age, his status as a free man, and his birth from two citizen parents. If rejected by the deme members, a candidate or rather his father or guardian could appeal to a jury-court, but the stakes were high, for if the deme members denied the appeal they could sell the boy into slavery; if the deme members accepted the appeal they had to enroll him. Candidates approved by the deme had to pass a further and final scrutiny by the council before officially becoming citizens.[77]

Now *kyrios*, the eighteen-year-old had taken his most significant step yet in his integration into the citizen community and on the road to manhood. Having raised his son to become a citizen, the father had fulfilled the bulk of his educational responsibilities. Yet his status as advisor and mentor to the young man might continue, as would of course the potential for conflict between the two men. First of all, Athenian and Greek culture generally accorded a young man a transitional stage, as an ephebe, between registration as a citizen (or its extra-Athenian equivalent) and participation in the public life of the city. The *ephêbeia* of the 330s, prescribing special military service for eighteen- and nineteen-year-olds, was a new institution, but it was based on ancient practice, and the term *ephêbos* was time-honored. As early as the 370s Athenian ephebes had a special military status, and during the Peloponnesian War the youngest soldiers (*neôtatoi*) had a distinct status. Furthermore, new citizens were not expected to participate in the assembly before the age of twenty, nor could they participate in the courts (except for inheritance cases) or the council or hold a magistracy until age thirty. As an ephebe, therefore, a young man was not quite a full-fledged member of the adult citizen community. Ephebes and *neoi* generally, therefore, might continue to seek (or shirk) the advice of an older man, perhaps their father.[78]

A second point concerns the son's continuing dependent status, both emotionally and financially. Until he married, came into his patrimony, and formed his own oikos, which might not happen until the age of thirty, a son might frequently turn to his father, and not merely for money. For example, he might ask for the older man's advice on finding a wife. The adopted son of the late Menekles, for instance, anxious (on the occasion of a legal challenge to his inheritance) to prove his close relationship with Menekles, has this to say:

> After this Menekles began to look for a wife for me and said that I should marry. I took the daughter of Philonides. Menekles displayed the forethought on my behalf that a father would naturally display on his son's behalf, and I tended and respected (*etherapeuon te kai aischunomên*) him in the way that I would my birth father – I and my wife, with the result that he praised us to all his demesmen.
>
> (Isai. 2.18)

Particularly if he continued to live in his father's house or to work on the family farm or in the family trade, the son might continue to treat his father as a mentor.[79]

This Isaios passage also points to the evolution of roles within the father–son relationship. As Menekles grew older (and if a twenty-year-old had a living father he was likely to be in his fifties or older) his son would take on an increasing responsibility of care and respect. As the boy became *kyrios* of his own *oikos* and a full-fledged member of the citizen community, his former *kyrios* would shift roles and become his charge, as well as an increasingly less active citizen.

To sum up, as his son matured, a father would play a central and supervisory role in the boy's education, but he would share that role with other individuals and institutions. He was expected to teach his son a *technê*, which presumably in most cases was his own *technê*. In most families, the burden of technical education fell on the father himself and his close relatives, although some fathers of ordinary income sent their sons out to an apprenticeship. Wealthy fathers could shift the burden to a large extent onto the shoulders of teachers and slaves but, as demonstrated by the many examples of professional continuity between wealthy fathers and sons, even wealthy fathers may have played a personal role in their sons' professional education.

The polis neither expected nor desired the father to have full responsibility for his son's integration into the political or religious communities. Much of the father's responsibility consisted of ensuring that his son participate in certain communal rites of passage, spaced at intervals during his growing years, that would teach the meaning of Athenian manhood. The interaction of father and fatherland in a boy's education was a vivid example of the interweaving of public and private; it prepared a boy for his future roles as practitioner of a *technê*, as *kyrios*, and as citizen, as well as future educator of his own son.

CONCLUSION

An Athenian son was expected to respect, honor, and obey his father, to take care of him in old age, to arrange for his burial and memorial rites. He was supposed to protect his father from his enemies and to defend his father's reputation, even beyond the grave. In doing so, the son would act out of both duty and self-interest, since his reputation was tied to his father's. The father was a model for the growing son to emulate. The son was likely to follow in his father's footsteps on the family farm or in trade or a political or military career. Rich or poor, every son would be expected to grow up to become *kyrios* of his own *oikos* someday, just as his father had been. Fathers could be affectionate or proud, but they could also be censorious and demanding, to the point that even when far away or when dead, their image still exerted great power over a son's behavior.

Unlike Roman sons, Athenian sons won legal independence from their father relatively early, at age eighteen. Society nonetheless accorded young men an "ephebic" period for military service, travel, experimentation, or, as was the case with many rich young Athenians in the late fifth century, study with a sophist. This period continued late into a man's twenties; a son usually did not settle down for marriage until around age thirty. In the canonical case, a son would not come fully into his patrimony until the age of marriage, at which point his father might retire. Given the prevailing Mediterranean marriage pattern, however, with its low life expectancy and late age of marriage for men, perhaps half of Athenian sons had lost their father by age eighteen, and so would inherit their patrimony then. Many others would come into their property between the ages of eighteen and thirty.

Athenian fathers had the responsibility and right to initiate a newborn baby into the oikos or to reject it as a bastard. After accepting the baby, a father could not change his mind later. He was expected to supervise his son's education and to arrange for the boy to learn to earn a living as he himself did. Fathers also played the important role of initiating their sons into the male world of the polis, by arranging for them to become members, in due course, of the inherited paternal phratry and deme. The sources afford frequent examples of paternal pride in their sons, a pride that was a complex combination of selfish and unselfish motives.

On the whole, the sources speak of harmony and cooperation between fathers and sons. Yet there was much potential for tension and conflict as well. Paradoxically, the better a father supervised his son's upbringing, the better he prepared the boy first to leave the paternal oikos for the world of the polis and then to create his own new oikos. On the other hand, there are complaints by grown sons about having received insufficient attention from their busy fathers. Teachers, friends, and lovers might have served as a buffer between son and father during the difficult teenage years. An eighteen-year-old who had attained legal independence might chafe at his continued financial dependence on his father. Add to this a strong undercurrent of admiration for youthful independence, which exists in ancient Greek culture at least as far back as the *Iliad*. Furthermore, the Peloponnesian War era had its own special characteristics which (a) exacerbated the general perception of father–son tension and (b) perhaps caused extra tension in a segment of the elite. We shall now turn to these tensions and to the reaction they engendered.

4

CONFLICT
The sons of Theseus

In the summer of my sixteenth year a strange voice sang in
my ears.
> George Seferis, "Ephebe" (from "Mr. Stratis Thalassinos
> Describes a Man"), tr. Keeley and Sherrard

Fifth-century Athens may represent an extraordinary moment in
the history of high culture, but there is nothing unique about the
theme of father–son conflict found in its literature. Father–son
conflict figures prominently not only in early and later Greek
literature, but in the literature, mythology, and art of many different cultures of different eras and different parts of the world.
Nor is Athens unique in putting this datum of social practice to
ideological use. What is unique and interesting are the details, the
particular ideological use which the Athenians made of the
conflict.

SOCIOLOGY AND MYTHOLOGY

Conflict between father and son may well be universal and inevitable, particularly at critical turning points in the life cycle: when
the boy (*pais*) becomes a man (*anêr*) and when the man (*anêr*)
becomes an old man (*gerôn*). Athenian culture had its own ways
of mediating and exacerbating the conflict. Mediation may have
come through participation in ritual (e.g. the Oschophoria),
through segregation by age (e.g. the ephebate), through the
creation of father-substitutes (e.g. teachers or lovers), through
the invocation of self-interest (conflict between father and son
would damage their shared and inherited reputation), through the
observation of dramatic re-creations of conflict (e.g. tragedy and

comedy) with a consequent release of emotion (*katharsis*) – and above all, of course, through the constant reinforcement of the lesson of father–son solidarity by means of the normative discourse discussed in the preceding chapter.

Normative discourse, however, spoke with a forked tongue. Granted, the fork was not precisely in the middle: the bulk of the tradition speaks of solidarity. Nevertheless, father–son conflict sounds a distinct and unforgettable minor key throughout Greek literature, art, and mythology. We shall presently turn to this subject and to one striking Attic example. First, let us reconsider two ways in which Athenian culture exacerbated father–son conflict: (1) through its abhorrence of the subordination of one male to another while, inconsistently, encouraging male assertiveness and aggression, and (2) through often making a son wait years after becoming *kyrios* at age eighteen until he finally obtained his patrimony. To make the second point in another way, by recognizing a boy's manhood and politico-jural independence at age eighteen, instead of putting off that turning point until the boy was in charge of his patrimony, Athenian culture created an opening for potential father–son conflict. Both property and appearance, both interest and emotion were grounds for conflict between Athenian father and son.[1]

The character of male–male relationships outside the family, to discuss the first point, could hardly help but influence the father–son relationship. The education of an Athenian male citizen prized equality, harmony, and cooperation, but not without also emphasizing a high degree of aggression, competitiveness, and hierarchy. Lysias, for example, praises the hero Herakles for leading a life devoted to hard work, ambition, and competition, making it clear that all three were laudable (Lys. 2.16). Athenians were acutely conscious of the difference between winning and losing, and all too often they acted as if one man's victory required another man's defeat. Athenians differentiated rigorously between active and passive positions: both in public and in private, in such diverse places as the Athenian empire, where hegemon and subject cities were distinct; in Athens's democratic regime, where governing and being governed alternated; and in the bedroom, where in both heterosexual and homosexual relations, "top" and "bottom" were strictly defined.[2]

Teach a boy to be fierce, aggressive, competitive, and a jealous guardian of his own, and you may find it difficult also to teach him to respect and obey his father. Such was the paradox of Athenian patriarchy, a system of male dominance that carried the seeds of its own, well, if not undoing, then at least destabilization: the likelihood of a challenge to older by younger males. Patriarchy? Perhaps one could even speak of "paidarchy."

In a perceptive study of kinship and male-centered relationships in the modern Middle East, Fredrik Barth offers an illuminating analogy. Barth notes the existence of considerable variation and contradiction among the different ideas of male behavior in different relationships. Difficulties consequently arise for the individual, which Barth believes are generally resolvable by avoiding simultaneous encounters with parties toward whom one has discrepant relationships. For example, males are supposed generally to behave toward other males with independence, courage, dominance, and a repudiation of superordinate authority; and husbands are supposed to treat their wives with assertiveness and in a dominating manner. On the other hand, sons are expected to treat their fathers with obedience, discipline, and respect. Barth zeroes in on the dilemma that arises for a male if he has to behave at the same time as an obedient son to his father and an assertive husband to his wife. The solution is the seclusion of women and the systematic separation of public and private activity, either physically through walls or symbolically through ritualized avoidance. The separation of different statuses and modes of behavior is rarely completely successful, however, as Barth notes, especially where parties to different relationships are simultaneously present, as they are in a domestic unit. The actor cannot always switch roles.[3]

What can be said of the separation of males and females could also be said of the separation of men and boys. The Athenians could, and did, use the physical and symbolic separation of young men from their fathers (as in boys' contests in poetry or athletics, religious rituals, education, pederasty, and the ephebate) to allow for the separation of filial obedience and developing manly assertiveness. There was, moreover, no difficulty in explaining the difference between the two *intellectually*. Barth's model, however, not to mention common-sense experience, demonstrates the *practical* difficulty of rendering such a separation effective. Even a regimented, authoritarian society like Sparta found it difficult to train citizens to keep separate such categories as public and private, command and obedience; how much greater the task of enforcing separation in the comparatively democratic and individualistic atmosphere of Athens. Athenian male culture oscillated between great coarseness about and hypersensitivity to the problem of being subordinate to another man. Keep the generations apart, invoke the principle of self-interest, appeal to tradition: all would help, but nevertheless some degree of father–son conflict in some families would probably be irrepressible. Promote male autonomy and independence as the cherished patrimony of every citizen, and the door to conflict becomes all but a flood gate.[4]

Let us now turn to the subject of the transmission of property. The Mediterranean marriage pattern prevailing in Athens entailed that only about half of Athens's males would have had to wait beyond the age of eighteen to obtain their inheritance, and many of them would not have had to wait very long. Furthermore, the duties and adventures of military service might have left them with their hands full enough without arguing with their father over the purse strings. Still, when it comes to ideology, perception is often more important than reality. Given Athenian hypersensitivity to autonomy, a few spectacular cases in the elite of sons champing at the bit of fathers' financial reins might have added greatly to the generalized perception of father–son conflict. Aristophanes' *Clouds*, for example, offers a memorable depiction of the struggle between horse-crazy, approximately nineteen-year-old Pheidippides and Strepsiades, the father whose purse he was dipping into. On the ideological plane, one performance of this play (produced in 423) might have outweighed hundreds of cases of harmonious intergenerational transmission of property.[5]

Goody has written of the generalized struggle between the generations over the transmission of property and rights, which he calls the "Prince Hal complex."[6] Fortes, also noting the existence of conflict and wariness over this issue, points out that among the Ashanti, where property is transferred through uterine kin, from uncle to nephew (sister's son) rather than agnatically from father to son, there is a proverb that goes "Your nephew is your enemy": that is, he is waiting for you to die to collect your property.[7] However easy and routine the transmission of property between Athenian father and son in most cases, the existence of prominent exceptions would exacerbate the inevitable tension in the minds of both older and younger generation about the changing of the guard. "Your son is your enemy." Not the sort of thing an Athenian father would be likely to admit openly but, after a performance of *Clouds*, the statement might have elicited at least a few knowing glances and nods.

Let us turn now to the evidence of myth, which demonstrates the existence not only of an inherited substratum of father–son tension in Greek culture, but of its continued usefulness and its specific adaptation by fifth-century democratic ideology. Father–son conflict is an important theme in Greek myth; the work of Lévi-Strauss helps to clarify its significance. In his study of myth, Lévi-Strauss has argued that the subjects of incest and patricide or fratricide, common mythological themes (mythemes) in Greece and elsewhere, are closely related: incest representing an "overvaluation of kinship," patricide or fratricide an "undervaluation of kinship." Stories containing these mythemes are in turn variations on a larger theme, a basic social message of which myth is only the poetic expression. For Lévi-Strauss, myth is both a kind of collective unconscious and a kind of collective pedagogy, a way of transmitting unpleasant and paradoxical realities across the generations. The particular, paradoxical message of the incest–patricide/fratricide mytheme has been expressed neatly by Leach: "If society is to go on, daughters must be disloyal to their parents and sons must destroy (replace) their fathers."[8]

A young person in classical Athens might have found this message to hand in many different places: in the myth of Kronos and his father Ouranos and son Zeus, readily accessible in Hesiod or in drama; in the relationships of Telemakhos, Odysseus, and Laertes in the *Odyssey*; in inverted form in the tragedy of Hektor in the *Iliad* and the pathos of Priam having to beg Achilles for the return of his son's body; in such Athenian adolescent rites of passage as registration with one's father's deme upon the age of eighteen; in the stories of innumerable Attic dramas (e.g. Oedipus, Antigone) whether seen at first hand or recounted by adults; in the ritual of a marriage ceremony. Indeed, myths of father–son conflict were sufficently prominent that the Athenian Stranger in Plato's *Laws* (886c) criticizes their influence on contemporary parent–child relations. Perhaps the best-known version of the story, the one most frequently encountered in classical Athens, is the myth of Theseus.

HERO OR PATRICIDE?

Theseus has aptly been called Athens's national hero. As the subject in the fifth century BC of monumental sculpture and painting, of hundreds of vase paintings, of tragedy and comedy, of history, of annual festivals, and of everyday recognition in gymnasia and wrestling schools, Theseus was a ubiquitous role model of prowess, patriotism, and manhood. An athlete-in-training (Paus. 4.32.1), a young man leaving home – especially on his way to war, the Athenian army flushed with victory over the Persians: all might have thought of themselves as following in Theseus's footsteps.[9]

A ubiquitous hero, but not a monolithic one: Athenian writers, artists, and politicians recrafted Theseus, as they did other figures of myth, to suit their various ideological purposes. Fifth-century drama and painting, fourth-century oratory, local history, and painting reshape myth to make Theseus the founder of Athenian democracy. Thucydides does not endorse that conclusion, but he does assert that Theseus was responsible for the unification of the separate villages of Attica into a national state (Thuc. 2.15; cf. Plut. *Thes.* 24). As the symbol of the state as a whole, Theseus could not have been co-opted by any one of its parts, but both his father Aigeus and his son Akamas were among the eponymous heroes of the ten Kleisthenic tribes. In tragedy, Athens is the "land of Theseus"; the Athenians are "Theseid" (Aesch. *Eum.* 1026; Eur. *Tro.* 208, 219; Soph. *OC* 1066). Theseus was considered a patron of the poor and humble, and his hero shrine became a refuge for runaway slaves (Plut. *Thes.* 36.4; Pherekrates frg. 49 Kassel and Austin; schol. Ar. *Kn.* 1312; *FGrH* 328 F 177). The Atthidographers, those writers of local histories of Athens from primeval times to their own day (ca. 350–250 BC), have much to say about Theseus; Istros and Philokhoros are the primary sources for the colorful life of Theseus which Plutarch wrote some four centuries later. In his discussion (1.2), Plutarch calls Theseus the "founder" (*oikistês*, the same word used for the founder, real or legendary, of a colony) of Athens and compares him to Romulus, the "father" (*patêr*) of Rome.[10]

Theseus was frequently depicted in art as a young athlete, was considered by many as the inventor of the art of wrestling, and was an honored patron of gymnasia and *palaistrai* (Paus. 1.39.3). The generic term that best befits the most common fifth-century conception of Theseus is ephebe.[11] Scholars have called Theseus the "Athenian ephebe par excellence,"[12] the "ephebe of ephebes,"[13] and referred to his myth as "the story of the Athenian ephebe system."[14] His various early deeds – the feats on the road from Troezen to Athens, the conquest of the Marathonian bull, the victory over the Minotaur, and other acts all of which preceded his assumption of the kingship of Athens – have long been recognized as initiatory in character. As Keuls has pointed out, Theseus makes an unsavory role model from the point of view of sexual ethics, since rape, abduction, mendacity, and abandonment are all characteristic of his treatment of women. It needs also to be recognized, however, what an ambiguous and problematic character Theseus was from the point of view of father–son relations.[15]

In the course of his mythological career, Theseus, who was born a bastard and abandoned by his father, raised fear in the mind of his father Aigeus at the news of his exploits on the road to Athens; expressed anxiety and unease over his parentage, whether of Aigeus or his reputed divine father, the god Poseidon; was indirectly responsible for Aigeus's death (from which he profited by inheriting the throne); was sentenced by King Minos to be among the young Athenians sacrificed to the Minotaur in revenge for the murder in Attica of Minos's son Androgeos, a murder caused by Aigeus in some versions of the myth; took credit as a defender of the oikos by killing the Minotaur and returning Athenian children to their parents; caused the death of his own son Hippolytos by begging it as a favor from his "other" father, the god Poseidon; and died in a way similar to that of his father Aigeus, by a fall from a cliff. In short, Theseus virtually embodies the ambiguities of the Athenian father–son relationship. Let us examine the ideological significance of the Theseus myth more closely, beginning with a survey of his position in Athenian popular culture of the Peloponnesian War era.[16]

HISTORY OF A MYTH

At first a relatively minor figure in Greek mythology, Theseus's rise to prominence began in the early fifth or possibly late sixth century, although some aspects of the saga, particularly the Cretan adventure, date back at least to the Mycenaean era. In the fifth century BC. Theseus became a symbol of Attic unity, democracy, and sympathy for the poor and downtrodden, all themes that began to become important under Kleisthenes and continued to dominate Athenian ideology for centuries. Hence, it has been argued that Kleisthenes and the Alkmeonid opposition to the Peisistratids played a major role in promoting the story of Theseus; the evidence, however, is inconclusive. We cannot be certain that any politician "sponsored" Theseus before the 470s.[17]

In that decade, Kimon undoubtedly championed the Theseus legend, and the hero's popularity probably reached a peak. Responding to an oracle, Kimon "found" the bones of Theseus on the island of Skyros around 475 and brought them triumphantly home to Athens, where they were buried in the center of the city in the hero shrine, the Theseion, which was adorned with painted walls depicting triumphs of Theseus's career (Plut. *Thes.* 36.3–4, *Kimon* 8.7; Thuc. 1.98.2; Paus. 1.17.6, 3.37; Diod. 11.60.2; *FGrH* 328 F 18). Kimon connected the career of Theseus the conqueror of the "barbarian" Amazons with his own victories over the "barbarian" Persians and with his father Miltiades' victory at Marathon. Theseus was promoted as a national hero; his victory in Crete taken as a symbolic precursor of Athens's naval hegemony; Kimon may even have claimed to be a descendant of Theseus. Bacchylides' two Theseus poems, which glorify his exploits as an Athenian and Ionian, have plausibly been dated to the Kimonian, early period of the Delian League. It has been suggested that the language of one of these poems, Bacchylides 18, recalls Kimon, his parents, and his sons; and that the poem was composed to inaugurate or commemorate the inauguration of the new Theseia, an annual state festival and athletic competition probably instituted under Kimon. The Histories of Pherekydes treat the Theseus legend in detail. Pherekydes was connected in some way with Kimon and his family, and his work, which certainly comes from the early fifth century, may well date to the 470s.[18]

In the era of Kimon's political prominence, Theseus became a popular subject for artists. Contemporary artwork depicts Theseus as a national hero, an ally of Kimon's family, an enemy of tyrants and friend of the people. The paintings of the Theseion provide evidence of the last theme. Bad history though it was, the tradition that the aristocrats Harmodios and Aristogeiton had killed the Peisistratid tyrants and established popular government was engrained in fifth-century Athenian popular culture. A famous pair of statues (replaced with a new pair in 477/476 BC after the Persians took the originals) symbolized the "tyrannicide" legend in Athens. It is precisely this legend that Kimon seems to have appropriated in the Theseion, where Theseus may have been represented in the likeness of a tyrannicide. Certainly the resemblance is clear in several vase paintings of the Theseus cycle in mid-century and again a generation later.[19]

There are other prominent Kimonian representations of Theseus in public art and architecture, both in the Athenian agora and in statues dedicated by Athens at Delphi. Among them are the Stoa Poikile (Painted Colonnade), built in the Athenian agora in the 460s BC under the sponsorship of a relative of Kimon's. The stoa shows, in one painting, Theseus fighting the Amazons; in another, Theseus appears with Miltiades at Marathon (Plut. *Kimon* 4; Paus. 1.15). Another example is the so-called Marathon Base, a group of statues by Phidias which Athens dedicated at Delphi in the second quarter of the fifth century. The scene shows Miltiades and the gods at one end, seven of the ten eponymous heroes of the Athenian tribes in the center, and at the far end, Theseus, the ancient Attic king Kodros, and probably Philaios, eponymous founder of Kimon's *genos* (Paus. 10.10.1–2). It appears that the sculptor replaced the tribal hero Ajax, whose connections with the island of Salamis might recall the victory of 480 by Kimon's rival Themistocles, with Theseus, a hero whose Marathonian connections might recall the victory in 490 by Kimon's father – Miltiades! In short, Kimon's use of the Theseus legend is a prime example of a member of the elite using a hero cult to legitimize his rule.[20]

Pericles did not make much use of Theseus, a figure associated with his rival Kimon. The cycle of Theseus's Isthmian deeds seems to have suffered a temporary loss of popularity in vase painting from the 450s to the 430s. Theseus also conspicuously fails to have a prominent position in the Periclean Acropolis building program, disqualified perhaps by his association with both Pericles' rival Kimon and Athena's rival Poseidon. On the other hand, Theseus appears in some architectural sculpture in public buildings in Athens and around Attica that may have been planned while Pericles was prominent, so he was not ignored entirely. These buildings are the Temple of Poseidon at Sounion, the Temple of Athena Nike on the Acropolis, the Temple of Nemesis at Rhamnous, and the Stoa Basileios in the Athenian agora.[21]

Around the beginning of the Peloponnesian War in 431, Theseus returned to popularity in vase painting, a reflection perhaps of the increased patriotism of the war years and of the death of Pericles in 429. We may note that after his victory in a naval battle in the

Corinthian Gulf in 429, the general Phormion dedicated a thanks-offering to Theseus and to Theseus's father Poseidon (Paus. 10.11.6).[22]

Other sites in the city of Athens, some perhaps of fifth-century date, also evoked Theseus. He was prominently represented in sculpture on the Acropolis. Pausanias claimed to have seen three sculptural groups: Theseus fighting the Minotaur, Theseus defeating the Marathonian bull, and Theseus lifting the stone at Troezen under which Aigeus had left his sword and sandals (1.24.1, 27.7–10). Whatever the date and style of the first two groups, the original (Pausanias saw a later copy) of Theseus lifting the stone has been dated ca. 475 BC. In the streets of the lower town north of the Acropolis, Pausanias saw a spot sacred to the loyalty oath taken by Theseus and Perithous, which is perhaps to be equated with a place called the Horkômosion (1.18.4; cf. Plut. *Them.* 27.5; Soph. *OC* 1594). Another precinct sacred to the heroes Theseus and Perithous was seen by Pausanias in the deme of Kolonos (1.30.4). Back in the city, the law court of the Delphinion, next to the shrine of Apollo Delphinios in southeastern Athens, was also associated with Theseus's arrival and early adventures in Athens (Paus. 1.19.1, 28.10; Plut. *Them.* 12.3, 14.1, 18.1).[23]

Whatever his position in monumental sculpture, Theseus was very prominent in late-fifth-century drama, having already appeared in the *Eleusinians* (Plut. *Thes.* 29.5) and *Herakleidai* of Aeschylus (died 456). He is a central figure in Euripides' *Hippolytos* of 428, and is quite important in *Suppliant Women* (ca. 424–420) and *Herakles* (ca. 416 or 414). Theseus is also a major figure in Sophocles' *Oedipus at Kolonos* of 406. Consider a sample of the now-lost plays in which Theseus appeared. Sophocles, Achaios, and Euripides all wrote plays, now lost, entitled *Theseus*; Sophocles and Euripides each also wrote an *Aigeus*. Old comedy has two plays entitled *Theseus* (by Aristonymos [frg. 1 Kock] and Theopompos [frgs. 18–21 Kassel and Austin]) and one *Aigeus* (by Phillylios [frg. 1 Kassel and Austin]). Theseus also appears in Kratinos's *Runaway Women* (frg. 53 Kassel and Austin).[24]

Images of Theseus, therefore, were all but ubiquitous in Athenian sculpture, wall and vase painting, drama, and ritual (to say nothing of media that have hardly survived, such as weavings and shield decorations). If somewhat out of fashion in the 440s and 430s, the Theseus motif was prominent again in the Peloponnesian War. In terms of paternal–filial ideology, images of Theseus were complex and problematic.

LIFE WITHOUT FATHER

The complex details of the story of Theseus's relations with Aigeus may represent elements of a political compromise on the part of Athens and Troezen (perhaps at the time of the formation of the Kalaureian amphictyony in about the ninth century BC) between two versions of the myth: the Attic tradition of Aigeus and the Troezenian tradition of Poseidon as the hero's father. (Classical Athenian authors generally prefer Aigeus, although they sometimes choose Poseidon [Isoc. 10.18] and sometimes are content with double parentage, as in Euripides' *Hippolytos*.) The story of father and son nonetheless is an indication of the Greek mythopoeic mentality, and contains elements of the traditional mythological themes of patricide and matricide. Aigeus's abandonment of the unborn Theseus, for example, is the kind of act of hostility that leads to patricide in other myths (e.g. Laius and Oedipus), and which here ends up in Theseus's indirect provocation of Aigeus's suicide. Aigeus's hostility to Theseus – whose identity is as yet unknown to him – upon Theseus's arrival in Athens and Aigeus's attempt in collusion with Medea to poison Theseus recall the mythic theme of averted matricide. As early as Bacchylides 18 (an early-fifth-century poem) we hear of Aigeus's nervousness about a rival as the news reaches Athens of the young hero's deeds in the Isthmus region. Many scholars – from Atthidographers and Plutarch (*Comp. Thes. Rom.* 5.2) to neo-Freudians, structuralists, and deconstructionists – have commented on Theseus's implicit guilt on the charge of patricide for having neglected to change sails when returning from Crete.[25]

Plutarch, relying on or embellishing the tradition of the classical Atthidographers, supplies other details of father–son tension or hostility: Theseus chose to take the dangerous overland route from Troezen to Athens in order to prove himself to Aigeus (Plut. *Thes.* 7.2); on the eve of his sad departure for Crete, Theseus boasted to Aigeus of what he expected to accomplish there (Plut. *Thes.* 17.4). Most of Plutarch's sources agree that years before Theseus arrived on the scene, Aigeus had arranged for the murder in Attica of King Minos's son, Androgeos, who had befriended Aigeus's political rivals, the sons of Pallas (Plut. *Thes.* 15.1, 17.1; cf. Diod.

60.4–5; Apollod. 3.209–210). Minos's imposition of a tribute of Athenian youths for the Minotaur was an act of revenge on behalf of his son – which adds irony to the cause of Aigeus's death, an indirect result of his son Theseus's victory over Minos.[26]

It is not surprising that young Theseus felt a need to prove himself to Aigeus. As a bastard who had been abandoned by his father, Theseus may have understandably felt both bitterness and unease about his paternity. Several of the surviving fragments of comic or tragic dramas on the theme of Theseus's arrival in Athens and meeting with Aigeus bring out this point. Fragment 1 (Nauck) of Euripides' *Aigeus*, for example, runs:

> What land shall we say that you have left to be a guest
> In this city? What fatherland's boundary?
> Who is your begetter? Who was announced as your father?

"What is your fatherland?" and "Who is your father?" might be trying questions for Theseus. Nor would the conventional sentiment of fragment 6 (Nauck) – "What is dearer to a man than his patrimonial land?" – be a mere cliché for a man who had to fight to acquire a patrimonial land. Theseus's concern over his parentage is perhaps the butt of humor in Philyllios's comedy *Aigeus*. Only one line has survived from this Old-Comedy-era play: "My grand-dad was a small shark" (frg. 1 Kassel and Austin). According to Stephanus Byzantinus (s.v. *Galeôtai*, 197.1) the playwright is playing on the shark's variegated color. If Theseus is speaking here, perhaps Philyllios is making fun of the hero's need to define his ancestry.

A somewhat different indication of father–son tension survives from Euripides' *Theseus*, a play produced before 422 (when it was parodied in Aristophanes' *Wasps*). The subject of the play is Theseus and the Minotaur; it is perhaps a chorus of Athenian children being sent as tribute to Crete who say, "Oh father, you have begotten a useless ornament (*anonêton agalm'*) for the oikos" (Eur. frg. 386 Nauck).[27] The "ornament" – the children themselves – was useless because it was being sacrificed. Of course, Athenian fathers did not give up their children willingly or happily (Plut. *Thes.* 17.1–3), but give them up they did: perhaps there are notes of bitterness or irony in the children's lament.

To sum up so far, the details of the myth are striking: Aigeus abandoned his unborn son; that son grew into Theseus, who as a youth felt a burning need to prove himself to his father; after conquering many evil-doers on the road, Theseus arrived triumphantly in Athens; not recognizing the heroic stranger as his own son, Aigeus was jealous of Theseus, and attempted to murder him; recognition led to reconciliation but not peace, because of other misdeeds by Aigeus; Aigeus's complicity in the murder of Minos's son led to the fathers of Athens having to sacrifice their children to Minos; Aigeus's son Theseus became one of the sacrificial victims, but saved the day by killing the Minotaur and bringing the other Athenians back home; Theseus accidentally sent Aigeus the wrong message; thinking his son dead, Aigeus committed suicide. Paternal–filial hostility, therefore, both overt and subconscious, plays an important part in the Theseus myth as known to fifth-century Athens.

THE MAN WITHOUT A MASTER

It comes as no surprise that Theseus was a great hero of Athens. Nor, given the tradition that Theseus was the first to unite the villages of Attica into one state, is it hard to fathom why the Athenians considered Theseus to have been the founder of their polis, an event which was celebrated annually in the Synoikia festival, the festival of Synoikismos, "Unification" or "Dwelling Together" or, to press a point, "Establishment of a Common Oikos" (Thuc. 2.15.2; Plut. *Thes.* 24.4). What is, however, rather opaque is the tradition that Theseus was the founder of Athenian democracy. By the mid-fifth century, Theseus was depicted as a tyrannicide in vase painting and possibly wall painting too, thereby preparing the way for the notion of Theseus the founder of Athenian democracy. Later in the fifth century, Theseus appears in tragedy as a democrat, and the identification seems to have grown increasingly popular in the fourth century. It is attested in Euripides (*Supp.* 353, 404–408, 433–441), Isocrates (10.36), the Demosthenic corpus (60.28), and – in what is probably a reflection of the Atthidographers – Plutarch (*Thes.* 24–25, *Comp. Thes. Rom.* 2.1), among others. In Sophocles' *Oedipus at Kolonos* (405 BC) Theseus is presented as a believer not only in the old heroic values of hospitality and kindness, but in the polis's values of law and justice and of the strict distinction between citizens and foreigners (562–568, 911–928). Aristotle's *Constitution of Athens* says that Theseus changed the constitution by inclining slightly away from monarchy (41.2; cf. Plut. *Thes.* 25.2) and it is also reported in the now-missing first part (according to the *Epitome of Heracleides*) that Theseus brought the Athenians together on the proclamation of terms of equality and concord. Plutarch reports a similar proclamation, and adds that Theseus promised the leading men that he would share power with them and virtually abolish the monarchy (24.2). He also reports that Theseus was a consistent champion of the little people (*hoi tapeinoteroi*, 36.2).[28]

It is true enough that Athenians liked to hallow their institutions with antiquity, but none of this is very much to go on; the historian must wonder why Theseus and not some other legendary figure (Erechtheus? Athena herself?) was made into a proto-democrat by the tradition of the classical era. Others have argued that Theseus's status as king gave democracy a royal pedigree, or that Theseus's antiquity endowed democracy with an element of permanence – a welcome change from the constitutional divisions of the late fifth century. These are good arguments, but again, Theseus was not the only time-honored Attic king. Perhaps after Kimon or Kleisthenes had promoted Theseus as the national hero or founder of Athens, it was all but inevitable that, as Athens grew more democratic, Theseus would be made into the first democrat.[29]

As an alternative, however, I would like to suggest that Theseus's peculiar relationship with his father had something to do with his acquisition of a reputation as a democrat. Athenian democratic ideology problematized the father–son relationship. Democracy needed assertive, energetic, public-spirited citizens who gave as well as took orders. By the same token, democracy was not about to promote the disobedient son as its ideal; outright rebellion of son against father went too far – that would be civil war, not democracy. What the mythmakers of Athenian democracy needed therefore was a heroic and assertive son who outstripped his father without direct competition. They needed to look no further than their own Theseus. Theseus was so useful as a symbol of democracy because he was a symbol of the assertive, but discreetly assertive, son, as evidence from Euripides and Isocrates makes clear.

In Euripides' *Suppliant Women* Theseus is an avatar of democracy, uttering one of the clearest statements of democratic ideology (including liberty, the absence of tyranny, the succession of ruling and being ruled, power-sharing between rich and poor, free speech, 399–408, 426–455) to have survived from the fifth century. At first glance, he is also a model of filial piety, willing to risk all to help

113

the mothers and fathers (as well as the widows and orphans) of the Seven Against Thebes recover the bodies of their sons (or husbands or fathers) from the battlefield. A closer look, however, shows a more complex and problematic character.[30]

Theseus's vision of democracy prominently includes an element that is absent from standard contemporary descriptions, for example, Pericles' Funeral Oration, but which resonates, loudly and ominously, in the second half of the 420s – the time of Alcibiades' emergence into prominence – which has been suggested as a date for the play: that element is youth.[31] For instance, Theseus says in praise of democracy:

> Nay more, when the demos is master (*authentês*) of the land
> It takes pleasure in youthful townsmen (*astois neaniais*) as its subjects;
> But when one man is king, he finds this hateful,
> And if he thinks that any of the nobles
> Are wise, he fears for his tyranny
> And kills them. How can a city become strong
> If someone takes away bold ventures
> Like ears of grain in a spring field
> And plucks off the young (*neous*)?
>
> (Eur. *Supp.* 442–449)

It is clear in the play that Theseus himself is one of the young men: both Adrastus and the Theban herald call him *neanias* (190, 580) and the chorus states that he is young (*en neoisi*, 250) and about the same age as the "children" (*paides*, 283) lying dead before Thebes. As a young man, Theseus is hot-blooded, emotional, rash, energetic, aggressive, and a lover of battle. When Adrastus and the chorus of Argive mothers ask him to rescue the Argive corpses at Thebes, Theseus dismisses them superciliously (113–285). Adrastus makes a point of the role reversal in which he, a "graybeard" (*polios anêr*, 166), has to clasp the knee of a young man (*neanias*, 190) and beg for help. Melodrama it may have been, but if Theseus had the least bit of respect for his elders, Adrastus's ploy should have worked.

It did not. Only when his mother Aithra points out that Theseus's own honor is at stake does he change his mind and agree to help (297–365). Theseus goes to war less to help the Argive mothers and fathers than to help his polis and himself.[32]

Our impression of Theseus's devotion to democracy likewise

changes complexion after careful scrutiny. Once he decides to go to Thebes, Theseus also decides to consult the Athenian demos. Not that the outcome on the Pnyx could be in doubt: "with me wanting it, they will approve," as Theseus tells his mother (350). The purpose of his going to the trouble of making a speech is merely to ensure the Athenian people's goodwill (351–352). Like charity, therefore, democracy becomes subordinated to Theseus's ego.[33]

The particular language used by Theseus to describe the power of the Athenian demos is noteworthy and revealing. In two circumstances in which he might have described the demos as *kyrios*, he uses other, loaded terms. In the long passage cited above, he calls the demos *authentês*, a much stronger word for "master" than *kyrios*, one that emphasizes power.[34] In his confident description to his mother of his political prowess, Theseus says that he has set the demos up in a monarchy (*katestês' auton es monarchian*, 352) because he freed the city to have an equal vote (*eleutherôsas tênd' isopsêphon polin*, 353). "Monarchy" is, to say the least, an intemperate description of the power of the people in a democracy. It is a word one might expect to hear from a scornful opponent of democracy rather than from a democratic champion. Theseus's diction thus reveals not only the intemperance of his youth but also his rather authoritarian view of democracy, in which the demos is either the tool of the king or itself a king who rides roughshod over others. It may be noted that many Athenians similarly suspected Alcibiades, that symbol of rebellious youth, of harboring a tyrannical view of democracy (e.g. Thuc. 6.15.4). To sum up, the Theseus of Euripides' *Suppliant Women* is a questionable hero. A youth made king by his father's death, he is disrespectful of age. He is an egotist, highly sensitive to his own reputation. As a democrat, he reveals a not-so-secret authoritarian fantasy.

The Theseus of Euripides' *Herakles* (ca. 416) is also a problematic character. This Theseus appears remarkably insouciant upon discovering that his old comrade Herakles has murdered his own wife and sons. Without apparent conflict or hesitation, Theseus exonerates Herakles and assigns all blame to the gods, specifically Hera (1186, 1232). He offers Herakles asylum in Athens, making it clear that friendship and the repayment of a debt (Herakles has saved Theseus from Hades) would outweigh any religious scruples (1234, 1236, 1322–1337). While acting generously, Theseus is not entirely an altruist, for he expects to win great glory among the Hellenes for his polis in return for helping Herakles (1331–1335). Although he has little choice but to accept, Herakles is not entirely taken with Theseus, particularly when Theseus offers the gods' own misbehavior toward their parents as a justification for Herakles' actions:

> Do not the gods commit adultery?
> Have they not cast their fathers into chains,
> in pursuit of power? Yet all the same,
> despite their crimes, they live up on Olympus.
>
> Eur. *Herakles* 1316–1318, tr. Arrowsmith

The stolid Herakles is horrified by Theseus's argument, and refuses to believe his defamation of the divinity (1341–1346). In short, while Herakles is a Dorian of old-fashioned piety, Theseus is an up-to-date Athenian rationalist: energetic and fast-talking, a sophistic wheeler-dealer, a type known all too well in Euripides' Athens.[35]

Theseus is much more independent-minded than Herakles, much less respectful of traditional authority, and much more willing to write his own rules. As such, he makes an appropriate ideological model for the citizens in Athenian democracy. The independence and imperiousness which Euripides saw in Theseus reappear, in tamer form, in Isocrates – if a look ahead to the fourth century be permitted. In his *Helen* Isocrates points out that while Herakles took orders from King Eurystheus (the famous Twelve Labors of Herakles) Theseus on the other hand performed his great feats as his own master: the word used is *kyrios* (*autos hautou kyrios ôn*, "being himself master of himself," 10.25). Shortly afterward Isocrates credits Theseus with having founded democracy, specifically by making the Athenian people "master" – *kyrios* – "of the constitution" (*dêmos kyrios tês politeias* 10.36).[36]

It is a small point, but Isocrates' emphasis on *kyrios* provides a neat insight into at least part of Theseus's appeal to the Athenian mentality. Isocrates has no interest in Theseus's obedience to his father who, the orator says, was Poseidon, not Aigeus; and he is untroubled by any filial disrespect in Theseus's destruction of the bull which his father Poseidon had sent to ravage Attica (10.25). What matters for Isocrates is that Theseus is his own master, just as the demos is master of the constitution: the latter point (about the demos, not Theseus) is made in Aristotle's *Constitution of*

Athens as well and in very similar language: "For the demos itself has made itself master (*kyrios*) of all things, and it administers everything through decrees and jury-courts, in which the demos is the ruler" (41.2, cf. 41.1, 27.1–2).[37] Compare Aristotle's *autos hauton pepoiêken ho dêmos kyrion* to Isocrates's strikingly if coincidentally similar *autos hautou kyrios ôn*. In both cases, the emphasis is on mastery through personal initiative; Theseus is master of himself, the demos is master of everything in the regime, and both through their own actions.

The Athenian people rid themselves of aristocrats, Theseus rid himself of a king; both become *kyrioi*. For king read father, for *kyrios* read son: it may be no accident that the less-than-model-son Theseus became the model for the less-than-docile people of Athens.

Like other figures of mythology – Herakles, Helen, Phaethon – Theseus had two fathers, one divine and one mortal. The tradition thought little of Theseus's mortal father. Classical Attic art is scarcely interested in Aigeus outside of his relationship with his great son Theseus. Aigeus is not a heroic figure; in fact, he is rather foolish, sneaky, and pathetic. He considers Androgeos, son of King Minos, to be a rival, but rather than face him openly, Aigeus arranges for someone else to murder him. His childlessness makes him an object of contempt on the part of his relatives and rivals, the sons of Pallas, and an object of pity on the part of Medea (Plut. *Thes.* 13.1; Eur. *Med.* 653–758). After receiving advice from Delphi about finally procreating a son in Athens, Aigeus is tricked by Pittheus of Troezen into fathering a son by Pittheus's daughter, Aithra (Apollod. 3.15.7; but see Plut. *Thes.* 2.3). He listens to the pleas of a woman: hardly an admirable trait according to the dominant Athenian protocols of manhood, especially considering that the woman was Medea (see Eur. *Aigeus* frg. 3 Nauck). Aigeus offers her asylum in Athens and eventually takes her as wife or concubine. Afraid of the reports of the prowess of the stranger who turns out to be Theseus, Aigeus declines to face him *mano a mano*, but instead resorts to poison, having been deceived again by Medea's wiles (Bacchylides 18.30; Schol. A Hom. *Il.* 11.741; Plut. *Thes.* 12.2–3; Apollod. 1.9.28, *Epit.* 1.5–6; Paus. 2.3.8; Ovid *Metamorphoses* 7.404–420; Bode, ed. *Mythographi Vaticani*, 1834, 1.48). Where Theseus is eager for adventure in Crete, Aigeus is pessimistic (Plut. *Thes.* 17.2). Aigeus's suicide upon the sight of the ship's black-masted trip home is pathetic, but not especially heroic, and not without an element of comedy: a sober man would have verified the facts before acting. One of the Atthidographers even suggests that Aigeus did not commit suicide, but rather slipped and fell (Plut. *Comp. Thes. Rom.* 5.2). In short, Theseus's mortal father was no Theseus.[38]

INITIATION RITUAL AND TEENAGE FANTASY

Further indication of Theseus as a symbol of assertive youth comes from the highly relevant evidence of vase painting. The images in question come mainly from fifth-century Attic red figure vases, where Theseus is often depicted, usually as an idealized youth or ephebe. Aigeus, on the other hand, is always depicted as a mature, bearded man. It may be, as Brommer argues, that whenever a youth dressed for travel (i.e. wearing a mantle, *petasos* hat, sandals, and carrying a spear) appears before a bearded king holding a scepter, the artist has Theseus and Aigeus in mind. Securely identified representations of Aigeus are relatively rare, as are those of Aigeus's recognition of Theseus; Kron's recent catalog lists twelve recognition scenes (or at least scenes of Aigeus and Theseus), from the fifth century, eight of them dated 440–430 or later. Dozens of extant vase paintings, however, depict Theseus as a beardless young man in the company of an older, bearded man or men. The context is frequently hostile: in many cases, these are scenes of young Theseus fighting the older villains (Periphetes, Sinis, Skiron, Kerkyon, Prokrustes) whom he defeated on the road from Troezen to Athens. The contrast between youth (handsome, victorious, fighting for the right) and maturity (ugly, defeated, evil) is vivid. An unusual work, a red figure ram's head rhyton from ca. 480–470, shows a beardless youth with several bearded men at a symposium. The scene has convincingly been interpreted as Theseus being welcomed by the previous Attic kings into their ranks. Here the context is of course friendly rather than hostile, but as in the scenes of fighting, the contrast between youth and age is again striking. Athenian democracy, a regime poised between novelty and tradition, between sons and fathers, created as its hero an assertive youth who replaced his father as a figure of authority.[39]

Scholars have long recognized the presence of initiation-ritual motifs in Theseus's story, from his lifting of the stone at Troezen to his adventures on the road to Athens, in Attica, and in Crete, until his replacement of his father and assumption of the throne.

Theseus may have been fifty years old when he abducted Helen, as Hellanikos states (Plut. *Thes.* 31.1) but most of his exploits were carried out well before the age of thirty. Pausanias makes Theseus only sixteen when he left Troezen (Paus. 1.27.8); Bacchylides similarly describes him as "a boy in the first flower of youth" (*paida . . . prôthêbon*, 17.56–57); Plutarch makes him a *meirakion* (Plut. *Thes.* 6.2). On their first sight of him, he was so boyish-looking that Athenians taunted him for resembling a girl (Paus. 1.19.1; see below).[40]

The notion of a sixteen-year-old leaving home, fighting and beating all comers including a bull and the fifty sons of Pallas, proving himself to his father, seducing and abandoning the princess of the most powerful country in the world, and becoming king, all by about the age of eighteen – not to mention supernatural feats like killing the Minotaur and visiting Poseidon's submarine palace – is, needless to say, an impossibility. What is possible, however, is to recognize Theseus's exploits as a prime example of adolescent male fantasy: the super-potent hero who beats everyone and is absolutely unrestrained by the adult world. The contemporary equivalent is the hero of comic-books or cartoons. No wonder that Theseus was honored, along with Hermes and Herakles, as patron of the gymnasium and palaestra, those adolescent hangouts (Paus. 4.32.1); no wonder that he was closely associated with the Athenian ephebeia and its rites of passage.[41]

Theseus's associations with adolescent initiation rites appear with particular clarity in a cluster of myths concerning the Athenian Delphinion, a precinct sacred to Apollo Delphinios and consisting of a small temple and a law court. Aigeus was the supposed founder of the precinct (Paus. 1.19.1). Apollo Delphinios was the patron god of the last stage of ephebic integration, during which the adolescent became a part of adult society. In classical Athens the Delphinion law court had jurisdiction over cases of allegedly justifiable homicide and was also the place where someone's Athenian citizenship could be affirmed by oath. Ancient etiologists traced both of these functions back to Theseus. He was supposedly tried and acquitted in the Delphinion for his justifiable homicides, either of the evil-doers of the Isthmus Road, of the Pallantidae, or of both (Paus. 1.28.10; *Etymologicum Magnum* 359.4; Schol. Dem. 23.74). Tradition made the Delphinion the site of Aigeus's palace and the place where he recognized Theseus as his son: in Plutarch's day the spot where Aigeus supposedly grabbed a flask of poison from Theseus's hand and spilled it on the floor was formally marked by an enclosure (Plut. *Thes.* 12.3).[42]

Aigeus's recognition was a kind of rite of passage for Theseus, as the affirmation of citizenship would be in the classical period for someone whose status as an Athenian was in doubt. The ritual-initiatory aspect is brought out even more strongly in another tale about the Delphinion and Theseus's arrival in Athens. The building was supposedly still new and unroofed when Theseus arrived; the workmen saw his beautifully combed hair and long robe reaching to his feet and called out insults along the lines of "hey, what's an unmarried girl like you doing out without a chaperone?" Theseus's reply was to unhitch the oxen from a nearby cart and toss them in the air higher than the roofline, thereby proving his manhood (Paus. 1.19.1). Two points are worth noting (aside from the saltiness of everyday language in Athens). First, Theseus's appearance in feminine garb calls to mind the frequency of transvestism in male initiation rites throughout ancient Greece: a "ritual of inversion" that dramatized the contrast between boys, who look feminine, and men, who do not.[43] Second, on several occasions during their two-year stint as ephebes, young Athenians in the fourth century participated in ceremonies in which they would join together in groups and lift an ox up to the altar for sacrifice; supposedly they were imitating Theseus.[44]

Clothing also connected Theseus and ephebes, in several different ways. First, Theseus is very frequently depicted in vase paintings in the garb of an Athenian ephebe: the broad-brimmed felt hat (*petasos*) and black traveling cloak (*chlamys*). Second, in the second century AD an etiology was provided for the ephebe's black cloak, which was supposed to commemorate the black sail which Theseus forgot to change on his return from Crete, thus indirectly provoking Aigeus's death (Philostratus, *Lives of the Sophists* 2.550, *IG* II² 3606). The etiology is probably wrong: the color black, like feminine clothing, is probably meant to mark off ephebes – youths going through an exciting but difficult period of transition – from ordinary society. It hardly matters: more significant for our purposes is the ancient (albeit post-classical) recognition of the connection between Theseus and the status of adolescence in transition. Both the black sail and the ephebeia itself denote the poignant but inevitable transition from boyhood to manhood, and from father to son.[45]

There is also an initiatory aspect to the patricide theme in the

Theseus saga. Jeanmaire compared the death of Aigeus and Theseus's succession as king to the ritualized murder of the king as part of coming-of-age ritual in certain traditional African societies. Aigeus's plunge, echoed both in Theseus's later death on Skyros and in his earlier dive into the Aegean to recover Minos's ring, is itself initiatory in character, having the quality of a test or ordeal. Theseus's ambivalent role in Aigeus's death, which combined ingenuity and incompetence, triumph and disaster, was read by later generations in the ritual of the Oschophoria, an annual festival of the wine harvest. This festival took place on the seventh day of the autumn month Pyanopsion, that is, one day before the Theseia. Instead of garlanding his head, the herald at the Oschophoria garlands his staff; the libations are met with mixed cries of triumph ("*Eleleu*") and of shock and disorder ("*Iou, iou*" [Plut. *Thes.* 22.2–3]). These peculiarities are supposed to mirror Theseus's mixed emotions as the conquering hero turned indirect patricide turned king. There may be a hint of this etiology in Euripides' *Hippolytos* (790–807). King Theseus returns to Troezen from a consultation of an oracle. His head is garlanded, and he expects a warm welcome, but he is shocked to find cries and shut doors. He fears that his grandfather Pittheus is dead; when he finds out that his wife Phaidra is the victim, he bemoans the irony of his garlands. The echoes of the Oschophoria ritual here suggest that by the late fifth century Athenians connected Theseus and the death of Aigeus with this festival.[46]

The connection of Theseus with the ephebate and with rituals of initiation, change of status, and death indicates that Athens's national hero was not merely a symbol of youth or assertiveness, but a symbol of the process whereby a boy became a man, a child became a citizen, and a dependent became *kyrios*. He was also, of course, a symbol of the reverse, the process by which a *kyrios* (the father) either became dependent (as an old man) on his son or died. Theseus was a symbol of alternation and change.

Athenian democracy depended on alternation and change: between the generations, but more directly between governors and the governed. As a projection of collective wishes, fantasies, and fears, Theseus was perhaps a symbol of the hope that the transition would go smoothly. When one considers the price that others paid for Theseus's power – Aigeus, Ariadne, Hippolytos – it becomes clear that Theseus was also a symbolic recognition of the reality that no matter how smoothly executed, transition and sharing always exact a price.

PATERNITY SUIT

Theseus was a bastard and an immigrant to Athens; he would have failed the test of Pericles' citizenship law (451 BC), which required that one have two citizen parents. The Delphic oracle had enjoined Aigeus to beget a son at his "patrimonial hearth" (*patrôian . . . hestian*, Eur. *Hipp.* 681; cf. Plut. *Thes.* 3.3–4), but the union which produced Theseus took place contrary to the god's wishes, outside the fatherland and with a foreign woman. Theseus had a dubious relationship to Aigeus's "patrimonial hearth." The results were twofold. For Aigeus, the oracle's warning proved true: his misbegotten son eventually provoked Aigeus's death. For Theseus, despite a whitewashing tradition to the contrary – the chorus of Sophocles' *Oedipus at Kolonos* calls Athens Theseus's "patrimony" (*patrôion astu* 297) – his legitimacy as king was shaky. Enemies in Athens threw the facts of Theseus's birth in his face (Plut. *Thes.* 17.1, 32.1). Nor was a resort to the other tradition, which made Poseidon Theseus's father, much of a help for Theseus, since that still left him illegitimate and since claims of divine parentage always create skeptics. In Bacchylides 17, for example, Minos challenges young Theseus, en route to Crete, to prove his divine parentage by diving into the sea to recover a ring which was the gift of Minos's father, Zeus. Theseus passes the test with flying colors. Even as a mature man in Euripides' *Hippolytos*, however, Theseus still has doubts. Ironically, not until Poseidon grants Theseus's request to kill Hippolytos is Theseus sure that Poseidon is really his father (1169–1170). As for Hippolytos, when the going gets rough with his father, he stings Theseus by expressing bitterness about Hippolytos's own bastard birth (1083, 1455). Aigeus had not been a bastard, but for many years he suffered from what was in a sense the opposite problem: childlessness. Aigeus knew his father but had no son (Eur. *Med.* 669–688; Plut. *Thes.* 3.3–5; Apollod. 3.15.5).[47]

Clearly, therefore, paternity was an issue in the family of Theseus, and one, moreover, with interesting consequences for Athenian ideology. We have already noted both the semiotic function of the *patêr* in Athenian culture and the symbolic function of assertive youth in Athenian ideology. In Theseus's case, the facts of paternity and the assertiveness of youth were in conflict. The fact of Theseus's bastardy might have crippled him psychologically and disqualified him culturally as an admired Athenian. Theseus was, however, a hero, and one index of his heroism is what he makes of his lack of the proper signifier (a secure patronymic). The hero learns to master the symbols of his paternity and to use them to win a major achievement: recognition from his father and from his fatherland. As we shall see, some ancient scholars indeed traced Theseus's very name to this recognition.

A great achievement, but in Theseus's hands inappropriate signifiers, whether of birth or of anything else, became a weapon. In a kind of Newtonian physics of semiotics, every action in the Theseus saga causes a reaction. Undervalued by his father, Theseus undervalues his father in turn and, by the misuse of symbols, indirectly causes Aigeus's death. Years later, belief in a misleading symbol causes Theseus to bring about the death of his son Hippolytos. The ironic stuff of Greek tragedy, to be sure; but we come back to the democratic ideology of sonship. Theseus's use and misuse of symbols are but another dimension of his status as an assertive son who, without rebelling directly, nevertheless overshadows and even destroys his father. Theseus's son Hippolytos too, for all his professed purity, is enough of a "chip off the old block" to shows signs of Theseus-like steel; Hippolytos merely had the bad luck of having Theseus and not Aigeus as father.

Let us look more closely at a recurrent motif in Theseus's relations with both his father Aigeus and his son Hippolytos, a motif that might be called the semiotic theme. Let us note first that the ancients generally derived Theseus's name from the verb *tithêmi*, "to place," "put," "set," "establish," "adopt," or "acknowledge" a child. Various etymologies were proposed, of which Plutarch cites two. According to Plutarch, some of his sources derived the name "Theseus" from the placing of tokens of recognition (*dia tên tôn gnôrismatôn* **thesin**, *Thes.* 4.1): the story goes that Aigeus left a sword and pair of sandals under a great rock at Troezen, with instructions that if Aithra gave birth to a son, he should attempt to lift the rock when he grew up. If the son passed the test, he should bring the sword and sandals – "tokens (or signs) of his father" (*patrôia symbola*, 6.2) – to his father, but proceeding in secrecy, because of Aigeus's rivals at home, the sons of Pallas (3.4–5, 6.1–3; cf. Diod. 4.59.1, 6). Others of Plutarch's sources derived "Theseus" from Aigeus's eventual acknowledgment of the boy at Athens (*Athênêsi paida* **themenou** [from *tithêmi*] *tou Aigeôs*, 4.1). In either case, Theseus's name would have to do with the notions of identity, recognition, and signs.[48]

Aside from the correctness of either proposed derivation, it is unclear if either was current in fifth-century Athens, although there is an intriguing case of wordplay on Theseus and *tithêmi* in Euripides' *Hippolytos* (520–521). In any case, Theseus's reputation in fifth-century Athens as the man who had lifted the stone at Troezen is of equal symbolic significance. The image of Theseus and the stone is attested several times in fifth-century Attic vase painting, with one example as early as the mid-fifth century and another possibly from the last decade of the sixth century. According to a plausible reconstruction, Theseus may have been depicted with the *gnôrismata* already in one of the metopes of the Athenian treasury at Delphi, which may date from the period of Kimon in the 470s. A sculptural group of Theseus lifting the stone (in bronze except for the stone) was visible on the Acropolis in the early Roman empire; a good case has been made for making this a Hellenistic replacement of an earlier work of the Severe Style with a date ca. 475. Hence, it was a commonplace in classical Athens that Theseus was the hero who lifted a heavy rock and claimed the symbols of his paternity and manhood. The sources make him an adolescent (Plut. *Thes.* 6.2; Paus. 1.27.8) at the time of his feat, and stone-lifting has been plausibly described as a traditional Troezenian manhood-initiation ritual. Athenians, who themselves entered manhood after an examination (*dokimasia*) of their paternity, would have warmed to the story of Theseus, who passed his *dokimasia* and claimed his *patrôia symbola* the heroic way.[49]

Signs (*symbola* or, more frequently, *gnôrismata*) play a central role in Theseus's relations with Aigeus and, eventually, with Hippolytos. When he finally reaches Athens after his adventures upon leaving Troezen, Theseus is received by Aigeus, but Aigeus plans to kill the dangerous young stranger; only when Theseus shows Aigeus a sign – his sword – does the older man recognize him and avert disaster (Plut. *Thes.* 12.2–3). After embracing Theseus, Aigeus recognizes him formally (*egnôrizen*, 12.3) before an assembly of citizens, who gladly accept the hero as their prince (12.3). The recognition scene seems to have been presented dramatically by Sophocles and Euripides in their respective *Aigeus* plays and it shows up in fifth-century Attic red figure vase painting, especially after mid-century.[50]

The next important sign in the legend is the sail flying on the ship that carries Theseus to and from Crete. As was the custom, the ship flew a black sail upon its departure from Athens, in recognition of its grim mission. Aigeus, however, gave the pilot a white sail, ordering him to hoist that if the ship returned with Theseus safe and victorious (as Theseus boasted to Aigeus that it would, Plut. *Thes.* 17.4). In a vivid alternative tradition, Simonides says that Aigeus's sail was not white but "a scarlet sail (*phoinikeon histion*) dyed with the tender flower of luxuriant holm-oak," and this was to be a sign (*sêmeion*) of the Athenians' safety (Plut. *Thes.* 17.5; Simonides F 550 Page). The color was a symbol of military action (LSJ s.v. *phoinikis*) and perhaps also, like the purple (*porphyreos*) of Aeschylus's *Agamemnon* (910, 918–922, 944–947), a dangerous symbol of power and death.

The sequel is well known. Theseus did return home safe and victorious, but he neglected to hoist the white (or scarlet) sail as a token (*gnôrimon*, Plut. *Thes.* 22.1) of his safety to Aigeus. Theseus forgot either because he and the pilot were so jubilant at the sight of home (Plut. *Thes.* 22.1) or because Theseus was so deep in grief over the loss of Ariadne (Diod. 4.61.6). In either case, Aigeus got the wrong message and committed suicide, by jumping either from the Acropolis (Diod. 4.61.7) or perhaps from Cape Sounion or some other cliff (Plut. *Thes.* 22.1). In some traditions, Aigeus gave his name to the Aegean Sea (*Aigaïkos*, Hyginus 43). Theseus, meanwhile, inherited the kingship (Diod. 4.61.8). According to Plutarch, it was he who named the city Athens (Plut. *Thes.* 24.3). Between them, therefore, father and son provided the permanent signifiers of the land and sea, with Theseus behaving in a characteristically active and Aigeus in a characteristically passive manner.[51]

Years later, Theseus, like Aigeus, is misled by a token: in this case, a writing-tablet (*deltos*, Eur. *Hipp.* 887), a suicide note in which his deceased wife Phaidra "signifies news" (*sêmênai neon*, Eur. *Hipp.* 888). Theseus is taken in by her slander of his son Hippolytos. Believing that the boy has indeed raped Phaidra – Hippolytos's stubborn silence about his innocence does not make matters easier – Theseus calls down a curse from his father Poseidon, and Hippolytos is fatally injured (Eur. *Hipp.* 885–1267). Theseus finally learns the truth from Artemis and repents, but too late (Eur. *Hipp.* 1282–1461).

There are many ironies in Euripides' *Hippolytos*, among them:

Phaidra's connections to that site of Theseus's past triumphs, Crete (she was Ariadne's sister, the Minotaur's half-sister, and Minos's daughter); Aphrodite's role in tricking Theseus, who had always been a lady's man; and Hippolytos's misplaced belief in a close and trusting relationship with his father (661–662). For the time being let us underline the irony of the false symbol, which tripped up Theseus as it had his father Aigeus. The play may even make a veiled reference to an earlier false symbol, the ship that brought Theseus back to Aigeus's Athens, a ship that failed to display a white sail. In its ode immediately preceding the announcement of Phaidra's suicide, the chorus recalls the "white-winged Cretan ship" (752–753) that brought Phaidra to her marriage in Athens; in spite of all hopes, that ship proved to be ill-omened for both Athens and Crete (755–759). Both Theseus and Hippolytos suggest that Hippolytos's fate might represent payment for some inherited familial crime; perhaps Aigeus's crime in procreating Theseus against the will of the gods, who wanted him to bed a woman in Athens, not Troezen (Eur. *Hipp.* 820, 831, 1379–1383). We might also suggest that Hippolytos's fate represents those two other interconnected familial traits: the transmission of paternity through illicit means and the misinterpretation of transmitted symbols.[52]

To sum up, in his use of and abuse of symbolic communication with his father and his son, Theseus reveals a strain of ambivalence in the Athenian father–son relationship. On the one hand, Theseus was the hero whose feats of strength, courage, and prowess against villains compelled his father and his fatherland to recognize him. On the other hand, the same ambition and energy – the same *philotimia*, as the Athenians might have said – that won Theseus a father also permitted him to go beyond accepted limits. Thus he was careless enough to cause his father's death and gullible enough to cause his son's. In both cases, it is impossible not to suspect him of "accidentally" fulfilling a deeply held hostility toward anyone claiming to share his manhood. The national hero, Theseus is unlikely to have been the only man in Athens to harbor ambivalent feelings about his father and his son.

CONCLUSION

In spite of his miserable record vis-à-vis his father and his son, a sanitized Theseus sometimes appears in the literature nonetheless. In Euripides' *Herakles*, for example, a grateful Herakles declares that Theseus is like a son to him (1400); one might say more accurately that by his dependence on the Athenian, Herakles, though older, is like a son to Theseus (1424–1425, cf. 613). Theseus is proud of his benefactions: he informs Herakles that he (Theseus) has won many gifts from his fellow citizens in return for killing the Minotaur and saving fourteen youths (1326–1327).[53] Isocrates tells a similar story in *Helen* (ca. 370): by conquering the Minotaur, Theseus "saved the children and returned them to their parents" (10.28). Nor did Theseus go to Crete to win glory, but rather to free Athens from its terrible tribute and to save the children and stop mourning (10.27). Isocrates likewise emphasizes Theseus's service to the children of Herakles by defeating the Peloponnesians in battle (10.31, cf. 4.56). In Sophocles' *Oedipus at Kolonos*, it is Theseus who defends the oikos by convincing Oedipus at least to listen to his own son Polyneikes, rather than to dismiss him out of hand (1173–1180, 1346–1351). Although the ensuing meeting is a disaster, Oedipus nonetheless shows his respect for Theseus both by making him a kind of surrogate son and heir and also by making him guardian (surrogate father, as it were) to his daughters (1629–1637). Oedipus agrees to show the mysteries of his death only to Theseus, although he denies the sight to his own children; and he tells Theseus to pass on this magical knowledge to his sons and grandsons forever (1518–1538). By agreeing to Oedipus's wishes, Theseus, we are told, is truly a noble man (*anêr gennaios*, 1636).

These cases, however, are best seen as exceptions that demonstrate the flexibility of mythology. Nor is it surprising that Sophocles' Theseus should defer more to normative discourse than Euripides'; nor, truth to tell, that Isocrates, the chameleon who praised democracy and aristocracy in the same breath and who alternately championed Athens, Sparta, and Macedon, should present contradictory images of Theseus (recall his notion of Theseus the champion of the *dêmos kyrios*).

What needs to be emphasized is the general thrust of the discourse, and in that regard the trend is clear. Theseus was the national hero who squared the circle of patriarchy and youth culture. As the embodiment of adolescent prowess, as a man without a master, Theseus symbolized the vigor and freedom of Athens's young democracy. Yet Theseus was no rebel, at least not overtly. He spoke the language of filial submission. Theseus fought to win his father's recognition and to make his father proud of him, not to destroy his father or to overshadow him with youthful heroics. Theseus did overshadow Aigeus, however. There were tears and embraces when Aigeus finally recognized his son, but not before Aigeus had revealed his own insecurity and fear of a young rival, as well as his dependence on a woman and foreigner (Medea). Theseus's optimism, spirit of adventure, womanizing, and heroic prowess as a killer make a stark contrast to Aigeus's pessimism, his staying at home, his infertility, and his suicide. Finally, Theseus's failure to change from black to white sails made him an indirect patricide, and surely reveals (through mythopoeic language) an underlying resentment of his abandonment years previously by Aigeus.

In short, Theseus, the young man of action, destroyed and replaced his father without attacking him directly. Overtly, he was the perfect son in word and deed; beneath the surface, he was a patricide. Theseus was no Telemakhos, that loyal ally of his father, but he was no Oedipus or Haimon either, young men who each physically attacked his father (Laios and Kreon respectively). Theseus was a figure of extraordinary suppleness and duality (though not quite duplicity, for surely his patricidal tendencies remained subconscious). Small wonder that the Athenians, those devotees of sophists, those lovers of art and elegance, constructed Theseus; nor should anyone be surprised to see reflections of Theseus in other characters of Athens in the era of the Peloponnesian War. Truly, the Athenians were, as Sophocles calls them, *Thêseidai*, the "sons of Theseus" (*OC* e.g. 1066).

We turn now, in the final two chapters, to several other representations of fathers and sons, representations either of or by Athenians, and dating from the Peloponnesian War era. Each of these images can be analyzed in terms of the themes developed in this chapter. By tracing certain general changes in the depiction of fathers and sons in the course of the era, important insights into the evolution of contemporary Athenian ideology can be gained.

Two basic periods can be discerned. From the 440s down to 413, Athenian culture gave ever increasing prominence to youth – a youth that, ironically, sometimes prefered oligarchy to democracy. Athens ca. 420 was, so to speak, a city of sons. After the Sicilian disaster, however, it was time for second thoughts. With freedom beginning to look unstable, the city turned back toward the image of the father. This trend can be seen in such developments as the call by many and various parties for an "ancestral" or "paternal" constitution, the *patrios politeia*, and in the depiction of one's political enemies as actual or symbolic patricides.

5

THE HOUR OF THE SON

CA. 450–414 BC

To slam doors, to rant and shout, was not in Father's character. Nor, for better or for worse – perhaps mostly for worse
– was it in mine. We fought not like wrestlers but like
diplomats, whose top hats and morning coats concealed a
wariness, a maneuvering for position, a knowledge that an
outburst of open anger might even be self-defeating if your
opponent remained calm. We would have made poor material
for a playwright.

Adam Hochschild, *Half the Way Home:*
A Memoir of Father and Son

From the perspective of two millennia, late-fifth-century Athens
seems like a golden age of youth. From Antigone to Alcibiades,
from Theseus to Iphigeneia, from the young men who flocked
around Socrates to the youthful indiscretion suggested by the
mutilation of the Herms, Athens seems like a youth culture. As
one approaches closer to the surviving documents, the impression
of youth in prominence remains, but the details become more
complex. Chronologically, the era seems to fall into two periods.
The first is marked by a combination of confidence in youth, some
good-natured irritation at youthful exuberance, and an undercurrent of doubt about the arrogance, egotism, and contempt for
everything traditional – including Athens's now traditional form
of government, democracy – on the part of some of the members of the wealthiest and most privileged generation in Athenian
history. This period dates from about mid-century to the Sicilian
Expedition of 415–413. After that disaster, sentiments become
reversed. Confidence in youth fades, the irritation loses its good
nature, and the older generation's worst fears about youth seem

confirmed. Suddenly, not youth but maturity, in the person of paternal authority, begins to become the byword of the day. This second period lasts from 413 at least to the trial of Socrates in 399. The second period is the subject of the next chapter; this chapter examines the first period, from ca. 450 to 414, especially the period 430–414.[1]

The first half of this chapter focuses on the two politicians whose public personas exemplify the extremes of paternal and filial ideology: Pericles and Alcibiades. It also considers the question of the generation gap of the 420s BC. The intergenerational tensions evident in the assembly and the salons of the sophists left their mark in the theater as well. Accordingly, the second half of this chapter examines four comedies of Aristophanes as well as one Euripidean tragedy. Taken as a whole, the evidence demonstrates that, at least within the Athenian elite, there was a perception of Athenian public life ca. 430–414 as a social drama of father and son.

THE PARADOX OF PERICLES

The drama of Athens in the Peloponnesian War era is, in many ways, a drama of father and son. At the outbreak of the war the leader of Athens was Pericles. Pericles cut a grand and complex public figure, one important facet of which was that of a father or paternal symbol. Consider three indices. First, Pericles was often nicknamed "Zeus" or "Olympian," and sometimes shown on the comic stage wielding a thunderbolt (Ar. *Ach.* 530; Kratinos frgs. 73, 118, 258, 259 Kassel and Austin [= Plut. *Per.* 13.9, 3.5, 3.4, 24.9]). The appellation reflects Pericles' majestic bearing, austerity, and haughtiness (Plut. *Per.* 5, 7, 8, 15). Like Zeus, Pericles was called a tyrant (Kratinos frg. 258 Kassel and Austin; Plut. *Per.* 3.4); wags said that he and his associates were "the new Peisistratids" (Plut. *Per.* 16.1). We should also recall that Zeus was the "father of gods and men," as Homer says, the god who watches over kinship and fatherhood (Pl. *Laws* 881d). Zeus-like Pericles was thus a paternal figure in Athens.

This is reflected in a second point, Pericles' leadership style as characterized by Thucydides, whom Plutarch follows. Pericles was one of Athens's leading politicians for more than thirty years. After the ostracism in 443 of his great rival Thoukydides son of Melesias, Pericles held an unbroken string of generalships until

430 (Thuc. 2.65.3–4; Plut. *Per.* 16). For Thucydides, Pericles was a consummate leader in complete command of the Athenian people. He "governed moderately and guarded it [Athens] securely" (Thuc. 2.65.5). There was no question in Thucydides' mind as to who ruled and who was ruled in Periclean Athens:

> Pericles, because of his position, his intelligence, and his known integrity, could respect the liberty of the people and hold them in check. It was he who led them, rather than they who led him, and, since he never sought power from any wrong motive, he was under no necessity of flattering them: in fact he was so highly respected that he was able to speak angrily to them and to contradict them. Certainly when he saw that they were going too far in a mood of over-confidence, he would bring them back to a sense of their dangers; and when they were discouraged for no good reason he would restore their confidence. So, what was nominally a democracy was really government by the first man.
>
> (Thuc. 2.65, tr. Warner)

Thucydides depicts Pericles managing information and advice, only doling it out to the demos when necessary (Thuc. 2.62). In short, Pericles treated the Athenian people the way a parent might treat a child.

A third point is the theme of fathers and fatherhood in Pericles' rhetoric and career. In each of the three speeches by Pericles which Thucydides presents in direct discourse, Pericles strengthens his argument by referring to the fathers of the current generation of Athenians (Thuc. 1.144.4, 2.36.2, 2.62.3). In his personal life, however, Pericles was not so successful a father. The gossipy Plutarch reports the tradition that Pericles' sons were his Achilles' heel. He had two legitimate sons, Xanthippos and Paralos, and one illegitimate son (by Aspasia), Pericles. Rumor says that Xanthippos lived with a male prostitute, Archestratos, and that Paralos frequented the company of a vulgar jokester, Euphemos (Antisthenes *ap.* Ath. 5.220d). A more serious problem was the quarrel between Xanthippos and his father over money and debts – an ugly quarrel, in which son ultimately accused father of seducing the son's wife.[2] The two men had not made up when Xanthippos died during the epidemic of 430–429 (Stesimbrotos *FGrH* 107 FF 10b, 11 *ap.* Plut. *Per.* 13.16, 36.6; Ath. 13.589d–e). Paralos died shortly thereafter, leaving only the illegitimate son Pericles. Pericles *père* was reduced to pleading before the assembly that an exception be made to his own citizenship law of 451, and that his illegitimate son Pericles be made an Athenian citizen, in spite of the circumstances of his birth. The request was granted (Plut. *Per.* 36.7–9).

Perhaps the most interesting of the anecdotes about Pericles and his sons concerns the death of Paralos. Plutarch claims that Pericles maintained a facade in the face of the death during the epidemic which claimed Xanthippos, Pericles' sister, and most of his kinsmen and friends. Then he cracked:

> he was not seen weeping even at the funeral rites or at the grave of any of his nearest kin, until at last his remaining legitimate son, Paralos, died. Although he was made to yield by this, he tried to hold true to his character and to maintain his greatness of soul; but as he laid a garland on the corpse, he was so overcome by suffering at the sight that he broke into sobbing and poured out masses of tears, something he had never done before in his life.
>
> (Plut. *Per.* 36.8–9)[3]

Zeus-like, tyrannical, austere, majestic; the paternalistic scolder, chider, booster, and controller of information; yet a man deeply concerned that he leave behind a son to carry on his oikos: such was Pericles.

At the end of Pericles' career the Athenian people rebelled: in 430 at the height of the epidemic an angry citizenry fined him and removed him from office. Then they changed their minds and reinstated him, but he died shortly afterwards, himself a victim of the epidemic (Thuc. 2.65.6; Plut. *Per.* 38.1). In Thucydides' estimation, Pericles had been a giant; his successors, however, were "more equal in regard to each other" (Thuc. 2.65.10). There would be no second Zeus bestriding the speaker's platform of the Athenian assembly.

The irony is that, Olympian father-figure though he may have been, Pericles himself bears some of the responsibility for the change in political style. Pericles resembled a tyrant in more ways than one, for, like many an absolute ruler before and since, Pericles made the mistake of failing to prepare adequately for his succession. Although his son Pericles eventually had a career as an Athenian general (cut short in 406 when he was one of the generals executed in the Arginousai affair), none of Pericles' sons attained anything near their father's eminence. Pericles was also famous for playing a quasi-paternal role to young Alcibiades, whose guardian he was. Alcibiades is hardly evidence of Pericles' success as a father; the sources are full of anecdotes about Alcibiades' obstreperousness, spoiled behavior, and smart-alecky antics. In short, Pericles may have ruled the polis like a father, but his failure to maintain paternal control of his sons within his own oikos points to his political failure to provide Athens with a strong paternal figure to succeed him.[4]

Herodotus, a contemporary of Pericles, takes up a theme reminiscent of Pericles' relations with his sons: the tyrannical ruler whose heart is broken by a never-healed breach with a son. In his Histories Herodotus (3.50–53) describes the quarrel of Lykophron, younger son of the Corinthian tyrant Periander, who snubs his father upon learning, from his maternal grandfather, of Periander's responsibility for the murder of his wife (Lykophron's mother). In return, Periander first banishes the boy, then repeatedly attempts a reconciliation; when after years he is finally on the verge of at least partial success, Lykophron is murdered. At the time of the quarrel, Lykophron was seventeen: in other words, a *meirakion* ripe for asserting himself against paternal authority.[5]

An even richer comparison exists between Pericles and the Kreon of Sophocles' *Antigone* (late 440s BC). Like Pericles, Kreon is called "tyrant" (Soph. *Ant.* 506, 1056) and his behavior is certainly tyrannical at times: authoritarian, mean-spirited, and opposed to free speech. Furthermore, Kreon sees himself, *qua* ruler, as a kind of father-figure. He compares his political position as king to his domestic position as *kyrios* of his oikos, assuming that he can demand the same obedience from the Theban demos that he can from the members of his own oikos. His lecture to his son Haimon on a son's duties is a model, if not a parody, of paternal authoritarianism:[6]

> Yes, my son, you must be prepared in your heart
> To back up your father's opinions (*gnômês patrôias*) in all
>   things.
> Men pray to raise obedient offspring
> In their home on account of this:
> That they both fight back hard against the enemy
> And honor the friend on a par with their father.
> Whoever begets unprofitable children –
> What would you say he had begotten

Except troubles for himself
And a lot of laughter for his enemies?

(Soph. *Ant.* 639–647)

Kreon's political philosophy similarly emphasizes obedience, with conscious reference to the model of obedience within the household:

Whoever is a firm man among the members of his oikos
Will be found to uphold justice in the polis too.
. . .
Whomever the polis might appoint must be obeyed
Even in small matters and whether right or wrong.
. . .
There is no evil worse than anarchy.
This destroys poleis, this leaves oikoi
Ravaged.

(Soph. *Ant.* 661–662, 666–669, 672–674)

An interchange with Haimon further highlights Kreon's authoritarian conception of his rule. When Haimon gently suggests that Kreon might consider muting his harsh sentence of execution against Antigone, Kreon takes offense at being advised by a younger man (726–727). Haimon retorts that he is mature beyond his years, and then invokes a generalized pro-Antigone sentiment in Thebes to support his case (728–729, 733). Father and son then argue:

Kr.: Is the polis to tell us how we should rule?
Hai.: Do you see that you have spoken like a very young
man (*hôs agan neos*)?
Kr.: Am I to rule this land for others or for myself?
Hai.: It's no polis if it's ruled by one man.
Kr.: Is not a polis governed by he who controls it?
Hai.: You'd make a good one-man ruler of a desert.

(Soph. *Ant.* 734–739)

As this interchange suggests, Haimon refuses Kreon's demand of blind obedience. Not only does he support Antigone, but he disobeys Kreon openly. Haimon ends up spitting in his father's face and threatening him with his sword, only then to commit suicide (Soph. *Ant.* 1231–1239).

Like Pericles, therefore, Kreon finds that the adoption of a stern,

135

paternal tone in public is no guarantee of obedience by his son. Kreon's failure was greater, but neither man was able to ensure either filial obedience or the survival of the tightly controlled rule which both advocated (to varying extents of course – Periclean Athens, unlike Kreon's Thebes, was a democracy). In many ways, therefore, Kreon's predicament foreshadows that of Pericles and of Pericles' generation more widely, for Athens was to abound in Haimons during the decade of the 420s.

THE "GENERATION GAP" OF THE 420s

As several scholars have noted, the 420s (and the following decade, down to the failure of the Sicilian Expedition in 413) was a period in which youthful and filial rebellion was very much on Athenians' minds, and in which a "generation gap" between young and old and fathers and sons was often noted. Clear evidence comes from tragedy (for example, Euripides' *Suppliant Women*), comedy (for example, Aristophanes' *Clouds* and *Wasps*) and history (Thucydides, especially the discussion of Athens's assembly debate in 415 about the proposed Sicilian Expedition).[7]

Neither filial rebellion nor generation gap were invented in 429. In Greek culture, to say nothing of earlier civilizations, they are as old as the story of Zeus, Kronos, and Ouranos. Even in the specific fifth-century BC Greek context, there is considerable father–son conflict in Sophocles' *Antigone* (late 440s) and Euripides' *Alcestis* (438), and latent conflict in Sophocles' *Ajax*, (440s?) all of which antedate the 420s by a decade or so. The troubles of Theseus and his father Aigeus were well known by Kimon's heyday (470s–460s). When faced with the sophistical cleverness of the teenaged (Xen. *Mem.* 1.2.40) Alcibiades, Pericles announced: "When I was your age, we were very clever too at these sorts of things" (Xen. *Mem.* 1.2.46). Taken at his word, Pericles means that there were clever young smart alecks even in Athens in the 470s. Whether in the 420s or earlier, therefore, themes of intergenerational conflict in Athenian texts can be explained in part as contemporary expressions of an age-old motif. Only in part, however.[8]

Types and causes of conflict

Specific characteristics of late-fifth-century Athenian culture made intergenerational conflict a particularly urgent and compelling theme. Some of these characteristics were in effect before the 420s, others only came to the fore during that decade. By mid-century, well before the 420s, the twin forces of empire and democracy had begun to transform Athenian society. Young Athenians were now wealthier than their fathers had been as young men, and were perhaps more confident and proud of their status as an imperial people. As Piraeus boomed and foreigners from all over the eastern Mediterranean poured into Attica, it became impossible to insulate young people from the shock of the new (Ps.-Xen. *Ath. Pol.* 1.10–12, 2.7–8). Moreover, between 480 and 461, the prestige of the Areopagos (Arist. *Ath. Pol.* 23.1, 25.1), which was the closest that Athenian political institutions came to a council of elders, might have been used to justify the authority of the older generation: the equation being something like "obey your fathers (*pateres*) the way you obey the elders (*presbuteroi*)." In Isocrates' idealizing reconstruction a century later, the Areopagos of the good old days had supervised the behavior of Athens's young men; he blames the reformers of the Areopagos ca. 461 for destroying the morals of the young (Isoc. *Areop.* 43–51). Perhaps there is a similar message in the arguments of the Furies in Aeschylus's *Eumenides* of 458: by their lack of respect for older gods, the new, young Olympians encourage matricide and patricide (Aesch. *Eum.* 149–154, 490–498, 640–643). At the end of the fifth century, the advocates of the *patrios politeia* drew a connection between government by elders and obedience among the young.[9]

To be sure, the reforming democrats of 461 are unlikely to have intended turning the state over to twenty-year-olds. Moreover, as Pericles' Funeral Oration (e.g. Thuc. 2.36.1–2) shows, and as one might expect anyhow in a slow-to-change pre-industrial society like Athens, the democrats appropriated the language of traditionalism, making the new regime seem like a hallowed and ancestral institution. Plato is surely exaggerating enormously, therefore, when he says that under democracy, young men lose all respect for their elders, and fathers fear their sons (*Rep.* 562e–563b). Still, the liberation of Athenians from what was, in fact, a traditional institution may have contributed in some measure to a sense of liberation on the part of the young from their elders.[10]

A third force for change was rhetoric. Its growing importance in democratic free speech rendered rhetoric a tool for questioning and challenging traditional customs and the authority of elders, especially with the boom in interest in the sophists following the visits to Athens of Protagoras in 433 and Gorgias in 427. By the mid-420s, it was common for ambitious young Athenian men of property to study with sophists.[11]

A final, if tentative, point is that around the year 420 there may have been an imbalance in the usual ratio of Athenian men in their twenties to Athenian men in their thirties. In 430–427 Athens suffered a great epidemic which, it is estimated, killed between one-fourth and one-third of the population. Men in their twenties are more vulnerable than teenagers to certain diseases, such as smallpox, which some (though by no means all) scholars believe the Athenian disease to have been. Furthermore, Athenian men in their twenties were in particularly close contact with each other, serving as they did as hoplites or rowers, and so particularly vulnerable to infectious disease. The teenagers of 430 would have been twenty-year-olds in 420; if the epidemic had hurt them less than the next older generation, they would have been particularly prominent in 420 and following years.[12]

We come, then, to the 420s. Scholars have carefully collected the literary evidence of intergenerational conflict in this period. A composite portrait of the new youth of the Athenian upper class and the traits which his elders found so offensive would look something like this: a taste for luxury and softness, and for expensive, profligate hobbies like horse-racing; a sophistic education which, by the age of about twenty or so, allowed a son to run rhetorical circles around his father; aggressive pursuit of a political career in one's twenties, which the older generation considered to be too early an age; disobedience toward one's father and disrespect for and even outright attacks on older men generally; philo-laconism and a preference for oligarchy (to be run, naturally, by the sophist-educated elite) instead of Athens's by now traditional regime, democracy.[13]

The social historian must approach this portrait cautiously. Let us begin outside the household and then look in. It is certain that a number of upper-class Athenian youths did study with the sophists, and that the result was sometimes such twisted geniuses as Alcibiades, Andokides, or Aristophanes' Pheidippides. The sophists were not a monolithic phenomenon, and their arguments varied considerably, but in general they proved to be quite destabilizing to traditional authority. For example, an argument that appears in Antiphon's fragmentary "On Truth," which was perhaps written in the 420s, is probably characteristic: that it is contrary to nature to treat parents well if one has not received good treatment from them (Antiphon frg. A Diels and Kranz = *Oxyrhynchus Papyrus* 1364.135–139). It is not at all clear that Antiphon is advocating maltreatment of parents, but nevertheless he raises unsettling questions. It is conceivable, for example, that such questions increased the chance that a son would litigate over his patrimony. Still, Alcibiades and Pheidippides are, in the nature of things, atypical; the average student of the sophists was probably considerably less prominent or radical.[14]

As, for example, Pseudo-Xenophon's *Constitution of Athens* demonstrates, the students of the sophists in the 420s included would-be oligarchs and admirers of Sparta (e.g. 1.4–5, 7–9, 11). Some affected Spartan hardiness (e.g. Ar. *Birds* 1281–1283), others were dandies, like the symposiasts in Aristophanes' *Wasps* (e.g. 1208–1264), most were probably more conventional sorts. Some professed to disdain rhetorical skill and to refuse to lower themselves by addressing the "mob" in the Athenian assembly: sentiments echoed by Euripides' Hippolytos and Aristophanes' Bdelykleon. Yet both these characters *were* in fact good speakers, which suggests an element of sour grapes in the aristocratic *topos* of withdrawal from the assembly. Like Antiphon, they might have addressed the assembly willingly had the demos not been so suspicious of them (Thuc. 8.68.1). To be sure, in the conspiratorial atmosphere of the aristocratic political clubs (*hetairiai*), young nobles plotted anti-democratic coups, which would come to pass in the following decades. Still, not all students of sophists were so inclined; much of the teaching of Protagoras, for example, was profoundly democratic (Pl. *Prt.* 322b–324d). While some noble youths withdrew from politics, others, like Alcibiades, leaped into the "acknowledged folly" (Thuc. 6.89.5) of democracy and tried to use it for their own ends.[15]

The new prominence of young men in Athenian politics is a similarly complex and interesting phenomenon. Let us note first that in contemporary Athens, a man was considered "young" until the age of thirty (Xen. *Mem.* 1.2.35). Other Greeks may have been even more conservative: Thucydides raises his eyebrows at Alcibiades' participation – at about age thirty-one – in the Athenian assembly and in international diplomatic negotiations in 420 when he was "still young ... in years for any other city" (*hêlikiai men eti ... ôn neos hôs en allêi polei*, 5.43.2). In the mid-fourth century men over fifty years of age had the right to speak first in the assembly, a sign of respect for age (Aeschin. 1.23).

The evidence for the involvement of young men in contemporary politics is considerable. Aristophanes speaks of young men active as sycophants against wealthy allies and as advocates for the prosecution (*synêgoroi*) in scrutiny (*euthyna*) trials (Ar. *Wasps* 686–695, 1096, *Birds* 1430–1431). The names of two young *synêgoroi* have survived, Kephisodemos and Euathlos; Kephisodemos, possibly in cooperation with Euathlos, scored the coup of a successful prosecution of Thoukydides son of Melesias when he was an old man (Ar. *Ach.* 702–712). The comic playwrights complain that Hyperbolos was still young when he began his career in the assembly (Kratinos frg. 283 Kassel and Austin; Eupolis frg. 252 Kassel and Austin). Phaiax too seems to have begun his political career as a young man (Plut. *Alc.* 13.1). In 425 at about age twenty-six, Alcibiades was one of the young orators criticized in Aristophanes' *Acharnians* for prosecuting old men (Ar. *Ach.* 716). Two years earlier, his diction had been sufficiently well known (though not necessarily because of political activity) to have been parodied in Aristophanes' *Banqueters* (frg. 205 Kassel and Austin). In 425 Spartan prisoners from Pylos were brought back to Athens. Over the next few years Alcibiades, whose family had hereditary ties to Sparta, was prominent in looking after their needs (Thuc. 5.43.1). In 425 he may also have been a member of the commission of ten reassessing allied tribute, although the tradition is questionable (Ps.-Andok. 4.11). Andokides was barely thirty when he delivered his speech "To His Comrades," usually attributed to the period before 415 (frg. 4 Blass). In Thucydides, in the assemblies of both Athens and its enemy-to-be Syracuse in 415, speakers complain of a division between young (*hoi neôteroi* or *hoi neoi*) and old (*hoi presbuteroi*) (Thuc. 6.12.2–13.1, 17.1, 18.6, 38.5–39.2). The sophist Thrasymakhos and the comic playwright Eupolis are just two of the voices from the end of the fifth century who idealized a past in which public affairs were run by older men, and young men kept their mouths shut.[16]

Euripides' *Suppliant Women*, which is probably to be dated in the second half of the decade of the 420s, pays considerable attention to the prominence of young men in the politics of Athens and Argos.[17] The chronological setting is the heroic age, but with the characteristic anachronism of Attic tragedy, the play gives Athens a democracy and a lively assembly; the leading character, Theseus, is as much a fifth-century demagogue as a Bronze-Age king. Hence the play is of considerable relevance to contemporary political perceptions of the 420s.[18] As noted in Chapter 4, the Theseus of *Suppliant Women* is an energetic and ambitious youth, but a selfish and cynical one. He has little respect for his elders, and has no compunctions about manipulating the assembly to serve his ends. Although Theseus approves of the special prominence of young men ("youthful townsmen": *astois neaniais*, 443) in democracy, he knows the excesses to which they are given; at least he is willing to cite those excesses to suit his rhetorical purpose. As a justification of his initial unwillingness to help the Argive elders, led by Adrastos, to recover their dead young men from the battlefield at Thebes, Theseus castigates the elders for having listened to young war hawks in the first place. First he elicits from Adrastos the information that a "clamor of young men" (*neôn ... andrôn thorubos*, 160) drove Argos into the expedition against Thebes; as Theseus comments, they unwisely put good courage (*eupsuchian*, 161) before good counsel (*euboulias*, 161). He renders a harsh judgment:

> You were led astray by glory-loving youngsters (*neois*),
> Promoters of unjust wars, who spoil the townsmen.
> One of them wants to be a general;
> Another to seize power and riot (*hubrizêi*) in it;
> A third is set on gain. They never think
> What harm this brings for the majority (*to plêthos*).
>
> (Eur. *Supp.* 232–237, tr. F. Jones)

Although something of an Alcibiades figure himself, here the nimble Theseus sounds much like Nicias does in 415 when he warns the assembly not to undertake an expedition to Sicily led by young Alcibiades and his young supporters (Thuc. 6.12.2–13.1). The two men make many of the same points: for example, Theseus says the youths rejoice at wars (*chairousi polemous*, 233) and want generalships (234), Nicias notes Alcibiades' joy in his command (*archein asmenos hairetheis*, 6.12.2); Theseus says that some youths seek gain (*kerdous*, 236) in war, Nicias says that Alcibiades is out to profit from office (*ôphelêthêi ti ek tês archês*, 6.12.2, cf. 6.15.2); Theseus says that young generals fail to look at (*ouk aposkopôn*,

236) the good of the majority, Nicias says that Alcibiades only looks at his own interests (*to heautou monon skopôn*, 6.12.2); Theseus says that young men promote wars without justice (*aneu dikês*, 233), Nicias says that Alcibiades will "do injustice to," that is, harm, the public interest (*ta men dêmosia adikein*, 6.12.2); Theseus contrasts courage with good counsel (*eupsuchia* vs. *euboulia*, 161), Nicias contrasts youthful passion with mature forethought (*epithumiai* vs. *pronoiai*, 6.13.1); Theseus says that the young corrupt the citizens (234), Nicias says that the young intimidate the old (6.13.1). Nicias does not refer specifically to *hubris* (violence, arrogance, assault, and battery) as Theseus does (235), but this was a common charge both against Alcibiades specifically and against young men generally. In short, Euripides' *Suppliant Women* paints a picture of young men coming into political and military power and using power for their own selfish ends. This picture is very similar to that of Nicias's denunciation of Alcibiades in 415, and recalls more generally other contemporary critiques of young men.[19]

The 420s saw both a decline in the political importance of the generalship and an increased emphasis on rhetoric as a tool of political success. Both trends would tend to ease the entry of young men into politics, since one could not be elected general until age thirty, but a student of the sophists could make a good speaker in his twenties. The circumstances of the Archidamian War (431–421 BC) perhaps also gave a boost to an early entry into politics on the part of wealthy youths. The relative infrequency of active service for hoplites and cavalrymen compared to thetes, the loosening of old mores and inhibitions after the epidemic of 430–427, the epidemic-induced manpower shortage, and the sense of importance which wartime gives soldiers all may have encouraged men in their twenties to play an unusually active role in public life. It should be noted that young men had indeed played a role in Athenian politics in an earlier generation: the archons of the early fifth century were sometimes young men; Pericles was about thirty when he prosecuted Kimon in 463 and in his early twenties when he served as *khorêgos* for an Aeschylean trilogy in 472. Perhaps never before, however, had as many young men been involved in Athenian politics as in the 420s.[20]

One other point needs to be made. Although there is no shortage of complaints about young men in the sources, it is clear that some older men were quite taken by the vigor of youth, and were sometimes persuaded to cede power to the young. In *Suppliant Women*, Argos listens to the "clamor of young men" and sends an expedition to Thebes; in real life, Athens listened to Alcibiades and his young supporters and sent an expedition to Sicily. Young prosecutors won cases, young orators swayed the assembly. Fathers may have been shocked by some of the novel habits of their sons, but there was also much that they admired about the new generation, and much that they were willing to wink at, having once been young themselves. The 420s were a season of youth not least because the older generation was willing to let them be.

Filial rebellion?

Wealth, luxury, study with sophists, ambition, unscrupulousness, an early entry into politics: many Athenians were impressed or troubled by these traits of some upper-class youths of the 420s. One of the most difficult questions for the historian of this era is that of whether the 420s also saw an unusual amount of filial rebellion in Athenian households. Satisfactory data for answering this question have not survived, but there is anecdotal evidence. The quarrel of Xanthippos with his father Pericles and (as we shall see) the case of Alcibiades are two spectacular examples in the Athenian elite. The case of Andokides, who turned informer on his father Leogoras in 415, is also striking, though inconclusive, since Andokides may have been an obedient son before betraying his father in a moment of crisis. Anecdotal evidence is not proof, but it is important nonetheless. Three considerations – Alcibiades' popularity with other young men, the explosive teachings of the sophists, and the frequency of the theme of father–son conflict in Aristophanes – suggest that many Athenians in the elite had father–son rebellion on their minds in the 420s. It goes without saying that the evidence tells us little about anyone outside of a narrow, relatively wealthy, urbanized, and mainly citizen elite. Moreover, even within that group, we can attempt little more than the most impressionistic statements about such intimate social realities as the father–son tie.

No one would be surprised if there was more filial rebellion than usual in contemporary Athenian households. That conclusion, however, does not bring us much further than our starting point, that is, the notion that trends *outside* of the household made the rebellious son into a powerful symbol in late-fifth-century Athens. It is impossible to go much beyond that, however, and write explicit intra-household social history.

Ideology

It is unclear that many Athenian sons rebelled against their fathers in the 420s. Why then do so many sources speak of filial rebellion or father–son conflict in this era? The answer is that an ideological conflict does not necessarily correspond to a real one. In 1861, for example, the majority of American Southerners did not own slaves, and yet that same majority considered the "peculiar institution" essential to their way of life and worth fighting a war over. Likewise, there is no reason to think that a majority (or even a significant plurality) of Athenian sons ca. 400 BC were in rebellion against their fathers. That such rebellions became a common theme of Athenian literature in the late fifth and early fourth centuries tells us, rather, that Athenians felt that their values had been challenged at the heart.[21]

To be sure, Athenian society did face genuine shocks in the late fifth century. The egalitarian ideology of democracy may well have led to some tension between father and son. The growth in wealth and increased access to the courts may have led to increased tension over patrimonies. The Peloponnesian War, as Thucydides and Euripides demonstrate, brutalized and corrupted Athenian morals, challenged old rules of behavior, and subordinated oikos ties to faction and vengeance. Sophists could and did argue that filial piety was contrary to nature.[22] Still, aside from a "where there's smoke there's fire" argument, there are no grounds for making this into a general social crisis.

Indeed, it is tempting, if seemingly perverse, to argue that the more widespread the perception of ideological conflict, the less likely the existence of real-life conflict. Consider an analogy from another period, England in the first half of the seventeenth century. Amussen discusses the almost universal emphasis on obedience within the family to the authority of the husband and father that is found in the pamphlets, manuals, sermons, and political philosophy of early-seventeenth-century England. Foucault similarly has discussed the centrality of the family as a model for governing the state in continental European ideology of the six-

144

teenth and seventeenth centuries.[23] In these cases, unlike that of fifth-century Athens, it is possible to compare the ideology of literary sources with the evidence of court records and such examples of popular culture as the charivari. Amussen's comparison reveals an interesting point: in reality, the man's authority in the family remained relatively strong in this period, if not completely unchallenged. What *was* under frontal attack was the authority of the local gentry. Rapid population growth, currency inflation, and changes in agriculture in this period disturbed English villagers and impelled them to challenge and criticize local governors. The governors, in turn, made use of the widespread analogy between family and state to buttress their own position. Amussen writes:

> Because of the ideological relationship between family and state, the control of gender disorder symbolically affirmed all social order. It may have been impossible to make all poor villagers accept the authority of their neighbours of "credit and estimation," but the affirmation and insistence on the father's role asserted the position of those local governors.[24]

Amussen's insights may be applied to Athens. Now, an Athenian conservative of the 420s might have got up and said "the rich and well-born should rule because they are the best," as indeed the Old Oligarch does. The trouble was, virtually no one in Athens would have obeyed, because the demos had acquired the firm conviction that the ordinary people were the best. If, however, that same conservative got up and said, in effect, "traditional political authority should be in power in Athens because, as we all know, the father's authority must not be challenged," he would then stand a chance of being listened to – and *precisely because the authority of the Athenian father was still basically intact*. The very strength of the oikos gave it an emotional power that made anxiety about its future the perfect material for political rhetoric. In other words, the existence of an ideological conflict between father and son may be evidence of precisely the opposite phenomen in real life: a relatively strong and traditional father–son relationship. For every Alcibiades or Pheidippides there were a dozen Athenian boys who displayed the traditional, grudging but obedient deference to the father.

Given the importance of father–son relations in Athenian culture, the subject was an excellent symbol of tension between old and new. In general we are better off taking contemporary statements about filial rebellion in late-fifth-century Athens less as sociological commentary than as symbolic expression. The same is true to an extent, though to a lesser one, of the evidence for intergenerational conflict outside the household. There is good reason to think that such conflict reached an unusual pitch in the 420s, and that it was the result of certain novel causes. Intergenerational conflict in Greece was not entirely without precedent, however, and it is unlikely that it was as sharp in the 420s as some of the sources (e.g. Aristophanes' *Clouds*) might suggest. Statements about filial rebellion and intergenerational conflict must be read, among other things, as a *façon de parler* about external political and social issues. They must be read, in short, as ideology.

One does not have to look far for reasons why filial rebellion might have seemed like an appropriate metaphor in Athens of the 420s. The decade witnessed a series of challenges to tradition. First, the sophists represented a potential revolution in the education of the young. A conversation with a *meirakion* who had wholeheartedly accepted the sophists' teachings might leave one convinced that sons were indeed in rebellion against their fathers. Second, Pericles' defensive strategy in the face of Spartan invasion was indeed a revolutionary departure from tradition. Instead of fighting the Spartans on the field of honor in the tradition of the Greek hoplite (or accepting the worst and suing for peace, as in 446), Pericles withdrew the citizen population behind the impregnable walls of the Athens–Piraeus complex whose construction he had overseen. This was a shock to a traditionalist, as was the experience of living under annual Spartan siege. In *Acharnians* (425) Aristophanes portrays a chorus of old men who claim to have fought at Marathon (barely possible in 425, when an eighteen-year-old at the time of Marathon would have reached the age of eighty-two) as the most ardent proponents of war with Sparta. This need not be taken literally, but rather as the symbolic expression of the conflict between the old and new styles of making war.[25]

Third and most important, the 420s were a watershed in Athenian political history. When Pericles died in 429, a period of over thirty years ended in which he had been a leading figure in Athenian politics; since the ostracism of Thoukydides son of Melesias in 443, Pericles had towered over the political scene. Born before Marathon, *khorêgos* in 472 of Aeschylus's *Persians*, a play that commemorated Athens's victory of Salamis, Pericles was some-thing of a personal link between the present and Athens's heroic past. There was no one of his political stature to replace him (Thuc. 2.65.10–12). Pericles' death marked a very major changing of the guard. A new breed of political leader, personified by Kleon, now came to the fore: a non-aristocrat whose family money came from small-scale manufacturing and trade rather than agriculture; more of an orator than a general and frequently a rhetorical show-man, one willing to escalate populist rhetoric against the upper classes; a man more at home in the assembly than in the aristocratic political clubs (*hetairiai*), more knowledgeable about budgets than blue blood; and a man more likely than the previous generation to achieve prominence at a relatively young age. Whether called "demagogues" or "new politicians," Athens's new leaders were a new breed. No wonder Aristophanes portrays conservatives (for example, in *Knights*, 424) as outraged over Kleon's break with what they saw as the glorious traditions of past Athen-ian leaders.[26]

In symbolic terms, Pericles' death also marked the loss of a father-figure: an event traumatic for some, liberating for others. Many Athenians were no doubt given pause by the "son" who, as the 420s progressed, showed an increasing interest in stepping into his shoes: Pericles' ward and Athens's bad boy, Alcibiades. Pericles' failure to discipline Alcibiades or his own son Xanthippos perhaps seemed like a symbol of the older generation's failure to produce sons and successors in its own image. The sophist-educated, politi-cally ambitious, and potentially oligarchic, if not tyrannical, young Athenian who, many feared, typified the youth of the 420s – it was a caricature, of course, but a powerful and emotive one – was quite different from his father. The difference is not entirely to be blamed on bad upbringing on the father's part. Change is inevit-able, particularly given the unprecedented dynamism of wealthy, democratic, imperial Athens, which made it likely that the world in which an eighteen-year-old entered manhood in, say, 425 would be enormously different from the world in which his father had entered manhood thirty years previously, in 455. Of course the world of 455 had in turn differed from the world of 485, but 455 lacked sophists, Aristophanes, or an "Old Oligarch" to express the sense of change consciously. Change may be inevitable, but nonetheless in 425 change might have seemed both disturbing and a sign of personal failure to an Athenian of the older generation.

In short, within a few years after the outbreak of the Peloponnesian War in 431, an older Athenian might have been forgiven for thinking that the world had been turned upside down. Pericles, the embodiment of what had become traditional government, was dead, replaced by a radical new breed of leader. Sparta had invaded the Athenian fatherland, and instead of doing what hoplites had done for centuries – that is, standing and fighting – Athenians hid behind their walls. A deadly epidemic had loosened moral inhibitions. War brutalized public discourse and behavior, as shown by Athens's near-willingness to execute all the men and enslave the women and children after the revolt of Mytilene in 427. Wealthy and ambitious young Athenians, masters of sophistic reasoning, were entering politics at a young age in unusual number, and they seemed to be speeding change even further.

For many, youth was a symbol of disruption. Contemporary political language affords an example. As several scholars have pointed out, the term "young men" acquired an ideological as well as literal meaning in the political discourse of this period. The elderly men of the chorus of *Wasps* (424), for example, castigate the "young men who steal" the tribute, but their *bête noire*, Kleon, was in his fifties and thus no young man (Ar. *Wasps* 1099–1100). In 415 Nicias attacked Alcibiades as an irresponsible young man leading a faction of young men in support of the proposed Sicilian Expedition (Thuc. 6.12–13). Nicias calls Alcibiades a rash youth and too young to lead an army, but Alcibiades was about thirty-five at the time. Compare Kimon, that conservative hero, who was only about thirty-one when he commanded the Athenian fleet at Mycale in 479! For some Athenians, therefore, "young" was a code word for immature and irresponsible rather than a literal description.[27]

What was true of politics was also true of the household. What symbol better evoked the dizzying and sometimes frightening change occurring in Athens than a son rebelling against or even beating his father? Who personified the change better than Alcibiades? What greater contrast than that between his personality and Pericles'?

ALCIBIADES: SONS IN CHARGE

From rule by the generation of the father, Athens entered a period of rule by the generation of the sons. If Thucydides does not use just this metaphor, he does emphasize the predominance of youth in the decision in 415 to invade Sicily (Thuc. 6.12.2–6.13.1; 6.18.6). The mutilation of the Herms of that same year, moreover, seemed to underline the dark side of youthful enthusiasm in politics: whether the mutilation was merely a drunken prank and a violent spree (Thuc. 6.28.1; Plut. *Alc.* 18.3) or a serious political conspiracy (Thuc. 6.27.3, 28.2, 60.1, 61.1; Plut. *Alc.* 18.4, 20.3, 21.1) the accused perpetrators of this act and of the profanation of the Mysteries included such diverse young men (young by Athenian standards) as Andokides (who was in his late twenties) and Kharmides son of Aristoteles (aged about twenty-five), not to mention Alcibiades.[28]

The metaphor of a generational change in politics – from old to young, from father to son – can be reconstructed from Thucydides and other contemporary sources: comedy, tragedy, and oratory.

Alcibiades had no living father: he had been orphaned as a young child, and was raised with his brother Kleinias as wards of Pericles; Pericles' brother Ariphron also seems to have played some role in raising the boys. As a teenager, Alcibiades troubled Pericles by running away from home to a lover's house; from time to time he peppered Pericles with sophistic questions and smart-alecky advice (Plut. *Alc.* 3, 7.2; Xen. *Mem.* 1–2.40–46; Diod. 12.38). Plutarch's anecdotal *vita* is full of tales of Alcibiades' insubordination toward various other surrogate fathers. Hence, Alcibiades can be considered an example of the rebellious son.[29]

Plutarch's stories include such details as Alcibiades' leading a students' rebellion against flute lessons; physical violence against a teacher, fisticuffs with the prominent man Hipponikos (later Alcibiades' father-in-law) on a dare, and the murder of one of his attendants (Plutarch does not believe this last story); and numerous insults and examples of outrageous behavior toward his many lovers (Plut. *Alc.* 2–4, 7–8). The truth of these stories hardly matters; much more important is that Alcibiades elicited them.[30]

While Pericles was teased, flattered, and criticized by a comparison with Olympian Zeus, Alcibiades had a different thunderbolt-wielding deity as his symbol. In his case, the deity was Eros, who appeared on his shield, in place of his ancestral blazon (*episêmon tôn patriôn*) in ivory inlaid on gold (Plut. *Alc.* 16.1–2; Ath. 12.534e). It has been argued that the shield was merely comic invention, and that, for the sake of a better story, Plutarch and Athenaeus concealed the tale's origin on the stage. The theory seems plausible, but even so, the shield is still significant evidence of Alcibiades' public image in the eyes of contemporaries. The absence on the shield of any sign of Alcibiades' father or ancestors is striking, and is perhaps symbolic of his independence. The choice of deity is also striking. It is conceivable that the thunderbolt was a conscious reference and riposte to Pericles. Whether so chosen or not, Eros made a stark contrast to Zeus: a youth instead of a mature man, hardly the image of prudence cultivated by Pericles, and more at home in the bedroom than the political or military arena (e.g. Hes. *Th*. 120–122, 201).[31]

Alcibiades acquired a reputation as an *enfant terrible*, but he was a child whom the Athenian assembly was willing to indulge for a very long time, through two exiles, treason, and numerous military disasters. Like Strepsiades, the father in *Clouds*, the demos would have to be very hard pressed indeed before losing its patience with its prodigal. One reason for this is that, in his public persona, Alcibiades presented a dimension of the Athenians' self-image that they craved seeing. He was the symbol of youth, of the liberated son ascendant.[32]

Alcibiades, of course, tried to get away with a more disreputable and libertine private life than the Athenian people proved willing to bear. In 415 he alienated that most conservative, most traditional, most *patrios* of all Athenian institutions: religion. He was only able to duck temporarily his palpable guilt in the parodying of the Eleusinian Mysteries and his suspected, though never-proven, guilt in the mutilation of the Herms. Although he came home to a hero's welcome in Athens in 407 (the Athenian fleet at Samos had received him in 411) his popularity proved to be exceedingly flimsy. At the first sign of defeat, at Notion, he was forced into a second exile, which suggests that the first charges against him still remained potent. Nor was Alcibiades able to talk his way back into the Athenian army's favor during his appearance at Aegospotami in the Chersonese on the eve of the climactic battle of 405.[33]

As Thucydides says of Alcibiades, "his way of life made him objectionable to everyone as a person" (6.15.4) because it was "generally unconventional and undemocratic" (6.28.2), especially because of a frightening quality in him that "was beyond the normal and showed itself both in the lawlessness of his private life and habits and in the spirit in which he acted on all occasions" (6.15.4, tr. Warner). People feared that Alcibiades would settle for nothing less than a tyranny (Thuc. 6.15.4) and so eventually they got rid of him in order to save the democracy.

This political explanation makes sense, but other levels of analysis are also worth pursuing. On the religious level, driving Alcibiades into exile in 415 was a matter of purifying the city. As one convicted of sacrilege against Demeter and Kore, Alcibiades was cursed publicly by priests and priestesses (Plut. *Alc.* 22.5, 33.3; Diod. 13.69.2; Nep. *Alc.* 4.5). His name was inscribed on stelai with those of other offenders as a mark of shame. A reward of one talent of silver was offered to anyone who killed Alcibiades or any other of the convicted who had taken flight (schol. Ar. *Birds* 766). On one level of analysis, therefore, Alcibiades was a figure of sinful pollution (*alitêrion*) or scapegoat (*pharmakos*) in the Greek tradition.[34]

The association of the Sicilian Expedition with the festival of Adonis is perhaps also of interest. According to Plutarch (*Alc.* 18.3, *Nic.* 13.2, 7; cf. Ar. *Lys.* 387–396) the Adonia fell at the time of the preparation of the departure of the Athenian fleet in June 415. Adonis was famous for his youth and good looks, for being loved by Aphrodite, and for his tragic, violent, and young death: in a contemporary version he was gored by a boar while out hunting (Eur. *Hipp.* 1420–1422). His was a woman's cult, organized informally by women, and celebrated by them on rooftops throughout Athens. The rites included the planting of rooftop gardens and nighttime dancing and chanting; activities on which Athenian men turned a suspicious eye. Scholars have suggested several different interpretations of how the festival afforded women a way to protest male domination or mock male pretensions. At the climax of the festival, female worshippers mourned Adonis by imitating funeral rites, by beating their breasts and singing dirges, and by carrying statuettes of dead men in preparation for burial. The statuettes and rooftop plants were thrown into the sea.[35]

Understandably, the sight of women mourning over the death of a youth was taken as a bad omen for the departure of a seaborne armada of young men. Perhaps the femininity of the festival and its temporary triumph over male control were also taken as a bad omen for what was considered the manliest of enterprises, war.[36] Perhaps the most interesting (if admittedly the most speculative) symbolic question about the Adonia is its problematic effect on Alcibiades' public persona. Thanks to his notorious erotic exploits, the would-be conqueror of Sicily might possibly have found himself identified with Adonis: both were handsome youths and both had a connection to Aphrodite. Adonis was Aphrodite's lover, Alcibiades was, as it were, her worshipper. Oratory, comedy, biography, gossip, and writings of the Socratic circle all testify to the widespread public perception of Alcibiades as a rake. In addition to the many male lovers of his teenage years, of whom the most famous was Socrates, Alcibiades is supposed to have had numerous affairs with women. For example, he is said to have dallied with courtesans in Athens and abroad (Plut. *Alc.* 8.5; Ath. 12.534f–535a; Lysias frg. 246 Thalheim = Ath. 15.574e; Antiphon *ap.* Ath. 12.525b), pursued other men's wives (Aeschines the Socratic *ap.* Ath. 5.220c), seduced and possibly impregnated the Spartan queen Timaia (Plut. *Alc.* 23.7–9; Xen. *Hell.* 3.3.1–4), and, according to gossip, slept with his mother, sister, and daughter (Ath. 5.220c). In addition there was an erotic quality to Alcibiades' political charisma (Plut. *Alc.* 24.6; cf. Ar. *Frogs* 1425; Thuc. 6.24.3).[37]

At the heart of the Adonis myth, it has been suggested, is the paradox of a goddess who adopts a young lover who prematurely dies in consequence. Perhaps the symbolic meaning drawn by the Athenian public from the ill-timed Adonia of 415, therefore, was this: that Alcibiades, Eros personified and the new favorite of Aphrodite, would come to an untimely end like Adonis. With Alcibiades in charge, therefore, the Sicilian Expedition was doomed.[38]

The Adonia was quickly overshadowed in 415 by the far more sensational affair of the Herms and the Mysteries, but we ought not to overlook thematic connections between the separate scandals. Keuls speculates that both the Adonia and the mutilation of the Herms represent symbolic attacks on male pretensions. Let us note that both the Adonis story and the parodying of the Eleusinian Mysteries of Demeter contain the theme of disharmony between goddess and mortal. If Adonis had died as a consequence of Aphrodite's *love*, what would happen to a mortal who incurred a goddess's *wrath*? In the mind of the ordinary Athenian, Alcibiades and the other sophisticated parodists of the Mysteries had incurred just this wrath by blaspheming the so-called Two Goddesses, Demeter and Kore (Persephone). The official indictment, preferred by a son of the famous Kimon, Thettalos (an older man, aged perhaps about sixty in 415), accuses Alcibiades of committing various crimes against the two goddesses (Plut. *Alc.* 22.3). Andokides, moreover, has this to say in 400 about the scandal of 415:

I have shown that I have never turned informer, that I have never admitted guilt, and that I have not a single offence against the Two Goddesses upon my conscience, whether serious or otherwise. And it is very important for me to persuade you. The stories of the prosecutors, who have shrieked out these awful and frightening versions of what happened and who have spoken about other earlier offenders and men guilty of impiety toward the Two Goddesses, how each of them suffered or was punished – what do these words or deeds have to do with me?

(Andok. 1.29)

Whatever Andokides' guilt or innocence, Alcibiades was convicted of blasphemy. As public opinion no doubt noted (in the spirit of *post hoc ergo propter hoc*), he did suffer. Two additional points of contact between the Adonia and the Two Goddesses are also worth noting. First, in one fifth-century version of the myth, Persephone too was a lover of Adonis. Second, Athenian women also celebrated a festival to Demeter – the Thesmophoria, similar in some (though not all) ways to the Adonia. There were thus a number of thematic connections between the parodying of the Mysteries and the ominous timing of the Adonia.[39]

By the end of summer 415, therefore, fortune's darling had turned into the accursed of heaven. The very qualities that had made Alcibiades so appealing in the public eye – youth, beauty, brains, and brashness – had turned out to condemn him. On the symbolic and social dramatistic levels, the avatar of youth had become Adonis, the victim as well as the beneficiary of divine love.[40]

On other levels of symbolic meaning, the expulsion of Alcibiades was not only a necessary step of purifying the city by ridding it of corruption, but also a way of announcing the end of the previously unfettered reign of youth. It marked the beginning of the restoration of the rule of the father. By declaring Alcibiades' antics unacceptable, Athenians were sending a message to other licentious and unscrupulously ambitious young men.

FATHERS AND SONS IN ARISTOPHANES

Unscrupulous young men and, at least in indirect references, Alcibiades himself fill the pages of Aristophanes. The conflict of the

153

generations is a theme in virtually all of his plays, as is the conflict between tradition and novelty. Conflict between father and son is also an important motif; indeed, it is a stock theme of ancient Greek comedy generally. The most important examples of father–son conflict in Aristophanes' plays before 413 are *Clouds* (423, partially revised shortly after 420) and *Wasps* (422), in both of which it is a major motif; *Knights* (424), where the theme has some interesting resonances; and *Birds* (414), where it appears briefly.[41] Our usual caution about not taking literary representation as a description of sociological reality must be even stronger in the case of Aristophanes. As a poet and comic playwright, Aristophanes maintains exaggeration, parody, inconsistency, and distortion as his stock in trade. His plays are a much better guide to Athenian fantasy, therefore, than to Athenian reality. One might even say that they are a better guide to what could *not* happen in Athens than to what could – one could not negotiate a private peace with Sparta (contrary to *Acharnians*); Kleon was not a Paphlagonian nor was he booted from office by a man with a hotdog stand (contrary to *Knights*); women could not take over the Acropolis (contrary to *Lysistrata*) nor establish communism in Athens (contrary to *Ecclesiazusae*); and up-to-date sons did not beat their fathers (contrary to *Clouds*).

Fantasy, however, has its uses for the historian. It serves as a guide to the hopes and fears of a culture or its representatives. Comedy bites best when it touches raw nerves, just as *Ecclesiazusae* exploits Athenian poverty in the 390s, or when it taps the most impossible wishes, just as *Acharnians* does with the war-weariness of 425. Aristophanes' use of father–son conflict does not in itself indicate that such conflict was prevalent, although it may demonstrate that it was feared by some (fathers) and wished by others (sons). No doubt the generation gap which generalized tension between young and old raised violent feelings between fathers and sons; through comic exaggeration, Aristophanes turns metaphorical into literal violence.

If fantasy is one element of Aristophanes' plays, another is political caricature, with a considerable amount of specific, often indirect or punning references to Pericles and Alcibiades, among others.[42] For all his authority, Pericles was not a king; his was not the royal family, nor was Alcibiades the heir apparent. The great interest, nonetheless, of Aristophanes and his audience in Pericles' family tells the historian something about the power of the oikos as a metaphor in fifth-century Athens. The fortunes and misfortunes of Athens's "first family" seemed to symbolize the ups and downs of the polis. Alcibiades' ungovernable rebelliousness and Pericles' peccadilloes were funny and momentous not only because they were the faults of leading politicians, but because disorder in the oikos seemed to correspond to disorder in the polis. References to Pericles' family are yet another example of the importance in Athenian ideology of the oikos–polis analogy, and more particularly of the father–son analogy. In any case, references to Pericles and his family only add flesh to the bones of a theme that is independently present in so many of Aristophanes' plays, the theme of father–son conflict.

Let us consider, in chronological order, Aristophanes' use of the theme of father–son conflict in *Knights*, *Clouds*, *Wasps*, and *Birds*, with particular attention to the contemporary Athenian debate about rebellious youth. Aristophanes is a notoriously complex author. The brief discussion that follows can hardly do full justice to his work, but it may shed additional light on the subject of father–son conflict in Athenian ideology during the Archidamian War and Sicilian Expedition.

One of the most interesting, if brief, uses of the father–son theme is in *Knights* (424). The conceit of the play is that the Athenian demos is a difficult and foolish old man (e.g. 42–43, 269–270, 737, 752–755, 1349) who is flattered and gulled by his household slaves, above all, by "the Paphlagonian," who represents Aristophanes' political *bête noire*, Kleon. The other slaves dragoon one Agorakritos, a vulgar, young (611, 750–751) sausage-seller, to outdo the Paphlagonian in flattery and gifts and replace him as Demos's favorite – literally as his lover or *erastês* (732–740). Agorakritos's allies are a chorus of young Athenian cavalrymen (731), while the Paphlagonian calls on the "elderly jurymen, phratry-members of the triobol payment" (255) to support him. Much is thus made in the play of the opposition of youth and age, good looks and ugliness, passive and active erotic roles, good government and demagoguery.[43]

What is most interesting for our purposes is the oikos metaphor. The demos is represented as the master of a household, and the leading politicians (Demosthenes and perhaps Nicias are depicted as well as Kleon) are his servants (*oiketai*, e.g. 5). This is yet another indication of the currency of the oikos–polis analogy in

Athenian discourse. In *Knights*, however, the oikos is reversed in the mirror of the polis. At home, Demos is old but intelligent, the master of his servants, but in the assembly, he becomes a fool (40, 752–755). Various demagogues compete for his favor, variously casting him as a child, an aged father, or an *eromenos* (737). Aristophanes makes much of the notion – as old as Homer (cf. Arist. *Pol.* 1259b12–14) and as recent as Sophocles' *Oedipus Tyrannos* (line 1) – the notion of the king as father. Agorakritos calls Demos "father" (*ô pater*, 725) and "daddy" (*ô pappidion*, 1215) and promises to "take good care [of him]" (*therapeusô kalôs*, 1215), using a verb, *therapeuô*, that refers both to a servant's ministrations (cf. 58–59) and to a son's care of his parents. Agorakritos's attitude is that of a grown son who needs to take care of an aged and infirm parent. The Paphlagonian, on the other hand, casts himself in the role of father and protector and Demos in the role of child (1037–1039). Just like Kleon to appropriate the kingly and paternal role for himself; yet even the more filial Agorakritos places Demos in a subordinate position.[44]

By eventually liberating Demos from this subordination Agorakritos acts more like a father than a son. Instead of sitting at Demos's feet and listening to his Nestor-like wisdom, Agorakritos boils his "father" in a pot and makes him young and beautiful again (1321, a parody of the myth in which Medea boils Jason's father Aison in a pot and rejuvenates him). In other words, instead of the normal pattern of son maturing and replacing his father, in the Aristophanic fantasy of *Knights*, the father becomes young again and replaces the son, who departs the scene. Aristophanes makes much of the "miracle."[45]

Although rejuvenated (1349, cf. 908), Demos is nothing like the smart young men of the 420s. Instead, Demos comes to "shine in old-fashioned costume" (*archaiôi schêmati lampros*, 1331), that is, to resemble Athens's noble leaders of old, like Miltiades and Aristides (1325, cf. 1323, 1327, 1387). A rejuvenated Demos immediately lashes out against *meirakia* and beardless youths who follow or take part in rhetorical displays in the agora when they should be out hunting (1373–1377). Through a curious rite of passage, Demos has left second childhood and crossed the threshold into adulthood. Demos is now a young man, a twenty-year-old, say, and one who has just come into his inheritance: the regime of his forefathers. Although formerly an old man, Demos was like a child, in that he needed someone (a demagogue) to serve as a guardian (*epitropeuein*, 212, 426, 949). As a result of Agorakritos's miraculous help, Demos can stand on his own; like a king (1330, 1333) he has no need of demagogic guardians.[46]

In political terms, Aristophanes' metaphor seems to be a call for a renovation of the Athenian constitution on the terms of the conservative democracy of a previous generation – something of a precursor of the *patrios politeia* movement of the period after the Sicilian Expedition. For the troubled demos of the Archidamian War to "grow up," it must become more like its ancestors; so Aristophanes seems to say. There are perhaps strong elements of Alcibiades in Agorakritos and of Pericles in Demos; it is the older politician who wins out in the end. In familial terms, Aristophanes likewise fantasizes about an earlier generation reemerging as *kyrios* of the Athenian household, a notion that he later expands in *Wasps*. *Knights* is a remarkable example of the use of familial metaphors to describe politics: from household management to paternal–filial relations to coming of age to generational alternation to eros.[47]

The better-known conflict between father and son in *Clouds* (423, but the extant version was partially revised several years later) should be read in light of Aristophanes' black humor and anarchic tendencies. The beating of father by son is a wicked symbol of the revolutionary potential of sophistic education. The opposition between, on the one hand, youth and novelty and, on the other, age and tradition is a major theme of the play, most notably in the contests (*agones*) between the Stronger Argument and the Weaker Argument (889–1111) and between Strepsiades and his son Pheidippides (1321–1475).

The circumstances of the play are well known. Strepsiades, an old man, perhaps in his sixties, has a son Pheidippides, a *meirakion* in the cavalry, perhaps eighteen or nineteen years old. While Strepsiades is rude and rural, he has an aristocratic wife, and their son is spoiled, lazy, disobedient, and runs with a horsey set. At the play's start, Strepsiades complains of the creditors plaguing him over Pheidippides' debts. The old man's solution is to force Pheidippides into lessons at the "think tank" (*phrontistêrion*) run by the sophist Socrates, so that he can learn how to make the weaker argument defeat the stronger and talk his way out of debts. The lessons work only too well, however, as the boy is taught to value arguments over family ties: Pheidippides "learns" to beat his father, to justify himself philosophically, and to threaten to beat his mother next. The play ends with a furious Strepsiades burning down Socrates' school.[48]

Let us consider *Clouds'* treatment of the father–son relationship. First of all, for all the role reversals and youthful misbehavior, there are many traditional elements in the interplay of Strepsiades and Pheidippides. When, for example, Strepsiades insists over Pheidippides' strong objections that he study with Socrates, the boy gives in, obedient to his father. Second, Strepsiades misses his son while Pheidippides is closeted away with Socrates, and is overjoyed upon the boy's homecoming. Third, Strepsiades fills up at first with paternal pride at Pheidippides' education and new skills. He calls his son a savior, bulwark, deliverer, and terror to the family's enemies, and he expects all his friends and demesmen to be jealous that Strepsiades has raised such a son (1161–1162, 1208). He is about to treat Pheidippides to a feast when the creditors arrive (1212/1213). Even later, after getting a beating at Pheidippides' hands, Strepsiades can still call the boy, rather conventionally, "most dear one" (*ô philtate*, 1464).[49]

Even before he enters Socrates' school, however, Pheidippides challenges his father's authority. When, early in the play, Strepsiades threatens to stop paying his son's bills, and in fact to throw him out of the house, Pheidippides replies that it doesn't matter because he can get all the help he needs from his maternal uncle Megakles (124–125, cf. 815). This is a multiple insult to Strepsiades: back-talk, invocation of the help of another adult male, and invocation of Pheidippides' mother's family. Strepsiades replies with a wrestling metaphor along the lines of "I've been thrown but I won't stay down" (126–127), and later we learn just how apt the metaphor is. Strepsiades confides to the chorus (the clouds of the title) that he is afraid of his son's superior physical strength (799). Shortly afterward he accuses Pheidippides of wanting him dead (838). Pheidippides in turn finds his father's behavior so odd that he toys with the idea of suing Strepsiades for mental incapacity (844–845). Socrates may give Pheidippides the philosophical tools to justify his attack on his father, but clearly the impulse was already present.

Pheidippides' offstage beating of Strepsiades results in a verbal contest (*agôn*) between the two. Finally, in this last part of the play, father–son tension is out in the open. Strepsiades calls his son a *patraloias*, a father-beater or patricide (1327). Fighting words, for the imputation of patricide could lead to legal action. Pheidippides' response, however, is to claim the title proudly and then to go on and justify father-beating philosophically (1328–1329, 1331–1475). Unreligious up to now, Strepsiades clutches at straws and invokes "Zeus of Fathers and Children" (*Patrôion Dia*, 1468), apparently quoting tragedy, but Pheidippides merely sneers at someone old-fashioned enough to believe in Zeus (1469–1470).[50]

In the previous *agôn* between the Stronger and Weaker Argument, the main battle lines are youth/novelty versus age/tradition, but here too the subject of fathers and sons appears as a subsidiary but interesting theme. The Stronger Argument speaks in favor of what he calls old education (961), the Weaker Argument advocates new ideas (e.g. 896), namely rhetoric and indiscipline. The Stronger Argument notes the tradition behind his teaching: his musical technique, for instance, has been "handed down by our fathers" (967). He has specific advice for young Pheidippides: give up his seat to his elders, don't be rude to his parents, and not one word of back-talk to his father (991–999).[51]

The last admonition contains the particular injunction not to call his father "Iapetos," because that would remind the father of just how old he had grown since taking care of his baby "nestling" son (998–999). In mythology, Iapetos was the brother of Kronos (Hes. *Th.* 134), so calling someone Iapetos was probably the same as calling him Kronos – and that insult is frequently tossed back and forth in the play. As a god even older than Zeus, and perhaps also as one whose festival (the Kronia) was no longer as popular as it had once been, Kronos was synonymous with "old-fashioned" or "out of date." In spite of the Stronger Argument's injunction, the Weaker Argument twice calls his opponent a Kronos, as Socrates has already called Strepsiades (398, 929, 1070). Furthermore, the word *archaios* ("old-fashioned") and its derivatives as well as similar charges are tossed out frequently by several different characters in the play (e.g. 821, 908, 915, 984, 1357, 1469; cf. Isoc. 4.30).[52]

Kronos plays another interesting thematic role in *Clouds*. The father of Zeus, Kronos had castrated *his* father Ouranos at the behest of his mother Gaia (earth), because Ouranos was jealous of his children and kept them all in Gaia's body (Hes. *Th.* 154–159; Apollodoros 1.3). Later on, Kronos proved to be afraid of his own children in turn, having heard that it was his destiny to be overcome by one of his sons. Kronos swallowed each of them upon birth, much to the distress of his wife Rhea. She contrived to save their son Zeus from Kronos. Zeus grew up, led a successful revolt against Kronos, and established his own kingship (Hes. *Th*. 71–73, 453–506, 851).

The Weaker Argument avails himself of the story of Zeus's binding of Kronos as proof that there is no justice: otherwise, a son would be punished for using violence against his own father (904–906). The implication, of course, is that Pheidippides should feel free to use violence against his father. The Stronger Argument announces his reaction: he wants to vomit (906–907), perhaps a coarse joke on the way Rhea tricked Kronos into vomiting up his children (Hes. *Th*. 467–491). The Weaker Argument responds that the Stronger Argument is a "silly old man" and "out of touch with the times" (908). A few more exchanges of insults, and the Stronger Argument calls his opponent *patraloias*, which term Weaker Argument accepts proudly, thus anticipating Pheidippides' future behavior (911–912, 1328–1329).

The Kronos theme ties together several of the major oppositions of *Clouds*: father vs. son, intergenerational conflict, novelty vs. tradition, and being *au courant* vs. being out of date. Kronos also points to one of the play's paradoxes. The new education of the sophists may threaten traditional Athenian education and the old order, as dramatized by Pheidippides' manhandling of his father. On the other hand, the old order itself was founded on Zeus's rebellion against his father Kronos. Perhaps an Athenian father who played Kronos to his son's Zeus was merely playing a traditional role.

In any case, we must shy from drawing either simple lessons (e.g. "Aristophanes the conservative") or sociological dicta from *Clouds*. Let us note, for example, how little interest Aristophanes has in drawing a consistent picture of the differences in generational tastes. Remember that, although Strepsiades ends up as the outraged defender of tradition, he starts out as a devotee of sophists who chides his son for being "old-fashioned" (398); Pheidippides has a reverse progression from horse-racing to sophistry. As previously in *Knights* and later in *Wasps*, Aristophanes explores the themes of rejuvenation and generational role reversal in *Clouds*. Perhaps there is even a suggestion in Pheidippides' *mot*, "old men are twice children" (1417), that age and youth are not so different after all. The sketch of generational characteristics is thus inconsistent, but to repeat a point, *Clouds* was not intended to be a sociological tract. What was intended was to use father–son conflict as a symbol of contemporary Athenian educational debate and intergenerational tension. As we have seen, Clouds does not demonstrate the existence of father-beating in contemporary Athenian households.[53]

Vickers calls attention to another dimension of the play, arguing that the characters of Strepsiades and Pheidippides lampoon Pericles and Alcibiades (with occasional references to other characters as well). This attractive suggestion strengthens the symbolic force of the play as a comment on intergenerational conflict, which Alcibiades so personified. It also heightens the element of fantasy in the comedy. In 423 Pericles was no longer alive. Before his death in 429, moreover, Pericles had banished Socrates neither from Alcibiades' life nor from Athens. Strepsiades' behavior thus is not a true-to-life copy of Pericles, but a comic distortion of what some Athenians (and perhaps Pericles himself at certain moments) might have wished Pericles had done.[54]

Father–son conflict is once again a theme in Wasps (422), but here Aristophanes goes even further in role reversal. The son is more responsible than the father who, during the course of the play, goes from crotchety old age to an irresponsible second childhood. At the beginning of the play, old Philokleon ("friend of Kleon") has evidently retired from control of the oikos and turned it over to his son Bdelykleon ("disgusted by Kleon") (67–70). Bdelykleon is older than Pheidippides, and, when it comes to the household, certainly more responsible. Although Bdelykleon frequently tires of his father he genuinely cares about him (114, 209–210, 478). Bdelykleon is no rebel. The chorus of old men indeed praises him for his *philopatria* ("love of father," 1465). The troublemaker in the household rather is the father, Philokleon, an irascible old man obsessed with sitting on juries and with condemning people, the perfect example of the incorrigible Aristophanic hero.[55]

Bdelykleon's goal – again, he is more responsible than Pheidippides – is to save his father from himself. Like Pheidippides at the start of Clouds, Bdelykleon is more interested in luxury than in rhetoric. Bdelykleon explicitly abjures politics; there is much in him of the refined young aristocrat who washes his hands of democracy and its perceived vulgarities. Bdelykleon wants his father Philokleon to give up the courts for a "noble life" (504–506) of dinners, drinking parties, and religious and theatrical events (1003–1006). Indeed, much of the thrust of Wasps is an attack on the politics of Kleon's Athens in the name of a retreat to private life by disillusioned young aristocrats. To save his father from Kleon, Bdelykleon keeps the old man under virtual house arrest (68–70). Philokleon calls to his aid the chorus of elderly jurors ("wasps" in temperament, 197). They too have bad relations with their sons, on whom they are dependent (248–315), but, after a long verbal *agôn* between Philokleon and Bdelykleon over the law courts (526–724), they are forced to concede victory to the younger man (726–727). Bdelykleon slowly convinces his father that there is more profit in *symposia* than in the law courts, but the result is not what Bdelykleon might have wished. Philokleon characteristically goes overboard in his new enthusiasm: by play's end, the former legal addict is a lascivious and over-rowdy party-going symposiast. Austere and crotchety old age is turned into swinging, luxury-loving youth (1450–1455). As one critic suggests, the structure of the play is a "reverse ephebeia," a passage from citizenship and responsibility to irresponsible youth, instead of the usual opposite course.[56]

Much of the humor in *Wasps* is an extended commentary on Pheidippides' dictum about old men being twice children. In contrast to Bdelykleon's sense of responsibility (it is no accident that the slaves call *him* "the master" and "the big man," 67–68) Philokleon cares far more about his hobbies (whether the law courts or *symposia*) than his household. When Bdelykleon addresses his father with affection ("daddy," *pappidion*, 655) and reasoned arguments, Philokleon threatens to kill him (652–654). After his conversion to youthful excess, Philokleon promises a flute-girl to make her his concubine when his son dies and he inherits the family fortune – a play of course on the usual situation, where a son would be waiting to inherit his patrimony (1351–1363). When Bdelykleon shows up to cool the old man down, Philokleon first "plays a youthful trick on him" (1362) and then eventually knocks him down, after recalling an Olympic boxing match when "the older man struck down the younger one" (*ho presbuteros katelabe ton neôteron*, 1385). To add to the irony, Bdelykleon himself is the source of the story, having told it to his father as an example of a clever anecdote to tell at a party (1185–1199).[57]

Intergenerational conflict works on several different levels in *Wasps*. First, the play sympathizes with the distress of old men too proud to go gently into dependence on their young sons; not the least of reasons why Philokleon loves serving on juries is that it gives him power and independence (238–258, 290–315, 548–630, 1133–1134). Second, the play dramatizes generational differences in public and private styles. As in *Clouds*, young wastrels are opposed to austere old men (1060–1070), but in his explicit withdrawal from politics into private life, Bdelykleon is more forcefully anti-democratic than Pheidippides and his horsey friends. Third, there may be something of Pericles in Philokleon and of Alcibiades in Bdelykleon, with a considerable role reversal at the play's end: father becomes more like Alcibiades, son more like Pericles. This schema highlights the anarchism of Aristophanes' "solution" to the problem of Kleon, for Alcibiades is hardly a better alternative. Fourth and finally, *Wasps* refuses to give either generation the last word. Like Strepsiades, Philokleon refuses to be constrained by the world in which he ends up at play's end: if he has to give up public life, then he will live the high life with a terrifying lack of restraint. Even more than in *Knights*, the cure is not clearly better than the disease: is there really much to choose from between Philokleon the hanging judge and Philokleon the rowdy? Aristophanes' point may be that if Kleon's demagoguery is a sad fate for the aged heroes of the Persian Wars (236–237, 1078–1090, 1097–1100), so is the play's program of youthful dissipation. The sharp-spirited, manly Attic character (403–455, 1075–1078, 1090) was made for neither drinking parties nor demagoguery, but for great deeds like Marathon. What Athens needs is the vigor of youth rededicated to the ideals of its forebears.[58]

Aristophanes returned to the father–son theme eight years later in *Birds* (414). In this play, two disillusioned citizens leave Athens and create a utopia ("Cloudcuckooland") among the birds. The place is typically Aristophanic in its reversals; as the Chorus of Birds says, whatever is illegal or considered shameful in Athens is considered noble among the birds (755–756). The first example is father-beating (*ton patera tuptein*, 757): shameful in Athens, it is "noble among us" (*kalon par'hêmin*, 758). Later in the play a young (1362) *patraloias* (father-beater or patricide) decides to take the birds at their word and to enjoy the delights of Cloudcuckooland (1337–1371).

The *patraloias* says that he is crazy about the birds (*ornithomanô*, 1344) and their laws, one of which, as he has heard, states that the birds consider it noble to strangle and bite one's father (1347–1348). Peisthetairos confirms the report:

163

And by Zeus we consider it quite manly (*andreion*),
If someone who is just a chick (*neottos*) beats (*peplêgêi*) his
   father.

(1349–1350)

Peisthetairos's remark is a pun on several levels. First, a chick cannot
literally be a man, and neither can a boy – not unless the act of
beating his father changes him into one. On the literal level, therefore, Peisthetairos might be saying that father-beating is, on the one
hand, a sign of being human and, on the other, a rite of passage
from childhood to manhood. Second, Zeus is both a wonderfully
appropriate and, *prima facie*, an inappropriate deity to invoke on
the subject of father-beating. As Zeus Patroios, he is the tutelary
deity of good parent–child relations. Zeus personally, however, had
rebelled against and bound up his own tyrannical father Kronos –
which marked the beginning of Zeus's own manhood. So of course
one would invoke Zeus in defense of father-beating! In any case, it
turns out that the birds admit a big exception to their permitted
father-beating. An old bird law says that a father who took care of
(*trephein*) his son during his childhood must be taken care of by his
son during his old age in turn – a parody of Solon's law about
humans to the same effect (1353–1356).[59]

   Having been enthusiastic to strangle his father and inherit all he
owned, the *patraloias* is disappointed to find out that, on the
contrary, he will have to support the man (1351–1352, 1358–1359).
The never-at-a-loss Peisthetairos has a solution, however. He will
declare the *patraloias* an orphan, which will entitle the boy to be
outfitted as a hoplite at public expense. Then, as Peisthetairos
advises,

> support yourself (*sauton trephe*) on your pay (*misthophorôn*),
> Let your father live (*ton pater' ea zên*). Since you are warlike
>   (*machimos*),
> Fly off Thraceward and fight there.

(1367–1369)

Once again, Peisthetairos employs puns. Not only will the *patraloias* be supporting (*trephein*) himself by earning soldier's pay, he
will cease having to be supported (*trephein*) by his father, and
he will avoid having to support (*trephein*) his father, having been
declared an orphan. The *patraloias* will indeed let his father live,

by ceasing to burden him financially and by leaving the man alone.

In Peisthetairos's opinion, the *patraloias* has an excess of aggression, which Peisthetairos suggests diverting in a military expedition rather than in an attack on his father. These were not idle words in 414, a year in which thousands of Athenians were exercising their aggression in military expeditions. Perhaps Aristophanes is alluding to Euetion's expedition to retake Amphipolis, which sailed (in vain) in summer 414 (Thuc. 7.9). He may be referring to Athenian military activity of that year more generally, the most prominent part of which was the armada that sailed to Sicily. The recently deposed commander of that expedition was, of course, Alcibiades.[60]

Alcibiades, so several scholars have argued, is alluded to in the main figures of *Birds*. It has been suggested that Peisthetairos ("persuader of comrades [*hetairoi*]," "persuader of whores [*hetairai*]," etc.) and Euelpides ("optimistic") each represents a side of Alcibiades. The *patraloias* might represent yet another aspect of Alcibiades.[61]

It is tempting to see the *patraloias* scene as (among other things) a commentary on the Sicilian Expedition, the underlying notion being that it is better to have the youth of Athens make trouble for enemies abroad than to have them make trouble for their fathers at home. Better to have young Athenians fight Syracusans than to mutilate the Herms, parody the Eleusinian Mysteries, or challenge their elders in the assembly, all of which they had done on the eve of the Sicilian Expedition's sailing in 415. Which is not to say that Aristophanes supported the Sicilian Expedition; his ultimate preference might have been an Athens that was orderly at home and so had no need to intervene abroad. As so often before, Aristophanes uses father–son conflict in *Birds* to dramatize Athens's political and cultural issues.[62]

Another, muted instance of father–son conflict in *Birds* may also refer to Alcibiades. The success of Cloudcuckooland has mortals desert the Olympian gods in droves to sacrifice to the birds instead. To regain his power, Zeus sends his brother Poseidon and son Herakles on an embassy to Peisthetairos. Peisthetairos in effect demands surrender – Zeus's scepter – but the gluttonous Herakles is happy to give in, in return for a meal. Poseidon, however, is properly horrified and asks Herakles, "Would you deprive your father of his tyranny?" (1605). As Peisthetairos explains, however,

Herakles is a bastard, and so he will never inherit his father's patrimony (1641–1675). In the end, therefore, Herakles takes the banquet and betrays the Olympians (1685–1687).

Alcibiades was neither a god nor a bastard, but he too had recently betrayed his fatherland, Athens, by defecting to Sparta, an infamous deed that some people thought might cost Athens its empire – or, as it was sometimes called, its tyranny (e.g. Thuc. 2.63.2). "Tyranny" is a term that was sometimes also used to describe the political preeminence of Pericles, Alcibiades' guardian (e.g. Kratinos frg. 258 Kassel and Austin [= Plut. *Per.* 3.4]). Aristophanes frequently parodies Alcibiades' defection in other sections of *Birds*, and Herakles' disloyalty to his father too may have been meant to bring Alcibiades' disloyalty to father-figure and fatherland to mind.[63]

To sum up, Aristophanes makes extensive use of the theme of father–son conflict in four plays from 424 to 414 (*Knights*, *Clouds*, *Wasps*, *Birds*). His descriptions are far from sociologically accurate accounts of Athenian households; in fact they are more indicative of what behavior did not occur rather than of what behavior did occur. Aristophanes' point is neither that all over Athens Bdelykleons were locking up Philokleons, nor that Pheidippides' beating of Strepsiades was a common scene in Athenian households, nor that young politicians generally spoke of the demos as their father. Father–son conflict in Aristophanes, rather, is used symbolically to dramatize the tensions and conflicts between the generations in contemporary Athens, generations which often differed in style and substance in regard to personal habits, education, politics, and war.

Father–son conflicts in Aristophanes can often be read as specific, if veiled, references to Alcibiades and Pericles, whose relationship was a paradigm of intergenerational conflict. Again, the playwright is not offering a sociologically accurate description of Athens's first family. Instead, he uses a fantastic, distorted, and humorous caricature of that family to symbolize the changes and tensions of Athenian society in an era of war and intellectual revolution.

EURIPIDES' HIPPOLYTOS: AN ANTI-ALCIBIADES?

Much the same could be said about Euripides' *Hippolytos* of 428, although the tone of tragedy is of course quite different from that of comedy, and the references to contemporary life are far more oblique. *Hippolytos* is nonetheless a most revealing text, with much to say about Athenian culture's construction of father–son conflict, about adolescent initiation, and about the challenge of youth to maturity. A revised version of a *Hippolytos* first presented several years earlier, the *Hippolytos* of 428 appeared a few years before Alcibiades' emergence on the political scene.[64] The drama nevertheless presages many of the themes that would unfold during his career. Although set in Troezen, it concerns a conflict in what might have been seen as the Athenian family *par excellence*, the family of Theseus. Hence, the play is worthy of attention here.[65]

Although conflict between father and son (Theseus and Hippolytos) is an important theme of *Hippolytos*, it is a far cry from similar conflicts in Aristophanes. Hippolytos is no Pheidippides. He is neither decadent nor lazy nor spoiled, but rather an austere and upstanding young man who is apparently dutiful toward his distant father. So it seems at first; in the course of the drama, however, certain similarities between Hippolytos and Pheidippides appear, in terms both of character and of relationship with the father. Like Pheidippides, Hippolytos is devoted to horses (though not particularly to horse-racing). The "child of the horse-loving Amazon" (581), Hippolytos has great familiarity and experience with horses; his very name may mean either "one who binds and loosens horses," "loosened by horses", or "unharnessing horses." Hence the irony of his death in a chariot mishap.[66]

Before their quarrel, it was possible to conceive of feelings of solidarity, duty, and trust between Theseus and his son (308–309, 464–465, 661, 690, 902–903, 1258–1260); Theseus seems to have believed in Hippolytos's piety and excellence before coming to the conclusion that Hippolytos had raped Phaidra (948–957, cf. 1455), and he seems to feel genuine grief at Hippolytos's death when he learns of his innocence (1409–1415). Nevertheless, a history of latent hostility seems likely. An illegitimate child, Hippolytos had been sent from his father's house in Athens to be raised in Troezen by his paternal great-grandfather Pittheus. He seems to have resented his status as a bastard (964–965). As for Theseus, beneath the surface lurks the suspicion that his son is a hot-blooded, randy, and untrustworthy youth (967–970), as attested by Theseus's readiness to believe Phaidra's accusation of rape. Theseus, of course, had been just such a youth himself; he is incapable of fathoming Hippolytos's supposed purity.[67]

In Theseus's eyes, therefore, Hippolytos's professed virtue and piety are nothing but an arrogant fraud, a cover for his lusts (948–951, 955–956). At the same time, however, Theseus concedes that Hippolytos may be genuinely pious, but only as a follower of the Orphic sect, for which Theseus expresses contempt. He accuses his son of practicing vegetarianism, of taking Orpheus as his lord, of celebrating Bacchic rites, and of wasting his time on the hot air of too many books (952–954). Although Hippolytos may have evinced an Orphic's mysticism and concern for purity, as a hunter, Hippolytos could hardly have been a convincing vegetarian; Theseus's gibe, therefore, has something of the force of "you're such a fraud that you don't even eat the meat you kill!" Theseus's outburst is an index of his anger and frustration. A man of action, he had no appreciation of his son's religious and mystic tendencies; to Theseus, such practices probably seemed unmanly if not effeminate. They have, moreover, nothing to do with Phaidra's charge against Hippolytos. It seems likely, therefore, that even before Phaidra's shocking accusation, Theseus had been watching Hippolytos with a wary eye.[68]

Theseus's comments point to the many other indices in the play of Hippolytos's peculiarities. Unlike his father, that democrat and citizen of citizens, Hippolytos is an aristocratic snob who claims to reject the normative Greek path of a political career (986–989). A hunter, a horseman, a "hail-fellow-well-met" type with many friends, Hippolytos was nonetheless the illegitimate and motherless child of an unnatural woman in Athenian eyes – of an Amazon. For all his familiarly Athenian characteristics, in many ways he lived on the margin of civilization.[69]

Recent scholarship has emphasized Hippolytos's rejection of the normal paradigm of an Athenian youth. Most notably, he is proud to be chaste (1003, cf. 14, 102, 106, 1302) with a "maiden soul" (1006) who not only rejects Phaidra's advances but entirely regrets the necessity of sex for procreation (616–627). Male chastity was not a virtue in Athens, for it left a man unfit for the role of procreator and head of the oikos. Hence, Hippolytos's emphatic chastity was a rejection of the normal male role in the oikos. So, for that matter, was his single-minded dedication to hunting. In the ideology of the Athenian male (or at least of the Athenian aristocrat), hunting normally marks the ephebe's passage from boy to man; by refusing to progress beyond the hunting stage, Hippolytos symbolically rejects the passage to manhood.[70]

Hippolytos resists simple mythological analysis: it is clear that a whole complex of mythemes, from the Egyptian tale of the Two Brothers to Potiphar's wife to Hymenaios, are conjoined in his character. One clear strand can, nevertheless, be detected: Hippolytos is one of several examples of "the ephebe gone awry"; like Melanion, Adonis, or Atalanta, Hippolytos flees marriage for the hunt. Like Narcissos, he rejects the knowledge of love that is part of an adolescent's initiation. Like Phaethon, he flees the loss of innocence required by adulthood. Hippolytos and his mythic cognates are all liminal figures who refuse to grow up.[71]

Psychoanalytic critics have reached similar conclusions. Unable to accept the reality of adult sexuality, Hippolytos is permanently stuck in a liminal phase. His sex drive is forced underground by deep Oedipal fear of the father, only to reemerge in repressed form as attachment to a non-threatening virginal goddess. Such critics also point out a paradox whose recognition might have fed the flames of Theseus's anger: simply put, Hippolytos's self-love and indifference to sex only made him more attractive to Phaidra. Not only does Hippolytos reject his father's model of manhood, but the very qualities which so offend Theseus prove seductive to his wife. Hippolytos's narcissism is strangely erotic and charismatic.[72]

Theseus accuses his son of rape, hypocrisy, and an unsavory devotion to a bookish, bacchanalian, and vegetarian cult. A young man in heat is less reliable than a woman, Theseus says (967–969), implying perhaps that Hippolytos's two-faced behavior (a common male slander of women in ancient Greece) and excessive religiosity (also commonly associated with women) were unmanly. As will become clear presently, these are not the only indications of Hippolytos's ambivalent gender.[73]

As for Hippolytos, he requires but little provocation to respond in kind, suggesting a history of hostility to his father, perhaps because of the "natural hostility of a bastard" (964–965). Hippolytos does not respond to Theseus's accusation with modesty, calm, or filial forbearance, but rather, talks back to his father rudely, sharply, and without apology (983–1035). He accuses Theseus of having gone wild with grief over Phaidra (923–924, 934–935). He insults Theseus's manhood, suggesting that he lacks "the guts" (*thumos*, 1086–1087, cf. 1051–1089) to send Hippolytos into exile with his own hands, and noting that he, Hippolytos, would insist on *killing* anyone whom he thought had slept with *his* wife

(1041–1044). Only on Hippolytos's deathbed, and even then only after the intervention of the goddess Artemis (note Hippolytos's accusatory language at 1409–1415), do the two men patch up their quarrel (*neikos*, 1442).[74]

Hippolytos's haughty and insolent tone to his father probably comes as little surprise to the audience. The quality of *semnotês*, which can mean either an august dignity or a dangerous haughtiness, has already emerged as one of his hallmarks, most strikingly in an interchange with a slave early in the play. Not only is Hippolytos untroubled by his slave's warning that he is behaving in a *semnos* (haughty) manner to that *semnos* (august) deity, Aphrodite (93–99), but he dismisses the whole matter by the haughty gesture of telling the slave to fix dinner and tend to the horses (108–113). His arrogance belies his claim of modesty and virtue (*sôphrosunê*, cf. esp. 1363–1367).[75]

Hippolytos's haughtiness, his disrespect toward his father, and his love of horses make him similar not only to Pheidippides but also to Alcibiades.[76] Alcibiades, of course, acquired a reputation for treating his lovers haughtily (Plut. *Alc.* 4.4–5) and for generally being disrespectful to older males. As for horses, he was famous as a horse-breeder and for his accomplishment of entering seven chariot teams and winning three prizes at the Olympic Games of 416.[77]

There are other similarities between Hippolytos and Alcibiades, although there are differences too and, as we shall presently discuss, it is highly unlikely that Euripides is simply identifying the two characters. In the meantime, let us consider the similarities further. Like Alcibiades, Hippolytos is raised in the household of a great political leader (Hippolytos of course is raised not in Athens but in Theseus's extended household in Troezen). Like Pericles, Theseus is sometimes referred to as *tyrannos* (843, 870, 1013). Both men, unlike Hippolytos, were great ladies' men. Like Alcibiades, Hippolytos is perceived as a young man (*neos*, 114, cf. 967, 1343; *huph' hêbê*, 118, cf. 970, 1096) with a young man's fierce emotions (118–119, 967–970). Like Alcibiades, he appears in the company of young men and is sometimes seen as representative of them (967–970, 987); for example, Hippolytos calls on the young men of his age cohort to bid him farewell before exile (1098, cf. 1179–1180). Like Alcibiades (Plut. *Alc.* 10.2–3; Dem. 21.145), Hippolytos is a very good orator (986–989); moreover, he is as ambitious as Alcibiades (Thuc. 6.15.2–4; Plut. *Alc.* 2.1, 6.3), and he aspires to a famous name (1028, 1299) and to first place in the contests of the Greeks (1016). Like Alcibiades (Thuc. 6.89.4–6), Hippolytos disdains the common people (986). Like Alcibiades (Thuc. 6.16), Hippolytos does not hesitate to sing his own praises, announcing that no one will ever find a more *sôphrôn* (prudent, modest, virtuous) man than himself (905, 1035, 1100–1101).[78]

Like Alcibiades, Hippolytos's gender is ambivalent. The sources contain several *mots* to the effect that the bisexual Alcibiades was every wife's husband and every husband's wife. As a boy, when he once resorted to biting to win a wrestling match, Alcibiades was accused of fighting like a woman ("no, like a lion," he supposedly replied; Plut. *Alc.* 2.2). As for Hippolytos, both structuralist and psychoanalytical analyses of Euripides' play emphasize the importance of Hippolytos's unusual feminine characteristics. As the bastard son of a mannish woman, an Amazon, Hippolytos starts off on the wrong foot, symbolically speaking. His extraordinary emphasis on hunting and horses recalls his Amazon mother more than his Greek father. His aspirations to be a virgin (*parthenos*) are more proper to a female than a male in Greek culture. His activity of picking flowers for Artemis in an inviolate meadow calls to mind a female image: Kore, daughter of Demeter. Hence, although Alcibiades and Hippolytos both exhibit masculine prowess, they each have certain feminine characteristics that make them ambivalent and abnormal characters in Athenian eyes.[79]

The similarity of misfortune between Hippolytos and Alcibiades may be even more striking. Both men offend goddesses: Alcibiades insults Demeter and Kore; Hippolytos offends the goddess Aphrodite. Both Alcibiades (Thuc. 6.27.2, 53.1) and Hippolytos (1050) are branded with the charge of impiety. Both men are driven into exile from their fatherland, "famous Athens" (1094). What the chorus says of Hippolytos could equally be said of Alcibiades: "we see the brightest star of Athena Hellanias banished . . . to another land" (1121–1125). True, Alcibiades, unlike Hippolytos, was not banished "by a father's anger" (1124), but he was banished by men of his father's generation who saw him as a dangerous youth.

Did Euripides model Hippolytos on Alcibiades? Perhaps in part, but only in part, since Hippolytos's personal qualities may have been shared widely among Athens's elite youth. In addition, the date of the play – 428 BC – not to mention an even earlier date for the original *Hippolytos*, imposes substantial cautions on this argument. In any case tragedians do not "model" their dramatic creations on real characters without considerable revisions. In 428, Alcibiades was at the beginning of his political career. Alcibiades' Olympic victories, his impiety, and his exile were far off in the future. To a large extent, therefore, Hippolytos must be independent of Alcibiades. On the other hand, Alcibiades was in his early twenties in 428. He was already well known as an obstreperous teenager, imperious to his lovers and often troublesome to his late guardian, Pericles. Indeed, he was already conspicuous as a lover of Socrates in the 430s, both in Athens and on campaign at Potidaea. In Aristophanes' *Banqueters* of 427, a father blames Alcibiades for his profligate son's overly refined speech (frg. 1205 Kassel and Austin); the same play lampoons Alcibiades' erotic appetite (frg. 244 Kassel and Austin) and perhaps his sophistic arguments (frg. 206 Kassel and Austin). All of this suggests that in 428 Alcibiades was well known and influential, a "role model" – albeit a bad one – for youth. Hence, Euripides' portrait of Hippolytos as the shining and talented youth who quarrels with his father may reflect something of Alcibiades.[80]

The picture is more complex, however, for certain of Hippolytos's qualities are anything but Alcibiadean. Unlike Alcibiades, Hippolytos emphatically rejects the notion of a political career in the city. He refuses to be clever (*kompsos*, 986) in speaking before a "mob" (*ochlos*, 986), although he admits to a reputation for wisdom among a small group of men of his own age (*eis hêlikas de kôligous sophôteros*, 987): words evoking contemporary Athenian politics. Hippolytos's self-deprecation as an orator is a variation on the "unaccustomed as I am to public speaking" motif, a common theme in Athenian public speeches. "Mob" was a standard oligarchic complaint about the assembly. Withdrawal from democratic politics into the small, age-graded groups of the *hetairiai* was a stance taken by some young aristocrats of the 420s. *Sophôteros* (followed by *en sophois*, 988) suggests the intellectual world of the sophists and their young aristocratic students. The overall picture is of a contemporary youth much like Alcibiades except for the refusal to plunge into the hurly-burly of democratic politics.[81]

There are other differences between the two men as well. As Socrates' companion, Alcibiades was not ignorant of philosophy, but he showed no signs of Hippolytos's mystic and meditative sides. Unlike Alcibiades, who parodied the Eleusinian Mysteries of Demeter, Hippolytos devotes a trip to Athens to being initiated into the Mysteries (25); his identification with Kore has already been noted. Most important, the quality on which Hippolytos prides himself above all is the quality in which Alcibiades displays the least possible interest: chastity. Alcibiades was the bisexual lover who in 428 was well on his way to amassing many and far-flung amorous conquests.

An Alcibiades figure and also an anti-Alcibiades figure; what, finally, is the significance of Euripides' Hippolytos? If we leave aside the matter of exact models, if we recall the multivalent nature of characters in complex poetry, and if we assume that Euripides was sketching not specifically Alcibiades in the character of Hippolytos but a more general Athenian type of whom Alcibiades was but one incarnation, then Euripides' Hippolytos takes on considerable significance as an Athenian cultural paradigm.[82] Hippolytos is a promising and talented young man who is destroyed by a quarrel with the older generation in which both parties misbehave: Theseus's jealousy is matched by Hippolytos's arrogance and implacability. In the end the young man is doomed to die and the old man to mourn his loss.

The differences between Hippolytos and Alcibiades are considerable, but in structural terms, the underlying similarities are even greater. Both men are perceived as impure and polluted: Hippolytos because of his alleged rape of Phaidra (946), Alcibiades because of his alleged profanation of the Mysteries. Both men represent impurity and pollution in the fundamental sense defined by Mary Douglas, that is, "matter out of place." The particular matter that Alcibiades and Hippolytos each wrenches out of place is that of age gradation. Hippolytos threatens civilized order by refusing to acknowledge the power of eros and thereby to pass from adolescence to adult manhood: to pass from the boy who yokes horses to the man who yokes maidens, as Zeitlin puts it. Alcibiades threatens Athenian civilization by threatening to replace the rule of elders with the rule of young men, to replace laws with unfettered eros, to replace *dêmokratia* with tyranny. Neither man recognizes the right relationship of youth and age.[83]

In the context of the 420s, the fate of Hippolytos is a reminder of the congenital inability of ancient Greek culture to integrate the genius of youth into a society governed by mature men. Hippolytos is far from the first instance of such a pattern in Greek culture. For Hippolytos read Achilles, for Theseus read Agamemnon, and a series of similarities becomes apparent. For that matter, the quarrel between Hippolytos and Theseus recalls the subterranean tension between Theseus and his father Aigeus. Nor was the notion that the most prominent man must be driven into exile foreign to Athenian culture: consider the institution of ostracism. In mythic terms, Hippolytos might call to mind such diverse but paradigmatic cases of asocial behavior as Adonis, Phaethon, and the Amazons, all of them symbols of liminality, of a failed adolescent initiation, of the refusal to mature.[84]

The story of Hippolytos and Theseus might possibly also call to mind another bit of contemporary gossip beside the case of Alcibiades: the quarrel between the (in 428) recently deceased Pericles and his son Xanthippos. As leaders of Athens and "tyrants," Pericles and Theseus have obvious similarities. Hippolytos ("unharnessing horses") and Xanthippos ("chestnut horse") have similar names, although admittedly hippos-names are common in the Athenian upper classes. The troubles of both households are sometimes ascribed to an inherited curse: that of Theseus and Hippolytos is nameless (820, 1379–1380), that of Pericles and his son the curse of the Alkmeonids (e.g. Thuc. 1.126–127). The main similarity, however, is in a quarrel over women, with the generations playing reversed roles. Theseus accuses his son of sleeping with his stepmother; Xanthippos accused his father of sleeping with his daughter-in-law, Xanthippos's wife (Plut. Per. 13.16, 36.6; Ath. 13.589d–e). Both sons, Hippolytos and Xanthippos, quarreled bitterly with their fathers (Plut. Per. 36.2–6). Both fathers, Theseus and Pericles, saw their sons die before them (Plut. Per. 36.6–9). Finally, it should also be noted that both Theseus and Pericles had a well-loved illegitimate son (in Pericles' case it was his son Pericles, Plut. Per. 37) in addition to their legitimate children. Hence, the action of Euripides' Hippolytos might conceivably be taken by the audience as referring not only to myth and epic but to the history of the house of their only recently deceased great leader, Pericles.[85]

The story of Euripides' Hippolytos can be fruitfully considered an example of Victor Turner's social drama: the notion that political conflicts, like dramas, pass through ritualized and culture-specific stages which are implicit in the minds of the actors.[86] In Turner's terms, Hippolytos and Theseus based their behavior, both consciously and unconsciously, on such "social dramas" as the Iliad, the myth of Adonis, and the subterranean tension between Theseus and Aigeus. Hippolytos recapitulates such profoundly resonant themes of Greek culture as the youth who threatens paternal authority, the adolescent who rejects initiation into adulthood, the dangerous man of unusual (in this case, wrongly focused) eroticism, the polluted leader who must be expelled, and the dying god.

In like manner, the interplay between Alcibiades and the Athenian people was based on preexisting cultural paradigms, so many of them summed up in the drama of Hippolytos and Theseus. Turner's notion might help us better to understand how Euripides' *Hippolytos* seems to presage Alcibiades' fate over a decade later. It might also help to confirm that sense that a reader of Thucydides may have that Alcibiades and his behavior were no accident. Alcibiades was the product, perhaps even the inevitable product, of Athenian culture: the brilliant son who quarrels over private matters with his father or with someone *in loco parentis* and hence destroys his public career, the youth who must die, the eternal adolescent, the dangerous man of unusual (in this case, excessive) eroticism, the polluted leader. If the cliché be permitted, we might say that if Alcibiades had not existed, the Athenians would have had to invent him.[87]

CONCLUSION

This chapter has covered disparate material, but what each section has in common, in addition to the themes of father–son and intergenerational relations in the 420s, is the figure of Alcibiades. The son of Kleinias and ward of Pericles surely stands for the rebellious youth and disobedient sons of Athens if anyone does. Not that Alcibiades – in either his wealth, status, talent, ambition, or career trajectory – was typical, even of the narrow and interlocking Athenian elites of birth, wealth, and education. The typical Athenian of the elite, if one existed, might have been some virtual supernumerary like Glaukon son of Ariston or Kharmides son of Aristoteles, and the "ordinary Athenian" of the masses perhaps survives as an individual merely as a name on a humble grave stele.[88]

Alcibiades was less the typical than the extreme case; the man who impressed his contemporaries for carrying youthful assertiveness to the limit, for acting out widespread fantasies. To be sure, Alcibiades never pushed those tendencies as far as they might have gone. He might have wanted to become a tyrant, but he never did. He might have struck his teachers, mistreated his lovers, and asked his guardian Pericles difficult and uppity questions, but he never struck him. Alcibiades, in short, was not Pheidippides, nor was he Haimon, nor was he Hippolytos, nor was he Adonis. He was not even Euthyphro, who supposedly hauled his father into court on a murder charge against a slave (Pl. *Euthphr.* 4a–e). What Alcibiades was, however, was a "youth" (ideologically if not chronologically speaking) who seemed to have the potential to turn into all of those characters. As such, he put on an extraordinarily appealing mask in the Athenian social drama. He and all the other lesser Alcibiades of his generation would find, however, that the same role that established their popularity also guaranteed their ultimate destruction. Athenian fathers enjoyed the spectacle of their sons pushing the potential of youth far beyond the point that they had in their own day; they even enjoyed the mixture of admiration and fear that they felt at watching their sons challenge their authority. All the more dramatic and awful the restoration of paternal authority in the final scene.

The hour of the son seemed glorious but it had within it the seeds of its own destruction. It was fundamentally unstable because Athenian admiration for youthful vigor was outstripped by the reassuring quality of paternal power. In the face of a radical decline in the fortunes of the polis, Athenians could not afford the indulgence of placing power in the hands of youth. Indeed, the destruction of the Sicilian Expedition in 413 brought with it a turn away from the fascination with youth that had marked the previous decade, and a turn back to the authority of the father. Age and maturity became the preferred qualities of the day. The *patrios politeia* – the "ancestral," "traditional," or "paternal" constitution – became a ubiquitous slogan at all points on the political spectrum. The campaign to restore Athens's traditional/paternal/*patrios* virtues gave rise to an oligarchic movement and to two prolonged *coups d'état* (in 411 and 404–403). It also left its mark on democratic politics. Any public figure who could be depicted as a threat to Athenian fatherhood was in grave danger. Andokides survived an attempt to tar him with this brush in his trial of 400; in his trial of 399, Socrates did not. He was condemned and executed on formal charges of challenging traditional religion and corrupting the youth – the latter including a commonly held notion that Socrates turned sons away from their fathers. Socrates' association with Alcibiades hardly helped him any at his trial.[89]

To sum up, the social drama of Athens in the Peloponnesian War era is characterized by the rule of a stern father who is deposed and replaced by an over-indulged and rebellious son of tyrannical, dangerous, and seductive passions. After giving the son great power, however, the people repent, destroy him, and attempt to reimpose the rule of a father.

The question of why the people repent is not easy to answer; let us venture two possibilities. First, the notion of the sacrifice of a young man is present in a whole complex of myths such as the stories of Adonis and Hippolytos. It may be, as Burkert has argued, that the sacrifice of these consorts or habitués of goddesses is meant to symbolize the contrast between male aggression, whose contribution to society is hunting and killing, and female fertility, whose contribution to society is procreation. In this vein, one could argue that the demos only gave Alcibiades his exalted position as ephebe *extraordinaire* – as the epitome of warlike aggression – in order to have a better victim to sacrifice to the gods.[90]

The second suggestion comes from a comparison of Alcibiades and Theseus. As our examination of Theseus in Chapter 4 showed, it was precisely the ambiguity of his rebelliousness that made him such a popular figure in Athens. Although his *actions* were patricidal, Theseus's *words* were filial obedience itself. Now, Alcibiades was aware of the need to temper his rebellious actions, as demonstrated by his conciliatory words about harmonizing age and youth at the assembly debate over Sicily in 415 (Thuc. 6.18.6). By his open ambition and by the indulgences of his private life, however, Alcibiades walked a very narrow line between rebellion and obedience; the scandals of 415 pushed him over the edge. Although he may have matched Theseus in cunning, Alcibiades fell short in self-control.

After Sicily, therefore, Athenians attempted to restore the ideology of paternal authority. Once destroyed, however, authority is not easily restored without a reinforcing show of force. As it turned out, the restoration of the Athenian *patrios politeia* required not merely the exile of Alcibiades and the execution of Socrates, but a civil war (in 404–403) and numerous other executions and decrees of exile. Such extreme actions were uncomfortably common in Athens in the last decade of the fifth and first decade of the fourth centuries BC: from the trial of the generals after Arginusae in 406, to the trial of Adeimantos in 393 on a charge of treason at Aegospotami in 405, to the exile or execution of numerous Athenian public figures during the Corinthian War. So stern were the means of restoring the firm, ruling hand of the Athenian father.[91]

6

THE RETURN OF THE FATHER, 413–399 BC

If a son has struck his father, they shall cut off his hand.
Code of Hammurabi

A country that sustains a major defeat, especially if it had started from a position of seemingly unassailable strength, tends to ask "why?" and "who?" and "how?" Athens in 413 was such a nation. The Sicilian Expedition had ended in disaster: it drained the treasury, wrecked the fleet, tipped the balance of power in the Aegean far enough for Persia to enter the war on Sparta's side and for many Athenian allies to revolt. Above all, the enormous loss of life might have seemed like a blood sacrifice of Athens's young men. A reasonable estimate is that close to 10,000 if not more Athenian citizens, out of a total citizen population of some 30,000 to 40,000, died in Sicily. If Pericles could have said of the heavy casualties after the reduction of Samos in 439 that it was as if the spring had been taken out of the year, what *mot* could his successors have possibly found to do justice to the losses in Sicily?[1]

Aristophanes' *Lysistrata* of 411 expresses in dramatic form some of the sentiments of loss. The play presents an image of Athens populated mainly by women and weak old men. "There isn't a man in the land," as Lysistrata complains, because the men are all off at war (Ar. *Lys.* 523). In the comedy the young men eventually come back and everyone lives happily ever after, but there is an undercurrent of recognition that reality was much less pleasant. When the chorus of old men complains that the women are meddling in public affairs, the chorus of women replies:

Do not begrudge me if I have been born a woman
So long as I have something to contribute to the current
circumstances.

179

I claim a share in public service, because I contribute men –
Something to which you wretched old men have no claim,
Since you have spent the so-called contribution of our
  grandfathers
From the Persian War era without paying any of it back.
Moreover, we've come close to being destroyed by you.

(Ar. Lys. 648–655)

Women contribute young men to Athens and old men use them up.[2]

Not everyone would have agreed, however, that the blame for Sicily should be laid on the shoulders of the old. Rather, a good case could be made for saying that the death of so many young men had been caused by "youth and folly" – to use a phrase that Andokides applies to his involvement in the mutilation of the Herms in 415 (*neotêtês te kai anoia*, Andok. 2.7). In 415 young men, not old men, had been the most enthusiastic supporters of the Sicilian campaign. Alcibiades, its chief proponent, was in many ways the embodiment of youth. The mutilation of the Herms, which cast a shadow of doubt over the expedition, had the feel of a youthful prank, however serious its purpose.[3]

From the nadir of 413 it might have seemed as if Athens's troubles could all be traced to the disobedience of youth. The Athenian religious calendar annually celebrated a day of role reversal, the Kronia: masters waited on slaves, just as if Kronos, the father who had been deposed by his son Zeus, had regained power and turned things topsy-turvy. Perhaps the Sicilian Expedition seemed in retrospect like a prolonged Kronia that had gotten out of hand. One could argue that in 415 the young of Athens, led by Alcibiades, had reversed roles with their elders, led by Nicias. The result was an anarchic and bloody adventure that lost all sense of restraint, and in which the Syracusans exchanged places with the Athenians. From the Athenian point of view, the only remedy was to restore the rightful masters to power, both at home and abroad.[4]

For many Athenians, therefore, the answer to the question of what caused the Sicilian disaster, and the Athenian weakness and defeat which eventually followed, might have been: an overdose of youth. The logical consequence would be to stop indulging Athenian youth and to reassert the power of the older generation. Perhaps the logic had a physical correlative in the relative absence of young Athenians after the Sicilian casualties. Athens might have suddenly seemed like a city with more fathers than sons.

In 413 BC a man who had been in his twenties at the beginning of the Peloponnesian War in 431 was now approaching the age of forty. By the end of the war in 404, he would be nearly fifty. Alcibiades, for example, born in about 451, was about 26 in 425, about 38 in 413, and about 47 in 404. Andokides was about forty at the war's end, Theramenes perhaps about the same, Kritias in his fifties. In other words, the generation of youth that had come to power in the 420s was no longer young. Its hold on power was still likely to be considerable between 413 and 404, especially considering the relative absence then of men in their twenties as a result of heavy casualties. The "graying" of the youths of the Archidamian War will not in itself explain the ideological shift after 415 from youth to maturity and from father to son, but it may have been a contributing factor.[5]

REFOUNDING FATHERS

In Athens, the decade following the Sicilian disaster was a period of reform, revolution, and restoration. Athenians were divided, sharply and at times violently, among loosely constituted factions of oligarchs, democrats, and middle-of-the-roaders. The one thing virtually everyone agreed on, however, was that his particular blueprint for a new and better Athens would really be just a return to the traditional order. As in other periods of change and disorder (the Augustan principate, the Protestant Reformation, Khomeini's Iran) revolutionaries tried to convince others and perhaps themselves that they were really seeking only to restore the past. The watchwords of the day in Athens between 413 and 403 were *ta patria*, *patrioi nomoi*, and especially *patrios politeia*: respectively, "the ancestral ways" (literally, "the ancestral things"), "ancestral laws," and "ancestral constitution," to use the most common English translations.[6]

The standard translations no doubt convey the meanings that most Athenians derived from these terms most of the time. It should be noted that *patrios* could also be rendered as "of our forefathers," which would yield, respectively, "the ways of our forefathers," "laws of our forefathers," and "our forefathers' constitution." Moreover, given the derivation of *patrios* from *patêr*, it is intriguing to consider a literal connotation of each term, something along the order of: "the ways of the father," "laws of the father," and "constitution of the father." I would not suggest that these connotations were uppermost in Athenian minds; *patrios* usually meant something more abstract and less immediate, that is, it meant "ancestral." By 413, however, after years of witnessing powerful images of filial disrespect and intergenerational conflict on the public stage, any connotation of "father" in a term of political discourse is likely to have been strong and evocative. An Athenian hearing in 411 that so-and-so advocated the *patrios politeia* did not take that to mean that so-and-so literally wanted to make his or anyone else's father the leader of Athens. The auditor might take the term to mean, however, that paternal symbolism was an important part of what so-and-so had in mind. The *patrios politeia* was a symbolic statement about using an image of the Athenian past as an authority for the present. The past was, as it were, a *patêr*, who would guide his wayward sons.[7]

In a putative Athenian assembly speech probably written in the period 411–403, the sophist Thrasymakhos comments:

> I wish I had lived in those olden times when the young men could remain silent because affairs did not require public discussion and the old men were administering the state correctly.... There is an uproar over the ancestral constitution (*patrios politeia*) which is in fact easy to understand and which all citizens have in common.
>
> (Thrasymakhos, Diels and Kranz 85 B frg. 1,
> tr. Finley [1975 (1971)] 37)

As Thrasymakhos's statement indicates, to advocate a return to the *patrios politeia* was to call not only for a regime of old, but for a regime in which old men ruled and young men remained silent. This was an implicit attack on the contemporary state of affairs in Athens, in which relatively young men did have a considerable say in politics. It was easy enough, for example, to blame the failure in Sicily on the young: on Alcibiades, on the young proponents of the expedition in the assembly of 415, even on the young mutilators of the Herms. In other words, the *patrios politeia* was a paternal regime in two ways. First, it used the authority of tradition as a quasi-parental corrective of current misbehavior. Second, it took power away from young men and returned it to old men – to the generation of their fathers.[8]

Symbolically, therefore, *patrios politeia* was the rule of the fathers (*pateres*) and of the elders (*presbuteroi*). Other evidence indicates that this equation, made by Thrasymakhos, was widespread. Eupolis's comedy *Demes*, for example, which probably dates to 412 or 411, makes such an equation. Although extensive fragments remain, the plot and most of the characters are still hazy. It is clear enough that ghosts of Athens's great leaders of the past (Miltiades, Pericles, Aristides, Solon, and possibly others) appear to offer advice to a foundering city. The play compares Athens's once-great leaders with "today's new breed of scoundrel" (frg. 99.116 Kassel and Austin, cf. frgs. 99.47–48, 101.6). It is noteworthy, incidentally, that politicians who advocated the *patrios politeia* around this time also often personified their admiration for the past. For example, the mandate to a legislative commission of 411 speaks of searching out the *patrioi nomoi* of Kleisthenes and apparently of Solon too (Arist. *Ath. Pol.* 29.2). The Teisamenos Decree of 403, specifying that Athens be governed "according to the ancestral ways" (*kata ta patria*), mentions Draco as well as Solon (Andok. 1.83). Hence, both playwright and politicians were nostalgic not just for the past abstractly but for its specific great leaders.[9]

Inevitably, the shades of the great men of old who appear in Eupolis's play become something of father-figures. First of all, their maturity stands in contrast to the childishness of the current crop of leaders. "Not for the child public affairs" (*mê paidi ta koina*), as one fragment says (frg. 133 Kassel and Austin), punning on the well-known expression, "not for the child the knife" (Photius *Lex.* 267.18). One character says, addressing heroes of old,

> Commander Miltiades and Pericles,
> don't let those young degenerates (*meirakia kinoumena*) rule
>   any longer,
> who let the generalship drag about their ankles.

(frg. 104 Kassel and Austin)

Several fragments (e.g. 129, 131, possibly 101.5–6 Kassel and Austin) make the point of how much better Athens was in the old days; as one of the risen heroes is told:

> [Right away] you will recognize how much [worse]
> [in every way] the demes are now disposed
> [than when] you and Solon used to rule over
> that youth, that intelligence and mind.

(frg. 99.45–49 Kassel and Austin)

Moreover, the difference between the generations of father and son seems to have been a motif of the play. Three fragments take up the theme of the Athenian leader whose sons were not as good as him: Aristides, Pericles, and the general Hippokrates (killed at Delium in 424), perhaps a more general comment on Athenian decline (frgs. 111, 112, 127 Kassel and Austin). Another fragment compares the magnitude of Miltiades' victory at Marathon to a very large sacrifice by a father on the occasion of enrolling his teenage son in his phratry – so large that all other such sacrifices seem too little by comparison (frg. 130 Kassel and Austin). Miltiades is thus a kind of founding father of Athenian manhood whose achievements are unparalleled.[10]

As Eupolis's great men and as the references in decrees to Solon *et al.* show, advocates of the *patrios politeia* did not leave things in the abstract, but identified the *pateres* (fathers) directly and sometimes quite visibly. After the end of the Peloponnesian War in 403, to take another example, when democracy was restored and a new codification of the ancestral laws (*patrioi nomoi*) had been prepared, the assembly voted to inscribe the code on a wall of the Royal Stoa in the Athenian agora (Andok. 1.84). This was the same place where Solon's legislation had been stored nearly two centuries previously (Arist. *Ath. Pol.* 7.1). Hence, the democrats vividly identified themselves with the *patrios politeia* and made themselves its perpetuators. At the same time, the assembly voted that any additional proposed laws had to be displayed in writing near the statues of the Eponymous Heroes (Andok. 1.83). Since the Heroes personified Athenians' mythical forefathers, the assembly required that amendments, like the code as a whole, seek the sanctity of tradition. (A more prosaic motive, of course, was the prominent position of these statues in the agora.) The Eponymous Heroes, too, personified *patrios politeia*.[11]

Another example of enthusiasm for rule by older men is that of the *probouloi*, "preliminary counselors" whose office was created in 413. The *probouloi* were ten magistrates, chosen one per tribe, whose purpose was to stabilize and check the activities of the council and assembly in the post-Sicilian crisis. The creation of the office is evidence of how severe the crisis was perceived to be. Each *proboulos* had to be over forty years of age (Arist. *Ath. Pol.* 29.2). Thucydides describes the *probouloi* as "a certain magistracy of elder men (*presbuteroi andres*) . . . who would take initial discussions about current events as occasion should arise" (8.1.3). In his opinion, the demos needed such firm, guiding hands. He describes the Athenian people as one caught up in a momentary panic (8.1.4). He uses the verb *sôphronizô*, "to control," "to chastise," to describe their concurrent financial cutbacks; the implication, perhaps, is that the childlike Athenian people required guidance from elder men if it was to survive its panic (8.1.3).[12]

The equation of old age and the heroes of old is achieved in the persons of the two *probouloi* whose names are known to us. Both were older men with strong connections to Pericles, that hero of the generation of the fathers of the young men of 413: Hagnon, who was about 57 in 413, and Sophocles the playwright, who was about 84. They seem to sum up the way that the rule by the old might return Athens to the glories of old; the way that rule by fathers (*pateres*) might return Athens to the glory of the forefathers (*pateres*).[13]

Patrios politeia and its cognate terms were probably the predominant political theme of 411, a year in which Athens experienced two oligarchies (the Four Hundred and the Five Thousand) before the eventual restoration of democracy. With commissions at work for most of the years from 411 to 399 whose job was to coordinate the previously disorganized collection of Athenian laws and to publish authoritative texts of the ancestral laws (*patrioi nomoi*), the theme remained alive. It continued to be a subject of great interest during the revolutionary times following Athens's defeat in the Peloponnesian War. The peace treaty negotiated with Sparta in 404 specified that Athens be governed according to the *patrios politeia* (Arist. *Ath. Pol.* 34.3; Diod. 14.3.2). The three main political tendencies in Athens at the time – oligarchic, democratic, and middle-of-the-road – each advocated its own version of *patrios politeia* (Arist. *Ath. Pol.* 34.3; cf. Diod. 14.3.3, 14.3.6). When they first came into office in 404, the Thirty, which would develop into a narrow oligarchy, received a mandate to "compose the ancestral laws (*patrioi nomoi*) under which to govern" (Xen. *Hell.* 2.3.2). When democracy was restored at the end of 403, the assembly voted that "the Athenians should be governed according to the ancestral ways (*kata ta patria*)" (Andok. 1.83). The search for the *patrios politeia* was thus a leitmotif of the period.[14]

While advocates of *patrios politeia* looked to the Athenian past for guidance, the Spartan present – or at least the self-image which the secretive Spartans presented to the rest of Greece – might provide inspiration for would-be oligarchs. Spartan society was renowned for the obedience of youth to older men, as well as for the ability of older male citizens to act as quasi-father to younger citizens who were not their sons or even their kin (Xen. *Lac. Pol.* 6.1–2). As Athens's fortunes in the Peloponnesian War fell and Sparta's rose, Athenian oligarchs were ever more impressed with Sparta as a social and political model. Spartan respect for paternal authority may have been part of the discourse of *patrios politeia* as far as Athenian oligarchs were concerned.[15]

The debate over the *patrios politeia* is interesting for its own sake, not least because of the light it sheds on Appadurai's dictum that the past is "a scarce resource," and hence something to be fought over. What makes the debate particularly interesting for us, however, is the way it stands in counterpoint to the imagery of the 420s or that of the even more recent assembly debate on the Sicilian Expedition in 415. It is understandable that a society that undergoes a defeat as severe as Athens's defeat in Sicily should become preoccupied with the past, promising as it might both an explanation of what went wrong and an ostensibly solid and unchanging blueprint for the future. The *patrios politeia* debate cannot be understood in its fullness, however, without considering the prominence of youth and disobedient sons in Athens during the previous decade or so.[16]

The *patrios politeia* was a sharp retort to the pretensions of young men and of independent-minded sons in the days before the Sicilian disaster, when Athens was still riding high. It was a way of saying that the tide had turned, that the season of youth was over, that the strong arm of the father would be called on to restore order. Solon, Kleisthenes, Pericles – the elders who were the *probouloi* – these were the heroes of the *patrios politeia*, not Alcibiades.

This is not to say that youth in general or Alcibiades in particular entirely ceased to have their charms for the Athenian public. The chorus of support for the *patrios politeia* was not universal, and even if it had been, the appeal of youth was too deep a part of the Athenian character to be wiped out by the Sicilian disaster. Alcibiades, for instance, managed to bounce back from exile (in 413) and collaboration with Sparta and Persia (413–411) to lead the Athenian fleet to victory in the Aegean (411–407) and then make a triumphal return to Athens (408), only to be forced into a new exile when he irresponsibly left the fleet in the hands of an inexperienced crony, who was defeated by Sparta (407). In spite of it all, Alcibiades continued to have a place not only in Athenian demonology but in Athenian hearts. As late as 405, he could still inspire this famous comment from Aristophanes in *Frogs*: "It [i.e. the demos] longs for him, detests him, but wants to have him" (Ar. *Frogs* 1425). Another well-known reference to Alcibiades in *Frogs* is Aristophanes' characterization of him as a lion reared in the *polis* (*leonta ...'n polei trephein*, 1431). In 405, Alcibiades was about forty-five, a father himself, and by no stretch of the imagination young anymore, and yet the emphasis is still upon his *rearing*. For the Athenians, it appears, Alcibiades would always be their son.[17]

Still, Alcibiades may have been an exceptional case. A reputation as a disobedient son was a dangerous thing in Athens at the end of the Peloponnesian War era. Not that it would have been helpful in the 420s, but what might have elicited merely a wink, nod, or groan then could now get a man into much deeper trouble. Consider the trial of Andokides in 400.

ANDOKIDES, HIS FATHER, AND HIS FATHERLAND

Compared to the trial of Socrates in 399 BC, which is one of the best-known events of European history, the trial of Andokides in 400 is a mere footnote (although it too involves the issues of impiety and the aftermath of defeat and civil war). Nevertheless, the case of Andokides has much to teach the historian. As often in Attic forensic oratory, Andokides's defense depends not only on his own (slanted) presentation of the facts, but on his attempt to present himself to the judges as a man of noble character. In pursuit of this end he mixes a generally ordinary and unsophisticated style with occasional and melodramatic borrowings from the vocabulary and narrative structure of tragedy: he attempts to endow his life story with the gravity of a tragic protagonist's dilemma. Andokides presents himself as a good citizen, a good friend, and – most interesting for our purposes – a good son. Andokides boldly manipulates the symbols of father and fatherland and skillfully deflects his opponents' allegations that he has trampled on *patêr*, *patris*, and *patrios nomos*. Andokides's rhetoric is thus an important datum in the study of Athenian paternal–filial ideology in the years after the Peloponnesian War.[18]

The main source of evidence for the trial is Andokides' defense speech, *On the Mysteries*. The survival of this text makes it possible to examine Andokides' defense strategy *in toto*, apart of course from an analysis of his rhetorical gestures. An analysis of the prosecution's strategy must be somewhat more speculative, although we are not completely in the dark. A cautious reconstruction can be made on the basis of Andokides' statements. Moreover, Lysias 6: *Against Andokides* has also survived. This text purports to be part of a speech made in support of the main prosecutor, Kephisios; most scholars today are inclined to accept the text as one indeed written on the occasion of the prosecution of Andokides, although it may have been a pamphlet that circulated at the time rather than a speech delivered at the trial. The author claims to belong to the Eumolpidai family, which provided priests for the Eleusinian Mysteries (Lys. 6.54); he certainly comes across as a religious zealot. There are strong, if not certain, grounds for identifying the speaker as Meletos, one of Kephisios's three supporting prosecutors (along with Agyrrhios and Epikhares) and allegedly the man who arrested Leon of Salamis under the Thirty (Andok. 1.94). He is perhaps the same Meletos who co-prosecuted Socrates in 399, but a firm identification is impossible. Other evidence for Andokides' trial includes a few relevant comments in Andokides' earlier speech *On His Return* (Andok. 2.6–9, 15, 23, 25–26), accounts in Thucydides (6.60.1–3) and Plutarch (*Alc.* 21.1–6) of the events of 415, and scholarly compilations of later centuries (especially *The Life of Andokides* and Tzetzes' *Historia* 49). Much can be said, therefore, about both prosecution and defense.[19]

The trial itself was quite complex and is not easy to summarize. The immediate, underlying issue, according to Andokides, was a quarrel between himself and Kallias son of Hipponikos (Andok. 1.117–123). Kin by marriage, both men were members of the Athenian elite. Their quarrel concerned money and the hand of a woman, one of the daughters of a certain deceased Epilykos, who brought with her his estate. Andokides wanted the bride for himself, Kallias for his son Hipponikos. As both men were related to Epilykos, each had a claim to the heiress (*epiklêros*).[20]

Threatened by a lawsuit from Andokides, Kallias allegedly acted first (Andok. 1.121). He arranged for Kephisios and his co-prosecutors to accuse Andokides of having illegally participated in the just-ended Eleusinian Mysteries (autumn 400). The official charge was an *endeixis*, that is, a charge of having exercised a right to which the acccused was not entitled; the broader moral, if possibly not legal, implication was impiety (Andok. 1.71–72, 121). The reason why Kallias could challenge Andokides' right to attend the Mysteries turns on events that transpired fifteen years earlier, in spring 415. Before turning to the intricate and much-debated narrative of that year, let us briefly note a pre-trial maneuver tried by the prosecutors.[21]

Kallias claimed that ancestral law (*nomos patrios*) had been violated by someone who had left a suppliant's bough on the altar of the Eleusinion (a temple at Athens associated with the Eleusinian cult) during the Eleusinian festival (Andok. 1.110–116). As a member of the family of the Kerykes, one of the two families who administered the Mysteries, Kallias brought this matter to the attention of the council. He did so in a scene of high drama, at the annual meeting of the council in the Eleusinion on the day after the celebration of the Mysteries. Dressed in his ceremonial robes, Kallias denounced the alleged culprit: Andokides. The penalty, Kallias claimed, was death, according to *patrios nomos*. High theater, but Kallias was not able to prove Andokides' guilt. His invocation of *patrios nomos*, moreover, was challenged by a reference to an officially inscribed law of Athens, which set a stiff fine, and not death, as the penalty. So Kallias and his colleagues were left with the charge of impiety, which brings us to the events of 415.[22]

Andokides had become notorious for his alleged role in 415 in the mutilation of the Herms and the parodying of the Eleusinian Mysteries, those two scandals that preceded the sailing of the Sicilian Expedition (Andok. 1.11–70, 2.6–9, 15, 23, 25–26; Thuc. 6.60.1–3; Plut. *Alc.* 21.1–6; Ps.-Plut. *Vita Andok.* 834). The facts are neither simple nor clear, and all too dependent on Andokides' highly tendentious accounts. It seems likely that Andokides was part of the initial plot to mutilate the Herms, though probably, as he claims, he did not take part in the deed itself (Andok. 1.61–64). There is good reason to think that he had participated in a parody of the Mysteries too. It is certain that Andokides was arrested and imprisoned (though whether on a charge of parodying the Mysteries as well as mutilating the Herms is disputed) and that in return for confessing his guilt and turning state's evidence, he was granted immunity and released from jail, while those he named were charged with having mutilated the Herms. Some fled, others were captured, tried, and executed (Andok. 1.60–68, 2.23; Thuc. 6.60.2–3; Plut. *Alc.* 21.2–4).

Andokides could not hide the fact that he informed on his fellow *hetairoi*, but the charges also arose – perhaps in 415, perhaps later – that he had informed on his kinsmen too, and even on his father, Leogoras (Andok. 1.52–53, 67; Lys. 6.23; Ps.-Plut. *Vita Andok.* 834e; Tzetzes *Historia* 49 = Chiliades 6.367–375). Andokides vehemently denied having denounced his father (Andok. 1.19–24). It seems likely that Leogoras was accused of both the mutilation and the parody in 415 (Andok. 1.17, 47). He was imprisoned but managed to gain his freedom and survive; Andokides takes credit for the outcome, but skepticism is in order (Andok. 1.48–68, 2.7–8).[23]

As a result of his immunity, Andokides avoided the prosecution, execution, or exile that others suffered in 415, but he incurred enormous opprobrium (see Andok. 2.6–7). As the speaker of *Against Andokides* says, Andokides was the man who reached the limits of shame by informing on his family and friends (Lys. 6.23). Andokides was castigated as the kind of man who, rather than follow the standard Greek dictum of "help your friends, hurt your enemies," followed the rule of not hurting his enemies but doing all the hurt he could to his friends (Lys. 6.7)![24]

It was probably this kind of opprobrium that led to the Isotomides Decree of 415 (Andok. 1.71; Lys. 6.9, 24), according to which anyone who had confessed to committing impiety would be barred from the temples of Attica and the Athenian agora: in other words, he would suffer a kind of public death. The decree applied to Andokides, in spite of his immunity from prosecution; it may have been an *ad hominem* attack. In any case, he went into exile, building up a fortune as a merchant over the years. An attempt to return to Athens under the oligarchy in 411 failed and landed Andokides in prison. After his release, he tried to return again one or two years later, but he was turned down. It was only with the amnesty of 403 that Andokides returned to settle in Athens and to play an important role in its politics and finances. The collision with Kallias followed three years later.[25]

Memory of the events of 415 had no doubt dimmed somewhat by 400, but the prosecution would be sure to fan what flames remained. *Against Andokides*, for example, gives great play to Andokides' impiety and his personal betrayal in 415 (Lys. 6 *passim*). A few years before the trial of 400, Andokides seems to have been well aware of the need to fend off his lingering ill-fame. The evidence is provided by one of his first acts upon returning to Athens in 403: he prosecuted one Arkhippos for mutilating a Herm dedicated by Andokides' family (Lys. 6.11). Andokides portrayed himself, in other words, as a defender of the family as well as of religion, and as a man who had changed since 415.

Like Socrates during his trial, Andokides probably knew that he would have to defend himself not only against the stated charge, but also against the "old accusers" (Pl. *Ap.* 18d9–10). The old accusations of 415 against Andokides might be thought of as four related offenses: that he had committed impiety, that he was a tattler, that he had betrayed his friends and family, and that he had betrayed his father. In his defense Andokides is careful to respond to each of these old accusations, as well as to the stated charge of illegally attending the Mysteries. Andokides' defense, in other words, is an *apologia pro vita sua* as well as a narrowly delimited brief. Let us focus on just one of Andokides' defense strategies, one that emerges, both directly and indirectly, as a prominent theme in *On the Mysteries*: Andokides' sterling reputation as a good son to both his father and his fatherland.

The paternal theme in Andokides' defense speech can, for the sake of analysis, be divided into five lines of argument. First, Andokides offers a revisionist account of the events of 415, according to which he was the savior rather than the denouncer of his father. Second, he invokes his love of his Athenian fatherland, equating his own triumph over exile after years of struggle and the Athenians' triumph over enemies after years of struggle. As Athens had returned to its ancestral ways (*ta patria*), so Andokides had saved his father (*patêr*) and regained his fatherland (*patris*). Third, Andokides attacks his prosecutors as enemies of fatherhood. Fourth, he calls on the great deeds of his forefathers as grounds for acquittal. Fifth, he invokes the jury's sympathy for him as a man who has lost his father (apparently Leogoras had died in the years since 415) and has no sons. Let us take each of these sub-themes in turn.

Andokides' first line of defense is his account of his treatment of his father in 415. He had to fight against the widespread belief that to save his own skin and get released from prison, he had turned informer on his own father as well as his friends and kinsmen. The charge had been alive and well when Andokides attempted vainly to return to Athens from exile several years after

411.[26] Furthermore, the *Hermokopidai* and the profaners of the Mysteries had a general reputation as arrogant and spoiled youths, which created a presumption of filial disobedience on the part of Andokides. He took great pains then to explain to the Athenian assembly that he had turned informer in 415 only to save his father's life; clearly, someone had accused him of jeopardizing his father's life (Andok. 2.7). The prosecution brought up the charge again in 400, and Andokides takes great pains again to portray himself as his father's savior in 415 (Andok. 1.17–24).[27] The later ancient tradition was not persuaded, however, and believed that Andokides had denounced Leogoras (Ps.-Plut. *Vita Andok.* 834e; Tzetzes *Historia* 49 = Chiliades 6.367–375).[28]

None of this proves anything other than that malicious gossip will always find an audience. Much more damning, however, is the flimsiness of Andokides' defense, which MacDowell has demolished. To outline his argument, Andokides claims first that one Lydos denounced Leogoras, hence Andokides could not have denounced him too (Andok. 1.17, 19). Multiple denunciations, however, were common in Athens. Andokides also claims that the survival of Leogoras past 415 proves that Andokides never denounced him: had Andokides denounced him Leogoras would have been tried, convicted, and executed – or, if acquitted, Andokides would have been executed (Andok. 1.20). This argument is clearly false. By Andokides' own admission, Leogoras blocked action on Lydos's charge by the technicality of a prosecution for an illegal decree (*graphê paranomôn*); Leogoras might have used the same tactic against any denunciation by Andokides (Andok. 1.17, 22). *The Life of Andokides* says that Andokides informed on his father and then got him off by promising that Leogoras would in turn denounce other malefactors, which he did (834e). In neither case would Andokides have been executed.

Andokides' argument in 400 therefore leaves a large loophole; would he not have closed it had the facts been on his side? Perhaps Andokides had done what his enemies alleged, and denounced his own father to the authorities in 415. No doubt he would have preferred not to include his father's name on the list of those he denounced, if only for reasons of self-interest (such behavior was bound to incur opprobrium) but perhaps Leogoras's guilt was too well known to deny or perhaps Andokides could not strike a deal without delivering such a relatively prominent person.[29]

Andokides' apparent guilt certainly complicated matters for him, but all was not lost. By 400, many of the men who had lived through the events of 415 were dead; many of the jurors were thus ignorant. In these relatively favorable circumstances, Andokides' strategy seems to have been the "big lie" technique: deny one's guilt boldy and often enough and people will come to believe you. Andokides thus hammers home the argument of his loyalty to his father. He refers to it often in *On the Mysteries*, particularly in his discussion of the furor in 415 over the profanation. To take the most striking example, in sections 17 to 24 of the speech (fifty lines in the Oxford text), he uses the word *patêr* (or *patera* or *patros*) fourteen times![30]

Having discussed the weakness of Andokides' arguments, let us note, with admiration, his ability to play on the jurors' emotions and on the sanctity of the father–son tie in normative discourse. First, Andokides emphasizes his role in persuading Leogoras to stay in Athens and fight rather than go into exile. He paints a vivid picture: "My father was denounced by Pherekles' slave Lydos, but he was persuaded by me to remain and not to go off into exile: it took many supplications as I held on to his knees" (Andok. 1.19). A grown son who so subordinates his pride to his father's best interests that he doesn't mind the self-abasing gesture of clinging to the old man's knees: what could be more touching? A son who keeps intact the tie between father and fatherland: who could be more pious?

Second, Andokides emphasizes the drama of his stay in prison – where denunciations had landed him and various family members – and his selfless decision to incur the opprobrium of denouncing his former comrades in order to save his imprisoned father and kinsmen. He makes much of the uproar in Athens before his statement put an end to a series of charges and counter-charges (there had already been five separate informers in the affair of the Herms and Mysteries), and the pitiful sight of his family members in prison, their women and children gathered outside, "the crying and weeping of those bewailing and lamenting their present evils" (Andok. 1.48). Andokides gave in to the plea of his cousin and fellow prisoner Kharmides, who urged him to save his kinsmen and his father Leogoras, "whom you [sc. Andokides] probably love most of all" (Andok. 1.50). Andokides claims that his confession only implicated four men who had not already been denounced, and all four of them survived to the present day in 400; in return, Andokides saved his father, brother-in-law, three cousins, and seven other kinsmen, all of whom, as he says dramatically, "owe it to me that they now see the light of the sun" (Andok. 1.68).[31]

Third, Andokides notes repeatedly that his self-interest and that of his father and of his kinsmen were completely at one with the best interests of Athens. He says:

> This is my greatest task in this trial, gentlemen, not to appear evil just because I was saved [in 415]; to make <first you> and then everyone else learn that I did nothing out of evil or lack of manliness, but rather on account of the disaster that struck the city and, to a lesser extent, us too; I said what I heard from Euphiletos out of forethought for my kinsmen and friends, out of forethought for the whole polis, out of virtue and not evil motives – so I think.
>
> (Andok. 1.56)

Although he denies any participation in the parodying of the Mysteries, Andokides admits that he was present when the plot to mutilate the Herms was hatched; he claims to have opposed it and to have played no part in the deed itself (Andok. 1.61). Had he kept silent in 415, Andokides argues, three hundred Athenians accused unjustly of mutilating the Herms would have been executed and Athens's turmoil would have continued. By coming forth with his denunciations, however, as Andokides says, "I saved myself, I saved my father and my other kinsmen, and I delivered the polis from fear and the greatest of evils" (Andok. 1.59). To sum up, Andokides not only denies that he denounced his father in 415, but he also denies having had any selfish motives then. He insists rather that he was guided by patriotism and filial piety, and that he was a model son.

Andokides' second defense argument draws an analogy between the depiction of himself as a son who loved his father and a depiction of himself as a citizen who loves his fatherland. Andokides claims that his enemies say that he would have preferred to go into exile rather than stand trial, could he have escaped from Athens (Andok. 1.4). He denies this indignantly:

> I would never accept a life elsewhere, cut off from all the good things of the fatherland (*steromenos tês patridos*). Even if the polis is in the condition that these enemies say it is, I would much rather be a citizen [of Athens] than of other

poleis which I may perhaps think are more prosperous at present.

(Andok. 1.5)

The orator establishes two things here. First, he is willing to stand by his fatherland in bad times as well as good. Second, he would suffer were he deprived of his fatherland, and suffer emotionally rather than materially, since other poleis are more prosperous.[32]

From the point of view of paternal symbolism, these two points might prove immensely valuable to Andokides. First, given the etymological connection between *patris* (fatherland) and *patêr* (father), a reputation as a citizen loyal to the *patris* could only help the orator's shaky status as a good son. Second, Andokides' particular crime against his father was, allegedly, to have abandoned him for the sake of his own self-interest. So by demonstrating his altruism in regard to his *patris*, Andokides implants the idea among the jurors that he was undoubtedly equally altruistic in regard to his *patêr*.

Third, and less tangible, was the whole matter of Andokides' exile. There is an element in the prosecution's case of a charge that Andokides was – if a twentieth-century expression might be permitted – a "rootless cosmopolite." His checkered wanderings around the Aegean are taken as signs both of divine disfavor and of Andokides' dismissal of the ancestral ways (*ta patria*) of his fatherland. *Against Andokides*, for example, makes the orator into a figure of Sisyphean suffering, whose life has been scarred again and again by pain and which lacks all charm. Men reject Andokides everywhere because he violated the most basic rule of civilization, treating one's own well. The gods refuse to save him because to do so would promote atheism: if impiety as grave as Andokides' goes unpunished, men will surely conclude that the gods do not exist (Lys. 6.28–32).

A man who prefers foreign countries to his fatherland is a man who has little regard for the traditions of his fathers – and probably also a man who would betray his own father for the sake of self-interest. So Andokides' prosecutors may have argued. *Against Andokides* at any rate lays great emphasis on the speaker's own piety, which he constantly compares to Andokides' impiety, noting the traditional piety of his family. He points out that his grandfather, Diokles son of Zakoros, was an offical of the Mysteries (a hierophant) who advised the Athenians on a case of impiety (Lys.

6.54). This makes a nice contrast with Andokides' father Leogoras, who had a reputation for high living, spendthrift ways, and profaning the Mysteries and mutilating the Herms (Ar. *Cl.* 109 with schol., *Wasps* 1269; Eupolis frg. 50 Kassel and Austin; Plato Comicus frg. 114 Kassel and Austin; Andok. 1.17, 47).[33]

Andokides is thus vulnerable to a smear as an exile from Athens's noble traditions. By countering with a portrayal of himself, however, as a good Athenian who never wanted to live abroad, Andokides turns the tables on this whole complex of charges. He makes himself, symbolically, a good son of both fatherland and father and, hence, a man deserving to be acquitted.

Andokides' third line of argument is to attack his prosecutors as enemies of fatherhood. As Meletos played a relatively small role in the prosecution, so Andokides does not devote much time to counter-attacking him. Andokides does mention the accusation that under the Thirty, Meletos had arrested Leon (perhaps the famous general Leon of Salamis), who was later executed. This only warms up the audience though for the scene of Leon's children (*paides*) who wanted to do their duty and avenge their father by prosecuting Meletos, but were prevented by the amnesty of 403 (Andok. 1.94). It was Meletos, Andokides implies, and not he who was a father-killer.[34]

Kallias was a bigger fish, both in the case against Andokides and in Athenian life generally, and accordingly Andokides enjoys reeling him in slowly. Apparently, Kallias had made much of Andokides' alleged violation of ancestral law (*nomos patrios*) in the affair of the suppliant branch; Kallias may have even emphasized the link between himself, his (Kallias's) father (*patêr*), and *nomos patrios*. According to Andokides, Kallias had informed the council that

> it was an ancestral law (*nomos patrios*) that if someone should place a suppliant branch in the Eleusinion, he should be executed without trial, and his father (*patêr*) Hipponikos had once made an official pronouncement on these things to the Athenians, and that he [Kallias] had heard that I [Andokides] had placed the suppliant branch.
>
> (Andok. 1.115)

Kallias accused Andokides of violating *nomos patrios*. By pointing, furthermore, to the solidarity between himself, his *patêr*, and the *nomos patrios*, Kallias also subtly reminded his audience of Andokides' offenses against his *patêr*, Leogoras.

Andokides' supporter Kephalos had already made short shrift of the *nomos patrios* argument by pointing out the superiority of Athens's written, inscribed law, which set the penalty for the alleged crime at a monetary fine, not execution (Andok. 1.116–117).[35] Not that it was possible to get rid of the argument entirely: Andokides' alleged violation of the *nomos patrios* no doubt emerged again in the trial. The author of *Against Andokides* puts it dramatically:

> You know well, men of Athens, that it is not possible for you to make use both of the ancestral laws (*nomoi patrioi*) and of Andokides, but either one or the other. Either the laws must be wiped out or this man must be got rid of.
>
> (Lys. 6.8, cf. 9–10)

Andokides, perhaps wisely, prefers to attack Kallias's record as a *patêr* rather than return to the *nomos patrios* argument. He focuses on Kallias's alleged lurid behavior in his own oikos.

According to Andokides, Kallias first of all had an affair with his wife's mother Khrysilla, from which union a son had been born. Kallias had refused to recognize the son as his own at the Apatouria, and perjured himself before relenting only several years later (Andok. 1.124–128). Second, although Kallias was claiming the daughter of Epilykos for his son (not the son of Khrysilla but a different son) he really wanted her for himself (Andok. 1.120–121). Third, Kallias had proven to be a bad son to his father Hipponikos, having damaged Hipponikos's fortune, his even keel, indeed his whole life (Andok. 1.131). In short, Kallias was a bad *patêr* to his son and a bad son to his *patêr*. Andokides paints Kallias and not himself as the true enemy of fatherhood.

A fourth line of argument concerns the Athenians' forefathers (*pateres*). Andokides points out, first, that observing an amnesty is a hallowed custom in Athens, hence the amnesty of 403, under which he claims to be protected, should invalidate the prosecution. Second, he notes the signal contributions of his particular forefathers to Athenian glory. He points out that his great-grandfather and great-great-grandfather had both played important roles in the expulsion of the Peisistratid tyranny about a hundred years before: presumably this might stand him in good stead in 400, with the expulsion of the Thirty still fresh in people's minds (Andok. 1.106–109, 141–143).

A fifth argument tried by Andokides evokes the jury's pity and sympathy. The orator points out that if he is condemned to death, his family, "the *oikia* of Andokides and Leogoras," will come to an end (Andok. 1.146). Andokides notes that his father has died in the years since 415, and that he himself has no brothers or sons. He is thus in a sorry predicament, and the solution he proposes is to implicate the jurors in a shared, quasi-paternal relationship. "You, then," he says, "must be mine in place of a father (*anti patros*) and in place of brothers (*anti adelphôn*) and in place of sons (*anti paidôn*)" (Andok. 1.149). It is a nice metaphor, perhaps calling to mind Andromakhe's statement to her husband Hektor in *Iliad* VI that since she is an orphan, he must be her father and mother (*Il.* 6.429–430). Assuming the jurors understood the allusion, then it would have helped Andokides strengthen his appeal to their paternal instincts with a reference to literary tradition.[36]

To sum up, at the end of the fifth century in Athens, the father and related concepts (fatherland, patrimony, paternal, inherited, ancestral) were rich in symbolic and ideological connotations. The figure of the son who was disobedient or disloyal to his father was connected in the public mind with such negative images as oligarchs who were disloyal to Athens's ancestral constitution (*patrios politeia*) and dissipated young aristocrats who treated the symbols of the Athenian demos (for example, Herms or the Eleusinian Mysteries) with violence and arrogance (*hubris*). Hence, the public perception in 400 that Andokides had not merely disobeyed but denounced his father Leogoras in 415 cast a dark shadow over his defense.

Andokides rose to the occasion, however, by denying the allegations that he had betrayed his father in 415. He counter-attacks by portraying himself, in vivid details, as rather a good son who saved his father's life. He also describes himself as a good citizen who moved heaven and earth to defend his fatherland and to regain it from exile. Furthermore, he attacks his prosecutors as bad sons and irresponsible fathers. He recites the great deeds of his forefathers and asks the jury's sympathy for his current status as an orphan without any sons of his own. In short, Andokides transforms his image from that of an arrogant, lawless youth who has trampled on *patêr* and *patrios politeia* alike to a sympathetic defender of democracy and his beloved father. Manipulative as these tactics may seem today, they were quite effective at the time.

SOCRATES VERSUS THE ATHENIAN FATHER

Why discuss the trial of Socrates in a book on fathers and sons in Athens? Scholarship has long demonstrated that many things were at issue in the trial, among them impiety, religious innovation, education, the sophistic revolution, the cultural consequences of the Peloponnesian War and the civil wars of 411 and 404–403, and Socrates' unique personality. No analysis of the trial places father–son relations at center stage, and I am not about to do so here. I would argue, however, that the continuing debate in Athens about fathers and sons is an important undercurrent, a secondary motif, in the hammering out of Socrates' fate.

Grote long ago pointed out the relevance to Socrates' trial of an anecdote in Xenophon's *Cyropaedia* (3.1.14, 38–40), that cranky and idiosyncratic "Persian" allegory of contemporary Greece. Xenophon's hero, Cyrus, is surprised to learn that the king of Armenia has had executed "a certain sophist" who was the constant companion of his son Tigranes. The official charge was that the unnamed sophist had "corrupted" the boy. The father, however, is rather blunt about his real motivation. Like a husband who kills a man simply for conversing with his wife, the father attacked his son's companion: "I was jealous of him," he said, "because I thought that he was making my son admire him more than me" (Xen. *Cyr.* 3.1.39). Grote suggests not only that Xenophon has Socrates in mind here, but indeed that much of the animus against Socrates in 399 came from paternal jealousy rather than from any genuine conviction that Socrates was a corrupter. In a similar vein, Nietzsche once wrote that "Socrates . . . was a sacrifice to the anger of the fathers at his 'corruption of the youth.' " These perspectives may be of considerable use in analyzing the trial.[37]

As a rhetorical commonplace has it, in discussing the trial of Socrates one is at a loss not as to where to begin but rather as to where to end. The trial is a vast subject, debated throughout antiquity and the object of considerable modern scholarly scrutiny. The following discussion shall be confined to the theme of Socrates and the Athenian father and confined primarily to one text, the central document about the trial, Plato's *Apology of Socrates*.

Again, a fuller discussion would also contain a thorough analysis of the other relevant texts: Plato's *Euthyphro*, *Crito*, *Phaedo*, and sections of *Republic*; Xenophon's *Memorabilia* and *Apology of Socrates*; a reconstruction of Polykrates' pamphlet attacking Socrates; and of course Aristophanes' *Clouds*. These texts have much to say about parent–child relations, but space demands that discussion be limited to brief references; the focus shall be on Plato's *Apology*.

Philologists have demonstrated that Plato wrote the *Apology* within a dozen years of the trial in 399, when the details were still relatively fresh. In what follows, it is assumed that Plato is relatively faithful to what Socrates actually said; a controversial position, but one with considerable scholarly support.[38]

Students of the trial often discuss motive: why was Socrates prosecuted? Politics, religion, and paternal ideology each played a part, as in Andokides' trial the previous year. Socrates had questioned some of the principles of Athenian democracy, although he was a solid citizen; whether his theoretical critique of democracy was matched by a desire for a practical alternative seems doubtful. In earlier years he had kept company with the oligarchs-to-be Kritias and Kharmides and especially with Alcibiades. Such behavior may have hurt Socrates, though it is hard to tell how much, since the amnesty of 403 should have kept politics in the background during the trial. Like Andokides, Socrates was formally accused of impiety. In addition, Socrates was formally charged with having corrupted the young, a subject which inevitably leads into the areas of education and paternal control.[39]

In the year 399, the relationship between young men and their elders was a highly charged subject. It was closely related to the themes of fathers and sons and of tradition and innovation. Chastened by Sicily and by a surfeit of oligarchic plots, Athens had had enough of bright, ambitious young men. Having held on to their democratic government by the skin of their teeth, and having just recently rededicated themselves to what was perceived as the ancestral constitution, Athenians were wary of any challenge to traditional authority. The ideological universe of Athens in 399 was thus not an ideal one for a teacher of bracing and innovative rhetoric: a sophist.

As teachers of the likes of Alcibiades and Andokides, and of Kritias, Theramenes and the oligarchs, sophists were vulnerable to the charge of having led a generation astray. Fifty years after

Socrates' trial, the orator Aeschines declared: "Men of Athens, you put to death Socrates the sophist because he was shown to have educated Kritias, one of the Thirty who abolished democracy" (1.173). True enough, this is not decisive evidence of what went on in 399, but consider the tenor of Athenian public culture in that year. It was an era in which a prosecutor could conjure up the hobgoblin of what might be called "the oligarchic personality": a rich young man who had contempt for ordinary citizens, against whom he did not hesitate to use violence, and contempt for the established laws, to which he preferred oligarchy (see Isocrates 20: *Against Lokhites*). Woe to the sophist who was accused of having instructed such a man; woe to Socrates, who could be tarred with the sophists' brush. He himself characterizes his "followers" as "young men who especially have leisure, the sons of the wealthiest men," even though he notes that they follow him spontaneously (Pl. *Ap.* 23c2–5). Socrates insisted on a great gulf between the sophists and himself, since he claimed neither to be a teacher nor to charge fees, but most people would have considered this distinction to be mere hair-splitting (Pl. *Ap.* 19d8–20c3). Besides which, the crucial thing was that Socrates challenged the traditional Athenian order as much as if not more than Antiphon, Gorgias, Protagoras, and Thrasymakhos.[40]

A further problem was Socrates' vulnerability to the charge of laconizing, that is, of following a Spartan way of life, in particular a life of frugality and toughness, and with little regard for personal hygiene. In *Birds* (414 BC) Aristophanes refers to laconizing as "Socratizing" (1282). The anti-democratic faction among the youth of Athens had long affected Spartan styles. To the extent that Socrates seemed to encourage such pro-Spartan ways, it might have seemed that he had indeed corrupted the youth, by turning them toward the national enemy.[41]

Socrates certainly raised questions that would disturb the traditional father–son relationship. In Plato's *Meno*, for example, he affirms that no father, however outstanding, can teach virtue to his son – and he is imprudent enough to say this before Anytos, one of his future prosecutors (93a–95a). Xenophon reports that on one occasion Socrates reproached Anytos for focusing his son's education on the family business, the tanning trade, an occupation at which snobs turned up their noses, but one in which Anytos's ancestors had made a fortune (Xen. *Ap.* 29). Anytos might indeed consider Socrates to have interfered in his relationship with his son. Socrates undermined the traditional Athenian assumption that a father would teach his trade to his son, thus rendering Socrates all the more problematic, especially in a period searching for the *patrios politeia*.[42]

Three men joined in prosecuting Socrates, and each gave a speech at the trial: Meletos, who made the official indictment, Anytos, and Lykon. Anytos, a prominent politician, may have been the driving force, but Plato's *Apology* focuses on Meletos, whom Socrates subjects to an interrogation. The precise wording of the indictment ran as follows:

> This indictment and affidavit is sworn by Meletos, the son of Meletos of Pitthos, against Socrates, the son of Sophroniskos of Alopeke: Socrates is guilty of refusing to recognize the gods the state recognizes, and of introducing other new divinities. He is also guilty of corrupting the youth. The penalty demanded is death.
>
> (D. L. 2.40)[43]

In the course of Socrates' questioning of Meletos, the thrust of the indictment becomes clearer: Socrates was being accused by Meletos of corrupting the young men of Athens by teaching them to be atheists.[44]

Much of Socrates' defense is based on the assertion of prejudice: in addition to the formal charges of the day, he claims to have faced the "first accusers" for a generation. Their accusations, and not Meletos's charges, are what Socrates says he is really up against in 399 (Pl. *Ap.* 18b). According to Socrates, the first accusations accused him of being dangerously clever, of inquiring into the things in the heavens and below the earth (and thus of challenging religious orthodoxy), of making the weaker argument the stronger, of doing wrong, and of teaching his insidious doctrines to others (Pl. *Ap.* 18b-c, 19b-c). He also mentions Aristophanes explicitly and alludes to *Clouds* (19c). Socrates does not remind the jury, but perhaps did not need to, that *Clouds* presented "a certain Socrates" (19c) – as Socrates says in 399, separating himself from the stage character – who corrupted young men by teaching them to disobey their elders and the laws.[45]

Socrates' direct response to Meletos is to deny being anyone's teacher and to deny being an atheist – a reply which also dismisses much in the first accusations. Through his interrogation, he demonstrates Meletos's ignorance about the education and well-being of young men, and his lack of expertise on the question of whether Socrates corrupts them (Pl. *Ap*. 24c4–26b1). He also makes an elitist argument about education (Pl. *Ap*. 25a12–c4) though he does not, as some construe, claim to be the only man in Athens who improves the youth. Well and good, but there was still the "Socrates" of *Clouds*, the sophist who taught young men to twist arguments, to ignore conventions, and to disobey their parents. Socrates needed to show clearly that he was not the man the play had depicted. One of the ways he does so (or at least attempts to: after all, Socrates lost the case) is by building up throughout his defense an image of himself as a good father and a good family man, an elder who, far from corrupting the young, makes sure that they defer to their seniors. Accordingly, familial themes are woven throughout Plato's *Apology*, sometimes subtly, sometimes not: fathers and sons, age and youth, children and childhood, and the education and corruption of young men.[46]

A difficulty in Socrates' defense, and no doubt one of the reasons he was put on trial, is that his activities certainly did shake belief on the part of the young in the wisdom and virtue of the elders of Athens. As Socrates explains, he was accustomed to spending his time examining the political, cultural, and technological leadership of Athens and to exposing their foibles and follies. A Socratic "examination" could be humiliating and infuriating for the examinee, but highly amusing for the audience, which usually included a high percentage of young men, many of whom went on to imitate Socrates by examining their elders (Pl. *Ap*. 23a–d, 24a, 33b–c, 37e). A liberal society would not prosecute Socrates for such behavior, but a reasonable person might conclude that he was indeed corrupting the young.[47]

He or she might also conclude that Socrates was making it more difficult for a father to do his job. How, for example, could a father elicit his son's respect and deference when Socrates had shown the boy that the father's generation was nothing but a bunch of fools? What was a father to think of a son who, instead of displaying the requisite respect, attempted to demonstrate his father's ignorance, and proudly admitted to having learned the technique from Socrates? Socrates does not help his case any by the anecdote of how he encouraged Kallias (Andokides' enemy) to find the right sophist to educate his sons (Pl. *Ap*. 20a–c); surely it would have been better for Socrates to tell the jury that he had encouraged Kallias to avoid sophists altogether and to educate his sons himself.[48]

Faced with the need to counter the (not unreasonable) belief that he turned sons against their fathers, Socrates presents himself as a good family man. Near the end of his first speech[49] he informs the jury that although he has three sons (one *meirakion* and two *paidia*, but who's counting?) he has no intention of demeaning himself by bringing them into court to plead for their father's life (Pl. *Ap.* 34d). In other words, Socrates engages in the well-known rhetorical trick of poisoning the wells. The penultimate passage of Socrates' final speech, the peroration of the *Apology*, is a plea to the jurors to look after his sons following his execution: in short, an appeal to traditional Athenian paternal values.[50]

Socrates makes much of his friendship with the late Khairephon, his "comrade . . . from youth" and a well-known supporter of democracy (Pl. *Ap.* 21a). The presence of Khairephon's brother in court to testify on Socrates' behalf is a subtle indication of Socrates' respect for family ties (Pl. *Ap.* 21a).

Nor is Socrates narrow in his familial outlook. Harsh as his "examinations" admittedly had sometimes been (he calls himself a gadfly, Pl. *Ap.* 30e), he says he always thought of himself as a kind of father or brother gently correcting his fellow man (Pl. *Ap.* 31b). Although he has examined foreigners from time to time, he always preferred citizens because they shared with him a common descent (*genos*, Pl. *Ap.* 30a). Nor is Socrates insensitive to the families of the young men who kept his company. He points out to the jury the presence in court of quite a few kinsmen of his young followers: mature men, the fathers, brothers, or other relations of the young he had supposedly corrupted (Pl. *Ap.* 33d, 34b). He notes with satisfaction that none of them has a word to say against him (Pl. *Ap.* 34a).[51]

One of the boldest of Socrates' appropriations of the familial metaphor is his comparison of himself to Achilles, whom he does not call by name but rather refers to as "the son of Thetis" (*ho tês Thêtidos huios*, Pl. *Ap.* 28c). Just as Achilles preferred death to the dishonor that would have been his had he failed to avenge Patroklos, so Socrates prefers death to the dishonor of abandoning his divine mission to pursue philosophy. Socrates quotes a discussion in the *Iliad* (18.95–98, 104) between Achilles and his mother Thetis.[52] She tries to dissuade Achilles from killing Hektor, pointing out that his death will follow inevitably, but Achilles is determined. Socrates' choice of this passage is striking, because although Achilles is heroic, he is not a very good son. He ignores Thetis's pleas here, and he pays very little attention to his father Peleus during the course of the *Iliad*. It is noteworthy that Socrates' familial role model is a headstrong and quasi-fatherless child who does not heed his mother; noteworthy and not particularly helpful to the defense.[53]

Socrates does better in his evocation of children and childhood as symbols of vulnerability. His "divine spirit" (*daimonion*) may be controversial and unorthodox, but he has heard it since childhood (Pl. *Ap.* 31c). In mythological terms, *daimones* are children of the gods (Pl. *Ap.* 27d). Childhood is part of Socrates' description of his opponents too. Socrates notes that many of the jurors have been hearing the "first accusers" since they were children, when they were impressionable; hence they have an ingrained prejudice against him (Pl. *Ap.* 18b–c).[54]

Finally, there is the wisdom and maturity of age, a winning subject for Socrates, who was sixty-nine or seventy years old in 399. He announces right off, in the *prooimion*, that he is a man of advanced age and a straight-talker, not some *meirakion* who concocts speeches (Pl. *Ap.* 17c). In other words, he is no Pheidippides and presumably he is no teacher of Pheidippides (no "Socrates") either! Having been accused of corrupting youth, Socrates tries to demonstrate that, on the contrary, he has been an influence for maturity and restraint. He returns to the point of his age in his appeal for a lesser penalty than death (Pl. *Ap.* 37d, 38c). Having failed, Socrates warns his condemners that after his death new and younger Socratics will appear, and being young they will be much more difficult men (like Pheidippides?) than old Socrates had been (Pl. *Ap.* 39c–d). Finally, Socrates does a fine job of turning the tables on Meletos. Meletos was a young man and not well known in Athens (*neos . . . kai agnôs*, Pl. *Euthphr.* 2b). Socrates accuses him of nonetheless having pretensions to greater wisdom than his elders, of whom he, Socrates, was one (Pl. *Ap.* 25d). In other words, Socrates depicts Meletos as just the kind of young troublemaker whom he himself is supposed to have created: a Pheidippides figure.

Socrates did not win his case, of course; many scholars believe that he never intended to, but had decided rather to make a vigorous and uncompromising defense of the philosophic way of life, win or lose. The defeat, however, ought not to be laid to a failure on Socrates' part to present himself as a good family man. Rather, at nearly every turn in his defense, Socrates tried to undermine the prosecution's implied argument that he had interfered with the Athenian father–son relationship. Hence, he offers up Socrates the respected elder, Socrates the concerned father, Socrates the Athenian who treats his fellow-citizens like family, Socrates the favorite of his young followers' fathers, Socrates the man still faithful to his childhood dreams, and Socrates the scourge of arrogant youth. It is true enough that glimpses of Socrates the disobedient son and the colleague of the sophists also appear in Plato's *Apology*, but even so, Socrates almost won his case (which he only lost by a narrow majority of thirty votes, Pl. *Ap.* 36a).[55]

So far we have focused on the charges against Socrates and his defense as reported in Plato's *Apology*. Three discussions in Xenophon, one from his *Apology of Socrates* and two others from his Socratic *Memorabilia*, as well as a point in Plato's *Euthyphro*, also shed important light on the role of paternal ideology in Socrates' trial, and they deserve a brief scrutiny.

In Xenophon's *Apology of Socrates*, a loose and brief set of anecdotes about Socrates' defense and his feelings about his trial, Xenophon reports the story that Meletos accused Socrates of corrupting the youth by turning them against their parents: "By Zeus, said Meletos, I know men whom you have persuaded to obey you [Socrates] rather than their parents (*hoi geinamenoi*)" (Xen. *Ap.* 20).[56]

Socrates is supposed to have admitted to the charge, but with his characteristic irony. On the subject of education, sons turn to him rather than parents for advice, Socrates says, but so they turn to physicians when the subject is health, to generals when the subject is war, and to the Athenian assembly when the subject is politics. Meletos accepts Socrates' analogies but only to a point; he insists on noting that Socrates' activities, unlike those of assemblymen, generals, or doctors, are neither advantageous (*sumpherei*) nor conventional (*nomizetai*). Maybe so, Socrates retorts, but his activities deserve to be recognized and honored, not prosecuted (Xen. *Ap.* 20–21).

A ready reply but not an adequate one, for Meletos has a valid point: to flesh out his argument, we might note that whereas doctors, generals, and assemblymen support the established order (*ta nomizomena*) Socrates challenges it. Socrates' "examinations," which so amused the young, were novel and therefore potentially unsettling. Furthermore, to make a point Meletos omits, a father was not supposed to be an expert on his son's health nor a legislator nor a military commander for his son, and hence need not feel displaced if his son consulted a doctor, assemblyman, or general. A father was, however, supposed to be the guardian of his son's education, as Socrates himself concedes in *Crito* (50d9–e1). True enough, Athenian fathers often appointed teachers for their sons, but Socrates was not a teacher, and no father had vetted Socrates' iconoclastic verbal displays held before the admiring young habitués of porticoes and gymnasia. Socrates' intervention in the father–son nexus was thus much more provocative and unsettling than a doctor's, a general's, or an assemblyman's. His admission of so intervening, if Xenophon is to be believed, would have been quite damning.[57]

Hegel concluded long ago that Socrates' reply was inadequate: "the real point of the accusation is the moral intervention of a third party in the absolute relationship of parents and children," he comments. "We can well suspect," he notes, that by his interventions with the young, Socrates raised "the germ of a feeling of unsuitability" between father and son; "raised, developed, strengthened, and stiffened." Thus Socrates strengthened discord between a young man and his father which became "the roots of his ruination." Hegel concludes that far from being unfounded, Meletos's accusation was "fully substantiated."[58]

Let us turn to a discussion in Xenophon's *Memorabilia* of one of the many pamphlets that followed in the wake of Socrates' trial, a pamphlet whose author, like Meletos, accuses Socrates of attacking paternal prerogatives. Xenophon relates these charges leveled by a pamphleteer of the 390s, considered by most scholars to be one Polykrates.[59] He wrote that

> Socrates taught sons to treat their fathers with contempt (*tous pateras propêlakizein*); he persuaded them that he made his companions wiser than their fathers: he said that the law allowed a son to put his father in prison if he convinced a jury that he was mentally incapable; and this was a proof that it was lawful for the wiser to keep the more ignorant in jail.
>
> (Xen. *Mem.* 1.2.49)[60]

According to Xenophon, Polykrates also accused Socrates of attacking kinship and friendship more generally, by making usefulness and knowledge more important than mere ties of blood, marriage or amity (Xen. *Mem.* 51–52).

Xenophon denies the charges, but admits that Socrates did discuss fathers, kin, and friends, and even that Socrates said that those who were not prudent and useful to them did not deserve their respect (Xen. *Mem.* 53–55). In a vivid image, Xenophon's Socrates compares a son, kinsman, or friend without prudence or utility to a corpse or corn or nail: something worthy of being buried or cut off (Xen. *Mem.* 53–54). Xenophon denies that, by this metaphor, Socrates was teaching a man to bury his father alive or to mutilate his own body (Xen. *Mem.* 55).

One wonders whether Polykrates indeed made this odd-sounding charge. If so, it might have been a striking symbol to use against Socrates. In Greek mythology, literal or figurative burial alive appears prominently in stories of father–son tension. Zeus, for example, buries his father Kronos and the other Titans in Tartaros. Previously, Kronos had swallowed his children alive, afraid – rightly, as it turned out – that if they grew up, they would displace their father. *His* father, Ouranos, had buried his children alive, for similar reasons, in the hollows of the earth.[61] The image of burial alive, therefore, helps to remove Socrates from the level of an actual, to a symbolic advocate of patricide.

Another passage in Xenophon's *Memorabilia* shows Socrates as a calming and maturing influence on rebellious youth, in this case on his eldest son Lamprokles. Lamprokles is angry at his mother, whom he thinks treats him more harshly than a wild beast would (Xen. *Mem.* 2.2.1, 7). Socrates gets the boy to admit that his mother means him well, and he reminds Lamprokles that children owe their parents a deeper debt for benefactions than they do to anyone else (Xen. *Mem.* 2.2.3, 9–10). Socrates also points out prudential considerations: if men hear Lamprokles bad-mouthing his mother they will think the worse of him for it, and they may even prosecute him for failing to support his parents (Xen. *Mem.* 2.2.13–14). Perhaps some Athenians might have found Socrates' reasoning to be objectionably selfish, but most would probably have held this discussion in Socrates' favor, seeing it as an indication of his good influence on the familial life of a young Athenian.[62]

The same point might have emerged from a reading of Plato's *Euthyphro*. In this dialogue, set on the eve of Socrates' indictment on Meletos's charge before a magistrate, Socrates learns that Euthyphro is prosecuting his own father for murder. Although shocked at first, Socrates later affects to admire Euthyphro's bold challenge to conventional morality (Pl. *Euthphr.* 4a, 15e). Socrates' probes, however, seem to have moved Euthyphro to see the error of his ways, and he apparently dropped his suit soon afterward (D. L. 2.29). Hence, the story of Socrates' run-in with Euthyphro, like that of his discussion with his own son Lamprokles, serves to exonerate Socrates of the charge of corrupting the youth or of turning them against their mother or father.[63]

To sum up, the trial of Socrates demonstrates the importance of paternal ideology in Athens in 399. Socrates was considered to be a religious innovator and a sophist who corrupted young men. Implicit in these charges, as Plato's *Apology* makes clear, was the notion that Socrates interfered with fathers who were trying to give their sons a traditional education. According to Xenophon's *Apology*, the prosecutor Meletos made this charge explicit; so, it seems, did Polykrates in a pamphlet circulated after the trial, though it is unclear how much of what the prosecutors said is reflected in this pamphlet. What is clear is that for the same reasons that the *patrios politeia* became a political rallying cry after 413 and that the wisdom of the elders became newly attractive, for the same reasons that the prosecution tried to depict Andokides in 400 as a man whose impiety was demonstrated by his mistreatment of his father, so the prosecution in 399 attempted to show that Socrates threatened the established religious and legal order in Athens by, among other things, usurping the proper role of the Athenian father. The refutation of this charge and the presentation of Socrates as a pious and traditional father and family man are an important part of his defense. Whether Socrates' prime goal was to secure acquittal or to go down fighting in defense of philosophy, his reputation as a good father and as a man who respected fatherhood was equally important, and so he does not neglect to demonstrate it.

CONCLUSIONS

In retrospect, the launching of the Sicilian Expedition in June 415 was the high-water mark of the power of Athenian youth, both in practice and in ideology. The Sicilian disaster weakened youth both demographically and politically. In 413 there may have been a relative imbalance of Athenians aged between 35 and 45 vis-à-vis

Athenians aged 25 to 35. Some of the older generation of 413 had themselves been radical youths in the 420s, but they had changed. Others, like Alcibiades, continued to be a symbol of youth in spite of their age. In any case, many Athenian elders came to the conclusion after Sicily that an overdose of youthful arrogance had been a prime cause of Athens's defeat. The remedy would be a "return" to the ways of their ancestors, the rule of elders, the regime of the fathers – to the *patrios politeia*.

The establishment in 413 of a board of ten senior statesmen, the *probouloi*, did little to stem debate about reforming the constitution. Democrats, oligarchs, and men in the middle argued over whose vision was the true version of the *patrios politeia*. In 411 and in 404–403 oligarchs had their chance, but both times democrats regained power. Still, even the democrats agreed as to the necessity of the recodification of the laws and a searching out of what the *patrioi nomoi* really said. For democrats as well as oligarchs, the last decade of the Peloponnesian War was a period of ferment, doubt, soul-searching, and a new beginning.[64]

The keynote of Athenian ideology at the end of the fifth century was the father; the son was a more problematic and questionable figure. This is not to say that the distinction was absolute: Alcibiades, for instance, continued to have considerable appeal. In general, however, sons and youthfulness were considerably less in vogue and more dangerous-seeming than before Sicily; fathers seemed more comforting. As an ideological lodestar, the father was also an ideological weapon. It became enormously useful to try to tar one's enemy with the brush of being an uppity son or of encouraging sons to rebel against their fathers.

Both Andokides and Socrates were vulnerable to such charges, for quite different reasons of course. Andokides, it seems, had betrayed his own father back in 415 to save his own skin. Socrates had done nothing of the kind, but he had indirectly but definitely encouraged young men to challenge everything taught them by their elders, including their fathers. As a consequence, both Socrates and Andokides had to "cover their flank" and belie the charges against them. Each man presented himself, in his own particular way, as a paragon of filial respect or paternal concern, as a traditional believer in the values of Athenian fatherhood.

The debate about the Athenian father was by no means over with the acquittal of Andokides in 400 and the execution of Socrates in 399. The two events (especially the latter) are sufficiently dramatic, however, and sufficiently indicative of the changes in Athenian ideology over a generation, that it is appropriate to end the narrative here and take stock.

CONCLUSION

Zeus, however, does not like this at all.
His beloved child – that he left
To be destroyed: so it was ordained –
At least he will do honor to it dead.
Constantine Cavafy, "The Funeral of Sarpedon"
(tr. John Mavrogordato)

In his Funeral Oration of 431/430 BC, Pericles attempts to subordinate the private oikos to the Athenian polis, largely by appropriating the symbols of the oikos. Have Athenian parents lost sons? They can produce new ones to serve not merely their own families but the polis. These new sons will prevent the polis from being "deserted"; Pericles uses the same word (*erêmousthai*, "to be deserted") that the orators frequently apply to the oikos, usually as a motive for adoption ("lest the oikos be deserted"). Have Athenian sons been orphaned by the death in battle of a brave father? The polis itself will raise the boys at public expense; Pericles uses *trephô* ("to raise"), the normal term for raising children (Thuc. 2.44–46). Pericles thus makes the polis a surrogate oikos and thereby asserts the polis's supremacy; much of the rest of classical Athenian funeral oratory follows suit.[1]

Some modern scholars and theorists have gone even further, describing Athens as a rare place that not merely absorbed the private in the public but actually erased petty private concerns from the high-minded world of politics. Yet one of the main themes of Thucydides' history is how the Peloponnesian War proved Pericles' attempt to be a failure. Thucydides argues that under the harsh pressures of war, Athenians showed their true selves, ones that chose private advantage in preference to the public

212

good. Similarly, the previous pages have tried to demonstrate that the alleged divorce of public and private in Athens is an idealized exaggeration.

It is true that classical Athens went a long way toward developing the notion of the separation of public and private that continues to influence us today. Under Athenian democracy, perhaps for the first time in history, the notion of politics came into its own as a category, as did the notion of the public sphere. So did the notion of the apolitical life, one chosen in conscious retreat from the perceived corruption of politics. If politics and public life were Athenian categories, however, they were not autonomous categories, divorced from private life. Athenian public discourse, in a way whose frankness may be surprising today, pays great attention to private life.

As an example, if we return to his Funeral Oration, we find Pericles explaining why parents of child-bearing age should have new children to replace sons lost in battle. Not only will these new children be both a private comfort and a public benefit, but they are valuable in another way as well: "for fair or just policy-making cannot be expected from those who are not, equally with others, risking the lives of their children" (Thuc. 2.44.3).[2] Here we have the champion of the polis conceding that men without children are in effect second-class citizens! Pericles, therefore, cannot be said to have wished to erase private life from politics; at most, he merely wished to make private life secondary.

Public and private were so thoroughly intertwined in Athens, however, that even that would have been a tall order. Athenian political categories were frequently defined in terms of the oikos. Pericles himself had sponsored a law in 451/450 that denied Athenian citizenship to those who were not of citizen descent on their mother's as well as their father's side. Athenians believed in a myth of common descent. They further believed that a man who misbehaved as father or son would probably misbehave in public life as well. They rewarded a man for being the son of a good father and thought the worse of the son of a bad father. Before admitting candidates to Athens's most honorific political office, the archonship, they asked them to prove that they honored their mother and father.

They also assumed that in times of great crisis, the citizens of Athens – even in their most public and masculine moments, that is, in war or in the assembly – would think of their oikos. For example, in his Funeral Oration of the Corinthian War era (395–386 BC) Lysias imagines the thoughts of Athenian rowers as they were about to begin fighting the battle of Salamis (480 BC). Among the mixture of fear, prayer, and courage, the rowers are supposed to have felt "pity for their children (*paidôn*), longing for their wives, and compassion for their fathers and mothers, and a reckoning of the evils to come should they fail" (Lys. 2.39).[3]

In short, the Athenian state used the metaphor of the oikos as one of its fundamental structuring principles. The good son, the good father, the *kyrios*, the legitimate child, the man born of Athenian parents, the children of Athena or Theseus: these described men *qua* citizens or soldiers. While the metaphor of the oikos structured the polis, the fact of the oikos, however, played relatively little role in Athenian politics. True enough, certain household data (bilateral parental citizenship, honoring father and mother, thinking less of citizens without children) had a significance in Athenian public life which might be unacceptable in a modern liberal state. More important, however, is that neither family ties, nor favors to cousins, nor hereditary offices, nor marriage alliances, in short, the stuff of "politics" in many a monarchy, tyranny, or aristocracy, were the fundamental issues in Athens. Though the Athenian notion of politics was imperfect, it was nonetheless a great achievement.

Metaphors, though, sometimes take on, Pirandello-like, a life of their own, especially when they involve very powerful emotions. The interesting thing about studying fathers and sons in Peloponnesian-War-era Athens is the way that, under the stress of war, the metaphor of that relationship became an unconscious driving force of politics, the underlying script in the social drama of public life.

Of the various relationships within the oikos, the father–son tie had a peculiar paradigmatic importance in the ideology of the polis. Like Athenian public life, the father–son relationship was restricted to males. In both oikos and polis, this restriction created both ideological conveniences and problems. As males and Athenians, citizens and fathers were masters: of imperial subjects, of metics, of slaves, of women, and of children. The notion of the *kyrios* or master was a root paradigm of both oikos and polis. The *locus classicus* is Aristotle's *Politics*, Book One, although Aristotle dissents from the common Athenian oikos–polis analogy. The *kyrios* was both the reciprocal element and the linchpin of the system: his lordship over wife, children, and slaves prepared and qualified him to be the lord of the Athenian constitution and the Athenian sphere of rule abroad. But masters make uneasy colleagues. Like the relationship among Athenian citizens, the father–son tie was a nexus of conflict, a locus where independence and obedience met tensely. Let us consider citizens and fathers and sons in turn.

The ideal Athenian male citizen was meant to be free, proud, independent to the point of autarchy (Thuc. 2.41.1); aggressive to the point of ferocity in his refusal to accept another man as master (Eur. *Supp.* 514–523); patriotic, ambitious, and energetic to the point of meddlesomeness (Thuc. 1.70.8–9; Eur. *Supp.* 576–577). In short, every Athenian citizen was a *kyrios*, his own master. Men with these characteristics could build an empire, but they could hardly organize a democracy without cultivating other, more cooperative virtues – which they perforce did. Athenians made the people as a whole the common *kyrios* of the polis, lauded the principle of cooperation in the military among hoplites and rowers, and followed the political principle of alternately ruling and being ruled in turn. Since every man was a *kyrios*, every man would respect every other *kyrios*'s right to have the opportunity to rule temporarily. The system was not without problems (e.g. faction, political trials, ostracism, assassination) but by and large it worked.

A boy prepared for his future role as a member of the ruling people (*dêmos kyrios*) of Athens by training under the *kyrios* of his oikos: his father. Should his father be dead, he would train under a guardian, usually his closest adult male relative; should his father have died in battle serving Athens, the polis itself would be responsible for his rearing. The *kyrios* would arrange for the newborn boy to be accepted as a legitimate member of the oikos. The *kyrios* would supervise the growing boy's education but other individuals and institutions – teachers, friends, kinfolk, lovers, schools, civic and cultic rituals and contests – would also play a role in initiating him into the ways of adulthood; the wealthier the family, the greater the boy's access to such institutions and individuals. Then, after the boy reached puberty, his *kyrios* would step in once again to arrange for his acceptance as a member first, at age sixteen, of the father's phratry and then, at age eighteen, of the father's deme. The eighteen-year-old boy would now become legally his own *kyrios* and a citizen of Athens. In the normative case, however, it would not be before about another dozen years of military service and perhaps travel, experimentation, and further education that he would settle down, marry, receive his patrimony, and found his own oikos. Should his father still be alive, the son would increasingly take on the role of protector of the aging man.

The Athenian father was faced with the same dilemma as the Athenian polis. The more successful the father was in supervising his son's education, the more likely he was to produce a future master. The better he bred his son for mastery, the less likely the son was to obey his father. The father was in the uneasy position of preparing his son to supersede him. The son, as he grew older, was in the uneasy position of having to depend on another man: legally until age eighteen, and financially often into his twenties.

One approach to the dilemma was to encourage age gradations in Athenian society, segregating (at least partially) boys in the company of other boys. Another solution was to encourage pederasty as a kind of surrogate father–son relationship, in which a teenage boy's hostility to his father could be sublimated in a relationship with another older man. A third solution was the *ephêbeia*, the notion that an eighteen-year-old was only a kind of apprentice citizen, who would be too busy with warfare for several years to meddle in either his father's oikos or the Athenian polis. A fourth "solution" was the frequency with which Athenian fathers (who married late and did not have a long life expectancy) died before their sons reached eighteen, thus freeing the eighteen-year-old to come directly into his patrimony.

To the extent that these various solutions worked in Athens before the Peloponnesian War era, they had to compete with certain countervailing tendencies in ancient Greek culture: the strain of admiration for unmastered, heroic youth; the patricidal motifs of the Olympian theogony; the disdain of old age; the preference of Odyssean adventure to the tedious work of staying home and raising a son. Troubling as these tendencies were, they could usually be managed. Consider the way official discourse in classical Athens makes Theseus into a national hero who is both an indirect patricide and a mouthpiece of the established order; the ephebe par excellence and a responsible governmental official; a king, and a tyrannicide and democrat. By the 420s, however, the uneasy stability of the Athenian father–son relationship faced new destabilizing threats.

The Peloponnesian War brought radical changes in traditional Athenian military strategy and a growing brutality, both in military tactics and in public speech. The annual summer migrations of countryfolk behind the Long Walls were both a socioeconomic and a cultural shock. An epidemic decimated the population and led to demoralization. With the death of Pericles, who symbolized the traditions of Athenian democracy, a new and unsettling kind of political leader took over the speaker's platform. The demographic consequences of the epidemic may have given unusual prominence to the age cohort of 25- to 35-year-olds. The sophistic revolution was both a cause and symptom of the political prominence of young Athenians in their twenties.

Troubling change seemed to be everywhere, and the new prominence of youth seemed to many to symbolize it. Through the war era and beyond, Athenians became conscious of what we would call a generation gap, a cultural and political gulf between young and old. In military terms the young were usually perceived as more aggressive than the old; in political terms, the young seemed less devoted to democratic equality and more willing to flirt with tyrannical powers. Aristophanes' choruses complain about the prominence of such youths and about their alleged predations (especially judicial prosecutions) on their elders. At the time of the debate on the Sicilian Expedition in 415, Nicias portrayed the supporters of the expedition as primarily young men and the opponents as primarily old. Thucydides makes clear the falseness of this dichotomy: many older Athenians supported the expedition. The very fact that Nicias chose to make such an argument, however, and that his opponent Alcibiades bothered to respond, demonstrates the sensitivity of the Athenian audience to generational differences (Thuc. 6.12.2–13.1, 18.6, 24.3).

It is far from clear that the generation gap led to a significant increase in father–son conflict or filial rebellion within private oikoi. Nevertheless, the image of the rebellious or disobedient son, a son who would even turn with violence on his father, became the symbol of both generational and other change brought on by the dislocations of the long Peloponnesian War. However firm the foundations of the Athenian oikos in reality, ideologically it was seen to be shaking.

Not least of the reasons for the ideological prominence of father–son conflict in this era were the troubles of Athens's most famous politician, Pericles. Beset with two independent-minded legitimate sons and an illegitimate son on whose behalf Pericles ultimately had to beg the favor of Athenian citizenship, Pericles faced the biggest problem of all in Alcibiades, son of the late Kleinias and ward of Pericles. A notoriously ill-behaved and undisciplined boy, Alcibiades grew into the symbol of brilliant and dangerous youth, at times the darling and at times the detestation of the demos.

Pericles' household, particularly Alcibiades, would not have played this role in Athenian consciousness, however, had not an appropriate script been awaiting them. The paradigm was present in the *Iliad*: Achilles, the brilliant and antisocial young hero without a father on the scene who defies older male authority, carries out a great deed, temporarily acknowledges the authority of the father in his brief rapprochement with Priam, and finally dies young before the danger he poses to society grows any greater. The Adonis myth adds the element of the young erotic hero who is destroyed by his own beauty.

Athenian culture, therefore, provided a paradigm in the oikos that was used by Athenians to understand their experience as a polis. Athenian democracy used symbols of the oikos to structure its government. Athenian writers described social and political change in terms of aggressive youths and rebellious sons. It was just a short step to the point where Athenians conceived of the fortunes of the fatherland in a disastrous war as a morality play in which a brilliantly rebellious son, a beautiful and eternal youth, is destroyed by his own ambition, and the authority of the father is restored.

In the early years of the Peloponnesian War the poets predicted the outcome. Euripides was prophetic. In *Hippolytos* a brilliant and educated but unyielding youth, the "brightest star of Athena Hellanias," would quarrel with his father, be driven into exile and killed. As it turned out, Aristophanes could see the future too. In *Clouds* a brilliant teacher, who gives a young man the rhetorical stick with which to beat his father, is finally destroyed by the father's anger. *Knights* presages the *patrios politeia* movement of a decade later. "Old Man Demos" is made young and beautiful again, but not as an up-to-date young upstart: rather he returns to the old-fashioned ways of an Athenian of the Marathon generation.

By the end of the war the predictions of the poets were well on their way to being fulfilled. Alcibiades had been exiled (twice). The prestige of the younger generation was waning, and that of the older generation (some of whose members had been obstreperous youths in the 420s) waxing. What Aristophanes had hinted at in *Knights* Eupolis calls for outright in *Demes*: back to the leadership of the past, away with the "young degenerates" who have been ruling Athens. In the elderly *probouloi* of 413 and the oligarchy of 411, and above all, in the generalized interest in a *patrios politeia*, a large number of Athenians showed that they agreed with Eupolis. The relatively non-violent coup of 411 was followed by a bloody civil war in 404–403. Even after the restoration of democracy in all of Attica between 403 and 401, there were still scores to be settled, still charges of crimes against the authority of the Athenian father. In 400, Andokides successfully defended himself against such a charge; in 399, Socrates failed, thereby ending up a victim of enraged Athenian fatherhood, like the fictional Socrates of Aristophanes' *Clouds*.

The tragic poets too, recognized the change in Athenian culture. The hero of Sophocles' last play, *Oedipus at Kolonos* (produced posthumously in 401), is a blind old man; his selfish and manipulative sons have no interest in their duty to their father. As for Euripides' last play, *The Bakkhai* (produced posthumously in 405), it would be hard to imagine a more powerful or more scathing portrait of the vain and self-destructive pretensions of youth than the story of the protagonist Pentheus.

No doubt things would have turned out differently had Athens conquered Syracuse, or at least had Athens avoided turning a defeat in Sicily into a disaster. Athens might have won the war and paternal authority might not have had to be restored so violently. Athens's love affair with youth, however, was never more than a flirtation. Given the parameters of Athenian culture – it admired youth, it idealized youth, and then it put youth in its place – there can be little doubt but that, one way or another, paternal authority would have been restored. Even without defeat in the Peloponnesian War, the futurology of Euripides and Aristophanes is likely to have come true. Their perception of the fickle love that their countrymen had for their scapegoats was quite profound.

After the execution of Socrates in 399, neither father–son conflict nor intergenerational differences disappeared. In his trial several years later, for example, Alcibiades' son Alcibiades makes a point of distinguishing the older men in the jury, who were well versed with his father's career, from the younger men, who were not (Isoc. 16.4). In his Funeral Oration of the Corinthian War era,

Lysias looks back nostalgically at Myronides' Megarid campaign of 458, in which the victorious Athenian army was made up of the youngest and the oldest men cooperating splendidly (Lys. 2.50–53; cf. Thuc. 1.105–106). The speaker of Lysias 19 (around 390 BC) makes a point of stating that even at the age of thirty he never talks back to his father (19.55), which suggests that some Athenians did talk back. In a court case around mid-fourth century, Mantitheos takes it for granted that sons quarrel with fathers (Ps.-Dem. 40.47). The phenomenon of children mistreating their parents is among the many subjects of legislation in Plato's *Laws* (930–932), a work of the mid-fourth century. In his day (the latter fourth century) Aristotle tells the story of a man accused of beating his father who defends himself on the grounds that although he is indeed guilty, the crime runs in the family (*Nic. Eth.* 7.1149b8). Finally, at the end of the fourth century, Menander's plays are chock full of quarrels between father and son.

Father–son conflict, therefore, continued past the Peloponnesian War era, just as it had existed before that era. What did change, however, with the changing Athenian political and social scene, was the particular ideological construction that contemporaries put on that conflict.

NOTES

1 INTRODUCTION: SOLIDARITY OR CONFLICT?

1 One could date the Peloponnesian War era by various means: aside from the dates of the war itself (431–404 BC), one might reckon the period from the Thirty Years' Peace (446/445) to the King's Peace (387/386) or from the birth of Alcibiades (ca. 450) to the death of Thrasybulus (390) or from the ostracism of Thoukydides, son of Melesias (443), to the latest-surviving rehashing of the debate over the Thirty in Lysias 26 (382) or from the birth-year of the cadre of males who turned eighteen at the outbreak of the war in 431 (449) to the year in which the first postwar cadre of babies turned eighteen (385). In any case, the period from roughly 450 to roughly 380 is what I have in mind.

2 On the *amphidromia* and the *dekatê*, and on the debate on exposure in Athens, see below, ch. 3.

3 For details, see below, ch. 3.

4 Orphans: Stroud (1971); Loraux (1986 [1981]) 26; Goldhill (1990) 105–106, 124–125.

5 Funeral and memorial obligations: see below, ch. 3. Claim to adoption: Isaios 2.10, 25, 36–7. Nikophemos and Aristophanes: Lys. 19 and below, ch. 3.

6 Plut. *Thes.* 17, 22–23; Deubner (1966 [1932]) 142–147; Parke (1977) 77–81; Sourvinou-Inwood (1979) 12–15, 21; Simon (1983) 89–92; Ampolo and Manfredini (1988) 231–232; Calame (1990) 143–148. I follow the argument of Calame (1990) 444–450 (cf. Podlecki [1975] 17–19) that the Oschophoria was a preexisting rite associated with Theseus at the time of the establishment of the Theseia festival in 475 BC. Plutarch cites Demon (a writer probably of the third century BC) as a source, but the Oschophoria is securely attested in fourth-century BC Athens: Hyp. frg. 88 Jensen, Philokhoros *FGrH* 328 F 16, Istros *FGrH* 334 F 8, *SEG* 21, 527 = 19 *Suppl.* Sokolowski; cf. Calame (1990) 177 n.7, 178 n.15. A fifth-century text, Euripides' *Hippolytos* (790–807), may also allude to the festival and its connection with Theseus and the death of Aigeus: see below, ch. 4.

7 See below, ch. 5.

8 See below, ch. 5.

9 See below, ch. 6.

10 See below, ch. 2.

11 Comparative dyadic data: Slater (1968) 471–473; cf. Humphreys (1983) 70–71 on the quantitative approach and its limits. Fathers and daughters: for comparative purposes, see Hallett (1984). Ancient conception of tyranny: Bonfante (1981). Seclusion of women, practice vs. ideology: Cohen (1989), (1991) 149–170. Theoretical statement: Lerner (1986); Scott (1986). For a rich comparison, see the study of women and the ideology of gendered republicanism during the French Revolution in Landes (1988).

12 Two kinds of patriarchy, priority of husband–wife relationship: see Pateman (1988) esp. 19–38.

13 Private life: Humphreys (1978) 197–200; Just (1989) 83–95. Funerary inscriptions: Humphreys (1983) 111, 128 n.48; Garland (1990) 156. See below, ch. 2, for detailed discussion.

14 *Kyrios* is a word with wide semantic range, referring both to household and polis, to persons and property, to slave and free, and to concrete and abstract notions of power or authority. Fifth-century usage includes references to the power of a master over a slave (Ant. 2.4.7), the power of a general to issue commands (Thuc. 8.5, cf. 5.63), the symbolic authority of a son as confirmation of his parents' marriage pledges (Aesch. *Ag.* 878), the authorities of the land (Soph. *OC* 915), the principal assembly (*kyria ekklêsia*: Ar. *Ach.* 19), the binding authority of judicial verdicts and decisions of arbitrators (Andok. 1.88), the supreme authority in the regime of laws and decrees (Ant. 3.1.1). On the father as *kyrios*, see e.g. Arist. *Rhet.* 1402a1; Lacey (1968) 21–22; Schaps (1979) 48–60. The translation of *kyrios* as "sovereign" is problematic: see Ober (1989b).

15 On women as Athenian citizens, see Patterson (1981) 128–129, 160–166.

16 The distinction between *homo politicus* and *homo economicus* was elucidated by Max Weber (1958) 212–213 and the insightful discussion by Humphreys (1978) 159–174.

17 Recent feminist theory: for example, see Lerner (1986); Nicholson (1986); Scott (1986); Norton (1987). Politics uses symbols . . . of family: a similar point is made by social historians in Medick-Sabean (1984) 6.

18 Barrett and McIntosh (1982) 26 n.17; cf. the often-cited but somewhat confusing discussion in Donzelot (1979).

19 For these terms, see Fortes (1969) esp. 89–99.

20 See the works of these scholars cited in the bibliography; see also my discussion of ritual in Athenian politics in Strauss (1985b).

21 Athenians as mythic children: below, ch. 2. Zeus and Kronos: below, chs. 5, 6. Theseus: below, ch. 4.

22 Recent revisions of nineteenth-century arguments: Bourriot (1976); Roussel (1976); Humphreys (1978) 177–208, (1983) 79–143; Kuper (1988). Nineteenth-century classics: Maine (1861); Fustel de Coulanges (1980 [1864]); Morgan (1964 [1877]); see the discussion of Trautmann

(1987) esp. 179–204; Kuper (1988) 15–75. For critique of notion of "idiom of kinship," see discussion of Schneider, below, ch. 2.

23 Kinship little influence: Humphreys (1978) 198. Emerging modern state: Stone (1979) 133; cf. Nicholson (1986) 116–117 for analogy with classical Athens. On separation of family and state in modern liberalism, beginning with John Locke, see Nicholson (1986) 133–166.

24 Arthur (1986 [1976]) 67, cited in Nicholson (1986) 116.

25 Arthur (1986 [1976]). Phratries: below, ch. 2.

26 Freud, anthropologists, ethnologists, historians of religion: see below, ch. 2.

27 On Foucault, see below, ch. 2.

28 Freud (1913), (1939); Brown (1966) esp. 3–31.

29 On Turner and social drama, see below, ch. 2.

30 For a discussion of the relative merits of synchronic and diachronic approaches, see Ober (1989a) 36–38.

31 Dover (1974) 1–8; Ober (1989a) 40.

32 Winkler (1990a) 19.

2 INTELLECTUAL PATERNITY

1 For Freud's ideas on the father and the law, see *Totem and Taboo* (1913) and *Moses and Monotheism* (1939); on the Oedipus Complex, Freud (1955) 260–264; cf. Juliet Mitchell (1974) 42–112, 364–398. On Freud's complicated and repressed relationship with his father and its importance for his thought (particularly in regard to the Oedipus Complex), see Balmary (1982). On fathers and sons in the New Testament, see Bornkamm (1976). For Lacan on the father and the Name-of-the-Father, see Lacan (1977) xi, 199, 217, 310; Gallop (1985) 58–61, 106–110, 157–160, 167–185; Ragland-Sullivan (1986) 42, 55, 115–116, 269–279, 290–291, 301. For a thoughtful psychological reading of the significance of the father–son relationship in the political culture of the Middle American Republic, see Forgie (1979).

2 See Pucci (1992) 203 n.29.

3 See the remarks of Lacan (1977) 199. On fatherhood as discourse, see Pucci (1992) 1–9.

4 Schneider (1984) 72–74; cf. Kuper (1988) 241–243. Schneider criticizes mainstream anthropology (including his own early work) for mistakenly privileging kinship and for directly imposing "the ethnoepistemology of European culture" on the other cultures. He calls instead for a heightened sensitivity to native formations and categories (77, 175–177). Trautmann (1987) discusses the nineteenth-century invention of modern anthropological theories of kinship, highlighting their artificiality; Kuper (1988) discusses the symbiosis of kinship and primitive society, both of which notions he criticizes.

5 LSJ s.vv. *Genetês* can also mean "ancestor" or "son." See ch. 3 for the *nomos kakôseôs goneôn*, the "law [against] harming one's parents."

6 On the etymology of *patêr* and its derivatives, see Benveniste (1969) 1:210, 270–274; Frisk (1970) 2:481–482; Chantraine (1974) 3: 863–865. On Zeus as father, see Pucci (1992) 26–27.

7 On Plato and the "father of the discourse," see Derrida (1984 [1972]) 75–84.

8 Most relevant examples: Ancient Greek has a multiplicity of *patêr*-derivatives. I restrict the survey mainly to Attic Greek and mainly to words with political and social significance. *Patris:* One's countrymen, however, were usually caled *politai, patriôtês* (LSJ s.v.) mainly being used for non-Greeks.

9 *Patriazein:* Pollux 3.10, cf. Dindorf comm. *ad loc. Patrios, patrikos, patrôios:* LSJ s.v. *patrios;* Chantraine (1974) 3:864. *Patrios politeia* and *patêr:* see Appendix A and ch. 6, below.

10 Patrimonial hearth, religious activities of oikos: De Schutter (1987) 110, 119.

11 On patronyms and epithets in Homer more generally, see Austin (1975) 11–80.

12 Paternity-affirming rituals: below, ch. 3. Name as a mark of status: for Homer's world, see Murnaghan (1987) 6 + n.5. Cleisthenes: Rhodes (1981) 81–82. Demotic, patronymic: Whitehead (1986) 69–72. Fourth-century inscriptions: personal communication by John Traill, director of ATHENIANS project, a database of over 100,000 ancient Athenians.

13 Compare the modern Greek custom of putting a woman's surname in the genitive: she is "of" someone, be it her father or husband.

14 See Pucci (1992) 4; on psychoanalytic theory, see above, n.1.

15 On the debility of being *anônymos* in classical Athens, see Eur. *Hipp.* 1028; cf. 1, 1429; cf. Eur. *Hel.* 16–17.

16 For another example of the *patêr*-theme in patriotic oratory, see Aesch. *Pers.* 401–405.

17 Etymology of *pais:* Golden (1985) 92, to which the following discussion of sons is much indebted. Various diminutives were formed from *pais:* e.g. *paidarion,* "young child," "little boy or girl," or "young slave"; *paidion,* "young child" or "young slave"; *paidiskos,* "young son," "boy," and possibly "young slave"; *paidiskê,* "young girl," "young female slave," "courtesan." LSJ s.vv.; Golden (1985) 91 n.3.

18 Male citizen not yet of age: Golden (1985) 93. *Teknon* vs. *pais:* Golden (1985) 95–96 + n.17.

19 Oedipus: Pucci (1992) 67–68, 162. Asclepiads: Pl. *Phdr.* 270c; Arr. *Anab.* 6.11.1; *SEG* 16.326; Burkert (1985) 215.

20 *Pais* as slave: Golden (1985) 104. *Pais* as *eromenos:* Dover (1978) 16–17; Golden (1984); Halperin (1990) 88.

21 The point has been made by Foucault (1985) from the perspective of the history of sexuality, and by Golden (1985) 101 from the perspective of philology and Athenian social history.

22 I have been particularly influenced by the discussions of Geertz (1973); Duby (1985 [1974]); Thompson (1984); Ober (1989a) 38–40.

23 Everyday life: Duby (1985 [1974]). Practice-oriented anthropology: Bourdieu (1977). Sociology: Giddens (1984). "Poetics of manhood": Herzfeld (1985). Historians of ancient Greece: for example, Schmitt–Pantel (1990).

24 These various points are discussed at greater length, and bibliographical citations are provided, in ch. 1, above.

25 Analogies between oikos and polis: see below, this chapter. Efficacious ideological symbol: see e.g. discussion of Theseus as father and son, ch. 4. Rituals: see e.g. discussion of fatherless children, above, ch. 1.

26 See for example Gluckman's (1963) much criticized model of rites of rebellion, which he saw as preserving the social order among the Swazi Ncwala; cf. Thompson (1984) 5, 61–63; Versnel (1987) 136–137; Lincoln (1989) 53–74.

27 *Eleutheria, isonomia, isêgoria*: Raaflaub (1985). *Archein/archesthai*: LSJ s.vv. and below, n.43. Roman patriarchal ideology: below, ch. 3.

28 Tension and balance: Ober (1989a) 17–35, 293–339.

29 Plasticity of terminology: Gernet (1955) 148–149; Bourriot (1976) on the manifold meanings of *genos*. Dem. 43: Sissa (1986) 182. Addition of aged parent: e.g. the married Euergos lived with his father, Dem. 47.34–35. MacDowell (1989) discusses the various meanings of oikos and *oikia*, arguing that oikos means "property" or "house" in Attic law but has no legal definition as "family" or "persons." *Suggeneia*: used generically by Aristotle, it can have the precise connotation of "collateral relative" (Isai. 8.30–33), Sissa (1986) 183–184. *Anchisteia*: a bilateral kindred extending perhaps to second cousins, and legally significant in acceding to inheritance and in the obligation to avenge a homicide. See Dem. 43.51; Isai. 11.11; Harrison (1968) 143–145; Davies (1977–78) 108–109; MacDowell (1989) 17–18. *Philoi*: usually translated as "friends," it can also mean "one's people" or "kinsmen," e.g. Xen. *Hell*. 1.14.18; cf. Connor (1971) 31. *Oikeioi*: Just (1989) 84. Other terms for extended family: Humphreys (1985b) 346, 348. Not letting the oikos die out: Asheri (1960); Lacey (1968) 97–99, 147; MacDowell (1989) 15–16. Religious significance: see Connor (1985). Meeting house, clubhouse, deme assembly: Hedrick (1990) 44–52, 80–85, whose arguments I follow.

30 Old Fustelian notion of ancestors no longer tenable: Humphreys (1983) 79–130, 131–143, (1986) 88. No interest beyond great-grandfather: Bourriot (1976) 223–233, 1037–1042. No family surname: Jameson (1990a) 112 n.26. Oikos an institution that recreates itself: Foxhall (1989) 28 + n.32; cf. Gernet (1955) 149. Father's responsibilities to legitimate sons: below, ch. 3.

31 "Household" rather than "family": a point often made, and nowhere better than in Humphreys' seminal work, especially (1983) 67–68. On the debate over terminology, see Netting *et al.* (1984) xix–xxi; on the ancient household from a medievalist's perspective, see Herlihy (1985) 2–5. Inheritance theme in tragedy: e.g. Orestes at *Eumenides* 754–761; Ion at *Ion* 1304–1305; Hecuba (concerning Astyanax) at *Troiades* 1192–1193; Herakles' pity for his dead children at *Herakles* 1367–1370. For an argument that such connotations of the modern middle-class "family" as privacy, intimacy, domesticity, and loving relationships radically different from the harsh give-and-take of the marketplace are a late development in human history, rooted in market capitalism, the Industrial Revolution, and individualism, see Shorter (1977). Good

general discussions of the oikos include: Lacey (1968) 15–32; Humphreys (1983) 66–67; Sissa (1986) 163–194; Foxhall (1989); MacDowell (1989).

32 Predominance of independent family, household architecture, religious cult: all discussed in Jameson (1990a and b); on religious cult, cf. Rose (1957); Harrison (1968) 123, 130; Lacey (1968) 27–28; Mikalson (1983) 89, 98; Burkert (1985) 170, 254–264; de Schutter (1987) 118–122. Hearth: Vernant (1983 [1969]), with Jameson (1990a and b) as a corrective. Limited importance of extended family in politics: Humphreys (1978) 197–202, (1983) 26–28; Hutter (1978) 33–36; Strauss (1986) 19–24. Aurenche (1974) pushes the evidence somewhat. Farber (1988) 17, 34, 104, 192 makes a stimulating argument for the "centripetal" and isolated nature of the oikos.

33 Public vs. private space: Vernant (1983 [1969]); Keuls (1985) 93–97; Cohen (1991) 72–74.

34 Public hearth: Gernet (1981 [1951]) downplays the oikos analogy; Vernant (1983 [1969]); Jameson (1990a). *Andrôn*: Keuls (1985) 162–163; Jameson (1990a) 106, (1990b) 188–191.

35 Meier (1990 [1979]) 146, see 141–145. Cf. review by Cartledge (1992). Arendt: (1958) 33. See similarly Rahe (1984).

36 Musti (1985); Hansen (1989) 17–21, 39 n.103. In an unpublished paper, Cheryl Cox (1990) provides graphic examples of the intermingling of citizens and non-citizens in private life.

37 Lanza and Vegetti (1975) 25, my translation. Similarly Osborne (1990); cf. Loraux (1986 [1981]) 25.

38 Humphreys (1983) 21, cf. 1–2, 27–28. Cf. Keuls (1985) 93–97; Konstan (1985) 41–45; Carter (1986).

39 Foucault (1985) 214–215. On this model, see the seminal study by Gouldner (1967); see also discussion of Athenian political culture in Strauss (1986) 31–36, which draws on Gouldner as well as on work by Adkins (1960), Walcot (1970), Connor (1971), and Dover (1974), among others.

40 On the body as a symbol, see Douglas (1966); Foucault (1985) esp. 70–76, 151–184, 215; Winkler, "Laying Down the Law: The Oversight of Men's Sexual Behavior in Classical Athens," in Winkler (1990a) 45–70; Halperin, "The Democratic Body: Prostitution and Citizenship in Classical Athens," in Halperin (1990) 88–112. On the regulation of sexuality by the Athenian polis, see the nuanced assessment in Cohen (1991) 221–231. On Mediterranean anthropology and the study of ancient society, see *inter alia* Walcot (1970); Winkler (1990a); Cohen (1991).

41 Ethos of equality: see Ober (1989a).

42 Herzfeld (1987).

43 Dover (1978) 84; Halperin (1990) 30–38. On the importance of the alternation of *archein/archesthai* in Athenian democratic ideology, see Hdt. 3.83.2; Arist. *Pol.* 1317a40-b17; cf. Eur. *Supp.* 404–407; Hansen (1989) 8–9. For a contrast between the *kyrios* and the slave, see Pl. *Laws* 700a.

44 Cf. Davies (1971) 467–468.

45 On the homology beteen oikos – particularly the father–son relationship – and polis, see Maffi (1983) 10.
46 Prevalent contemporary argument: Finley (1983) 137; Cambiano (1987).
47 I follow Salkever (1991); cf. Lord (1991) esp. 71–73.
48 All part of general problem: Golden (1985) 100–101.
49 "Having a share in" polis and oikos: I follow the discussion of Patterson (1981) 164–167, cf. (1990) 41, 56–57, 70.
50 Oikos essential to citizenship: Wolff (1944) 93, (1978) 12; Sissa (1986) 168–169. Qualifications for citizenship: see Rhodes (1981) 496–500; Manville (1990) 7–9. Citizenship requirements in fifth century: Patterson (1981). Adoption: Harrison (1968) 82–96; MacDowell (1978) 99–108; Sissa (1986) 175. *Poiêsis: p.* also has more general meaning of "recognition" of a (birth) child as legitimate by its father; see Rudhardt (1962). Properly married: on Athenian marriage, see Wolff (1944); Redfield (1982); Just (1989) 40–75. Exceptions to phratry membership: Manville (1990) 63 n.42. Witness: Humphreys (1985b) 346–347.
51 The revisionists on the phratry, *genos, and phyle* ("tribe") began with Bourriot (1976) and Roussel (1976). See Manville (1990) 58–67; Hedrick (1991). Political function: there is some reason to think that deme assemblies could intervene in phratry affairs, at least in times of crisis. See Hedrick (1990) 84–85. Father or guardian: Isai. 8.19; Ar. *Birds* 1669–1670. Phratry as legitimizing institution: Davies (1977–78) 109–110. Male solidarity: Jane Harrison's discussion (1927) 499–502 is based on outdated theories of patriarchy replacing matriarchy, but is nonetheless perceptive and instructive.
52 Wolff (1944) 50, 83–84, 93. MacDowell (1989) 20 is an overly harsh critique. Each generation reconstitutes oikos: Foxhall (1989). Bilateral but with strong patrilineal bias: Just (1989) 89–95.
53 Cf. Rhodes (1981) 617–618; Humphreys (1983) 121. Apollo Patrôios: De Schutter (1987); Hedrick (1988). Zeus Herkeios: De Schutter (1987) 118–119; cf. Jameson (1990a) 105.
54 *Nomos goneôn kakôseôs:* see ch. 3. Juror's oath: Dem. 24.149, 54.41; Bonner and Smith (1938) 2:149, 153–155.
55 Loraux (1981) esp. 40, 66, 120, 128–129, 145–146; Davies (1977–78) 110; Strauss (forthcoming).
56 Athena, funeral oratory: Loraux (1981) 65–68, 130–131, 143–146, (1986 [1981]) 26, 275, 283–284. Apollo Patrôios: De Schutter (1987); cf. Hedrick (1988). Euripides, *Ion:* Loraux (1981) 197–253; De Schutter (1987) 123–124. Date: Loraux (1981) 221 n.91, with earlier literature cited.
57 On the good-in-the-oikos, good-in-the-polis topos, see Dover (1974) 302–303. Private behavior . . . public reputation: Cohen (1991) 83–97. On the prosecution of Timarkhos, see Dover (1978) 19–110; Halperin (1990) 88–112; Winkler (1990a) 45–70. Fifth-century text: Sophocles' *Antigone,* which Aeschines supposedly knew well (Dem. 19.246).
58 Kleon brags in *Knights:* see Dover (1978) 141; Winkler (1990a) 54–55.
59 Public and private: Halperin (1990) 11, 95; Cohen (1991) 22.
60 Cf. Dem. 10.40–41, discussed below.
61 Personifications of polis as a mother are less common but not unheard

of: e.g. Isoc. 4.25, Hdt. 6.107 (Hippias's dream of Athens as his mother). Misbehavior toward one's mother is not as frequently cited as evidence of general wickedness as is mistreatment of one's father, but it is cited from time to time: e.g. Lys. 30.20–22; Dem. 24.54–55.

62 At 1.36 Euphiletos calls the vote of the jurors "the most authoritative (*kyrios*) thing of all in the polis" (*pantôn en têi polei kuriôtatê*). Cf. Arist. *Pol.* 1252a5.

63 Andokides: see below, ch. 6.

64 Bringing family to court: see e.g. Lys. 20.34–36; Dem. 25.76–77; Pl. *Ap.* 34c; Humphreys (1985b) 346–347. Family's record of public service: When the facts convict them, as Demosthenes (25.76–77) notes, defendants often "take refuge" in the alleged moderation of their private life or in the supposed deeds and liturgies of their ancestors, for example, their father. As Demosthenes also knew, the strategy did not always work: elsewhere (24.135–136) he cites Myronides son of Arkhinos (one of the liberators of 403) as a man who was convicted in spite of his father's many good deeds. Demosthenes himself came up with an excellent response to the "virtuous father" defense: as he says (24.127) of Timokrates, the father's virtues make the son's vices all the more inexcusable! An enemy of course might attack a man by blackening his father's name: see below, ch. 3.

65 "Root paradigms": Drawing on earlier work by Turner, Ortner, and Schneider, among others, Wagner-Pacifici (1986) 164–169 discusses the use of competing paradigms by politicians. She defines root paradigms as "appeals to what . . . [were posited] as the most salient and transcendent cultural values" and "symbolic weapons in . . . [an] ongoing action" (164) or "condensed myths" (167) that aim at political legitimation.

66 Geertz, "Deep Play. Notes on the Balinese Cockfight," in Geertz (1973) 450.

67 Geertz and symbolic anthropology: see also the other essays in Geertz (1973) as well as Geertz (1980) which offers a different analysis from Turner's of politics as drama, and (1983). For an introduction to symbolic anthropology and other recent anthropological movements, see Ortner (1984). Turner's followers: in addition to Turner's works on social drama cited below, I have also profited from MacAloon (1982); Herzfeld (1985); and Wagner-Pacifici (1986) 1–18. On symbolic anthropology, social drama, politics, and ritual in classical Athens, see also Strauss (1985b).

68 Turner (1957) 94.

69 See Wagner-Pacifici (1986) 9. On Turner's notion of the social drama, see also Turner (1957), (1974) 23–155, (1980), (1982) 11–30.

70 Turner (1974) 123.

71 Turner (1974) 123. Cornford (1971 [1907]) argued for a similar process of what he calls "infiguration" (132, cf. viii) by which Thucydides had been unconsciously influenced by the mythic paradigms of Aeschylean drama.

72 On applying modern theoretical perspectives to ancient history, see Ste. Croix (1981) 81–98, esp. 81–82. Theater as fundamental metaphor of Athenian culture: a point that has often been made, recently by

Humphreys (1983) 18, (1985b) 323, 355; and Ober-Strauss (1990). Aristotle and "social drama": Wagner-Pacifici (1986) 12–13. Orators and tragedy: Ober-Strauss (1990) 250–258. Thucydides and tragedy: Cornford (1971 [1907]).

73 Humphreys (1983) 69–74; Goldhill (1986) 63–78; Segal (1988) 52–53, 67.
74 Herzfeld (1985) 8–19; cf. Goffman (1959).

APPENDIX TO CHAPTER 2: PATRIOS AND PATÊR

1 In his study of Anaximenes, Wendland (1905) 7–13 concludes that A. borrowed freely from Demosthenes and imitated his style closely. The most relevant text here, section 22 of Ps.-Dem. 11, is an imitation of Dem. 18.67–68, with a suggestion of Dem. 7.7 as well.
2 On this trope, see Loraux (1981) 49–52, 66–68.

3 SOLIDARITY: PROUD FATHERS, OBEDIENT SONS

1 On *kyrios*, see above, ch. 1 n.14.
2 See Golden (1990) 28.
3 Recent reappraisals of *patria potestas* include Saller (1986), (1988), and Dixon (1988) 26–30, 41–44, 51–60.
4 Trade, phratry, deme, citizenship, legally independent: see below for sources and discussion. Legally required to leave to sons: see below. Squandering property: Harrison (1968) 79–81.
5 No contract, child represented by father: Harrison (1968) 73–74. Adoption, guardian, selling children: Harrison (1968) 73, 82–121. Child labor: Golden (1990) 32–36. Beating: see below.
6 *Amphidromia* and *dekatê*: for sources and discussion, see Harrison (1968) 70–71; Golden (1986) 252–256; Garland (1990) 93–94, 313. Exposure: Beauchet (1897) 2:85–93; Harrison (1968) 70–73; for summary of recent debate, with bibliography, see Patterson (1985). Julian Pitt-Rivers (1977) has argued that concern over the fidelity of one's wife and hence the paternity of one's child is an obsession among males in both ancient and modern Mediterranean (cf. Gardner [1989]). Perhaps the right of the Athenian father to reject a child is a reflection of this concern. Other considerations – the limitation of family size, a bias against daughters, and a rejection of babies born with deformities – were no doubt also important.
7 Plut. *Them.* 2; Harrison (1968) 63, 75–77.
8 Old age: for discussion and sources, see Harrison (1968) 77–78; Finley (1990); Garland (1990) 261–262. Richardson (1933) is still charming on Greek attitudes and sense of duty toward elderly. *Therapeia*: see Raepset (1971) 91. Gorgias: see Loraux (1986 [1981]) 227. Funerals and memorial rites: see e.g. Aesch. *Cho.* 22–585; Eur. *Supp.* 1114–1179; cf. Humphreys (1983) 84–88; Garland (1985) 21–37, 104–120. Laws of Solon and *dokimasia* for archonship: for other ancient evidence, see Rhodes (1981) comm. *ad* 55.3 and 56.6. Rhodes considers questions about parental support in the *dokimasia* to be part of an ancient

procedure. *Atimia*: Harrison (1968) 78. Orators: for the so-called *dokimasia rhêtorôn*, see Hyp. 4.7–8; and Ober (1989a) 110, 126.

9 The fifth-century context is provided in 496f.

10 Division of estate: Levy (1956), (1963). Harrison (1968) 122–162 discusses legal aspects of Athenian succession; Golden (1990) 106–114 is a witty and perceptive discussion of its psychology. For general discussion of intergenerational property transmission and the family, see Goody (1962), (1976); and Sabean (1976).

11 Lys. 32: see Davies (1971) 151–154. Konon: Lys. 19.39–40; Harrison (1968) 151; Davies (1971) 508–509. Another famous case is that of the orator Demosthenes: Dem. 27.5, 11–13, 42–43; 28.15; cf. Harrison (1968) 151; Davies (1971) 126–133; Schaps (1979) 78. Other cases: Dem. 36.34, 45.28; Dem. 41.6; Lys. 32.6; cf. discussion in Harrison (1968) 152. In my opinion, Harrison is pressing the point (and Asheri [1963] even more so) when he says that the hoary principle that a man with legitimate sons should not leave his estate to others "had been considerably eroded by the fourth century" (152). Based on the case of Konon, Gernet suggests that a father could dispose as he saw fit of property that he himself had acquired (as opposed to his patrimony), but this is speculative (Gernet and Bizos [1926] note on Lys. 19.39–40, Budé edition; cited by Harrison, 151 n.4).

12 Age of enrollment in phratry: Labarbe (1953) with Golden (1990) 26–29. Age of enrollment in deme: Golden (1979). Inheritance not automatic at eighteen: Following Whitehead (1986) 35 n.130, the word *lêxis* in *lêxiarchikon grammateion* refers not to the possession of a *klêros* (inheritance) but to the capacity to inherit a *klêros* one day. Hence, Pollux 8.104 misconstrues *lêxis* in saying that the eighteen-year-olds registered on the *lêxiarchikon grammateion* had "already taken possession of their patrimony" (*êdê ta patrôia parelambanen*). Son of *epiklêros*: Ps.- Dem. 46.20; Schaps (1979) 26, 34. Father already dead: Arist. *Ath. Pol.* 42.5 states that inheritance and *epiklêroi* were the only two matters in regard to which ephebes could sue or be sued in court.

13 In general, see Saller's seminal (1987) article: Golden (1990) 111–112 applies Saller's arguments to Athens. Relevant ancient evidence includes: Dem. 40.12–13; Xen. *Oec.* 7.5; Arist. *Pol.* 1335a28–32; cf. Hesiod *Op.* 696–698; Plut. *Mor.* 496e; cf. Davies (1971) 336–337; Pomeroy (1975) 64. Life expectancy of ca. twenty-five years: see Hansen (1985) 11. Mortality after fifty: Saller (1987) 30. Living father: Based on Roman epigraphic evidence, a model life table with a life expectancy of twenty-five years of birth, and comparative evidence from eighteenth-century England on frequency of births for women, Saller (1987) 31–33 has generated through computer simulation a model population of families in the Roman empire. Assuming a median age at marriage of 30 for men and 25 for women, the result is that 54 percent of 15-year-olds and 41 percent of 20-year-olds would have a living father; assuming median ages at marriage of 25 and 15, the result is 55 percent of 15-year-olds and 43 percent of 20-year-olds with a living father.

14 Living father: Saller's (1987) 33 estimates are: assuming marriage ages

of 30 for men and 20 for women, about 30 percent of 25-year-olds, about 19 percent of 30-year-olds, about 12 percent of 35-year-olds, and about 6 percent of 40-year-olds would have a living father; assuming marriage ages of 25 and 25 respectively, the figures for living father are respectively 32, 20, 12, and 6 percent. Old age: Richardson (1933); Finley (1990). *Wasps*: see MacDowell (1971) and Sommerstein (1983) comm. *ad loc.*; cf. below, ch. 5.

15 See Beauchet (1897) 3:639. Examples of dissension: Isai. 9.17; Dem. 48.12–14. On quarrels between brothers over the division of estates, see more generally Plut. *Mor.* 482e, 483b.

16 Date: Davies (1971) 79.

17 Retirement: cf. Arist. *Pol.* 1275a14–19. Lysis: see Davies (1971) 359–361.

18 Campbell (1964) 68, 171; cf. Golden (1990) 108–109.

19 Hirschon (1989) 151.

20 Hirschon (1989) 228. Common: for Euboea, see DuBoulay (1974) 20; for Cyprus, Loizos (1975) 65. Not invariable rule: for Boeotia, Friedl (1962) 58; also the more general reflections in Dimen-Friedl (1976). See also Levy (1956) and Walcot (1970) 45–56, comparing ancient and modern practices. For other examples of "the transmission of basic resources between the living," both in western Europe and in Africa, see Goody (1962) 277–278. Compare the African society in which a father gives up considerable property and rights to his sons in stages as they mature and marry: Stenning (1966 [1958]).

21 On this paradigm in the ancient Mediterranean in general, see comments in Goody (1983) esp. 31–33, 59, 207–210.

22 Slights in old age: see Schaps (1979) 84.

23 Note that the speaker of Lysias 19 may be exaggerating a father's tendency to hold property in reserve, since his main point is that one particular father, Nikophemos, left little to his son Aristophanes or to the speaker's late brother-in-law. Wealthy and poor: Lacey (1968) 129.

24 Konon and Nikophemos: Each man had a second family in Cyprus who looked after their property there. Euktemon and Philoktemon: As Lacey (1968) 129 points out, the son's ability to carry out liturgies in his own name indicates that he was *kyrios* of his allotted portion of the paternal estate. Cf. Schaps (1979) 48 n.3. A less clear example is that of Polykrates and his adopted son Leokrates (Dem. 41). Killed in battle probably in the 370s, Philoktemon died before his father (ca. 364): Isai. 6.14; cf. Davies (1971) 562–563. Leokrates was able to make a contract concerning the disbursement of the estate after Polykrates' death, but Leokrates had brought money of his own into the estate, and it is unclear what financial powers Leokrates had while Polykrates was still alive. Dem. 41.4–5; cf. Schaps (1979) 48 n.3.

25 Menekles retired: As Lacey (1968) 117 suggests. Cf., however, Lys. 19.37 where father is cared for by son but father still controls a substantial portion of his estate. Cf. Davies (1971) 225–226.

26 Saller (1987) 33.

27 Apollodoros and Pasion: Davies (1971) 427–442; Humphreys (1985b) 328. Polystratos and son: Davies (1971) 467–468.

28 Pheidippides' age: see Dover (1968a) xxvii. Property as cause of father–son conflict: see below, ch. 4.

29 Homer, Pindar: Kurke (1991) 15–21, 35–43. Andokides: Davies (1971) 27. Platonic youths: e.g. Pl. *Chrm.* 157e–158c, *Lys.* 205c, *Prt.* 316b.

30 Children dear: cf. Dem. 28.20; Dein. 1.99; Lyk. 1.2; cf. Charlier and Raepset (1971) 602. "Lion of a boy": This is not to say that a father was unhappy to hear the news that his wife had given birth to a daughter. On Athenian father–daughter relations, see Charlier and Raepset (1971) 594–595; Golden (1990) 94–97, 117–118.

31 Emphasis on material factors, symbolic significance: Raepset (1971) 81–87, 108–109. Tellos's distinction was also due to the flourishing state of his country and to his glorious death in battle, earning him a public funeral and the highest honors (Hdt. 1.30.4–5).

32 Raepset (1971) and especially Charlier and Raepset (1971) are aware of this sentimental dimension of Athenian parenthood but emphasize the other motivations for parenthood cited above.

33 Orators, playwrights, and philosophers: among the most important sources are Aeschin. 2.156–158; Ar. *Ach.* 326–329; Soph. *OC* 1529; Xen. *Oec.* 7.23; Pl. *Lys.* 207d, *Laws* 754b; Arist. *Eth. Nic.* 8.12, *Pol.* 1259b11–12; Plut. *Mor.* 496f; see Raepset (1971) and Charlier and Raepset (1971) for other references. Doting father: Plut. *Mor.* 497a-c; Raepset (1971) 596 n.34.

34 In the *Iliad*, Odysseus is proud of something slightly different, that is, of the very fact of his parenthood. At two moments of high emotion he makes vows on his status as the father of Telemakhos (*Il.* 2.260, 4.354; cf. Walcot [1970] 46).

35 See Lacey (1968) 77–78; Raepset (1971) 81, 86–87. Peisistratos's comment was politic but insincere: cf. Hdt. 1.61.

36 On Karkinos and his family, see Davies (1971) 283–285; MacDowell (1971) comm. *ad* 1501; Sommerstein (1983) comm. *ad* 1501. For fathers and sons with same profession, see also below.

37 Ar. *Wasps* 1275–1283; see MacDowell (1971) and Sommerstein (1983) comm. *ad loc.* Ariphrades: Ar. *Kn.* 1280–1287, *Peace* 885, *Eccl.* 129; Ps.-Ar. frg. 926 Kassel and Austin; Arist. *Poet.* 1485b31; Ath. 220b.

38 Vase: Boston, Museum of Fine Arts, 63.1246, William Francis Warden Fund. The vase is the work of the Dokimasia Painter. See Beazley (1971) 373, 34 *quater*; Boardman (1975a) 137. Antiphon: the speech, *Against the Stepmother, for Poisoning*, may be a rhetorical exercise.

39 Pindar: trans. Kurke (1991) 35, cf. discussion 35–37. Help living father fight: Raepset (1971) 92. Inherited friendship and enmity: see *inter alia* Lys. 14.2; Lys. frg. 78 (Thalheim) and Herman (1987) 28; Isoc. 1.2, 16.10–11, 19.10, 50; Pl. *Lach.* 180e; Dover (1974) 182, 276. A father's good reputation did not always help a son: for example, the good name of Nicias did not prevent the arrest of his son Nikeratos under the Thirty (Xen. *Hell.* 2.3.39). Sins of father: consider, for example, the curse of the house of Atreus, the curse of the Alkmeonidai (invoked against Pericles in 431, Thuc. 1.126–127), and the case of Alcibiades' son Alcibiades below (especially Isoc. 16.2, 3, 44).

40 Schol. Ar. *Wasps* 1007 (= Andok. frg. 5 Blass); Theopompos *FGrH*

115 F 95; Plato Com. frg. 182 Kassel and Austin; Davies (1971) 517; Ostwald (1986) 215.

41 Theomnestos: note that T. had previously accused his opponent, the speaker of Lys. 10 (and a later abstract = Lys. 11), of patricide (Lys. 10.2, 11.1). Date of prosecution of Alcibiades *fils* ca. 395: Lys. 14.4, 7–8, 15, which fits the Haliartus campaign of 395; Blass (1887) 488–489. Date of other prosecution after Alcibiades *fils* came of age in 390s: Davies (1971) 19, 21. For another example of son defending father's reputation, see discussion of trial of Polystratos in 411 BC, above, ch. 2.

42 Demosthenes' father's property: Dem. 27.9–12; Davies (1971) 126–135. Attacks on fathers of public figures: Ober (1989a) 273–274.

43 Redeem reputation of oikos: Pindar *Nemean Odes* 6.17–24; cf. Kurke (1991) 37. Inscription: Peek (1955) no. 1815; cited by Dover (1968a) xxvi n.2.

44 Compare the internal struggle of Henry James (father of the novelist) with the memory of his censorious father William for many years after William's death: Feinstein (1984) 59–66, 77–88, 114–115, cf. 325–326.

45 On Telamon and his sons, see Blundell (1989) 70, 76–77, 79, 81.

46 Obedience: Soph. *Ant.* 639–642; Ar. *Clouds* 860–861 and Dover (1968a) comm. *ad loc.* Corporal punishment: Arist. *Eth. Nic.* 1149b8; Dio Chrysostom 15.20; Beck (1964) 104–105; Golden (1990) 64–65, 101, 103, 214 n.99. Lysis's age: since he is too young to come into his patrimony, Lysis is not yet eighteen, and since he is Hippothales' would-be *eromenos*, he is probably at least thirteen (Pl. *Lys.* 204b-e, 209a and below). Double meaning of *pais*: above, ch. 2. Father-beating in comedy: Reckford (1976) 89–118; Golden (1990) 161–163); see below, ch. 5.

47 Age groups: Garland (1990) 288–289; Winkler (1990b) 28. Educational function of communal institutions: see Loraux (1986 [1981]) 144–145; Ober (1989a) 158–165. Son sue father: Dem. 39.2; 40.9–11; Harrison (1968) 78–79.

48 Cited by Marrou (1956) 58.

49 Cf. Pl. *Apol.* 49d; Xen. *Mem.* 1.5.2.

50 Emphasis of culture on familial reputation: see e.g. Dover (1974) 226–229, 236–242.

51 Nurses, teachers, etc.: Pl. *Prt.* 325c–326e. Education of wealthy different from that of ordinary boys: Pl. *Prt.* 326c. Cf. Marrou (1956) 65–67; Ober (1989a) 187–191. Father teaching *technê*: cf. Pl. *Prt.* 328a, *Rep.* 421e. Destitute minority: for an estimate of gradations of wealth and poverty in Athens, see Strauss (1986) 42–43. Eating, telling stories: Pl. *Lach.* 179b–c refers to one such scene among the rich, but it could have been repeated, with a much humbler menu, even among the very poor. Taking to theater: cf. Theophr. *Char.* 9.5, 30.6.

52 Cf. Isai. 8.15–16, where a grandfather brings his grandsons to festivals and sacrifices.

53 Harris (1989) 65–115, esp. 101–102, argues that primary education and literacy were relatively limited in Athens; for arguments that they were more widespread, see Harvey (1966); Ober (1989a) 157; Golden (1990) 63.

54 On Athenian education, see Girard (1889) 63–270; Freeman (1932 [1907]) 42–156; Marrou (1956) 63–136; Beck (1964) 72–146; Garland (1990) 133–136. Education usually ended in mid-teenage years: Pl. *Lach.* 179a; Xen. *Lac. Pol.* 3.1; Freeman (1932 [1907]) 54; Beck (1964) 95–96; Dover (1968a) lxi. Higher education with sophists: Freeman (1932 [1907]) 157–178; Beck (1964) 147–187; Dover (1968a) lxi; Guthrie (1971a) 35–44.

55 Apprenticeship: Pl. *Prt.* 38a, *Cltphon.* 409b, *Rep.* 421e, *Grg.* 514b; Ar. *Ach.* 1032; Freeman (1932 [1907]) 44–45; Dover (1968a) lxi. Mother's knee: Pl. *Rep.* 376e–378e; Garland (1990) 131. Gymnasia: on the democratization of the gymnasia in the fifth century, see Ps.-Xen. *Ath. Pol.* 2.10; Marrou (1956) 65–67. On lack of formal training for hoplites before the fourth-century institution of the ephebeia, see Hanson (1989) 31–32. Rowers: Jordan (1975) 103–106. Religion: children served in choruses and participated in a number of religious rituals. See Garland (1990) 144–147; Golden (1990) 41–46, 65–67.

56 Socrates similarly criticizes Pericles, Aristides, and Thoukydides: *Meno* 94a–e. See also Pl. *Alc.* 1.118e, *Prt.* 320a–b, *Theages* 126d. The Socratic circle perhaps took a certain *Schadenfreude* in the troubles that Socrates' prosecutor Anytos had with his son: see Xen. *Ap.* 30–31. For another criticism of sons not as great as their fathers, see Eupolis *Demes* frgs. 111, 112, 127 Kassel and Austin.

57 Thoukydides (ostracized in 443) was Pericles' most prominent conservative political opponent. Aristides (ostracized in 482) played a prominent role in the foundation of the Athenian empire.

58 Some scholars: Marrou (1956) 56–57; Slater (1968) 4–14.

59 See Davies (1971) 302–308.

60 Timotheos: Davies (1971) 508.

61 Pericles' sons: Davies (1971) 457–459. Kleinias: Davies (1971) 16. Alcibiades' brother Kleinias: Davies (1971) 17–18. On Alcibiades, see ch. 5, below.

62 Andron: *FGrH* 342 F 5a; cf. Ps.-Plut. *Mor.* 833e–f; Pl. *Grg.* 487c, *Prt.* 315c. Androtion: Davies (1971) 33–34. Hagnon: Lys. 12.65; Arist. *Ath. Pol.* 29.2, 39.2 with comm. of Rhodes (1981); Thuc. 8.68.4; Xen. *Hell.* 2.3.30; Davies (1971) 227–228. Hipponikos and Kallias: Davies (1971) 262; Xen. *Hell.* 4.5.13, 6.3.4. Diotimos, Strombichides, Autokles: Davies (1971) 161–162. Nikophemos and Aristophanes: Lysias 19 and Davies (1971) 201–202. Another example of father–son solidarity in military service is that of Stratokles and his son Euthydemos, who served as syntrierarchs in 357 and 356. Davies suggests that at the time Euthydemos had not yet married or set up a separate household. See *IG* II² 1612.136–137, 271–272; Davies (1971) 494–495.

63 Athenians ... stages of child's growth: Golden (1990) 13–22 offers a fine assessment of the complex and often imprecise ancient terminology. Segalen (1986) 173–177 provides a succinct survey of the different phases of parent–child relations over the course of the life cycle in traditional European society. For comparative purposes, the definition of age classes in Sparta is worth examining: see Tazelaar (1967). Sallares (1991) 160–192 offers provocative but extravagant ideas on the

importance of "age class systems" as the fundamental organizing principle of the Greek polis.

64 Usually argued: e.g. Garland (1990) 134; Golden (1990) 123–135. Idealist argument: e.g. Girard (1889) 76; cf. above, ch. 1. Psychological exposé: Slater (1968) 4–14; cf. above, ch. 1. Ancient evidence on fathers and infants: Hom *Il.* 6.466–485; Ar. *Wasps* 291–316, *Clouds* 863–864, 1380–1385; Theophr. *Char.* 20.6; Hdt. 1.136.2 and discussion by Garland (1990) 153. Women's quarters and Athenian houses: Cohen (1989), (1991) 149–170; Jameson (1990a and b).

65 Paternity, naming: above, n.6. Registration of infant in phratry: Parke (1977) 88–93; Garland (1990) 121; Golden (1990) 26–27; see below, n.75.

66 *IG* II-III² 1368.130; Parke (1977) 108; Golden (1981) 12–15, (1990) 41–43; Burkert (1985) 237; Garland (1985) 82–83, 161–162, (1990) 122.

67 In general: Garland (1990) 144–147, 320; Golden (1990) 41–44, 65–72. At City Dionysia and Thargelia: Ar. *Ath. Pol.* 56.3. At Hephaisteia and Prometheia: *IG* II² 1138.11. Competition at Apatouria: Pl. *Ti.* 21b. Bearers of *eiresiônê* boughs at the Pyanopsia: Plut. *Thes.* 22.6–7; Suda s.v. *eiresiônê* and *diakonion*; Hesykhios s.v. *diakonion*; Ar. *Kn.* 729, *Eccl.* 1053; Parke (1977) 76. "Hearth child": Porphyry *On Abstinence* 4.5; Harpokration s.v. *aph' hestias mueisthai*; Golden (1990) 44. Role in household religion: Golden (1990) 29–32; cf. above, ch. 2.

68 The absence of Kritias's father is noteworthy. Was he dead, or is Kritias's failure to mention him a commentary by Plato on his lack of filial piety, ironic in light of the following story, which accuses the Greeks in general of a lack of respect for tradition (Pl. *Ti.* 22b)? On genealogical background of Kritias's family, see Davies (1971) 325–327.

69 Quotation: Freeman (1932 [1907]) 65. *Paidagôgos*: Garland (1990) 65–66; Golden (1990) 62, 147. Availability of primary education: see above, n.53.

70 Age of *eromenos*: Dover (1978) 84–87; Halperin (1990) 88. On Athenian homosexuality, see Dover (1978); Foucault (1985); Halperin (1990); Winkler (1990a) esp. 45–70.

71 Father's mixed message: Dover (1978) 88–90, 202.

72 Cf. Halperin (1990) 93.

73 Aristophanes: see below, ch. 5.

74 Plato: see also *Symp.* 206b–e, 209b–e. Substitute paternity: e.g. Marrou (1956) 56; Devereux (1967) 78–79; Humphreys (1978) 202; Cartledge (1981) 22; Halperin (1990) 144. Criticize father: e.g. Marrou (1956) 56. Counteracting competition: Slater (1968) 59; Humphreys (1978) 203.

75 Hdt. 1.147; Isai. 6.22; Dem. 39.4, 40.11, 43.82; *IG* II² 1237 = W. Dittenberger, *Sylloge Inscriptionum Graecarum*, 3rd edn., Leipzig, 1915–24: 921 (the Demotionid Decree); Pollux 8.107; Hesykhios s.v. *koureôtis*; Suda s.v. *koureôtês*. Cf. Labarbe (1953); Parke (1977) 89; Garland (1990) 179–180; Golden (1990) 26–28. Previous registration: see above.

76 Eighteenth birthday: Golden (1979); Rhodes (1981) 497–498.

77 Arist. *Ath. Pol.* 42.1; Ar. *Wasps* 578; Dem. 39.2, 40.9–11; Harrison (1968) 79 and n.1; Rhodes (1981) 493–502; Whitehead (1986) 97–104.

78 *Ephêbeia*: Thuc. 1.105.4, 2.13.7; Aeschin. 2.167; Pélékidis (1962) 7–79; Reinmuth (1971) 123–138; Rhodes (1981) 494–495; Ober (1985) 90–95; Vidal-Naquet (1986a) 106–128; Winkler (1990b) 23–37. Assembly: Dem. 44.35; Xen. *Mem.* 3.6.1; Rhodes (1981) 494–495. Age of thirty and eligibility for office: see Develin (1985).

79 Arist. *Pol.* 1304a4–13 discusses a Mytilenian father's failed attempt to win his sons rich heiresses as brides. Cf. Schaps (1979) 33.

4 CONFLICT: THE SONS OF THESEUS

1 On reconstructing the interplay of interest and emotion in the historical family, see Medick and Sabean, "Interest and Emotion in Family and Kinship Studies: A Critique of Social History and Anthropology," in Medick and Sabean (1984) 9–27.

2 Sexuality, status, hierarchy: Foucault (1985) 210–211, 221; Golden (1985) 101; Keuls (1985) 6–8; Halperin (1990) 31–37.

3 Barth (1971) 89–94. Barth's explanatory model draws from Goffman's role theory (Goffman [1959]).

4 Sparta: see Hodkinson (1983).

5 Saller (1987) 33. On property as cause of father–son conflict in Athens, see Golden (1990) 106–114.

6 Goody (1962) 282, cf. 91–93, 274–282, 416–430; cf. Goody (1966b) 53–91.

7 Fortes (1969) 177.

8 Leach (1973) 81, cf. 54–73. Lévi-Strauss (1963) 213–218; (1970) 35–48; Sourvinou-Inwood (1979) 15.

9 The literature on Thesus is vast. The fundamental introductory works on the literary evidence are Herter (1936), (1939), (1940), and (1973); and on the evidence of art and archaeology, Dugas and Flacelière (1958); Brommer (1982); and Neils (1987). Calame (1990) is a thorough study of the interplay of Athenian history and the elaboration of the myth and ritual of Theseus. More accessible introductions for the anglophone are Ward *et al.* (1970), especially the essays by Connor (143–174) and Edwards (7–50); Kerényi (1979) 209–246; Carpenter (1991) 160–167. Because the evidence of art is very important for understanding Theseus in fifth-century Athens, I refer to it frequently in the following pages. I am, however, no art historian; the reader is referred to the various secondary sources cited for full discussion and references.

Ubiquitous: Connor (1970) 143. Festivals: Herter (1939) 293–295, 304–306; (1973) cols. 1220–1231. Athlete: Herter (1973) cols. 1235–1236. Young man leaving home: Sourvinou-Inwood (1979) 69 n.122; Scheibler (1987) 92–93. Athenians victorious over Persia: Sourvinou-Inwood (1979) 48–58. National hero: Agard (1928); Dugas (1943) 21; Edwards (1970) 32–33; Kron (1976) 224; Shapiro (forthcoming a).

10 Reshaping of myth in fifth-century Athens: for general discussion, see Kirk (1974) 103–112; Calame (1990) 406–450. Founder of democracy: below. Eponymous heroes: Kron (1976) 224. Patron of poor and humble: Herter (1939) 289. Hero shrine: Herter (1973) cols. 1223–1225. Unification: Herter (1936) 177–180, (1973) cols. 1212–1215. "Land of

Theseus," "Theseid": Herter (1936) 177–178, (1973) cols. 1213–1214. Atthidographers and their influence on Plutarch: Herter (1973) cols. 1047–1048; Frost (1984) 65–73. On Plutarch's *Theseus*, see comm. and intro. in Ampolo and Manfredini (1988).

11 Athlete: Agard (1928) 85–89. Theseus usually presented in art as young ephebe: Brommer (1982) 144. Ephebeia in fifth century: above, ch. 3.

12 Sourvinou-Inwood (1987) 135; (1990) 397.

13 Vidal-Naquet (1986a) 112.

14 Jeanmaire (1939) 245.

15 Initiatory: see below, n.40. Keuls: (1985) 57–62, 303–305.

16 See above, n.10, for the various versions of myth.

17 Mycenaean tradition: Nilsson (1972 [1932]) 163–180; Kirk (1974) 152, cf. 156. Kleisthenes: Schefold (1946) 65–67, 89–91; Sourvinou-Inwood (1971) 94–100, (1979) 27; Davie (1982) 26; Neils (1987) 149–150. Herter (1939) 284–286, (1973) col. 1046, and Connor (1970) 147–149 among others have argued that it was the Peisistratids who promoted Theseus, but Boardman's work on the Heracles–Peisistratus connection argues against this thesis ([1972]) 57–72, [1975b] 1–12). Kron (1976) 224 argues that Theseus was not assigned to any one of Kleisthenes' ten tribes because he represented the polis as a unified whole. Vidal-Naquet (1986a) 313, 322 n.77 argues vehemently nonetheless against the Theseus–Kleisthenes connection. Walker (1989) 18–50 makes a good case for skepticism about assigning the origin of Theseus's popularity to any one politician or faction. Calame (1990) 417, 420, 431 argues that the elaboration of the Theseus myth is less the result of individual political action than of a social process. Some speak of Alkmeonid sponsorship of an epic *Theseid*, but there is no good evidence for such an early date for that (now lost) poem: Neils (1987) 11–12.

18 Kimon: Connor (1970) 157–163; Podlecki (1971) 141–143; Barron (1980); Francis (1990); Shapiro (forthcoming b). Bacchylides: Snell (1970) 48; cf. Ferretto (1985) on the Theseus myth and Delian League propaganda; Francis (1990) 53, 55–57, on Bacchylides 18. Theseion: Wycherley (1957) 113–119, (1978) 64; Connor (1970) 159–160; Barron (1972) 20–45. Pherekydes: Jacoby, *FGrH* 3 F 148–153; Davies (1971) 306–307; Huxley (1973); Sourvinou-Inwood (1979) 55. Theseia; Deubner (1966 [1932]) 224–226; Herter (1939) 293–295, (1973) cols. 1225–1229; Connor (1970) 158–159; Parke (1977) 81–82; Calame (1990) 153–156.

19 Theseus popular subject: Sourvinou-Inwood (1979) 48; Brommer (1982) 149; Neils (1987) 151. Tyrannicide legend in fifth-century Athens: Taylor (1991). Appropriation of tyrannicide symbol in Theseion: Barron (1972) 39; Francis (1990) 69–70. Depiction of Theseus as tyrannicide in vase painting: Taylor (1991) 36–70. Taylor (1991) 59–60 makes Ephialtes and the new democracy the inspiration for the depiction of Theseus as tyrannicide, but Kimonian propaganda is perhaps the likelier source.

20 Stoa Poikile: Connor (1970) 162–164; Wycherley (1978) 38–41. See also Hephaistion: Neils (1987) 127, 151; cf. discussion in Connor (1970) 153–155; Wycherley (1978) 68–71; Ridgway (1981) 85–88.

Marathon base: Kron (1976) 205–227; Vidal-Naquet (1986a) 302–324. Marathon (Kimon's family) vs. Salamis (Themistocles): Podlecki (1971) 141–143. Legitimization through hero cult: Bérard (1982) 90–91, 96–98.

21 Absence of Theseus from Periclean Acropolis building program: Boardman (1985) 169; cf. Harrison (1966) 107–133; Connor (1970) 167–170. Sounion: Ridgway (1981) 84–85. Rhamnous, Athena Nike: Boardman (1985) 170; Wycherley (1978) 127–129. Stoa Basileios: Paus. 1.31; Wycherley (1978) 31. Doubts have been raised as to the presence of Theseus in all of these sculptures except for the acroterion of the Stoa Basileios: Boardman (1985) 170.

22 Return to popularity: Neils (1987) 129.

23 Acropolis sculpture: see below. Possible Horkômosion: Wycherley (1978) 185. Delphinion: Wycherley (1978) 185; Graf (1979) 13–19. It is unclear whether or not these shrines existed in the fifth century.

24 On the tragic fragments, see Pearson (1917); Nauck (1964); Herter (1973) col. 1047; for Theseus in drama generally, see Bertelli and Gianotti (1987) 43–48. For a speculative reconstruction of Sophocles' *Aigeus*, see Sourvinou-Inwood (1979) 55–57 who suggests a date in the 460s. Euripides' *Theseus* is parodied in Aristophanes' *Wasps* 312–314, and hence predates 422. For the date of *Suppliant Women*, see below, n.31; *Herakles*, Bond (1981) xxx–xxxii.

25 These points are all made by Sourvinou-Inwood (1979) 13–15, 18–28. On the death of Aigeus as a case of indirect patricide that exists in direct, undiluted form in Bororo mythology, see Lévi-Strauss (1970) 35–48; Burkert (1979) 14; Bremmer (1987b) 47–48; Neo-Freudians: see Slater (1968) 388–396; Green (1980); cf. Calame (1990) 122–123. Date of Bacchylides 18, see above, n.18. On Aigeus more generally, see the fundamental works on Theseus (above, n.9) and Wernicke (*RE* I [1894]) cols. 952–955; Radermacher (1938) 237–241; Kron (1976) 120–140, 264–269.

26 Note too that the closely related story of Daedalus the Athenian also contains a number of details of conflict between father and son or son surrogate. Daedalus's son Icarus dies because he disobeys his father's instructions and flies too near the sun (Xen. *Mem.* 4.2.33; Apollod. *Epit.* 1.13). The reason why Daedalus was in Crete, where he built the labyrinth for Minos, was his flight from justice in Athens. There he had been convicted by the court of the Areopagus for murdering his nephew (his sister's son) and apprentice Talos, whom he feared might surpass him as a craftsman. The manner of the crime is reminiscent of Aigeus's death: Talos was thrown from the Athenian Acropolis (Apollod. 3.214–215; cf. Diod. 4.76) or was flung into the sea (Ovid *Met.* 236). In Lévi-Straussian terms, both Daedalus and Theseus undervalue kinship; each man is the cause, direct or indirect, of the death of a close male relative, either a father or son surrogate.

27 Cf. Ar. *Wasps* 303–316, schol. *ad* 313; MacDowell (1971) comm. *ad* 314; Sommerstein (1983) comm. *ad* 303–316.

28 Why founder of democracy Theseus: Jane Harrison's explanation is unconvincing, but she underlines the problem ([1927] 316–317, 327).

Preparing the way: Bertelli-Gianotti (1987) 46. Literary tradition: see discussion and citation of ancient sources in Rhodes (1981) 73–77. Euripides is the earliest extant literary source to make Theseus the founder of democracy; the claim is also found later in some Atthides: Jacoby, *FGrH* comm. 328 F 11, p. 311; Davie (1982) 28. The Stoa of Zeus in the Athenian agora contained three paintings of the mid-fourth century BC by Euphranor: the twelve gods, the contemporary battle of Mantineia, and Theseus with Demos and Demokratia (Paus. 1.3.3–4; Robertson [1985] 174). Pausanias 1.3.3. rejects the tradition of Theseus as a democrat. Parke (1977) 81–82 speculates that if the generous distribution of meat to the populace that marked the late-fourth-century Theseia began in the fifth century, it becomes more understandable why Theseus was considered a friend of the common person.

29 Royal pedigree: Jacoby, *FGrH* comm. 323a F 23, p. 58 n.50. Antidote to constitutional debates, response to Kimon: Walker (1989) 73, 144, 157–158. Theseus in fifth century BC as democrat or oligarch: Ampolo and Manfredini (1988) XXXII. In general, see Davie (1982).

30 As Burian (1985a) 214–215 n.12 points out, interpreters of *Supp.* tend to be either idealists, who see the play as an encomium of Athens, or realists, who emphasize Euripides' satiric, ironic, and bitter intentions. I lean toward the realist position, though Burian's essay stakes out middle ground impressively. Also useful are: Greenwood (1953) 92–120; Zuntz (1955) 3–25; Fitton (1961) 430–461; Conacher (1967) 93–108; Gamble (1970) 385–405; Collard (1975) 23–30, 207–263; Shaw (1982) 3–19; Raaflaub (1990) 45–46.

31 A date between 424 and 420 has been suggested by Zuntz (1955) 88–93; Collard (1975) 8–14. On theme of youth in *Supp.*, see Collard (1975) comm. *ad* 190, 250, 426–462, 447–449; Shaw (1982); Burian (1985a) 143.

32 I argue in the realist vein of Greenwood (1953) and Fitton (1961).

33 The similarity between Theseus's position as *primus inter pares* within a democracy and Pericles' position as described by Thucydides (2.65) has often been noted. See e.g. Podlecki (1975–76) 22–27. Calame (1990) 436–437, cf. 222–223, is skeptical.

34 On *authentês*, LSJ s.v.; Collard (1975) comm. *ad* 442.

35 Date of *Herakles*: see Bond (1981) xxx–xxxii. Theseus as contemporary Athenian: see Bond comm. *ad* 1163, 1248, 1254, 1334. Theseus's use of divine *exempla* (1316–1318) has been compared to the similarly sophistic argument of Phaidra's nurse at Eur. *Hipp.* 451; see Bond *ad* 1314. On *Herakles* more generally, see Conacher (1967) 78–92; Gregory (1977); Foley (1985) 147–204.

36 On Theseus in Isocrates' *Helen* and in the fourth century generally, see Calame (1990) 412–415.

37 On this passage, see Rhodes (1981) 488–489.

38 Art: Kron (1976) 139–140. Indicative of Aigeus's reputation is the Athenian hero shrine to him (probably in the vicinity of the Ilissos) that recalled not his life but his death. Paus. 1.22.4–5; Harpokration, Suda, Photius s.v. *Aigeion*; Kron (1976) 124–127. Androgeos: see above. Medea: see Sourvinou-Inwood (1979) esp. 22–26, 48–58.

39 The evidence: Before ca. 510, representations of Theseus in vase painting are relatively few and generally restricted to his Cretan exploits.
Afterward with the promotion of Theseus as a national hero, scenes
of other deeds, notably those on the road from Troezen to Athens
and the capture of the Marathonian bull, begin to appear frequently
on vase painting, mainly red figure. See Boardman (1974) 225–226,
(1975a) 223–224, 228–229. From fifth century on, Theseus usually
depicted in art as beardless youth or ephebe: Brommer (1982) 144.
Aigeus mature: Kron (1976) 139–140, 207, 243. Youth and bearded
king: Brommer (1982) 126. Theseus and Aigeus: Kron (1976) 128–138,
264–266; Sourvinou-Inwood (1979) 30–31 + nn.119, 122, (1990)
422–424; Shapiro (1982) 292. Theseus versus villains: see e.g. red figure
kylix by Kodros painter, found at Vulci and dated ca. 430 BC, British
Museum E 84 ARV^2 1269 no. 4 (= Neils [1987] no. 111); red figure
calyx crater by Dinos Painter, found at Spina and dated ca. 425 BC,
Ashmolean Museum ARV^2 1153, no. 13 (= Neils [1987] 126). Ram's
head rhyton: signed by Charinos as potter, attributed to Triptolemos
Painter. Collection of Virginia Museum of Fine Arts, Richmond, The
Williams Fund (79.100); J. Neils in Shapiro (1981) 84–87.

40 Jeanmaire (1939) e.g. 243–245, 324–337, 338–363, interprets much of
the Theseus legend as an initiation ritual. See also Brelich (1969)
376–377, 471–472; Graf (1979) 13–19; Segal (1979a) 31–32; Bremmer
(1987b) 47–48; Calame (1990) 432–435 suggests limits to the interpretation. On the initiatory and ephebic motifs in Bacchylides' Odes 17
and 18, both of which concern Theseus, see: Merkelbach (1973); Segal
(1979a) 31; Ieranò (1987).

41 Ephebeia: see above, n.11. Rites of passage: see previous note. Gym-
nasiums and palaestras: Graf (1979) 13 n.108.

42 On these points, see Graf (1979) 13–19, whom I follow closely.

43 Graf (1979) 14–15; Vidal-Naquet (1986a) 114–117; Winkler (1990a) 35;
cf. Van Gennep (1960 [1909]) 171–172. Note too that transvestism
played a role in the ritual of the Oschophoria festival, which tradition
connected to Theseus's return from Crete. See Deubner (1966 [1932])
142; Jeanmaire (1939) 338–340; Simon (1983) 90–91; Vidal-Naquet
(1986a) 114–116.

44 Pélékidis (1962) 223. Similar ceremonies outside Attica: Graf (1979)
14 and n.115.

45 Vidal-Naquet (1986a) 113–116; Winkler (1990a) 35 n.43.

46 Death of Aigeus and initiatory ritual: Jeanmaire (1939) 314–316,
365–369; Calame (1990) 257–258; see above, n.40. Oschophoria: see
above, ch. 1 n.6.

47 Oracle comes true: Kron (1976) 127.

48 On this story, with full scholarly citations, see Sourvinou-Inwood
(1971) 94–109; Herter (1973) cols. 1049–1050; Ampolo and Manfredini
(1988) XXIII–XXIV.

49 Wordplay: *Thêseôs* and *thêsô* are juxtaposed at Eur. *Hipp.* 520–521;
Herter (1973) col. 1049 doubts the relevance of this evidence, but see
more generally Ahl (1985) on the importance of wordplay in classical
poetry. Delphi metopes: Neils (1987) 47–49. Date in 470s: Francis

(1990) 101–103. Vase painting, sculpture, initiation ritual: Sourvinou-Inwood (1971) 101–109; Neils (1987) 135.

50 Pearson (1917) i, 15; Kron (1976) 128; Sourvinou-Inwood (1979) 55–57; Neils (1987) 119–120.

51 See Herter (1936) 206–207, (1973) cols. 1145–1146; Kron (1976) 122–123.

52 Inherited familial crime: see Barrett (1964) comm. *ad locc.*

53 On these passages, see Bond (1981) comm. *ad locc.*

5 THE HOUR OF THE SON, CA. 450–415 BC

1 For a provocative, if idiosyncratic, analysis of Athens as youth culture, see Devereux (1967) 77, 90–92.

2 Plutarch (*Per.* 13–16) doubts Stesimbrotos's story about Xanthippos's alleged accusation. See comm. *ad locc.* in Stadter (1989) and pp. lxii–lxiii.

3 An alternative anecdote has Pericles maintain his Olympian demeanor in spite of the loss: Ps.-Plut. *Consolatio ad Apollonium* 118e; Valerius Maximus 5.10 ext. 1; Aelian *Varia Historia* 9.6; Stadter (1989) comm. *ad loc.* Plutarch's interpretation may be Stoic, but classical authors too note the presence or absence of emotion upon the loss of a son or kinsman: e.g. Xen. *Hell.* 6.4.16.

4 Alcibiades: see below. On Pericles' paternal rule, cf. Arist. *Ath. Pol.* 28.5 and Rhodes (1981) comm. *ad loc.*; Aristid. 46 *Quatt.* (2.161 Dindorf).

5 A short description cannot do justice to Herodotus's account: Gould (1989) 52–53. The Periander–Lykophron tale also suggests Theseus and Hippolytos, for whose details see below. Sourvinou-Inwood (1988) discusses the theme of father–son hostility in Herodotus's tale.

6 Kreon as tyrant: see Ober and Strauss (1990) 261–263, with references to previous discussions. Date of *Antigone* (late 440s BC): Ehrenberg (1954) 135–136; Fornara (1971) 48–49; Ostwald (1986) 149 n.36; Sourvinou-Inwood (1989) 134 n.3. Comparison of Kreon and Pericles: Ehrenberg (1954). As Sourvinou-Inwood (1989) 144–145 argues, a fifth-century BC audience would have had greater sympathy with Kreon's notion of paternal power than would a modern audience, but traditional notions of filial obedience had already become problematic by the time of the play's production, hence coloring the audience's response to the conflict between Kreon and Haimon.

7 Generation gap: Forrest (1975) 37–52 first applied this evocative term, drawn from the Euroamerican context of the 1960s, to late-fifth-century Athens. Ostwald (1986) esp. 229–250 has carefully examined what he aptly calls "the polarizations of the 420s."

8 Earlier civilizations: e.g. Egypt and the Hittites, see Reinhold (1976) 18–19. Ostwald (1986) 229 considers the intergenerational conflict of the 420s unprecedented in Athenian history; Reinhold (1976) 28, unprecedented in human history. For father–son conflict as a theme in Aeschylus, see Reinhold (1976) 30; cf. Strauss (1990a) n.24.

9 *Patrios politeia* argument: see below, ch. 6. On the ideology of the Areopagos, see Wallace (1989) 77–83, 145–173.

10 Reforms of ca. 461: Rhodes (1981) comm. *ad* Arist. *Ath. Pol.* 25.2; Wallace (1989) 83–93.

11 Marrou (1956) 78–94; Guthrie (1971a) 35–54, 262–264, 269–271; Reinhold (1976) 32–34; Ostwald (1986) 238 n.149, 243, 245, 365; Rusten (1989) comm. *ad* Thuc. 2.36.1–2.

12 Thuc. 2.47–55; Diod. 12.58.1–7; Plut. *Per.* 34.5, 36.7–9, 38.1, 3; Plut. *Nic.* 6.3; Strauss (1986) 75–77; see Sallares (1991) 244–262, esp. 258–260, for interesting speculations on the demographic consequences, though his identification of the disease as smallpox is unlikely to end the debate.

13 For these traits, see Ehrenberg (1962) 95–112; Connor (1971) 147–151; Forrest (1975); Reinhold (1976) 32–37; Ostwald (1986) 230–237; and the discussions below of Aristophanes, Thucydides, and Euripides. Considering Sparta's vaunted respect for elders (below, ch. 6), youthful philo-laconism was oxymoronic, but ideology is not necessarily consistent.

14 On reading Antiphon "On Truth": Guthrie (1971a) 107–108, 110. Date: Ostwald (1986) 363 + n.106; (1990) 302–303. Patrimonies: Gadamer (1976) 109–112.

15 Influence of the sophists on the "Old Oligarch": see Forrest (1975) 43–45. Date: composition early in the Archidamian War seems most likely; see Forrest (1970). Withdrawal from assembly, Hippolytos, Bdelykleon: Carter (1986) 52–75; below. I suspect that more young aristocrats groused about the assembly and talked about withdrawing from politics than actually withdrew. See Forrest (1963) 1–12. *Hetairiai*: still useful is Calhoun (1913).

16 On young men under thirty in public office, see Connor (1971) 147–151; Develin (1985) esp. 152–153. Kephisodemos and Euathlos, Hyperbolos: Ostwald (1986) 232–233; Athens, Syracuse, Thrasymakhos, Eupolis: see below, ch. 6. Alcibiades' age: Davies (1971) 18 argues for 451/450; Vickers (forthcoming) argues for 453. Alcibiades as tribute assessor (*taktês*): Hatzfeld (1951) 68–69; Ostwald (1986) 292–293; Develin (1985) 153, 159, (1989) 131. Andokides' birth year: Davies (1971) 30. Andokides "To His Comrades": Ostwald (1986) 327–328.

17 Date of play: see ch. 4, n.31.

18 The treatment of contemporary, societal concerns in fifth-century tragedy has received considerable scholarly attention. See in particular the French school, with its roots in structuralism: a good starting point is Vernant and Vidal-Naquet (1981 [1972]). See also Vickers (1973) 100–164; Segal (1984a); Goldhill (1986), (1990); Zeitlin (1990); and in general the essays in Winkler and Zeitlin (1990). On the prominence of the oikos as a theme in tragedy, see Vickers (1973) 109–119; Knox (1979) 20–23; Humphreys (1983) 18–21, 69–74.

19 *Hubris* and Alcibiades: e.g. Plut. *Alc.* 3, 7.1, 8.1; Andok. 4.20–21, 27. *Hubris* and young men: Isoc. 20.4, 11, 21–22. Aggressive *neoi* vs. prudent *presbuteroi*: Ant. *Second Tetr.* 4.3.2, 4.4.2. The similarity between the speeches of Theseus and Nicias raises the question of whether one was modeled on the other; or were these *topoi* simply in the air? Collard (1975) comm. *ad* 232–237 notes the similarity of these verses

to Aristoph. *Peace* 441–450; cf. Arist. *Rh.* 2.12–13. On *eupsuchia* and *euboulia* in *Supp.*, see Shaw (1982).

20 Connor: (1971) 147–151. Hoplites and cavalrymen vs. thetes: Ostwald (1986) 229–230. Moral consequences of epidemic: Thuc. 2.53. Archons of early fifth century: Badian (1971) 13–14. Pericles: Davies (1971) 457.

21 Only about one-third of the white population of the antebellum South owned slaves, according to Owsley (1965 [1949]) 8.

22 Causes of conflict: Havelock (1952) 95–109 (on sophists); Gadamer (1976) 109–112 (on patrimonies, sophists); Reinhold (1976) 29–30; Ostwald (1986) 229–250.

23 Amussen (1988). Family as model: Foucault (1979). On patriarchalism in seventeenth-century English ideology and elite political thought, see Schochet (1975).

24 Amussen (1988) 182.

25 On the challenge to traditional hoplite tactics posed by Pericles' defensive strategy, see Hanson (1989) 32–35. On the political turmoil in Athens caused by Pericles' unconventional strategy, see Kagan (1974) 51–57.

26 Pericles' birth: Davies (1971) 457. *Khorêgos* for Aeschylus: *IG* II² 2318.9–11. Pericles' dominant position in Athens: Kagan (1974) 54–56. Changing of the political guard: Arist. *Ath. Pol.* 28.1; Isoc. 8.126–127; Connor (1971) 139–175; Kagan (1974) 118–119, 124–132; Strauss (1986) 12. As Connor points out (119–134), Kleon's methods were not completely novel: indeed Pericles had anticipated some of them himself. On the whole, however, Kleon's style was a radical departure.

27 Reinhold (1976) 35–36. Kimon: Davies (1971) 302.

28 Affair of Herms/parody of Mysteries: among the best recent accounts are Gomme *et al.* (1970) 264–288; Kagan (1981) 193–209; see below, n.33, for Alcibiades' role, and ch. 6, for Andokides' role. Age of Alcibiades: above, n.16. Age of Andokides and Kharmides: Davies (1971) 30. Mutilation of Herms as a non-adult mode of behavior: Ostwald (1986) 325–326, 541, 549–550.

29 Guardianship of Pericles and Ariphron: Hatzfeld (1951) 29–30; Davies (1971) 18.

30 For the biographical details, see Hatzfeld (1951) 59–60; Davies (1971) 17–21; Ellis (1989) 18–20.

31 Eros: Rose (1959) 123. Comic invention: Russell (1966) 45. Russell points out that Plutarch's description of the shield uses comic meter. Even if this suggests that Plutarch is paraphrasing a reference in comedy, it does not prove that a comic poet fabricated the notion of the shield.

32 Cf. Keuls (1985) 383.

33 Alcibiades' role in mutilation and profanation: Thuc. 6.28, Andok. 1.11; Plut. *Alc.* 22.4, 19.1–3; Ellis (1989) 59–61; *contra* Hatzfeld (1951) 177–181, 191.

34 Purifying the city: Parker (1983) 168–170. Stelai: see Ellis (1989) 121 nn.82–83. Scapegoat: Andok. 1.11, Lys. 6.53; cf. the judicious remarks of Parker (1983) 257–280, esp. 267–268.

35 Atallah (1966) 93–140; Dover in Gomme *et al.* (1971) 223–271; Detienne (1977); Burkert (1979) 105–108, (1985) 177; Powell (1979) 18; Kagan (1981) 193; Keuls (1985) 23–30, 394; Ellis (1989) 58; Winkler (1990a) 188–209.

36 Omen: arguably the omen seemed less significant in 415 than when remembered after 413, when the Sicilian Expedition had turned into disaster. On female pacifism and male aggression in Athens in 415, see Keuls's [(1985) 16–32, 381–403] provocative remarks.

37 On Alcibiades' amours, see Littman (1970) 263–276; Ellis (1989) 18–20, 33, 50. On Alcibiades' erotic political charisma, see Cornford (1971 [1907]) 201–220, esp. 208–209; Bloedow (1990). Timaia: Littman (1969) 269–277 argues against the conventional view that the product of Alcibiades' affair with Timaia was the future Leotychidas. For a survey of secondary literature, see Ellis (1989) 122 n.96.

38 Heart of Adonis myth: Burkert (1979) 101–102. Relevance of Eros to Adonia: Eros appears as a hovering figure in fifth- and fourth-century vase paintings of the Adonia. See Keuls (1985) 23–30; Winkler (1990a) 191 with bibliography.

39 Keuls: (1985) 23–32, 381–403. Thessalos: Davies (1971) 307. Andokides and events of 415: see below, ch. 6. One fifth-century version of myth: Panyassis of Halikarnassos, *ap.* Apollod. 3.183–185; Atallah (1966) 53–55; Matthew (1974) 120–125; Burkert (1979) 109–110, 197 n.15. Thesmophoria and Adonia: Detienne (1977), with the critique in Winkler (1990a) 198–209.

40 One might also say that Alcibiades had become Hippolytos, the *theomachos*. On the parallels (as well as the contrasts) between Adonis and Hippolytos, see below, n.71, and discussion in text of Euripides' *Hippolytos*.

41 Conflict between generations in Aristophanes: Ehrenberg (1962) 207–211; Ostwald (1986) 231. Stock motif: Ehrenberg (1962) 208. Strauss (1966) e.g. 37–44, 104, 123, 181–182, emphasizes father-beating as motif in Aristophanes. For date and nature of the revision of *Cl.*, see Dover (1968) lxxx–xcviii and (1972) 103–105. Intergenerational or father–son conflict was also an important theme in *Banqueters* (427) to judge by the surviving fragments 205–248 Kassel and Austin; it is a minor motif of *Acharnians* (425 BC; see esp. 676–718), *Peace* (421 BC; see 110–149), and *Frogs* (405 BC; see 274–276), to say nothing of the generational conflict (mainly among females) over sex in *Ecclesiazusae* (ca. 393 BC; see 877–1111).

42 Carrière (1979) and others correctly note the carnivalesque aspects of Attic comedy. Equally important, Old Comedy was intensely political: see Ste. Croix (1972) 355–371; Konstan (1985); Henderson (1990); Redfield (1990). Pericles and Alcibiades: see the provocative discussion by Michael Vickers.

43 Whitman (1964) 143–166 is a good introduction to *Knights*; both Somerstein's (1981a) and Neil's (1901) commentaries are useful.

44 On the oikos metaphor in *Kn.* and its inconsistent application, see Dover (1972) 93–94. Home vs. assembly: Kraus (1985) 143. Father–son as political metaphor in *Kn.*: Strauss (1966) 92–93, 102–105, 317 n.18.

Demos as father: cf. Lys. 13.91, discussed above, ch. 2. *Therapeuô* and son's care of father: above, ch. 3.

45 Medea: *Nostoi* frg. 6 Allen; Ovid *Met.* 7.159–293; Sommerstein (1981a) comm. *ad* 1321. Rejuvenation: Kleon too had promised Demos that he would make him young and attractive again (908), though by the unpleasant method of plucking out the old man's white hairs.

46 Landfester (1967) 103; Kraus (1985) 163–164, 191; Brock (1986) 15 n.2, 23; Edmunds (1987) 43–49; Hubbard (1990) 100–101.

47 Alcibiades in Agorakritos, Pericles in Demos: Vickers (forthcoming).

48 On age and status of Strepsiades and his family members, see Dover (1968) xxv–xxix. Among many good discussions of the accuracy of portrayal of Socrates and his school in *Cl.*, see Ehrenberg (1962) 273–278; Dover (1968) xxii–lvii, (1972) 116–120; Guthrie (1971b) 41–67; Edmunds (1986); and especially Nussbaum (1980). See further below, ch. 6. On fathers and sons in *Cl.*, see Harriott (1986) 165–170.

49 Strepsiades' obedience: Dover (1968) xxviii.

50 Beating: Whitman (1964) 131; Strauss (1966) 37–44; Reckford (1976). *Agôn* between father and son: cf. Ar. *Banqueters* (427), frgs. 205, 233 Kassel and Austin. Legal action: Clay (1982) 277–298; Bremmer (1987b) 49. On quoting tragedy, and on meaning of Zeus Patrôios in this context, see Dover (1968) comm. *ad Cl.* 1468.

51 On conflict between the Stronger and Weaker Argument, and on old vs. new education, see Marrou (1956) 63–75, 83; Ehrenberg (1962) 292–296; Dover (1968) lvii–lxvi; Guthrie (1971a) 114; Nussbaum (1980) 50–67.

52 Iapetos: Dover (1968) comm. *ad* 998. Kronos as "old-fashioned": Dover (1968) comm. *ad* 398. Kronia: see below, ch. 6. *Archaios*: Dover (1968) comm. *ad* 821.

53 Role reversal: Whitman (1964) 125–126.

54 See Vickers (1993), (forthcoming), who notes that the identification of Pheidippides as Alcibiades was made long ago by J. W. Süvern (1836) as well as by other nineteenth-century scholars and more recently by V. Boruchovich in 1959.

55 Philokleon retired: see comm. *ad.* 67–70 in MacDowell (1971); Sommerstein (1983). Bdelykleon older than Pheidippides: a *meirakion* like Pheidippides would not be in charge of the household if his father were still alive. Bdelykleon is still young (531); his authority over the oikos points to an age in his twenties. Aristophanic hero: Whitman (1964) 21–58. On the characters of *Wasps*, see Ehrenberg (1962) 53–54, 211; Whitman (1964) 143–166; MacDowell (1971) 7–12; Dover (1972) 125–127; Harriott (1986) 142–149.

56 Refined aristocrat out of politics: Konstan (1985) 41–45; Carter (1986) 63–70. Chorus and sons: Banks (1980) 81–84. Reverse ephebeia: Bowie (1987) 115, 123.

57 Philokleon's inheritance: see MacDowell (1971) comm. *ad.* 1352; Sommerstein (1983) comm. *ad* 1352–1359.

58 Independence, politics of the play, Marathon ideals: Konstan (1985) 31, 35. Pericles and Alcibiades: Vickers (forthcoming). Ending: Vaio (1971) 335–351.

59 *Patraloias*: see Strauss (1966) 181–182. On Solon's law, see above, ch. 3.
60 Reference to Euetion: see Sommerstein (1987a) comm. *ad* 1369.
61 Allusions: Vickers (1989b) 267 n.4. Alcibiades in *Birds*: Vickers (1989b) 268–270, 277–278; cf. Süvern (1836); Katz (1976). For an argument against political allusions in *Birds*, see Whitman (1964) 167–170.
62 On Aristophanes and Sicily, see Katz (1976), which offers a good summary of various theories to that date.
63 Alcibiades' defection to Sparta parodied in *Birds*: Vickers (1989b) *passim*. Katz (1976) 361–362 sees the Athenian general Lamakhos rather than Alcibiades in Herakles. Perhaps Aristophanes is referring to both men.
64 In the earlier version of *Hippolytos* (which survives in a few fragments, in later reports, and possibly in echoes in Roman poetry), Phaidra apparently attempted to seduce Hippolytos on stage, which seems to have shocked and outraged the public. The revised, milder version of 428 (here the nurse acts as offstage go-between) won first prize at the Dionysia. See Barrett (1964) 11–12, 15–45; Lesky (1966) 370.
65 Hippolytos was probably originally worshipped at Troezen and later, perhaps in the sixth century, brought to Athens; a major hero in Troezen, he was only a minor figure in Athens. See Barrett (1964) 2–10. The scholarly literature on Euripides' *Hippolytos* is quite large. I have been particularly influenced, on the one hand, by the structuralist and psychoanalytical readings of Zeitlin, Devereux, and especially Segal; and, on the other, by the sensitivity to contemporary political references found for example in the work of Knox (1957) and Vickers.
66 On meaning of name "Hippolytos," see Burkert (1979) 111–118; Zeitlin (1985) 59, 191 n.16.
67 Bad relationship between Theseus and Hippolytos: Winnington-Ingram (1960) 183; Devereux (1985) 20, 145. Pittheus: Segal (1984c) 276–278. Bastard theme: Segal (1979b) 160–161; Devereux (1985) 41. Differences in sexuality between father and son: Segal (1970b). On Theseus's youthful sexual exploits, see above, ch. 4. As Golden (1990) 105–106 points out, sexual rivalry exists more in the mind of the father (Theseus) than in that of the son (Hippolytos); a conclusion Golden also draws about similar cases of conflict in Greek literature.
68 Orphics: Barrett (1964) 172–173, 342–345; Burkert (1985) 296–301 with references to specialized literature. Hippolytos's hearty appetite: Segal (1969). Active Theseus vs. intellectual Hippolytos: Knox (1952) 21–23.
69 Hippolytos's rejection of civic life: see Knox (1952) 21–23; below. As a bastard (*nothos*), Hippolytos would have found it difficult, though perhaps not impossible, to become a citizen: see Rhodes (1981) 496–497; Hansen (1985) 73–76; Manville (1990) 12 n.47; Patterson (1990) 41. Contrast with Theseus: compare Aristophanes' *Wasps*, with its contrast between Philokleon's hearty support for democracy and his son Bdelykleon's aristocratic withdrawal from public life (above). Symbolic consequences of Hippolytos's illegitimate and Amazon heritage: Goldhill (1986) 127. Amazons: du Bois (1982); Segal (1984a) 30–31; Tyrell (1984).

70 Chastity and manhood: Goldhill (1986) 118–121; cf. Vidal-Naquet's two essays in Vernant and Vidal-Naquet (1981 [1972]); Foley (1985); Zeitlin (1985).

71 Complexity of mythological background: Zeitlin (1985) 107. Hymenaios: Séchan (1911) 117. "Ephebe gone awry": Tyrell (1984) 73; cf. Sourvinou-Inwood (1988). Melanion, Adonis, Atalanta as liminal figures and cognates of Amazons: Detienne (1977) and (1979); Vidal-Naquet in Vernant and Vidal-Naquet (1981 [1972]); Tyrell (1984) 73–85. Hippolytos and Adonis: Atallah (1966) 79, 82. Hippolytos and the Near Eastern origins of Adonis and Attis: Burkert (1979) 111, 118. Narcissos: Sergent (1986) 82–83. Phaethon: Reckford (1972) 421–425; Segal (1979b) 151–152.

72 Rankin (1974); Smoot (1976); Segal (1984c and d); Devereux (1985) esp. 59–84, 110–113.

73 Women as two-faced: e.g. the "woman from the sea" of Semonides 7 (Diehl) or the portrait of Helen in *Odyssey* 4. Women as particularly religious: Keuls (1985) 301–302; cf. Pomeroy (1975) 75–78; Just (1989) 23–24.

74 The reconciliation of Theseus and Hippolytos serves as a reminder of importance of father–son tie to Euripides and his audience. As in many other myths (e.g. *Odyssey*), the son finally finds his true father. See Knox (1952) 31; Segal (1979b) 160; (1988) 67.

75 See Barrett (1964) comm. *ad loc.*; Conacher (1967) 31–32, 42–43; Segal (1969) 297–305.

76 The following discussion focuses on hints of Alcibiades and the *jeunesse dorée* in *Hippolytos*. It is not a thorough analysis of all contemporary references in the play. Among additional contemporary subjects, one might, for instance, consider the drama in the context of the epidemic: a topic touched on in Dimock (1977) 239–240.

77 Disrespectful to older males: see above. Chariot victories: Thuc. 6.16.1–2; Plut. *Alc.* 11–12, etc. (see Ellis [1989] 50–52 + nn.).

78 Pericles *tyrannos*: see above. Pericles the ladies' man: Ath. 13.589d; cf. Vickers (forthcoming).

79 *Mots* about Alcibiades: Pherekrates frg. 154 Kassel and Austin; Bion *ap.* D.L. 4.49; cf. Eupolis frg. 171 Kassel and Austin; Littman (1970) 270. Hippolytos's gender identification with Amazon mother: Devereux (1985) 20–28, 73–74. Hippolytos's appropriation of feminine models of *korê* and *parthenos*: Zeitlin (1985) 66–67, 95, 110.

80 Lover of Socrates in the 430s: Pl. *Prt.* 309a; *Alc.* 1.131c–d. Potidaea: *Symp.* 219e–220e, *Chrm.* 153b; Isoc. 16.29; Thuc. 1.56–65, 2.66–70. Cf. Hatzfeld (1951) 32–58, 63–65; Ellis (1989) 20–27.

81 Grene (1939) 51, 53; Barrett (1964) comm. *ad loc.*, Connor (1971) 183–190; Carter (1986) 52–56.

82 On multivalent nature of Greek tragedy: Segal (1984c) 293. Perhaps Hippolytos's chastity was an inevitable substratum of the myth which Euripides had no choice but to include. Perhaps the comic writer in Euripides also enjoyed the humorous contrast between Hippolytos's un-Alcibiadean virginity and his other quite Alcibiadean characteristics.

On comic elements in Euripides, see Beye (1987) 187–192 + 315 for bibliography.

83 Douglas (1966) 53; Zeitlin (1985) 56. On Alcibiades, youth, and tyranny, see Thuc. 6.12.2, 6.15.4; Plut. *Alc.* 16.5; Paus. 1.22.7; Ath. 12.534.

84 Theseus and Aigeus: above, ch. 4. Ritual roots of ostracism: Parker (1983) 269.

85 The theme of Hippolytos's status as a bastard among legitimate children figures prominently in the play: see 962–963, 1083, 1169–1170, 1455. For an analysis of references to Pericles in Sophocles' *Oedipus Tyrannos*, a play close in date to Euripides' *Hippolytos*, see Knox (1957) 63–77, 103–107.

86 See above, ch. 2.

87 On Euripides as a futurologist or prophet, see Knox (1952); Segal (1969) 304–305; Devereux (1985) 17–18.

88 Glaukon son of Ariston: Plato's brother. Se Pl. *Rep.* 368a–b; Xen. *Mem.* 3.6.1–18; Davies (1971) 332. Charmides son of Aristoteles: Andokides' cousin. See Davies (1971) 30.

89 Trials of Socrates and Andokides: see below, ch. 6.

90 Sacrifice of young male: see Burkert (1983 [1972]) 77–81.

91 Trials, executions, and exiles: Strauss (1985).

6 THE RETURN OF THE FATHER, 413–399 BC

1 Population statistics: Strauss (1986) 72–73, 75–77, 179–181; Hansen (1988) 14–16, 22–28. Pericles: Arist. *Rh.* 1365a31–33.

2 On the old men, see Henderson (1987) xxvii, 98–100.

3 Youthful prank: Ostwald (1986) 325–326.

4 On Kronos and the Kronia, see the excellent analysis of Versnel (1987) 121–152. Kronia festival in Athens: Philokhoros, *FGrH* 328 F 97; Accius *Annals* frg. 3 Morel; Plut. *Thes.* 12.1; Deubner (1966 [1932]) 22; Parke (1977) 29–30.

5 On the men's ages, see Davies (1971) 30, 228, 327; above, ch. 5 n.16.

6 For other historical comparanda, see Finley (1975 [1971]). On the *patrios politeia* debate at the end of the fifth century I have found the following most useful: Fuks (1971 [1953]); Ruschenbusch (1958) 398–424; Cecchin (1969); Finley (1975 [1971]); Bourriot (1976) 703–709; Harding (1978) 179–183; Ostwald (1986) esp. 337–411; Wallace (1989) 131–144.

7 For a discussion of Athenian consciousness of the derivation of *patrios* from *patêr*, see ch. 2, Appendix.

8 In this and the following several paragraphs I am greatly in debt to the excellent discussion of Ostwald (1986), especially. 342–343, which underlines the importance of the past as a model in Athenian political debate from ca. 413 to ca. 403. Date of Thrasymakhos's speech: see Wallace (1989) 136–137, 140.

9 Edmonds's ingenious restoration of the play, which makes Alcibiades into the hero, is far too speculative to inspire confidence. See Edmonds (1939), (1957–61) 1:978–994; with reservations in Schmid and Staehlin

(1946) 124 n.6; Sartori (1975) 9 n.7; Ostwald (1986) 341–342. On Solon, see Arist. *Ath. Pol.* 31.1; Ostwald (1986) 370–371.

10 All translations from Eupolis' *Demes* are by Ralph Rosen in Henderson *et al.* (forthcoming); I am grateful to the authors for permitting me to see and cite unpublished material. On *topos* of unillustrious sons, see above, ch. 3.

11 On the inscription of the law code in the Royal Stoa and its symbolic significance, see Clinton (1982); Ostwald (1986) 519, with bibliography. Eponymous Heroes: the same publication procedure was followed during the fourth century for legislation, Dem. 20.92–94, 99; Ostwald (1986) 515. On the Heroes generally, see Kron (1976).

12 *Probouloi*: Gomme *et al.* (1981) comm. *ad* Thuc. 8.13; Ostwald (1986) 337–343; Kagan (1987) 5–10 (both with references to earlier discussion).

13 General with Pericles in the Samian campaign of 440/439, Hagnon supported Pericles in the Pheidias scandal in 438/437. See Davies (1971) 227–228; Ostwald (1986) 340. Sophocles served as general with Pericles in the Samian campaign of 441/440 and had been a *hellênotamias* in 443/442: Androtion *FGrH* 324 F 38; Ion of Chios *FGrH* 392 F 6; Strabo 14.1.18; Plut. *Per.* 8.8; *ATL* 2, list 12.36; cf. Kagan (1969) 150–153, 175; Ostwald (1986) 340 nn.15–16 for scholarly bibliography. For an argument for a broad intellectual and philosophical kinship between Sophocles and Pericles, see Ehrenberg (1954).

14 Ostwald (1986) 342–343. Peace treaty of 404: McCoy (1975).

15 On Sparta as a model for the Athenian oligarchs of 404 BC, see Krentz (1982) 63–68.

16 Appadurai (1981).

17 Alcibiades in *Frogs*: Moorton (1988) 349–359 + references to earlier scholarship.

18 On the date and the style of Andokides' defense speech (1: *On the Mysteries*) see Blass (1887) 1:319–322; Jebb (1893) 1:95–96, 112–125; MacDowell (1962) *passim*; Kennedy (1963) 147. On elements of tragedy in the diction and narrative of the speech, see Blass (1887) 1:319–322; Jebb (1893) 1:95–96; Opelt (1979) 210–218; Ober and Strauss (1990) 256–258. For examples of Andokides' use of vivid and colorful details in *On the Mysteries*, see Harvey (1984); Sommerstein (1987b).

19 Sources of evidence: MacDowell (1962) *passim*; Marr (1971); Furley (1989). Meletos: Burnet (1924) 10–11; Gomme *et al.* (1970) 78–83; Marr (1971) 334 n.1; Blumenthal (1973) 167–178; Keaney (1980) 296–298. Keaney argues convincingly that Pl. *Ap.* 32c8–d3 hints that Socrates' prosecutor Meletos is the same Meletos who arrested Leon of Salamis under the Thirty, and therefore the Meletos of Andokides' trial (Andok. 1.94). A strong argument, but not decisive, because Plato or Socrates might have been trying to confuse the judges by attempting to blame Socrates' accuser Meletos for the crimes of another man named Meletos.

20 See MacDowell (1962) 10–11, 206–207; Davies (1971) 31, 264–265, 268–269.

21 *Endeixis*: MacDowell (1962) 13–14; cf. Ostwald (1986) 536 n.41.

22 Ostwald (1986) 161–169.
23 MacDowell (1962) *passim* offers the most detailed account of Andokides' activities in 415. Marr (1971) and Seager (1978) are far more skeptical about Andokides' credibility, as was Thucydides (6.60.3, assuming as is likely, that this passage refers to Andokides). Other details are discussed by Hatzfeld (1951) 173–177; Dover in Gomme *et al.* (1970) 264–276, 285–286; Aurenche (1974) 108–110; Fornara (1980); Kagan (1981) 209; Raubitschek (1981); Ostwald (1986) 327–328; Furley (1989).
24 On the opprobrium which Andokides' behavior incurred, see Mac-Dowell (1962) 3–4; Pecorella Longo (1971) 47.
25 On the vicissitudes of Andokides' career up to the time of his trial, see Davies (1971) 31; Ostwald (1986) 546–547; Strauss (1986) 99–100.
26 Date: MacDowell (1962) 4 n.9; Marr (1971) 33 n.1.
27 *Hermokopidai* and profaners as arrogant youths: Ostwald (1986) 541, 549–550. *Against Andokides* mentions the betrayal of kinsmen (*suggeneis*) and friends (*philoi*) without specifying Andokides' father (Lys. 6.23). A curious omission, but it is a quirky speech, far more interested in the issue of impiety against Eleusis than anything else, and fragmentary to boot. See Dover (1968b) 169 + n.23. Marr (1971) 336 cites the silence of this passage as evidence that Andokides' alleged denunciation of his father was a slander that was not universally alleged.
28 Later sources: MacDowell (1962) 172.
29 Flimsiness of Andokides' defense, multiple denunciations, Leogoras freed on technicality: MacDowell (1962) 169–171.
30 No other part of the speech even comes close in the frequency of use of the word *patêr*. The word appears seven times in sections 41–47, but five of those are in lists of degree of kinship (e.g. "cousin of my *patêr*") in section 47.
31 Drama: see Ober and Strauss (1990) 256. For the possibility that Andokides denounced as many as twenty-two men, see Seager (1978) 223.
32 Note the emotional connotations of *steromai* (LSJ s.v.). On Andokides' hatred of exile, cf. Hyp. 1.20.
33 Piety of *Against Andokides*: Dover (1968b) 78–83. Leogoras: Davies (1971) 30; Ostwald (1986) 542.
34 Andokides' charge may have been a smear: "Meletos" was a common name, and it is not certain that the Meletos of Andokides' trial is the same Meletos who arrested Leon. See MacDowell (1962) 208–209; Davies (1971) 382; above, n.19.
35 Ostwald (1986) 161–169.
36 Allusion to *Iliad*: see MacDowell (1962) comm. *ad loc.* I translate *paides* as "sons" rather than "children" because here the emphasis is on males and the continuity of the oikos.
37 Grote (1884) 8:272 n.2. Nietzsche: cited by Reeve (1989) 184.
38 For a recent and cogent discussion, see Brickhouse and Smith (1989) 2–10.
39 For recent discussions of political motives behind the prosecution, see Vlastos (1983) 495–616; Kraut (1984) ch. 6; Irwin (1986), (1989); Strauss

(1986) 94–96; Stone (1988); Reeve (1989) 97–107, 155–160. Stone's Socrates seems to me to have much more to do with late-twentieth-century AD America than with fifth-century BC Athens, but the book is a stylistic tour de force even so. Irwin (1989) points out the major problems with the book. I am unpersuaded by Brickhouse and Smith (1989) 84–87 that the political context only became important with Polykrates' accusations after the trial. On religious motives for the prosecution, see Connor (1991).

40 Date of Isoc. 20: *Against Lokhites*: Blass (1887) 2:217 argues for a date shortly after 403, based in large part on section 11 of the oration. Socrates challenged the traditional order: demonstrated poignantly in Nussbaum (1980) who notes the relevance of Pl. *Rep.* 538d–e. Most people considered Socrates a teacher: see Vlastos (1991) 296–297. Hegel's discussion in *Lectures on the History of Philosophy* is still relevant: see Hegel (1989 [1825–1826]).

41 I follow closely the discussion in Connor (1991) 54–55.

42 Anytos's family fortune: Davies (1971) 40–41; on Anytos more generally, Strauss (1986) 89–92, 94–96. Just before his death, Socrates prophesied that Anytos's ne'er-do-well son would accomplish nothing in life, and Xenophon is pleased to report that the prediction proved true (*Ap.* 30–31).

43 Trans. Brickhouse and Smith (1989) 30; cf. Xen. *Mem.* 1.1.1; Pl. *Ap.* 24b–c.

44 See Brickhouse and Smith (1989) 31–33; Reeve (1989) 74–82.

45 Ar. *Clouds*: Brickhouse and Smith (1989) 66, 68, 110; Reeve (1989) 16–21; on the portrait of Socrates in *Clouds*, see above, ch. 5 n.48.

46 Elitist argument, some construe: Reeve (1989) 90.

47 Brickhouse and Smith (1989) 198–199; cf. Strauss (1966) 41–42, 52; Nussbaum (1980); Reeve (1989) 164–169.

48 See Havelock (1952); Brickhouse and Smith (1989) 198–199.

49 Socrates' first speech (Pl. *Ap.* 17a–35d) is a defense against Meletos's indictment; Socrates' second speech (Pl. *Ap.* 35e–38b) follows the jury's guilty verdict and concerns Meletos's proposed penalty of death; Socrates' third speech (Pl. *Ap.* 38c–42a) follows the imposition of the death penalty, and offers last words to friends and enemies on the jury respectively. For the canonical divisions of the *Apology* see Reeve (1989) 3.

50 Socrates' plea is, to be sure, ironic, both since the convicted corrupter of youth entrusts his own sons to the hands of his prosecutors, and since he asks them to treat the boys the way he has treated the people of Athens (Pl. *Ap.* 41e).

51 This argument does not exculpate Socrates, however, for he may have hand-picked his supporters in the courtroom. The prosecution seems not to have any kinsmen of corrupted youth to testify against Socrates (Pl. *Ap.* 34a), but these kinsmen may have been reticent to call public attention to their families, as West (1979) 197 notes.

52 Plato or Socrates changes the Epic *tekos* (= Attic *tokos*, "offspring") of the original (*Il.* 18.95) to the ordinary Attic *pais*, hence making the quotation more accessible. Burnet (1924) comm. *ad loc.*

53 For a more optimistic reading of the analogy, see Reeve (1989) 108, 186; and, in a different vein, West (1979) 151–166.

54 On the *daimonion*: Reeve (1989) 68–70, 76–78, 180–182.

55 Was Socrates indifferent to winning his case? Xenophon asserts that Socrates was ready to die (Xen. *Ap.* 22–23, 31) and Epictetus believes Socrates intended to provoke the jury (*Discourses* 2.2.18). Grote thought likewise ([1884] 8:280–286). Reeve (1989) 6–8 offers a vigorous counter-argument; see Brickhouse and Smith (1989) 39 n.140 for bibliography.

56 Xenophon claims to have obtained his anecdotes from Socrates' friend Hermogenes son of Hipponikos (*Ap.* 2), who was half-brother to Kallias (Davies [1971] 269).

57 On Athenian education, see above, ch. 3.

58 Hegel (1989 [1825–1826]) 158–159.

59 Other traces of Polykrates' accusation are found in Isocrates' *Busiris* 5; D. L. 2.38–39; Libanius's *Apology*; and perhaps Aeschin. 1.173. On Polykrates' pamphlet, see Chroust (1957) 69–100; Brickhouse and Smith (1989) 71–72; Irwin (1989) 193. For the identification of Xenophon's accuser with Polykrates, see Chroust (1957) 90; Brickhouse and Smith (1989) 71 n.31.

60 On the law that permitted a son to sue his father on grounds of mental incapacity, see Harrison (1968) 79–81.

61 See Kerényi (1979 [1951]) 20–25. For an analogous story, consider Sophocles' Kreon, who punishes Antigone, the rebellious representative of the younger generation, by burying her alive (Soph. *Ant.* 74–80).

62 On prosecution for failing to support one's parents, see above, ch. 3.

63 See Brickhouse and Smith (1989) 37 + n.132.

64 See Ostwald (1986) 497–524.

CONCLUSION

1 Deserted oikos: Asheri (1960). Supremacy of polis as theme of Athenian funeral orations: Loraux (1986 [1981]). Lacey (1968) 78–79 emphasizes, on the contrary, the importance of families in this oration.

2 Cf. Dein. 1.71. In hindsight, Pericles' is a sadly ironic comment, since he would shortly lose his two legitimate sons in the epidemic; see above, ch. 5. My translation relies on Crawley and Gomme (1956) comm. *ad loc.*

3 Cf. Aesch. *Pers.* 403–405; Thuc. 7.69.2 (see above, ch. 2); Lacey (1968) 78.

BIBLIOGRAPHY

JOURNAL TITLES ABBREVIATED IN THE BIBLIOGRAPHY

AC   *L'Antiquité Classique*
AHR   *American Historical Review*
AJA   *American Journal of Archaeology*
AJAH   *American Journal of Ancient History*
AJP   *American Journal of Philology*
AncSoc   *Ancient Society*
BICS   *Bulletin of the Institute of Classical Studies of the University of London*
CA   *Classical Antiquity*
CB   *The Classical Bulletin*
CJ   *Classical Journal*
CPh   *Classical Philology*
CQ   *Classical Quarterly*
CR   *Classical Review*
CW   *The Classical World*
G&R   *Greece and Rome*
GRBS   *Greek, Roman, and Byzantine Studies*
JHS   *Journal of Hellenic Studies*
MH   *Museum Helveticum*
PCPhS   *Proceedings of the Cambridge Philological Society*
REG   *Revue des Etudes Grecques*
RhM   *Rheinisches Museum*
TAPA   *Transactions of the American Philological Association*
YCls   *Yale Classical Studies*
ZPE   *Zeitschrift für Papyrologie und Epigraphik*

Adkins, A.W.H. (1960). *Merit and Responsibility. A Study in Greek Values.* Oxford.

Agard, W.R. (1928). "Theseus, a National Hero." *CJ* 24:84–92.

Ahl, Frederick M. (1985). *Metaformations: Soundplay and Wordplay in Ovid and Other Classical Poets.* Ithaca.

Ampolo, Carmine and Mario Manfredini (1988). *Plutarco. Le Vite Di Teseo e di Romolo.* n.p.

Amussen, Susan Dwyer (1988). *An Ordered Society. Gender and Class in Early Modern England.* Oxford.

Appadurai, Arjun (1981). "The Past as a Scarce Resource." *Man* n.s. 16:201–219.

Arendt, Hannah (1958). *The Human Condition.* Chicago.

Arrowsmith, William (1956). Trans. Euripides *Heracles.* In D.Grene, ed. *The Complete Greek Tragedies.* Vol. V: *Euripides I.* Chicago.

Arthur, Marilyn (1986 [1976]). "Aphrodite Denied: Classical Greece." In Renate Bridenthal, Claudia Koonz, and Susan Stuard, eds., *Becoming Visible: Women in European History.* 2nd edn. Boston: 80–91.

Asheri, D. (1960). "L'*oikos eremos* nel diritto successorio attico." *Archivo Giuridico* 159:12–24.

—— (1963). "Laws of Inheritance, Distribution of Land, and Political Constitutions in Ancient Greece." *Historia* 12:1–21.

Atallah, W. (1966). *Adonis dans la littérature et l'art grecs.* Paris.

Aurenche, O. (1974). *Les Groupes d'Alcibiade, de Léogoras, et de Teucros: remarques sur la vie politique athénienne en 415 av. J.-C.* Paris.

Austin, Norman (1975). *Archery at the Dark of the Moon. Poetic Problems in Homer's Odyssey.* Berkeley.

Badian, E. (1971). "Archons and *Strategoi.*" *Antichthon* 5:1–34.

Balmary, Marie (1982). *Psychoanalyzing Psychoanalysis: Freud and the Hidden Fault of the Father.* Trans. Ned Lukacher. Baltimore.

Banks, Thomas (1980). "The Ephemeral, the Perennial and the Structure of Aristophanes' *Wasps.*" *CQ* 56:81–84.

Barrett, Michèle and Mary McIntosh (1982). *The Anti-Social Family.* London.

Barrett, W. S. (1964). *Euripides Hippolytos. Edited with Introduction and Commentary.* Oxford.

Barron, John P. (1972). "New Light on Old Walls: The Murals of the Theseion." *JHS* 92:20–45.

—— (1980). "Bakchylides, Theseus and a woolly cloak." *BICS* 27:1–8.

Barth, Fredrik (1971). "Role Dilemmas and Father–Son Dominance in Middle Eastern Kinship Systems." In Francis L.K. Hsu, ed., *Kinship and Culture.* Chicago: 87–95.

Beauchet, Ludovic (1897). *Histoire du droit privé de la république athénienne.* Vol. 2: *Le droit de famille*; Vol. 3: *Le droit de propriété.* Paris.

Beazley, J.D. (1971). *Paralipomena: Additions to "Attic Black-Figure Vase Painters" and to "Attic Red-Figure Vase Painters."* 2nd edn. Oxford.

Beck, Frederick A.G. (1964). *Greek Education 450–350 B.C.* London.

Benveniste, E. (1969). *Le Vocabulaire des institutions indo-européennes.* Vols. 1–2. Paris.

Bérard, Claude (1982). "Récupérer la mort du prince: héroïsation et formation de la cité." In Gherardo Gnoli et Jean-Pierre Vernant, eds., *La Mort, les morts dans les sociétés anciennes.* New York and Paris: 89–106.

Bertelli, Lucio and Gian Franco Gianotti (1987). "Teseo tra mito e storia politica: un' Atene immaginaria?" *Aufidus* 1:35–58.

Bertman, Stephen (1976). Ed. *The Conflict of Generations in Ancient Greece and Rome*. Amsterdam.

Beye, Charles Rowan (1987). *Ancient Greek Literature and Society*. 2nd edn., revised. Ithaca and London.

Blass, Friedrich (1887). *Die Attische Beredsamkeit*. Vol. 1: *Von Gorgias bis zu Lysias*. 2nd edn. Leipzig.

Bloedow, Edmund F. (1990). " 'Not the Son of Achilles, But Achilles Himself': Alcibiades' Entry on the Political Stage at Athens II." *Historia* 39:1–19.

Blumenthal, H. (1973). "Meletus the Accuser of Andocides and Meletus the Accuser of Socrates: One Man or Two?" *Philologus* 117:167–178.

Blundell, Mary Whitlock (1989). *Helping Friends and Harming Enemies. A Study in Sophocles and Greek Ethics*. Cambridge.

Boardman, John (1972). "Herakles, Peisistratus, and his Sons." *Revue Archéologique* 15:57–72.

—— (1974). *Athenian Black Figure Vases*. New York.

—— (1975a). *Athenian Red Figure Vases, the Archaic Period, a Handbook*. London.

—— (1975b) "Herakles, Peisistratus, and Eleusis." *JHS* 95:1–12.

—— (1985). *Greek Sculpture. The Classical Period*. New York.

Boegehold, A. (1990). "Andokides and the Decree of Patrokleides." *Historia* 39:149–162.

Bond, Godfrey W. (1981). *Euripides Heracles*. Oxford.

Bonfante, Larissa (1981). "Etruscan Couples and their Aristocratic Society." In Foley, ed., *Reflections on Women in Antiquity*. New York: 323–342.

Bonner, R.J. and G. Smith (1930–38). *The Administration of Justice from Homer to Aristotle*. Vols. 1–2. Chicago.

Bornkamm, Guenther (1976). "Das Vaterbild im Neuen Testament." In Hubertus Tellenbach, ed., *Das Vaterbild in Mythos und Geschichte*. Stuttgart: 136–154.

Bourdieu, Pierre (1977). *Outline of a Theory of Practice*. Trans. Richard Nice. Cambridge.

Bourriot, F. (1976). *Recherches sur la nature du génos: étude d'histoire sociale athénienne – périodes archaique et classique*. Paris.

Bowie, A. M. (1987). "Ritual Stereotype and Comic Reversal: Aristophanes' *Wasps*." *BICS* 34:112–125.

Brelich, Angelo (1969). *Paides e Parthenoi*. Vol. 1. Rome.

Bremmer, Jan (1987a). Ed. *Interpretations of Greek Mythology*. London.

—— (1987b). "Oedipus and the Greek Oedipus Complex." In Jan Bremmer, ed., *Interpretations of Greek Mythology*. London: 41–59.

Brickhouse, Thomas C. and Nicholas D. Smith (1989). *Socrates on Trial*. Princeton.

Brock, R.W. (1986). "The Double Plot in Aristophanes' *Knights*." *GRBS* 27:15–27.

Brommer, Frank (1982). *Theseus*. Darmstadt.

Brown, Norman O. (1966). *Love's Body*. Berkeley.

Burian, Peter (1985a). "*Logos* and *Pathos*: the Politics of the *Suppliant*

Women." In Peter Burian, ed., *Directions in Euripidean Criticism.* Durham: 129–155.

—— (1985b). Ed. *Directions in Euripidean Criticism.* Durham.

Burkert, Walter (1979). *Structure and History in Greek Mythology and Ritual.* Berkeley and Los Angeles.

—— (1983 [1972]). *Homo Necans. The Anthropology of Ancient Greek Sacrificial Ritual and Myth.* Trans. Peter Bing. Berkeley.

—— (1985). *Greek Religion.* Trans. John Raffan. Cambridge, Mass.

Burnet, John (1924). *Plato's Euthyphro, Apology of Socrates and Crito.* Oxford.

Calame, Claude (1990). *Thésée et l'imaginaire athénien. Légende et culte en Grèce antique.* Lausanne.

Calhoun, G.M. (1913). *Athenian Clubs in Politics and Litigation.* Austin.

Cambiano, G. (1987). "Aristotle and the Anonymous Opponents of Slavery." In M.I. Finley, ed., *Classical Slavery.* Totowa, NJ: 21–41.

Campbell, J.K. (1964). *Honour, Family, and Patronage. A Study of Institutions and Moral Values in a Greek Mountain Community.* Oxford.

Carpenter, T.H. (1991). *Art and Myth in Ancient Greece.* New York.

Carrière, Jean Claude (1979). *Le Carnaval et la politique. Une introduction à la comédie grecque suivie d'un choix de fragments. Annales littéraires de l'université de Besançon v. 212.* Paris.

Carter, L.B. (1986). *The Quiet Athenian.* Oxford.

Cartledge, Paul (1981). "The Politics of Spartan Pederasty." *PCPhS* n.s. 27:17–36.

—— (1992). "The Emergence of 'The Political.'" Review of Christian Meier, *The Greek Discovery of Politics* (1990 [1979]). *CR* n.s. 42.1:99–101.

Casson, Lionel (1976). "The Athenian Upper Class and New Comedy." *TAPA* 106:29–59.

Cecchin, S.A. (1969). *Patrios Politeia. Un tentativo propagandistico durante la guerra del Peloponneso.* Turin.

Chantraine, Pierre (1974). *Dictionnaire étymologique de la langue grecque. Histoire des mots.* Vol. 3. Paris.

Charlier, Marie-Thérèse and Georges Raepset (1971). "Etude d'un comportement social: les relations entre parents et enfants dans la société athénienne à l'époque classique." *AC* 40:589–606.

Chroust, Anton-Hermann (1957). *Socrates, Man and Myth.* London.

Clay, Diskin (1982). "Unspeakable Words in Greek Tragedy." *AJP* 103: 277–298.

Clinton, Kevin (1982). "The Nature of the Late Fifth-Century Revision of the Athenian Law Code." In *Studies in Attic Epigraphy, History, and Topography Presented to Eugene Vanderpool. Hesperia* Supplement 19:27–37.

Cohen, David (1989). "Seclusion, Separation, and the Status of Women in Classical Athens." *G&R* 36:3–15.

—— (1991). *Law, Sexuality, and Society. The Enforcement of Morals in Classical Athens.* Cambridge.

Collard, Christopher (1975). *Euripides Supplices. Edited with Introduction and Commentary.* Vols. 1–2. Groningen.

Conacher, D.J. (1967). *Euripidean Drama. Myth, Theme and Structure.* Toronto.

Connor, W.R. (1970). "Theseus in Classical Athens." In Anne C. Ward, W.R. Connor, et al., *The Quest for Theseus.* London: 143–174.

—— (1971). *The New Politicians of Fifth-Century Athens.* Princeton.

—— (1985). "The Razing of the House in Greek Society." *TAPA* 115: 79–102.

—— (1991). "The Other 399: Religion and the Trial of Socrates." In M.A. Flower and M. Toher, eds., *Georgica. Greek Studies in Honour of George Cawkwell. BICS* Supplement 58:49–56.

Connor, W.R., M.H. Hansen, K.A. Raaflaub, B.S. Strauss, with a Preface by J. Rufus Fears (1990). *Aspects of Athenian Democracy.* Classica et Mediaevalia Dissertationes XI. Copenhagen.

Cornford, Francis MacDonald (1971 [1907]). *Thucydides Mythistoricus.* Philadelphia.

Cox, Cheryl (1988). "Sibling Relationships in Classical Athens: Brother–Sister Ties." *Journal of Family History* 13:377–395.

—— (1989–90). "Incest, Inheritance and the Political Forum in Fifth-Century Athens." *CJ* 85:34–46.

—— (1990). "Family, Friends, Slaves, and Prostitutes: The Household in Classical Athens." Unpublished paper.

Davie, John N. (1982). "Theseus the King in Fifth-Century Athens." *G& R* 29:24–34.

Davies, J.K. (1971). *Athenian Propertied Families, 600–300 B.C.* Oxford.

—— (1977–78). "Athenian Citizenship: The Descent Group and the Alternatives." *CJ* 73:105–121.

Delaisi de Parseval, G. and Françoise Hurstel (1987). "Paternity à la Française." In Michael E. Lamb, ed., *The Father's Role. Cross-Cultural Perspectives.* Hillsdale: 59–87.

Derrida, Jacques (1984 [1972]). "Plato's Pharmacy." In *Dissemination.* Trans. Barbara Johnson. Chicago: 61–172.

De Schutter, Xavier (1987). "Le culte d'Apollon Patrôios à Athènes." *AC* 56:103–129.

Detienne, Marcel (1977). *The Gardens of Adonis. Spices in Greek Mythology.* Trans. Janet Lloyd. Atlantic Highlands, NJ.

—— (1979). *Dionysos Slain.* Trans. M. Muellner and L. Muellner. Baltimore.

Deubner, Ludwig (1966 [1932]). *Attische Feste.* Berlin.

Develin, Robert (1985). "Age Qualifications for Athenian Magistrates." *ZPE* 61:149–159.

—— (1989). *Athenian Officials 684–321 B.C.* Cambridge.

Devereux, George (1967). "Greek Pseudo-Homosexuality and the 'Greek Miracle.'" *Symbolae Osloenses* 42:69–92.

—— (1985). *The Character of the Euripidean Hippolytos: An Ethno-Psychoanalytical Study.* Chico, Calif.

Dimen, M. and E. Friedl (1976). Eds. *Regional Variation in Modern*

Greece and Cyprus: Towards a Comparative Perspective on the Ethnography of Greece. New York.

Dimock, George E. Jr. (1977). "Euripides' *Hippolytus*, or Virtue Rewarded." *YClS* 25:239–258.

Dixon, Suzanne (1988). *The Roman Mother*. London.

Dodds, E.R. (1925). "The *Aidôs* of Phaedra and the Meaning of the *Hippolytus*." *CR* 39:102–104.

Donzelot, Jacques (1979). *Policing the Family*. Trans. Robert Hurley. New York.

Douglas, Mary (1966). *Purity and Danger. An Analysis of Concepts of Pollution and Taboo*. Harmondsworth.

Dover, Sir Kenneth J. (1968a). *Aristophanes "Clouds"*. Oxford.

—— (1968b). *Lysias and the Corpus Lysiacum*. Berkeley.

—— (1972). *Aristophanic Comedy*. Berkeley.

—— (1974). *Greek Popular Morality in the Age of Plato and Aristotle*. Berkeley.

—— (1978). *Greek Homosexuality*. New York.

du Bois, Page. (1982). *Centaurs and Amazons*. Ann Arbor.

DuBoulay, J. (1974). *Portrait of a Greek Mountain Village*. Oxford.

Duby, Georges. (1985 [1974]). "Ideologies in Social History." Trans. David Denby. In Jacques LeGoff and Pierre Nora, eds., *Constructing the Past. Essays in Historical Methodology*. Intro. Colin Lucas. Cambridge: 151–165.

Dugas, C. (1943). "L'évolution de la légende de Thésée." *REG* 56:1–24.

Dugas, C. and R. Flacelière (1958). *Thésée: images et recits*. Paris.

Edmonds, J.M. (1939). "The Cairo and Oxyrhynchus Fragments of the *Dêmoi* of Eupolis." *Mnemosyne* 3rd ser. 8:1–20

—— (1957–61). Ed. and trans. *The Fragments of Attic Comedy*. 3 vols. in 4. Leiden.

Edmunds, Lowell (1986). "Aristophanes' Socrates." *Proceedings of the Boston Area Colloquium in Ancient Philosophy* 1:209–230.

—— (1987). *Cleon, "Knights," and Aristophanes' Politics*. Lanham and London.

—— (1990). Ed. *Approaches to Greek Myth*. Baltimore.

Edwards, Ruth B. (1970). "The Story of Theseus" and "The Growth of the Legend." In Anne C. Ward, W. R. Connor, *et al.*, *The Quest for Theseus*. London: 7–50.

Ehrenberg, Victor (1954). *Sophocles and Pericles*. Oxford.

—— (1962). *The People of Aristophanes. A Sociology of Old Comedy*. 3rd edn. New York.

Ellis, Walter M. (1989). *Alcibiades*. New York.

Falkner, Thomas M. and Judith de Luce (1990). Eds. *Old Age in Greek and Latin Literature*. Albany, NY.

Farber, Bernard (1988). *Conceptions of Kinship*. New York.

Fauth, Wolfgang (1958–59). "*Hippolytos und Phaidra. Bemerkungen zum religiösen Hintergrund eines tragischen Konflikts I.*" Akademie der Wissenschaften und der Literatur in Mainz: Abhandlungen der Geistes- und Sozialwissenschaftlichen Klasse 9:515–588.

Feinstein, Howard (1984). *Becoming William James*. Ithaca and London.

Ferretto, C. (1985). "Enopio fra mito e propaganda." *Civiltà classica e cristiana* 6:155–159.

Finley, M.I. (1975 [1971]). "The Ancestral Constitution." In M. I. Finley, *The Use and Abuse of History*. New York: 34–59.

—— (1983). *Politics in the Ancient World*. Cambridge.

—— (1985). *Ancient History. Evidence and Models*. New York.

—— (1990). "The Elderly in Classical Antiquity." In Thomas M. Falkner and Judith de Luce, eds., *Old Age in Greek and Latin Literature*. Albany, NY: 1–20 [= *G&R* 28 (1981):156–171].

Fisher, N.R.E. (1976). *Social Values in Classical Athens*. London.

Fitton, J. (1961). "The *Suppliant Women* and the *Herakleidai* of Euripides." *Hermes* 89:430–461.

Flandrin, Jean-Louis (1979). *Families in Former Times*. Trans. R. Southern. Cambridge.

Foley, Helene P. (1981a). "The Concept of Women in Athenian Drama." In Helene P. Foley, ed., *Reflections on Women in Antiquity*. New York: 127–168.

—— (1981b). Ed. *Reflections of Women in Antiquity*. New York.

—— (1982). "The 'Female Intruder' Reconsidered: Women in Aristophanes' *Lysistrata* and *Ecclesiazusae*." *CPh* 77:1–21.

—— (1985). *Ritual Irony. Poetry and Sacrifice in Euripides*. Ithaca and London.

Forgie, George B. (1979). *Patricide in the House Divided: A Psychological Intepretation of Lincoln and His Age*. New York.

Fornara, C.W. (1971). *The Athenian Board of Generals from 505 to 404. Historia* Einzelschrift 16. Wiesbaden.

—— (1980). "Andocides and Thucydides." In S.M. Burstein and L.A. Okin, eds., *Panhellenica. Essays in Ancient History and Historiography in Honor of Truesdale S. Brown*. Lawrence, KA: 43–56.

Forrest, W.G. (1963). "Aristophanes' *Acharnians*." *Phoenix* 17:1–12.

—— (1970). "The Date of the Pseudo-Xenophontic *Athenaion Politeia*." *Klio* 52:107–116.

—— (1975). "An Athenian Generation Gap." *YClS* 24:37–52.

Fortes, Meyer (1969). *Kinship and the Social Order. The Legacy of Henry Lewis Morgan*. Chicago.

Foucault, Michel (1977). *Discipline and Punish: The Birth of the Prison*. Trans. Alan Sheridan. New York.

—— (1978). *The History of Sexuality*. Vol. 1: *An Introduction*. Trans. Robert Hurley. New York.

—— (1979). "On Governmentality." *Ideology and Consciousness* 6:5–22.

—— (1980). *Power/Knowledge: Selected Interviews and Other Writings, 1972–1977*. Ed. Colin Gordon. New York.

—— (1985). *The History of Sexuality*, Vol. 2: *The Uses of Pleasure*. Trans. Robert Hurley. New York.

Fox, Robin (1983). *Kinship and Marriage: An Anthropological Perspective*. Cambridge.

Foxhall, Lin (1989). "Household, Gender and Property in Classical Athens." *CQ* 39:22–44.

Francis, E.D. (1990). *Image and Idea in Fifth-Century Greece. Art and Literature after the Persian Wars*. Ed. Michael Vickers. New York.

Freeman, Kenneth J. (1932 [1907]). *Schools of Hellas. An Essay on the Practice and Theory of Ancient Greek Education from 600 to 300 B.C.* Ed. M.J. Rendall. London.

Freud, Sigmund (1913). *Totem and Taboo*. New York.

—— (1939). *Moses and Monotheism*. New York.

—— (1955). *The Interpretation of Dreams*. Ed. and trans. James Strachey. New York.

Friedl, Ernestine (1959). "Dowry and Inheritance in Modern Greece." *Transactions of the New York Academy of Science* 22:49–54.

—— (1962). *Vasilika. A Village in Modern Greece*. New York.

—— (1963). "Some Aspects of Dowry and Inheritance in Boeotia." in J. Pitt-Rivers, ed., *Mediterranean Countrymen. Essays in the Social Anthropology of the Mediterranean*. Paris: 113–136.

Frisk, Hjalmar (1970). *Griechisches Etymologisches Wörterbuch*. Heidelberg.

Frost, Frank J. (1984). "Plutarch and Theseus." *CB* 60:65–73.

Fuks, A. (1971 [1953]). *The Ancestral Constitution*. Westport, Conn.

Furley, W.D. (1989). "A Note on [Lysias] 6, *Against Andocides*." *CQ* 39 n.s.:550–553.

Fustel de Coulanges, N.D. (1980 [1864]). *The Ancient City: A Study on the Religion, Laws, and Institutions of Greece and Rome*. New foreword by Arnaldo Momigliano and S.C. Humphreys. Baltimore.

Gadamer, Hans Georg (1976). "Das Vaterbild im Griechischen Denken." In Hubertus Tellenbach, ed., *Das Vaterbild in Mythos und Geschichte. Aegypten, Griechenland, Altes Testament, Neues Testament*. Stuttgart: 102–115.

Gallop, Jane (1985). *Reading Lacan*. Ithaca.

Gamble, R.B. (1970). "Euripides' *Suppliant Women*: Decision and Ambivalence." *Hermes* 98:385–405.

Gardner, Jane (1989). "Aristophanes and Male Anxiety. The Defense of the *Oikos*." *G&R* 36:31–62.

Garland, Robert (1985). *The Greek Way of Death*. Ithaca.

—— (1990). *The Greek Way of Life. From Conception to Old Age*. Ithaca.

Geertz, Clifford (1973). *The Intepretation of Cultures*. New York.

—— (1980). *Negara. The Theatre State in Nineteenth-Century Bali*. Princeton.

—— (1983). *Local Knowledge. Further Essays in Interpretive Anthropology*. New York.

Gernet, Louis (1955). *Droit et société dans la Grèce ancienne*. Paris.

—— (1981 [1951]). "Political Symbolism: the Public Hearth." In Louis Gernet, *The Anthropology of Ancient Greece*. Trans. John Hamilton and Blaise Nagy. Baltimore: 322–339 [= "Sur le symbolisme politique en Grèce ancienne: le foyer commun." *Cahiers internationaux de Sociologie* 11: (1951)21–43].

—— (1983). "La famille dans l'antiquité grecque. Vue générale." *AION* (arch.) 5:173–195.

Gernet, Louis and Marcel Bizos (1924–26). *Lysias, Discours.* Vols. 1–2. Paris.

Giddens, Anthony (1984). *The Constitution of Society. Introduction to the Theory of Structuration.* Cambridge.

Girard, Paul (1889). *L'Education athénienne. Au Ve siècle et au IVe siècle avant J.-C.* Paris.

Gluckman, Max (1963). *Order and Rebellion in Tribal Africa.* New York.

Goffman, Erving (1959). *The Presentation of Self in Everyday Life.* New York.

Golden, Mark (1979). "Demosthenes and the Age of Majority at Athens." *Phoenix* 33:25–38.

—— (1981). "Demography and the Exposure of Girls at Athens." *Phoenix* 35:316–331.

—— (1984). "Slavery and Homosexuality in Athens." *Phoenix* 38:308–324.

—— (1985). "*Pais,* 'Child' and Slave." *AC* 54:91–104.

—— (1986). "Names and Naming at Athens: Three Studies." *EMC* 30: 245–269.

—— (1990). *Children and Childhood in Athens.* Baltimore.

Goldhill, Simon (1986). *Reading Greek Tragedy.* Cambridge.

—— (1990). "The Great Dionysia and Civic Ideology." In John J. Winkler and Froma I. Zeitlin, eds., *Nothing to Do with Dionysos? Athenian Drama in Its Social Context.* Princeton: 97–129 [= revised version of *JHS* 107 (1987):58–76].

Gomme, A.W., A. Andrewes and K.J. Dover (1945–81). *A Historical Commentary on Thucydides.* 5 vols. (Vol. 1, 1945; Vol. 2, 1956a; Vol. 3, 1956b; Vol. 4, 1970; Vol. 5, 1981). Oxford.

Goody, Jack (1962). *Death, Property and the Ancestors: A Study of the Mortuary Customs of the Lodogaba of West Africa.* Stanford.

—— (1966a). Ed. *The Developmental Cycle in Domestic Groups.* Cambridge Papers In Social Anthropology no. 1. Cambridge.

—— (1966b). "The Fission of Domestic Groups Among the Lodagaba." In Jack Goody, ed., *The Developmental Cycle in Domestic Groups.* Cambridge Papers in Social Anthropology no. 1. Cambridge: 53–91.

—— (1976). *Production and Reproduction. A Comparative Study of the Domestic Domain.* Cambridge.

—— (1983). *The Development of the Family and Marriage in Europe.* Cambridge.

Gould, John (1989). *Herodotus.* London.

Gouldner, Alvin (1967). *Enter Plato. Classical Greece and the Origins of Social Theory.* London.

Graf, Fritz (1979). "Apollo Delphinios." *MH* 36:2–22.

Green, A. (1980). "Thésée et Oedipe. Une interprétation psychanalytique de la Théséide." In D. Anzieu, F. Carapanos, *et al.*, *Psychanalyse et culture grecque.* Paris: 109–158.

Greenwood, L.H.G. (1953). *Aspects of Euripidean Tragedy.* Cambridge.

Gregory, Justina (1977). "Euripides' *Heracles.*" *YClS* 25: 259–275.

Grene, David (1939). "The Interpretation of the *Hippolytus* of Euripides." *CPh* 34:45–58.

Grote, George (1884). *A History of Greece.* New Edn. London.

Guthrie, W.K.C. (1971a). *The Sophists*. Cambridge. [= first part of W.K.C. Guthrie, *History of Greek Philosophy*. Vol. III. Cambridge: 1969].

—— (1971b). *Socrates*. Cambridge. [= second part of W.K.C. Guthrie, *History of Greek Philosophy*. Vol. III. Cambridge: 1969].

Hallett, Judith (1984). *Fathers and Daughters in Roman Society. Women and the Elite Family*. Princeton.

Halperin, David M. (1990). *One Hundred Years of Homosexuality and Other Essays on Greek Love*. New York and London.

Hansen, Mogens Herman (1985). *Demography and Democracy. The Number of Athenian Citizens in the Fourth Century B.C.* Herning, Denmark.

—— (1988). *Three Studies in Athenian Demography*. Royal Danish Academy of Sciences and Letters. Historisk-Filosofisker Meddelelser 56. Copenhagen.

—— (1989). *Was Athens a Democracy? Popular Rule, Liberty and Equality in Ancient and Modern Political Thought*. Royal Danish Academy of Sciences and Letters. Historisk-Filosofisker Meddelelser 59. Copenhagen.

Hanson, Victor Davis (1989). *The Western Way of War. Infantry Battle in Classical Greece*. New York.

Harding, P. (1978). "O Androtion, You Fool!" *AJAH* 3:179–183.

Harriott, Rosemary M. (1986). *Aristophanes: Poet and Dramatist*. Baltimore.

Harris, William V. (1989). *Ancient Literacy*. Cambridge, Mass.

Harrison, A.R.W. (1968). *The Law of Athens*. Vol. 1: *The Family and Property*. Oxford.

Harrison, E.B. (1966). "The Composition of the Amazonomachy on the Shield of Athena Parthenos." *Hesperia* 35:107–133.

Harrison, Jane (1927). *Themis. A Study of the Social Origins of Greek Religion*. 2nd edn. Cambridge.

Harvey, F.D. (1966). "Literacy in the Athenian Democracy." *REG* 79: 585–635.

—— (1984). "The Wicked Wife of Ischomachos." *Echos du Monde Classique (Classical Views)* 28:68–70.

Hatzfeld, Jean (1951). *Alcibiade. Etude sur l'histoire d'Athènes à la fin du Ve siècle*. Paris.

Havelock, Eric (1952). "Why Was Socrates Tried?" In M. White, ed., *Studies in Honor of G. Norwood. Phoenix* Supplement 1:95–109.

Heath, Malcolm (1987). *Political Comedy in Aristophanes. Hypomnemata*. Heft 87. Göttingen.

Hedrick, Charles W. Jr. (1988). "The Temple and Cult of Apollo Patroos in Athens." *AJA* 92:185–210.

—— (1990). *The Decrees of the Demotionidai*. American Classical Studies 22. Atlanta.

—— (1991). "Phratry Shrines of Attica and Athens." *Hesperia* 60.2:241–268.

Hegel, Georg Wilhelm Friedrich (1989 [1825–26]). *Vorlesungen über die*

Geschichte der Philosophie. Teil 2. Griechische Philosophie I. Thales bis Kyniker. Ed. Pierre Garniron and Walter Jaeschke. Hamburg.

Henderson, Jeffrey (1987). *Aristophanes Lysistrata.* Oxford.

—— (1990). "The *Dêmos* and Comic Competition." In John J. Winkler and Froma I. Zeitlin, eds., *Nothing to Do with Dionysos? Athenian Drama in Its Social Context.* Princeton: 271–313.

Henderson, J., D. Konstan, R. Rosen, J. Rusten and N. Slater (forthcoming). *The Birth of Comedy: Fragments of Greek Plays, ca. 500–250 B.C.*

Henning, E.M. (1982). "Archaeology, Deconstruction, and Intellectual History." In Dominick Lacapra and Steven L. Kaplan, eds., *Modern European Intellectual History. Reappraisals and New Perspectives.* Ithaca: 153–196.

Herlihy, David (1985). *Medieval Households.* Cambridge, Mass.

Herman, Gabriel (1987). *Ritualized Friendship and the Greek City.* Cambridge.

Herter, Hans (1936). "Theseus der Ionier." *RhM* 85:177–239.

—— (1939). "Theseus der Athener." *RhM* 88:244–326.

—— (1940). "Theseus und Hippolytos." *RhM* 89:273–292.

—— (1973). "Theseus." In Pauly, *RE* Supplement 13:1045–1238.

Herzfeld, Michael (1985). *The Poetics of Manhood. Contest and Identity in a Cretan Mountain Village.* Princeton.

—— (1987). *Anthropology through the Looking Glass: Critical Ethnography in the Margins of Europe.* Cambridge.

Hirschon, Renee (1989). *Heirs of the Greek Catastrophe. The Social Life of Asia Minor Refugees in Piraeus.* Oxford.

Hodkinson, Stephen (1983). "Social Order and the Conflict of Values in Classical Sparta." *Chiron* 13:239–281.

Hubbard, Thomas K. (1990). "Old Men in the Youthful Plays of Aristophanes." In Thomas M. Falkner and Judith de Luce, eds., *Old Age in Greek and Latin Literature.* Albany, NY: 90–113.

Humphreys, S.C. (1978). *Anthropology and the Greeks.* London.

—— (1983). *The Family, Women, and Death. Comparative Studies.* London.

—— (1985a). "Law as Discourse." *History and Anthropology* 1:241–264.

—— (1985b). "Social Relations on Stage." *History and Anthropology* 1:331–369.

—— (1986). "Kinship Patterns in the Athenian Courts." *GRBS* 27:57–91.

Hunter, Virginia (1989). "The Athenian Widow and Her Kin." *Journal of Family History* 14:291–311.

Hutter, H. (1978). *Politics as Friendship.* Waterloo, Ont.

Huxley, George (1973). "The Date of Pherekydes of Athens." *GRBS* 14: 137–43.

Ieranò, Giorgio (1987). "Osservazioni sul Teseo di Bacchilide (Dith. 18)." *Acme* 11:87–103.

Irwin, T.H. (1986). "Socratic Inquiry and Politics." *Ethics* 96:400–415.

—— (1989). "Socrates and Athenian Democracy." *Philosophy and Public Affairs* 18:184–205.

Jacoby, F. (1923–58). *Die Fragmente der griechischen Historiker* [*FGrH*]. 3 Teile in 14 vols. Berlin and Leiden.

Jameson, Michael (1990a). "Domestic Space in the Greek City-State." In Susan Kent, ed., *Domestic Architecture and the Use of Space. An Interdisciplinary Cross-Cultural Study.* Cambridge: 92–113.

—— (1990b). "Private Space and the Greek City." In Oswyn Murray and Simon Price, eds., *The Greek City from Homer to Alexander.* Oxford: 171–195.

Jeanmaire, Henri (1939). *Couroi et Courètes.* Lille.

Jebb, R.C. (1893). *The Attic Orators.* Vol. 1. 2nd edn. London.

Jordan, Borimir (1975). *The Athenian Navy in the Classical Period.* Berkeley.

Just, Roger (1989). *Women in Athenian Law and Life.* New York.

Kagan, Donald (1969). *The Outbreak of the Peloponnesian War.* Ithaca.

—— (1974). *The Archidamian War.* Ithaca.

—— (1981). *The Peace of Nicias and the Sicilian Expedition.* Ithaca.

—— (1987). *The Fall of the Athenian Empire.* Ithaca.

Kassel, R. and C. Austin (1983–). Eds. *Poetae Comici Graeci.* Berlin and New York.

Katz, Barry R. (1976). "The Birds of Aristophanes and Politics." *Athenaeum* 54:353–381.

Keaney, J.J. (1980). "Plato, *Apology* 32c8–d3." *CQ* 30 n.s.:396–398.

Kennedy, George (1963). *The Art of Persuasion in Greece.* Princeton.

Kerényi C. (1959). *The Heroes of Greece.* New York.

—— (1979 [1951]). *The Gods of Greece.* New York.

Keuls, Eva (1985). *The Reign of the Phallus. Sexual Politics in Ancient Athens.* New York.

Kirk, G.S. (1974). *The Nature of Greek Myths.* Harmondsworth.

Knox, Bernard (1952). "The *Hippolytus* of Euripides." *YClS* 13:3–31.

—— (1957). *Oedipus at Thebes. Sophocles' Tragic Hero and His Time.* New Haven.

—— (1979). "Myth and Attic Tragedy." In Bernard Knox, *Word and Action. Essays on the Ancient Theater.* Baltimore: 3–24.

Konstan, David (1985). "The Politics of Aristophanes' *Wasps.*" *TAPA* 115:27–46.

Kovacs, D. (1987). *The Heroic Muse: Studies in the Hippolytus and Hecuba of Euripides.* Baltimore.

Kraus, Walter (1985). *Aristophanes Politische Komödien. Die Acharner/Die Ritter. Österreichische Akademie der Wissenschaften. Philosophisch-Historische Klasse. SB 453.* Vienna.

Kraut, R. (1984). *Socrates and the State.* Princeton.

Krentz, Peter (1982). *The Thirty at Athens.* Ithaca.

Kron, Uta (1976). *Die Zehn Attischen Phylenheroen. Geschichte, Mythos, Kult und Darstellungen. Mitteilungen des Deustchen Archäologischen Instituts, Athenische Abteilung: 5. Beiheft.* Berlin.

Kuper, Adam (1988). *The Invention of Primitive Society.* London.

Kurke, Leslie (1991). *The Traffic in Praise. Pindar and the Poetics of Social Economy.* Princeton.

Labarbe, J. (1953). "L'age corréspondant au sacrifice du *koureion* et les données historiques du sixième discours d'Isée." *Bulletin de la Classe des Lettres de l'Académie Royale du Belgique* 39:358–394.

Lacan, Jacques (1977). *Ecrits. A Selection*. New York.

Lacey, W.K. (1968). *The Family in Classical Greece*. Ithaca and London.

Landes, Joan B. (1988). *Women and the Public Sphere in the Age of the French Revolution*. Ithaca and London.

Landfester, M. (1967). *Die Ritter des Aristophanes. Beobachtungen zur dramatischen Handlung und zum komischen Stil des Aristophanes*. Amsterdam.

Lanza, Diego and Mario Vegetti (1975). "L'ideologia della città." *Quaderni di storia* 1.2:1–37 [Reprinted in slightly altered form in Diego Lanza, M. Vegetti, *et al.* (1977). *L'ideologia della città*. Naples: 13–28].

Lateiner, Donald (1982–83). " 'The Man Who Does Not Meddle in Politics': A *Topos* in Lysias." *CW* 76:1–12.

Lattimore, Richmond (1951). *The Iliad of Homer*. Chicago.

Leach, Edmund (1973). *Lévi-Strauss*. London.

Lemke, Werner (1976). "Das Vatesbild in der Dichtung Griechenlands." In Hubertus Tellenbach, ed., *Das Vaterbild in Mythos und Geschichte. Aegypten, Griechenland, Altes Testament, Neues Testament*. Stuttgart: 116–135.

Lerner, Gerda (1986). *The Creation of Patriarchy*. New York and Oxford.

Lesky, Albin (1966). *A History of Greek Literature*. Trans. Willis and Cornelis de Heer. New York.

Lévi-Strauss, Claude (1963). *Structural Anthropology*. New York.

—— (1970). *The Raw and the Cooked. Introduction to a Science of Mythology*. Vol. 1. Trans. John Weightman and Doreen Weightman. Chicago.

—— (1981). *The Naked Man. Introduction to a Science of Mythology*. Vol. 4. Trans. John Weightman and Doreen Weightman. New York.

Levy, Harry L. (1956). "Property Distribution by Lot in Present-Day Greece." *TAPA* 137:42–46.

—— (1963). "Inheritance and Dowry in Classical Athens." In Julian Pitt-Rivers, ed., *Mediterranean Countrymen. Essays in the Social Anthropology of the Mediterranean*. Paris: 137–144.

Lewis, D.M. (1966). "After the Profanation of the Mysteries." In E. Badian, ed., *Ancient Societies and Institutions: Studies Presented to Victor Ehrenberg on His 75th Birthday*. Oxford.

Lincoln, Bruce (1989). *Discourse and the Construction of Society*. New York.

Littman, Robert (1969). "A New Date for Leotychidas." *Phoenix* 23:269–277.

—— (1970). "The Loves of Alcibiades." *TAPA* 101:263–276.

—— (1979). "Kinship in Athens." *AncSoc* 10:5–31.

Loizos, Peter (1975). *The Greek Gift. Politics in a Cypriot Village*. Oxford.

Loraux, Nicole (1981) *Les Enfants d'Athéna: Idées athéniennes sur la citoyenneté et la division des sexes*. Paris.

—— (1986 [1981]). *The Invention of Athens: The Funeral Oration in the Classical City.* Trans. Alan Sheridan. Cambridge, Mass.

Lord, Carnes (1991). "Aristotle's Anthropology." In Carnes Lord and David K. O'Connor, eds., *Essays on the Foundation of Aristotelian Political Science*: Berkeley: 49–73.

Lord, Carnes and David K. O'Connor (1991). *Essays on the Foundations of Aristotelian Political Science.* Berkeley.

MacAloon, John (1982). "Sociation and Sociability in Political Celebrations." In Victor Turner, ed., *Celebration. Studies in Festivity and Ritual.* Washington, DC: 255–271.

McCoy, W.J. (1975). "Aristotle's *Athenaion Politeia* and the Establishment of the Thirty Tyrants." *YClS* 24:131–145.

MacDowell, D.M. (1962). *Andokides. On the Mysteries.* Oxford.

—— (1971). *Aristophanes: Wasps.* Oxford.

—— (1978). *The Law in Classical Athens.* Ithaca.

—— (1989). "The *Oikos* in Athenian Law." *CQ* 39:10–21.

Maffi, A. (1983). "Padri e figli fra diritto positivo e diritto imaginario nella Grecia classica." In Ezio Pellizer and Nevio Zorzetti, eds., *La Paura dei padri nella società antica e medievale.* Rome: 3–28.

Maine, Sir Henry James Sumner (1861). *Ancient Law.* London.

Manville, Philip Brook (1990). *The Origins of Citizenship in Ancient Athens.* Princeton.

Marasco, G. (1976). "I processi d'empietà nella democrazia atenese." *Atene & Roma* 21:113–131.

Marr, J.L. (1971). "Andocides' Part in the Mysteries and Hermae Affairs 415 B.C." *CQ* 21 n.s.:326–338.

Marrou, H.I. (1956). *A History of Education in Antiquity.* Trans. George Lamb. New York.

Matthew, V.J. (1974). *Panyassis of Halikarnassos.* Leiden.

Medick, Hans and David Sabean (1984). Eds. *Interest and Emotion: Essays on the Study of Family and Kinship.* Cambridge and Paris.

Meier, Christian (1990 [1979]). *The Greek Discovery of Politics.* Trans. David McLintock. Cambridge, Mass.

Meiggs, Russell and David Lewis (1969). Eds. *A Selection of Greek Historical Inscriptions to the End of the Fifth Century B.C.* Oxford.

Merkelbach, R. (1973). "Der Theseus des Bakchylides (Gedicht für ein attisches Ephebenfest)." *ZPE* 12:59–62.

Mikalson, J.D. (1983). *Athenian Popular Religion.* Chapel Hill.

Mitchell, Juliet (1974). *Psychoanalysis and Feminism.* New York.

Moore, John (1957). *Ajax.* In *The Complete Greek Tragedies. Sophocles II.* Chicago: 1–62.

Moorton, Richard F. Jr. (1988). "Aristophanes on Alcibiades." *GRBS* 29: 345–360.

Morgan, Henry Lewis (1964 [1877]). *Ancient Society.* Ed. Leslie A. White. Cambridge, Mass.

Murnaghan, Sheila (1987). *Disguise and Recognition in the "Odyssey."* Princeton.

—— (1988). "How a Woman Can Be More Like a Man: The Dialogue

Between Ischomachus and His Wife in Xenophon's *Oeconomicus*." *Helios* 15:9–22.

Murray, Oswyn and Simon Price, (1990). Eds. *The Greek City from Homer to Alexander*. Oxford.

Musti, D. (1985). "Pubblico e privato nella democrazia periclea." *Quaderni Urbinati di Cultura classica* 20:7–17.

Nauck, A. (1964). *Tragicorum Graecorum Fragmenta*. Supplementum adj. B. Snell. Hildesheim.

Neil, R.A. (1901). *The Knights of Aristophanes*. Cambridge.

Neils, Jenifer (1987). *The Youthful Deeds of Theseus*. Rome.

Netting, Robert McC., Richard R. Wilk, and Eric J. Arnould (1984). *Households: Comparative and Historical Studies of the Domestic Group*. Berkeley.

Nicholson, Linda J. (1986). *Gender and History. The Limits of Social Theory in the Age of the Family*. New York.

Nilsson, Martin P. (1941). *Geschichte der griechischen Religion*. Munich.

—— (1972 [1932]). *The Mycenaean Origins of Greek Mythology*. Berkeley.

Norton, Mary Beth (1987). "Gender and Defamation in Seventeenth-Century Maryland." *William and Mary Quarterly* 3rd ser. 44:593–619.

Nussbaum, M. (1980). "Aristophanes and Socrates on Learning Practical Wisdom." *YClS* 26. Jeffrey Henderson, ed., *Aristophanes: Essays in Interpretation*: 43–97.

Ober, Josiah (1985). *Fortress Attica. Defense of the Athenian Land Frontier 404–322 B.C.* Leiden.

—— (1989a). *Mass and Elite in Democratic Athens. Rhetoric, Ideology, and the Power of the People*. Princeton.

—— (1989b). "The Nature of Athenian Democracy." Review of Mogens Herman Hansen, *The Athenian Assembly in the Age of Demosthenes* (1991). *CPh* 84:322–334.

Ober, Josiah and Barry S. Strauss (1990). "Drama, Political Rhetoric, and the Discourse of Athenian Democracy." In John J. Winkler and Froma I. Zeitlin, eds., *Nothing to Do with Dionysos? Athenian Drama in its Social Context*. Princeton: 237–270.

Opelt, Ilona (1979). "Zur politischen Polemik des Redners Andokides." *Glotta* 57:210–218.

Ortner, Sherry B. (1984). "Theory in Anthropology since the Sixties." *Comparative Studies in Society and History* 26:126–166.

Osborne, Robin (1985). *Demos: The Discovery of Classical Attika*. Cambridge.

—— (1990). "The *Demos* and Its Divisions in Classical Athens." In Oswyn Murray and Simon Price, eds., *The Greek City from Homer to Alexander*. Oxford: 265–294.

Ostwald, Martin (1962). Trans. Aristotle. *Nicomachean Ethics*. Indianapolis.

—— (1986). *From Popular Sovereignty to the Rule of Law. Law, Society and Politics in Fifth-Century Athens*. Berkeley.

—— (1990). "*Nomos* and *Phusis* in Antiphon's *Peri Alêtheias*." In M. Griffith and D.J. Mastronarde, eds., *Cabinet of the Muses*. Atlanta: 293–306.

Owsley, Frank L. (1965 [1949]). *Plain Folk of the Old South*. Chicago.

Parke, H.W. (1977). *Festivals of the Athenians*. Ithaca.

Parker, R. (1983). *Miasma*. Oxford.

Pateman, Carole (1988). *The Sexual Contract*. Stanford.

Patterson, Cynthia (1981). *Pericles' Citizenship Law of 451–50 B.C.* Salem, NH.

—— (1985). " 'Not Worth the Rearing': The Causes of Infant Exposure in Ancient Greece." *TAPA*: 115:103–213.

—— (1990). "Those Athenian Bastards." *CA* 9:40–73.

Pearson, A.C. (1917). *The Fragments of Sophocles*. Cambridge.

Pecorella Longo, C. (1971). *"Eterie" e Gruppi Politici nell'Atene del IV Secolo a.c.* Florence.

Peek, W. (1955). *Griechische Vers-Inschriften*. Vol. 1: *Grab-Epigramme*. Berlin.

Pélékidis, C. (1962). *Histoire de l'ephébie attique*. Paris.

Perlitt, Lothar (1976). "Das Vaterbild im Alten Testament." In Hubert Tellenbach, ed., *Das Vaterbild in Mythos und Geschichte. Aegypten, Griechenland, Altes Testament, Neues Testament*. Stuttgart: 50–101.

Pitt-Rivers, Julian (1963). Ed. *Mediterranean Countrymen. Essays in the Social Anthropology of the Mediterranean*. Paris.

—— (1977). *The Fate of Schechem, or the Politics of Sex: Essays in the Anthropology of the Mediterranean*. Cambridge.

Podlecki, Anthony (1971). "Cimon, Skyros, and Theseus' Bones." *JHS* 91:141–143.

—— (1975). "Theseus and Themistocles." *Rivista storica dell'Antichità* 5:1–24.

—— (1975–76). "A Pericles *Prosopon* in Attic Tragedy?" *Euphrosyne* 7: 22–27.

Pomeroy, Sarah (1975). *Goddesses, Whores, Wives, and Slaves: Women in Classical Antiquity*. New York.

Powell, C.A. (1979). "Religion and the Sicilian Expedition." *Historia* 28:15–31.

Pucci, Pietro (1992). *Oedipus and the Fabrication of the Father: Oedipus Tyrannus in Modern Criticism and Philology*. Baltimore.

Raaflaub, Kurt A. (1985). *Die Entdeckung der Freiheit. Zur historischen Semantik und Gesellschaftsgeschichte eines politischen Grundbegriffes der Griechen. Vestigia*, Bd. 37. Munich.

—— (1990). "Contemporary Perceptions of Democracy in Fifth-Century Athens." In W.R. Connor, M.H. Hansen, *et al.*, *Aspects of Athenian Democracy*. Classica et Mediaevalia Dissertationes XI. Copenhagen: 33–70.

Rabinow, Paul. (1984). Ed. *The Foucault Reader*. New York.

Radermacher, L. (1938). *Mythos und Sage bei den Griechen*. 2nd edn. Vienna and Leipzig.

Raepset, Georges (1971). "Les motivations de la natalité à Athènes aux Ve et IVe siècles avant notre ère." *AC* 40:80–110.

Ragland-Sullivan, Elie (1986). *Jacques Lacan and the Philosophy of Psychoanalysis*. Urbana and Chicago.

Rahe, Paul A. (1984). "The Primacy of Politics in Classical Greece." *AHR* 265–293.

Rankin, Anne V. (1974). "Euripides' Hippolytus: A Psychopathological Hero." *Arethusa* 7:71–94.

Raubitschek, A.E. (1981). "Andocides and Thucydides." In G. Shrimpton, ed., *Classical Contributions. Studies in Honor of Malcolm Francis McGregor.* Locust Valley, NY: 121–123.

Reckford, K.J. (1972). "Phaethon, Hippolytus, and Aphrodite." *TAPA* 103:405–432.

—— (1976). "Father-beating in Aristophanes' *Clouds.*" In Stephen Bertman, ed., *The Conflict of Generations in Ancient Greece and Rome.* Amsterdam: 89–118.

Redfield, James (1982). "Notes on the Greek Wedding." *Arethusa* 15:181–201.

—— (1990). "Drama and Community. Aristophanes and Some of His Rivals." In John J. Winkler and Froma I. Zeitlin, eds., *Nothing to Do with Dionysos? Athenian Drama and Its Social Context.* Princeton: 314–335.

Reeve, C.D.C. (1989). *Socrates in the "Apology." An Essay on Plato's "Apology of Socrates."* Indianapolis and Cambridge.

Reinhold, Meyer (1976). "The Generation Gap in Antiquity." In Stephen Bertman, ed., *The Conflict of Generations in Ancient Greece and Rome.* Amsterdam: 15–54.

Reinmuth, O.W. (1971). *The Ephebic Inscriptions of the Fourth Century B.C. Mnemosyne* Supplement 14:123–138.

Rhodes, P.J. (1981). *A Commentary on the Aristotelian "Athenaiôn Politeia."* Oxford.

Richardson, Bessie Ellen (1933). *Old Age among the Ancient Greeks. The Greek Portrayal of Old Age in Literature, Art, and Inscriptions.* Baltimore.

Ridgway, B.S. (1981). *Fifth Century Styles in Greek Sculpture.* Princeton.

Robertson, M. (1985). "Greek Art and Religion." In P.E. Easterling and J.V. Muir, eds. *Greek Religion and Society.* Cambridge: 155–190.

Rose, H.J. (1957). "The Religion of a Greek Household." *Euphrosyne* 1:95–116.

—— (1959). *A Handbook of Greek Mythology.* New York.

Roussel, Denis. (1976). *Tribu et cité.* Annales littéraires de l'université de Besançon v. 193. Paris.

Rudhardt, J. (1962). "La reconaissance de la paternité, sa nature et sa portée dans la société athénienne." *MH* 19:39–64.

Ruschenbusch, E. (1958). "*Patrios politeia.*" *Historia* 7: 398–424.

Russell, D.A. (1966). "Plutarch, 'Alcibiades' 1–16." *PCPhS* 12:37–47.

Rusten, J.S. (1989). *Thucydides, The Peloponnesian War, Book II.* Cambridge.

Ste. Croix, G.E.M. (1972). *Origins of the Peloponnesian War.* Ithaca.

—— (1981). *The Class Struggle in the Ancient Greek World from the Archaic Age to the Arab Conquests.* Ithaca.

Sabean, David (1976). "Aspects of Kinship Behaviour and Property in Rural Western Europe before 1800." In Jack Goody, Joan Thirsk, and

FATHERS AND SONS IN ATHENS

E.P. Thompson, eds., *Family and Inheritance. Rural Society in Western Europe, 1200–1800.* Cambridge: 96–111.

Salkever, Stephen G. (1991). "Women, Soldiers, Citizens: Plato and Aristotle on the Politics of Virility." In Carnes Lord and David K. O'Connor, eds., *Essays on the Foundations of Aristotelian Political Science.* Berkeley: 165–190.

Sallares, Robert (1991). *The Ecology of the Ancient Greek World.* Ithaca.

Saller, Richard P. (1986). "*Patria Potestas* and the Stereotype of the Roman Family." *Continuity and Change* 1:7–22.

—— (1987). "Men's Age at Marriage and Its Consequences in the Roman Family." *CPh* 82:21–34.

—— (1988). "*Pietas*, Obligation and Authority in the Roman Family." In *Alte Geschichte und Wissenschaftsgeschichte. Festschrift für Karl Christ zum 65. Geburtstag.* Darmstadt: 393–410.

Sartori, Franco (1975). *Una Pagina di Storia Ateniese in un Frammento dei "Demi" Eupolidei.* Rome.

Schaps, David M. (1979). *Economic Rights of Women in Ancient Greece.* Edinburgh.

Schefold, Karl (1946). "Kleisthenes." *MH* 3:59–93.

Scheibler, Ingeborg (1987). "Bild und Gefäs. Zur ikonographischen und funktionalen Bedeutung der attischen Bildfeldamphoren. Mit 39 Abbildungen und 1 Tabelle." *Jahrbuch des Deutschen Archäologischen Instituts.* 102:57–118.

Schmid, W. and O. Staehlin (1946). *Geschichte der griechischen Literatur.* Munich.

Schmitt-Pantel, Pauline (1990). "Collective Activities and the Political in the Greek City." in Oswyn Murray and Simon Price, eds., *The Greek City from Homer to Alexander.* Oxford: 199–214.

Schneider, David (1984). *A Critique of the Study of Kinship.* Ann Arbor, Mich.

Schochet, Gordon J. (1975). *Patriarchalism in Political Thought. The Authoritarian Father and Attitudes Especially in Seventeenth-Century England.* New York.

Scott, Joan W. (1986). "Gender: A Useful Category of Historical Analysis." *AHR* 91.5:1053–1075.

Seager, Robin (1978). "Andocides' Confession; a Dubious Note." *Historia* 27:221–223.

Séchan, Louis (1911). "La légende d'Hippolyte dans l'antiquité." *REG* 24:105–151.

Segal, Charles (1969). "Euripides *Hippolytus* 108–112: Tragic Irony and Tragic Justice." *Hermes* 97:297–305.

—— (1970a). "The Order of Lines in *Hippolytus* 1452–1456." *GRBS* 11: 101–107.

—— (1970b). "Shame and Purity in Euripides' *Hippolytus*." *Hermes* 98: 278–299.

—— (1979a). "The Myth of Bacchylides 17: Heroic Quest and Heroic Identity." *Eranos* 77:23–37.

—— (1979b). "Solar Imagery and Tragic Heroism in Euripides *Hippolytus*."

In G. Bowersock, W. Burkert, and M. Putnam, eds., *Arktouros: Hellenic Studies Presented to B.M.W. Knox.* 151–161.

—— (1984a). "Greek Tragedy and Society: A Structuralist Perspective." In Charles Segal, *Interpreting Greek Tragedy: Myth, Poetry, Text.* Ithaca: 21–47.

—— (1984b). *Interpreting Greek Tragedy: Myth, Poetry, Text.* Ithaca.

—— (1984c). "Pentheus and Hippolytus on the Couch and on the Grid: Psychoanalytic and Structural Readings of Greek Tragedy." In Charles Segal, *Interpreting Greek Tragedy: Myth, Poetry, Text.* Ithaca: 268–293.

—— (1984d). "The Tragedy of the *Hippolytus*: The Waters of Ocean and the Untouched Meadow." In Charles Segal, *Interpreting Greek Tragedy: Myth, Poetry, Text.* Ithaca: 165–221.

—— (1988). "Theatre, Ritual and Commemoration in Euripides' *Hippolytus*." *Ramus* 17:52–74.

Segalen, Martine (1986). *Historical Anthropology of the Family.* Trans. J.C. Whitehouse and Sarah Matthews. Cambridge.

Sergent, Bernard (1986). *Homosexuality in Greek Myth.* Trans. Arthur Goldhammer. Boston.

Shapiro, Alan (1981). Ed. *Art, Myth, and Culture: Greek Vases from Southern Collections.* New Orleans.

—— (1982). "Theseus, Athens, and Troizen." *Archäologischer Anzeiger* 2:291–297.

—— (forthcoming a). "The Hero in Archaic Greece."

—— (forthcoming b). "Theseus in Kimonian Athens: The Iconography of Empire."

Shaw, Michael H. (1982). "The *êthos* of Theseus in *The Suppliant Women*." *Hermes* 110:3–19.

Shorter, Edward (1977). *The Making of the Modern Family.* New York.

Simon, Erika (1983). *Festivals of Attica. An Archaeological Commentary.* Madison.

Sissa, Giulia (1986). "La famille dans la cité grecque (Ve-IVe siècle avant J.-C.)." In André Burguière *et al.*, eds., *Histoire de la famille, I: mondes lointains, mondes anciens.* Paris.

Slater, Philip (1968). *The Glory of Hera. Greek Mythology and the Greek Family.* Boston.

Smoot, J.J. (1976). "Hippolytus as Narcissus: An Amplification." *Arethusa* 9:37–51.

Snell, B. (1970). *Bacchylidis Carmina cum fragmentis.* 14th edn. Leipzig.

Sommerstein, Alan H. (1981a). Ed. and trans. *The Comedies of Aristophanes.* Vol 2: "*Knights.*" Warminster.

—— (1981b). Ed. and trans. *The Comedies of Aristophanes.* Vol. 3: "*Clouds.*" Warminster.

—— (1983). Ed. and trans. *The Comedies of Aristophanes.* Vol. 4: "*Wasps.*" Warminster.

—— (1987a). Ed. and trans. *The Comedies of Aristophanes.* Vol. 6: "*Birds.*" Warminster.

—— (1987b). "Phrynichos the Dancer." *Phoenix* 41:189–190.

Sourvinou-Inwood, Christiane (1971). "Theseus Lifting the Rock and a Cup Near the Pithos Painter." *JHS* 91:94–109.

—— (1979). *Theseus as Son and Stepson. A Tentative Illustration of the Greek Mythological Mentality. BICS* Supplement 40. London.

—— (1987). "A Series of Erotic Pursuits: Images and Meanings." *JHS* 107:131–153.

—— (1988). " 'Myth' and History: On Herodotus III.48 and 50–53." *Opuscula Atheniensia* 17:11, 167–182.

—— (1989). "Assumptions and the Creation of Meaning: Reading Sophocles' *Antigone.*" *JHS* 109:134–148.

—— (1990). "Myths in Images: Theseus and Medea as a Case Study." In Lowell Edmunds, ed., *Approaches to Greek Myth.* Baltimore: 393–445.

Stadter, Philip (1989). *A Commentary on Plutarch's "Pericles."* Chapel Hill, NC.

Stenning, D.J. (1966 [1958]). "Household Viability among the Pastoral Fulani." In Jack Goody, ed., *The Developmental Cycle in Domestic Groups.* Cambridge Papers in Social Anthropology no. 1. Cambridge: 92–119.

Stone, I.F. (1988). *The Trial of Socrates.* Boston.

Stone, Lawrence (1979). *The Family, Sex and Marriage in England 1500–1800.* New York.

Strauss, Barry S. (1985a). "The Cultural Significance of Bribery and Embezzlement in Athenian Politics: The Evidence of the Period 403–386 B.C." *The Ancient World* 11:67–74.

—— (1985b). "Ritual, Social Drama, and Politics in Classical Athens." *AJAH* 10.1:67–83.

—— (1986). *Athens after the Peloponnesian War. Class, Faction and Policy 403–386 B.C.* Ithaca and London.

—— (1990a). "*Oikos/Polis*: Towards a Theory of Athenian Paternal Ideology 450–399 B.C." In W.R. Connor, M. H. Hansen, *et. al.*, *Aspects of Athenian Democracy.* Classica et Mediaevalia Dissertationes XI. Copenhagen: 101–127.

—— (1990b). Review of John J. Winkler, *The Constraints of Desire*, (1990). *Anthropological Linguistics* 30.2:268–270.

—— (forthcoming). "The Melting Pot, the Mosaic, and the Agora." In J. Peter Euben, Josiah Ober, and John Wallach, eds., *Educating Democracy: The Contemporary Significance of Athenian Political Thought.*

Strauss, Leo (1966). *Socrates and Aristophanes.* New York.

Stroud, Ronald S. (1971). "Greek Inscriptions: Theozotides and the Athenian Orphans." *Hesperia* 40:280–301.

Süvern, J.W. (1836). *Two Essays on "The Clouds" and on the "Geras" of Aristophanes.* Trans. W.R. Hamilton. London.

Taylor, Michael W. (1991). *The Tyrant-Slayers. The Heroic Image in Fifth Century B.C. Athenian Art and Politics.* 2nd edn. New York.

Tazelaar, C.M. (1967) "PAIDES KAI EPHÊBOI. Some Notes on the Spartan Stages of Youth." *Mnemosyne* 20:127–153.

Tellenbach, Hubertus (1976). Ed. *Das Vaterbild in Mythos und Geschichte. Aegypten, Griechenland, Altes Testament, Neues Testament.* Stuttgart.

Thompson, John B. (1984). *Studies in the Theory of Ideology.* Berkeley.

Thompson, W.E. (1971). "Attic Kinship Terminology." *JHS* 91:110–113.

—— (1981). "Athenian Attitudes toward Wills." *Prudentia* 13:13–23.

Thury, Eva M. (1988). "Euripides' *Alcestis* and the Athenian Generation Gap." *Arethusa* 21:197–214.

Trautmann, Thomas R. (1987). *Lewis Henry Morgan and the Invention of Kinship*. Berkeley.

Turner, Victor (1957). *Schism and Continuity in an African Society*. Manchester.

—— (1969). *The Ritual Process: Structure and Anti-Structure*. Ithaca.

—— (1974). *Dramas, Fields, and Metaphors: Symbolic Action in Human Society*. Ithaca.

—— (1980). "Social Dramas and Stories about Them." *Critical Inquiry* 141–168.

—— (1982). Ed. *Celebration. Studies in Festivity and Ritual*. Washington, DC.

Tyrell, William Blake (1984). *Amazons. A Study in Athenian Mythmaking*. Baltimore.

Vaio, John (1971). "Aristophanes' *Wasps*. The Relevance of the Final Scenes." *GRBS* 12: 335–351.

Van Gennep, Arnold (1960 [1909]). *The Rites of Passage*. Trans. M.B. Vizedom and G.L. Caffee. Chicago.

Vernant, J.-P. (1983 [1969]). "Hestia-Hermes: The Religious Expression of Space and Movement in Ancient Greece." In J.-P. Vernant, *Myth and Thought among the Greeks*. London: 127–175.

Vernant, Jean-Pierre and Pierre Vidal-Naquet (1981 [1972]). *Tragedy and Myth in Ancient Greece*. Trans. Janet Lloyd. Atlantic Highlands, NJ.

Versnel, H.S. (1987). "Greek Myth and Ritual: The Case of Kronos." In Jan Bremmer, ed., *Interpretations of Greek Mythology*. London: 121–152.

Vickers, Brian (1973). *Toward Greek Tragedy*. London.

Vickers, Michael (1984). "Dates, Methods and Icons." In C. Bérard, ed., *Actes du colloque international "Images et sociétés en Grèce ancienne: l'iconographie comme méthode d'analyse," Lausanne 1984*. Lausanne.

—— (1987a). "Aristophanes on Stage: *Philoctetes* and *Cyclops*." *Historia* 36:171–197.

—— (1987b). "Lambdacism at Aristophanes *Clouds* 1381–2." *Liverpool Classical Monthly* 12:143.

—— (1989a). "Alcibiades on Stage: *Thesmophoriazusae* and *Helen*." *Historia* 38:41–65.

—— (1989b). "Alcibiades on Stage: Aristophanes' *Birds*." *Historia* 38: 267–299.

—— (1993). "Alcibiades in Cloudedoverland." In R.M. Rosen and J. Farrell, eds., *Nomodeiktes: Greek Studies in Honor of Martin Ostwald*. Ann Arbor.

—— (forthcoming). *Pericles on Stage. Historical Comedy in Aristophanes' Early Plays*.

Vidal-Naquet, P. (1986a). *The Black Hunter: Forms of Thought and Forms of Society in the Greek World*. Trans. A. Szegedy-Maszak. Baltimore.

—— (1986b). "The Black Hunter Revisited." *PCPhS* 212 n.s. 32:126–144.

Vlastos, Gregory (1983). "The Historical Socrates and Athenian Democracy." *Political Theory* 2:495–516.

—— (1991). *Socrates, Ironist and Moral Philosopher*. Ithaca.

Wagner-Pacifici, Robin Erica (1986). *The Moro Morality Play. Terrorism as Social Drama*. Chicago.

Walcot, Peter (1970). *Greek Peasants Ancient and Modern*. Manchester.

Walker, Henry J. (1989). "Myth and Politics: The Role of Theseus in Athenian Ideology." Dissertation, Cornell University. Ithaca.

Wallace, Robert W. (1989). *The Areopagos Council to 307 B.C.* Baltimore.

Walsh, G.B. (1978). "The Rhetoric of Birthright and Race in Euripides' *Ion*." *Hermes* 106:301–315.

Walters, K.R. (1976). "The 'Ancestral Constitution' and Fourth-Century Historiography in Athens." *AJAH* 1:129–144.

Ward, Anne C., W. R. Connor, Ruth B. Edwards, Simon Tidworth, with a Preface by Reynold Higgins (1970). *The Quest for Theseus*. London.

Warner, Rex (1954). Trans. Thucydides. *"History of the Peloponnesian War."* Harmondsworth.

Wasserman, Felix (1976). "The Conflict of Generations in Thucydides." In Stephen Bertman, ed., *The Conflict of Generations in Ancient Greece and Rome*. Amsterdam: 119–122.

Weber, Max (1958). *The City*. Trans. and ed. Don Martindale and Gertrud Neuwirth. New York.

Webster, T.B.L. (1969 [1936]). *An Introduction to Sophocles*. London.

Wendland, Paul (1905). *Anaximenes von Lampsakos. Studien zur ältesten Geschichte der Rhetorik. Festschrift für die 48. Versammlung deutscher Philologen und Schulmänner in Hamburg*. Berlin.

West, Thomas G. (1979). *Plato's "Apology of Socrates." An Interpretation, with a New Translation*. Ithaca.

Whitehead, David (1986). *The Demes of Attica 508/7–ca. 250 B.C. A Political and Social Study*. Princeton.

Whitman, Cedric (1964). *Aristophanes and the Comic Hero*. Cambridge, Mass.

Wilkins, John. (1990). "The Young of Athens: Religion and Society in the *Herakleidai* of Euripides." *CQ* 40:329–339.

Winkler, John J. (1990a). *The Constraints of Desire. The Anthropology of Sex and Gender in Ancient Greece*. New York and London.

—— (1990b). "The Ephebes' Song: *Tragôidia* and *Polis*." In John J. Winkler and Froma I. Zeitlin, eds., *Nothing to Do with Dionysos? Athenian Drama in Its Social Context*. Princeton: 20–62 [= revised version of *Representations* 11 (1985):26–62].

Winkler, John J. and Froma I. Zeitlin (1990). Eds. *Nothing to do With Dionysos? Athenian Drama in Its Social Context*. Princeton.

Winnington-Ingram, R.P. (1960). *"Hippolytus*: A Study in Causation." *Fondation Hardt pour l'étude de l'antiquité classique. Entretiens*. Tome VI: *Euripide*. Geneva.

Wolff, Hans Julius (1944). "Marriage Law and Family Organization in Ancient Athens. A Study on the Interrelation of Public and Private Law in the Greek City." *Traditio* 2:43–95.

—— (1978). "Polis und Civitas." *Zeitschrift der Savigny-Stiftung für Rechtsgeschichte (Romanistische Abteilung)* 12:1–23.

Wycherley, R.E. (1957). *The Athenian Agora*. Vol. 3: *Literary and Epigraphical Testimonia*. Princeton.
—— (1978). *The Stones of Athens*. Princeton.
Young, Michael and Peter Willmott (1957). *Family and Kinship in East London*. Harmondsworth.
Zeitlin, Froma I. (1985). "The Power of Aphrodite: Eros and the Boundaries of the Self in the *Hippolytus*." In Peter Burian, ed., *Directions in Euripidean Criticism*. Durham: 52–111, 189–208.
—— (1990). "Thebes: Theater of Self and Society in Athenian Drama." In John J. Winkler and Froma I. Zeitlin, eds., *Nothing to Do with Dionysos? Athenian Drama in Its Social Context*. Princeton: 130–167.
Zuntz, G. (1955). *The Political Plays of Euripides*. Manchester.

INDEX